Four Walls and a Roof

Four Walls and a Roof

The Complex Nature of a Simple Profession

Reinier de Graaf

Harvard University Press
CAMBRIDGE, MASSACHUSETTS
LONDON, ENGLAND
2017

Library of Congress Cataloging-in-Publication Data
Names: Graaf, Reinier de, 1964– author.
Title: Four walls and a roof : the complex nature of a simple profession /
    Reinier de Graaf.
Description: Cambridge, Massachusetts : Harvard University Press, 2017. |
    Includes bibliographical references.
Identifiers: LCCN 2017010016 | ISBN 9780674976108 (cloth : alk. paper)
Subjects: LCSH: Architectural practice. | Architecture.
Classification: LCC NA1995 .G69 2017 | DDC 720—dc23
    LC record available at https://lccn.loc.gov/2017010016

It is life that is right and the architect who is wrong.

—Le Corbusier (toward the end of his life)

Contents

Four Walls and a Roof

Preface

Why this book? Most architects are lousy theorists; I am no exception. Whenever we offer theories, they should be mistrusted. We go where our work leads us and develop thoughts along the way. Revelations about the larger things in life, if they come at all, are incidental by-products of our (often banal) labor.

That doesn't mean, however, that what architects have to say is without value. Architecture's utter dependence on outside forces provides it with intimate knowledge of those forces. Professional experiences give architects eyes and ears, even if they mostly insist on using their hands. Recorded and collated, these experiences amount to a revealing X-ray of the present.

These forty-four essays offer snapshots of a world usually invisible to outsiders. They voice doubts and talk of failed efforts and aborted attempts—of things that we thought would happen, but that never did. Their profound incoherence is a reflection of the world they describe; they are a personal record of the twenty-first century so far—a mix of tragicomic anecdotes from the field and larger reflections on the nature of our work. What does it mean to be an architect right now?

Roughly half the essays were written for prior publication without ever considering their placement in a book; the other half were written with this book solely in mind. The relations among the essays are therefore partially intentional and partially accidental. *Four Walls and a Roof* can be read like a book or browsed like a website—consumed in stages or even incompletely. Each of its seven parts addresses a myth looming over the profession of architecture: its presumed authority (Part I), its reliance on individual inspiration (Part II), its commitment to good causes (Part III), its control of its own professional practices (Part IV), its independence from external powers (part V), its mastery of the large scale (Part VI), and, finally, its unrelenting devotion to progress (Part VII).

Perhaps the overriding myth debunked by this book is that of the architect as a hero. Serving the same powers that it strives to critique, architecture is condemned to a perpetual conflict of interest. Together, architects, clients, politicians, and consultants make up an embroiled world in which it is forever unclear who calls the shots.

Four Walls and a Roof

I. AUTHORITY

Nikolai Ladovsky's Space Studio, VKhUTEMAS, Moscow, 1927
Selim Omarovitch Khan-Magomedov, *VHUTEMAS: Moscou, 1920–1930*, presented and
annotated by Arlette Barré-Despond (Paris: Éditions du Regard, 1990)

I Will Learn You Architecture!

I remember my first job: Harbour Exchange Buildings 4, 5, 7, and 8, London Docklands, 1988. A building frenzy had engulfed the city during the last years of Margaret Thatcher's reign, allowing many young architects a first taste of practice. The buildings that we worked on were referred to only by their numbers, and their quality was bland—not quite the postmodern pastiche of Canary Wharf but rather a dumbed-down form of modernism: straightforward moneymaking machines. They were commissioned under so-called design-and-build contracts, which meant that the architect essentially answered to the contractor, producing drawings on demand with no further say in how the work would be executed. My first task had been to amend the ceiling plans of the lower and upper ground floors of office buildings that were still under construction. These ceilings had to be redesigned so they could hold chandeliers. The investor had calculated that with retail use on the ground floors (rather than more office space), the buildings would generate substantially larger financial returns, and so a partial conversion had been launched before the buildings were even finished. Among the junior architects there was a perverse delight in the thought that if we drew fast enough, the conversion of the building's interior might work its way up and eventually overtake the ongoing construction of the upper floors.

I had graduated only six months earlier, and in many ways, that first job came as a shock, not so much because of the quality of the buildings that I worked on or the nature of clients' decisions as because of the fact that practicing as an architect appeared to have nothing—and I mean *absolutely* nothing—to do with studying architecture. The first emotional state I recall having as a practicing architect was a feeling of utter uselessness. My technical knowledge fell far short of what was needed; at the same time, nobody was interested in the elevated philosophical considerations I had developed during my studies. I was both over- and underqualified for my job. My education had instilled near-megalomaniacal ambitions but had left me unprepared for the world in which to exercise them.

This was a feeling that I shared with other recent graduates, but we kept our spirits up and tried to feel good about ourselves. Admittedly, we worked on garbage, but it was straightforward and quantifiable garbage. Pay was good, and working days were neatly confined between the hours of nine and five. Still, given the never-ending stream of seemingly pointless tasks, every day seemed to last a lifetime. I was confident that things would change with time. As soon as I was no longer bound to execute the questionable design decisions made by others (which, in architecture, they are by definition), things would get better. Ultimately, there would be room to put into practice some of the idealism I had developed in school.

Once I began working for myself, things hardly improved. I quickly discovered that economic needs render the architect a largely powerless figure. Saying no or questioning a client's directives is at best a matter of gentle persuasion and never a battle of equals. As a profession, architecture presents a paradox. In economic terms, it is mainly a reactive discipline, a response to preformulated needs; in intellectual terms, it is the opposite: a visionary domain that claims the future, aspiring to set the agenda and precede needs. Architecture is a form of omniscience practiced in a context of utter dependency.

A former employer (shortly before firing me) once declared that "the most important thing for an architect is to have charisma!" This statement seemed inescapably fatalistic. You either had charisma or you didn't, and if you didn't, there was no way to get it. Up to that moment, I had progressed by copying the skills and following the directions of others before me, but this particular trait did not lend itself to imitation. If charisma was acquirable at all, it remained a distant prospect for when my career was over and I would have no further use for it. The whole notion seemed highly unfair.

Aldo van Eyck had charisma; so did Aldo Rossi, and so does Peter Eisenman. Given the differences among these men (I'm sorry that they are all men), it seems safe to conclude that charisma is unrelated to any particular approach to the practice of architecture. The only common element linking these three architects was that they appeared to know something we didn't, even if they never quite revealed what. As professors, they inspired their students, but certainly not through reason. Most of what they said hardly made sense. Van Eyck habitually lost himself in rage, nobody understood Rossi's English, and Eisenman's openly professed dilemmas were (and are) as impenetrable as his building designs. None of that interfered with the contagious effect they had on their audiences. Truth is everything that is strongly believed, and whenever they spoke, we certainly believed, regardless of what they said.

I guess we admired these men because we felt that they had somehow defied the realities of practice—we all knew such realities existed, but as students, we preferred to ignore them as long as we could—and had shown that a heroic role for architects was possible, provided one was persistent enough to hold one's own against the ever-increasing army of skill-specific experts who claimed "our" profession. They were our heroes primarily because they didn't give a damn about what else we were being taught. It was their manifest, brazen sense of irresponsibility in advocacy of strong beliefs, coupled with their blatant indifference to the consequences of their statements, that was so appealing. They were living proof that prolonged defiance eventually paid off and could conquer all the odds that architecture faced.

Little did I know what I was in for. Architecture differs fundamentally from what architects are taught to expect; it is a pinball manipulated by considerations and interests of which architects are often least aware. Buildings are more than just a means to organize space; they are vehicles for investment, an indispensable pillar of the current economic system, and, as we saw in the financial crisis of 2008, a potential source of its instability. Buildings emerge as the result of interactions among investors, quantity surveyors, real estate consultants, and other "experts." In hindsight, the charisma of those revered professors primarily served as a deferral of certain inevitable confrontations with the truth: as a stance not of heroism but of desperation, as a last line of defense, and as an effort to preserve architecture as an autonomous domain in the absence of conclusive arguments why.

In a context increasingly dominated by financial experts and technical specialists, only a leap of faith can rival the power of numbers. And that is what charisma is: a knowing in the absence of knowledge. The more it abandons the notion of evidence, the more potent is its effect. Arguments must neither be validated nor be disproved. Like a state of hypnosis, charisma obscures established relations of power. It allows architects to temporarily suspend the disbelief of their patrons and get the upper hand in the absence of a real mandate—to speak with authority even when they have no clue what they are talking about.

"I will learn you architecture," Herman Hertzberger used to tell us as students at the Berlage Institute. Somehow his flawed English carries great profundity and demonstrates deep knowledge of the architect's ultimate secret: packaging dependency as authority—the art of deferring the question of who ultimately needs whom, preferably forever.

More Specifically, Everything!

"Please welcome 'Urban Man', a hero like no other, greater than Batman, Superman, Spiderman, and Iron Man!" The moderator is clearly a fan, glowing with admiration as he invites the next speaker up to the podium. Urban Man is in every way the moderator's role model, modelled on the supernatural characters of his childhood comic books—a superhero simply because he has had the superhuman courage to push cities to the top of everyone's agenda.

It takes a considerable stretch of the imagination to recognize a super-hero in the figure who approaches the stage. He trips as he makes his way up the small steps and clumsily bumps into the stool that has been placed for him. Given his seventy-seven years, the organizers thought that, like Frank Sinatra in his twilight years, he might prefer to perform from a sed-entary position.

The speaker is having none of it. During his presentation the stool never becomes more than an inconvenient obstacle while Urban Man wobbles and lurches enthusiastically about the stage. We hear his heavy breathing amplified through the microphone of his jaunty Madonna-style headset. Endearingly, that microphone has been switched on throughout the introduction, making the audience privy to his impatient murmurings that the moderator "get on with it!"

It is Thursday, January 21, 2010. We are at the World Future Energy Summit in Abu Dhabi. As the home of the all-new, carbon-neutral Masdar City, Abu Dhabi has gathered a certain momentum on green issues, al-though to call it credibility would be a stretch. Abu Dhabi's wealth largely stems from fossil fuels. A small army of world and industry leaders, policy makers, and researchers have flocked to the small emirate to discuss today's big questions: energy and the environment. The recent Copen-hagen Climate Summit has critically failed to produce results, and the world is wondering where to go from here.

The keynote speaker—Urban Man—is none other than Lord Richard Rogers of Riverside, the architectural eminence behind the pioneering Centre Pompidou in Paris; the equally emblematic Lloyd's building in London; the Millennium Dome, redubbed the O2 Arena; Heathrow's hardest-working Terminal Five; the Senedd or Welsh National Assembly in Cardiff; and the European Court of Human Rights building in Strasbourg. He is the winner of the Royal Institute of British Architects (RIBA) Gold Medal, the Thomas Jefferson Medal, the RIBA Stirling Prize, the Minerva Medal, and the Pritzker Prize, and is a Labour peer in the House of Lords.

His list of accomplishments is long, and therefore, inevitably, Lord Rogers is old. During the later part of his career, he has shared leadership of his firm with a number of name partners and has thus been able to devote his attention to the city, acting as adviser to various municipal governments and as writer of urban manifestos, both solicited and unsolicited. The design of cities and their role in creating sustainability are the subjects he will address today.

It is the fourth and final day of the convention. Rogers's appearance offers a Hail Mary, a last redemption. In a world dominated by pragmatism and compromises, the architect is often framed as a strange source of optimism, a wizard offering a potential magic, cure-all design solution to banish the more mundane and pervasive struggles. The moderator's introduction of the speaker as a superhero, silly as it sounds, is by no means accidental.

We the audience have been looking forward to this keynote with great anticipation; eager for content, for a message, we exercise patience. Still, we are not sure what to make of its opening. Our doubts are reinforced by Rogers's way of speaking. It is striking how closely a posh English accent can resemble the slurred speech caused by excessive alcohol intake. It is as though the upper classes have intentionally perfected the similarity over successive generations.

Rogers kicks off with a long thank you, congratulating Abu Dhabi and the rest of the United Arab Emirates (UAE) for their urban development so far and their foresight for the future. He is extremely impressed with the city for having mushroomed from nothing almost overnight and for having expressed full commitment to sustainable plans. He goes on to describe the UAE as "a crossroads between east and west, between north and south, and fully conscious of that." For him, visiting the global summit has been "a delight more than a business trip."

Later, when I watch videos of his other talks online, I discover that it is only the name of the city that varies in his opening remarks. The formula and structure of the talks are invariably the same. Lord Rogers is impressed and delighted wherever he goes.

Suddenly, he starts talking about history. We are startled. His praise for the organizers has continued for so long that embarking on the actual subject feels like a rude digression. "Citieaaahhzz." He pronounces his topic as if he is tasting vintage wine, rolling the word on his tongue, holding it in front of his throat while the following clauses take form. Citieaaahhzz . . . are places where people meet; that is their primary function. He smiles. The audience can rest easy, for he has only nice things to say. Whether from the Hellenic Peaahhriod (different wine, same fruity roll) or from Mesopotamia, where they started six thousand years ago, cities have always been about that. Less has changed about cities than we might think. Cities are about trade; they are where the majority of our wealth is created. Citieaaahhzz are most extraordinary places.

Twelve minutes into what is supposed to be a twenty-minute talk, it is becoming apparent that we are not going to hear anything particularly challenging. We instead decide to focus on the slides, which thus far have been advancing on their own. The speaker does not have a clicker or control. Even though a monitor has been set up in front of him, in addition to the large projection screen behind, he seems fully oblivious of the imagery that accompanies his oration. The subjects he addresses seem starkly out of sync with the visuals: his call for lush green landscapes and verdant parks is illustrated by dense urban conglomerations; his vision of a carbon-free atmosphere is accompanied by the smoking chimneys of what appear to be Soviet-era factories; his evocation of absolute horror—of all that should be avoided—is backed by a romantic depiction of the Garden of Eden.

Urban Man has big plans for the world; indeed, his aspirations seem to have no bounds. With each new sentence, a new location, topic, or domain is added to the theoretical competence of architecture, culminating in a crescendo that can scarcely be summed up: more specifically, everything! Rogers personifies the twenty-first-century *homo universalis* and is encouraging everyone to follow suit. But regarding concrete solutions, he invariably defers. "We don't know how to do that yet, but I am sure someone does."

When, during the afterglow of the Q&A, someone from the audience addresses him as Norman Foster, he does not balk or bat an eye. Instead, he smiles amiably and proceeds to answer with great confidence. Why object? He has just been credited with another significant body of work, that of his friend, classmate, and former colleague. Lord Rogers of Riverside remains professional until the end.

They had interesting careers once, Rogers, Foster, and Renzo Piano— perhaps the last members of a generation of true modernists, capable of surrendering preconceptions about the look of architecture to the technical realities of our time and often achieving fresh and surprisingly beautiful results. Forty years after its construction, the Centre Pompidou, a collaboration between Rogers and Piano, stands, at least in this author's opinion, as an undisputed masterpiece.

But something odd happened to each of them. Rogers chose to dedicate himself to the city, which he viewed as the pursuit of a larger social good, but its complexities landed him out of his depth (and evidently still do); Foster turned architecture into big business, unconditionally embracing, if not reifying, the vacuous marketing-speak that comes with doing so (witness the alleged carbon neutrality of his Masdar City); Piano's industrially produced, technology-championing constructions now tend to be hidden under thick layers of moss, meant to demonstrate his commitment to the green cause. Promising explorations have turned into a relentless devotion to cliché that lordships, knighthoods, and other forms of regalia and recognition have done little to obscure.

Lord Rogers regularly makes the headlines still, mostly over clashes with the Prince of Wales, another slurring, self-appointed advocate of the greater architectural good. These clashes are generally read as a conventional opposition: modern and progressive (Rogers) versus traditional and conservative (HRH the Prince of Wales). Rogers is labeled the anti-establishment voice—a rebel despite his age. Still, watching these two men, one wonders: are they going at each other, or are they keeping each other going? Are we witnessing two separate establishments or two parts of the same whole?

3

Let Me Finish!

"Can I see some hands raised? Who in the audience thinks of Frank Gehry's Pritzker Pavilion in Millennium Park as contextual?"

(No hands raised.)

"Who thinks it is not?"

(No hands raised.)

"Since none of you seem to know, let me tell you!"

What follows is a lengthy exposé on what, according to the interrogator, is a highly contextual piece of architecture. Speaking is Jeffrey Kipnis, theorist, designer, filmmaker, curator, educator, founding director of the Architectural Association's Graduate Design Program, and currently, professor at Ohio State University's Knowlton School of Architecture.

The exchange, if one can call it that, takes place as part of a panel discussion during the first Chicago Architecture Biennial. The theme of this inaugural biennial is to question architecture's status quo. In addition to Kipnis, the panel includes Patrik Schumacher, design director at Zaha Hadid Architects; Peter Eisenman, principal of Eisenman Architects and a pivotal figure in American academia (present and past positions too many to mention); Theodore Spyropoulos, founder of Minimaforms; and me, a partner at the Office for Metropolitan Architecture—all assembled to reflect on a potential agenda for twenty-first-century architecture. The composition of the panel is conspicuously homogeneous: all of us except Spyropoulos are over fifty, most of our formative and professional lives played out in the twentieth century, and we are from parts of the world that, if current indicators are not mistaken, may lose their dominance in the twenty-first century.

The venue is the Gold Room in the Congress Plaza Hotel. Tickets have sold for $50, but although that price suggests that the event is in high demand, the room is only half full, rendering its grandeur perfectly inappropriate for the occasion. One of Africa's rising architectural stars, speaking next door, appears to have drawn a larger crowd. Still, the modest turnout doesn't faze the panelists: the epicenter of American academia thrives even in the absence of an audience.

The prediscussion briefing has been suitably vague, allowing for free-form postulations: "Panelists are invited to reflect on the problematics, principles, values, and heuristics that will drive design in the next two decades. They are encouraged to tread into one another's territories and challenge each other's assumptions in order to unleash a fertile debate, inspiring new and seasoned generations to collectively question the architectural status quo." The speakers' cues suggest that we could be here to respond to a leading question.

Schumacher's opening salvo is a proclamation of the end of pluralism (delivered with an impeccable German accent) and of the imminent global dominance of a single remaining master style: his own. (In the race to establish opinion, Schumacher's pole position may be due to his ties with the Chicago Biennial's organizer, an avid promoter of his particular brand of architecture.) Eisenman, who follows, suggests a change of format: "Only Patrik should present, while the rest of us put up a collective resistance." His request is denied, and Eisenman has to content himself with "agreeing to disagree." His presentation calls for "heroes instead of stars in architecture." On an all-male, all-white stage, his call leaves a somewhat dubious taste.

After Eisenman's talk there is open season, not just for each of the panelists' individual obsessions (in order of appearance: parametricism, Alberti, Gehry, Piketty, and robots) but also for the audience. Someone who introduces himself as "a humble teacher at a humble university" asks why there are no women on the stage. With near-Trumpian bravado Kipnis replies that he loves women but is dumbfounded by the stupidity of such a question, which he takes to be indicative of the inquirer's career progress (or lack thereof). In an attempt to rescue the situation, Eisenman murmurs that women have become so popular these days that they have become unaffordable. (We must simply assume that he means as panelists.)

It is Kipnis's turn at the wheel. His idea of offering the audience "value for money" is to subject it to a kind of intellectual waterboarding. Positions are invariably introduced via the same discursive formula: "Did you know . . . ? You did not . . . ? You should! Since you don't, let me tell you." It is unclear to what extent, if at all, he is seeking a discussion. Kipnis tempts the audience with long pauses, invariably followed by "Let me finish!" when someone dares to interject.

The main topic of his presentation is the recent and much-discussed competition to design the Guggenheim Helsinki museum—a competition that to date has not produced a building and that, because of shrinking coffers, doesn't look like it will any time soon. Kipnis displays the many entries to the Helsinki competition as a repository of contemporary design intelligence; his anonymized, meticulously categorized, and digitally database based inventory reveals simultaneously emergent "families" of design solutions applied in response to a very particular problem. Akin to genres of contemporary music, various "new waves" are identified and (hash)tagged with names. Links to individual authors are discarded as trends take priority over signatures. Originality is no longer a paradigmatic feature; in the context of a Guggenheim commission, the myth of individual genius is dismantled in favor of viewing architects as a virtual but largely unaware collective.

His argument takes a bizarre turn when he digresses into an enthusiastic endorsement of Frank Gehry, who in many ways personifies the exact opposite. Unlike the nameless souls of the Helsinki competition, Gehry is the ultimate signature architect. His approach to architecture is his and his alone, permitting no following other than through imitation. In bringing up Gehry, Kipnis burns his own portrayal of architecture as a form of collective progress into scorched earth before it can ignite a discussion.

Kipnis seems blissfully unaware of the contradiction as he proceeds to explain and interpret Gehry's design intentions as if he were the oracle of Zeus. The silence after his question about the Pritzker Pavilion is less a sign of the audience's ignorance than it is of its bewilderment. Don't all Gehry buildings look the same? It is clear to everyone in the room (at least to those who have built) that whatever contextual intentions might have gone into the building's design, they ultimately yield to the simple perception of the autonomy of its physical presence—at which point the only correct answer to Kipnis's question is that it is irrelevant. If legacy is ultimately a question of numbers, what constitutes the more significant intellectual fact: one person's supposed insight into Frank Gehry's nuanced design intentions or the vast majority's utter indifference toward them? Who holds the key, the oracle or the Simpsons?

As the evening progresses, the event turns into an unpleasant X-ray exposing the current state of American academia—a strangely insular world that is governed by its own autonomous codes, is dominated by antiquated pecking orders and estranged value systems, and has little hope of finding correctives from within. The often grandiose tone of the discussion contrasts starkly with the marginal importance of what is being debated. The Western architectural ivory tower has become a theater of the absurd, self-obsessed, blind to its own decline, and largely oblivious to real forces that determine the general state of the built environment. Kipnis's definition of context doesn't go beyond the immediate physical surroundings of the architectural object. Any notion that architecture might be shaped by a larger political, societal, or economic context does not seem to register on his radar. It is as though America's architectural establishment is preoccupied with studying footnotes under a microscope in the hope that they will eventually turn into a critically acclaimed novel.

At the special-invitation dinner afterward, guests are cautious about their alcohol intake. Even with the debate officially concluded, it is wise to remain alert. Dinners serve as extra time for the settling of undecided intellectual battles—a last chance to turn defeat into victory. When all other subjects appear to have been exhausted, conversation at the table turns to the human brain, and the question arises whether it ought to be discussed as an organ or as a muscle. Just when the vision of a brain without a skull is about to make me lose my appetite, Kipnis turns to a young woman at the table and asks her to "guess his favorite organ." When she looks at him aghast—she must be less than half his age—he smiles: "Rest assured, my favorite organ is my mouth." Eisenman points out that the mouth is not an organ. For the first time that evening, Kipnis looks genuinely unsettled, prompting Eisenman to ask the question of the day: "Jeff, have you been drinking?"

Four Walls and a Roof

Someone asked me shortly after I graduated, "Why did you study so intensively for so long? Isn't architecture basically just four walls and a roof?" The bluntness of this question took me aback, and twenty-five years later I still struggle to come up with an answer.

Throughout my career I have tried to justify to others—particularly to those outside my profession—why my job is important and why it should qualify as a source of pride, especially in the face of much of our built reality. Even while writing this (on a train, on my way to work), I cannot help but be overcome by a sense of shame when I pause to look out the window. The vast majority of the built environment is unspeakably ugly: an infinite collection of cheaply made buildings engaged in a perpetual and bloodless contest over which can generate the most "interest" for the lowest budget. Nothing more, nothing less. "Modern" architecture—the kind of architecture most of us claim to profess—hasn't helped; it has mainly proved to be a facilitator, an extension of the means to conduct this pointless contest, only at a faster pace.

Why do we—contemporary architects—wallow so deeply in the grand visions we offer? Where does it come from, this God complex—the inclination to view ourselves as authoritative on virtually everything? Despite a century of architectural mission statements, earnest treatises, and urgent manifestos, the world seems disenchanted. I have yet to meet a client, a public official, or any user who is truly interested in the grand promises we make, the lofty motivations we offer for our decisions (apart from costs), or, indeed, much of what we say. Let's face it: architects speak to architects, and as far as the rest of the world is concerned, they can remain forever silent. They should simply get on with their job of designing buildings, which, if they are any good, should speak for themselves.

I often wonder whether we would be better off if we were a little more discreet about our profession, like the old guilds of masons, secretive sects of builders who acted as custodians of centuries-old trade secrets, shared through mystic handshakes, rather than imagining ourselves as the great inventors and knowing announcers of "radical" revolutions (which, in architecture, happen approximately once a week).

The focus on the importance of individual figures in architecture primarily masks architecture's failing as a collective. The hype around contemporary architecture and the myth of the individual genius that comes with it are convenient decoys that allow us to shed any notion of collective responsibility and to engage in a disingenuous crusade against what are ultimately our own sins. But how much longer can we boast of the relevance of our profession before our complicity in what is being done in its name catches up with us?

Statistics indicate an alarming trend: an ever-growing number of architectural offices of ever-shrinking size, with ever fewer projects in the pipeline. Imagine the ultimate outcome of this trend: a fully atomized sector in which the number of practices equals the number of architects, all desperately in search of clients willing to give them serious responsibilities. Most of their working day will be consumed by writing mission statements. What better way to fill the time between one project (some time ago) and the next (not any time soon)? The smaller the offices, the smaller the audiences for the architects to address. In the short term, a professional scene of many small offices will lead to more visionaries to whom fewer people will listen. From architects speaking to architects, we will evolve to every architect talking to himself.

There is a scene in the film *Paris, Texas* by Wim Wenders in which a clearly deranged man delivers prophecies from a highway overpass to six lanes of passing traffic below. He screams at the top of his lungs, and the contents of his speech are eloquent and persuasive, but the drivers below, shielded by their steel shells, remain immune to his words. The man goes unheard, but that only inspires him to raise his voice further.

To what extent does this man resemble the contemporary architect—a person purporting to possess privileged knowledge, to which everyone around him appears deaf; a person who stands motionless while everything around him is in motion; a person who prophesies from a bridge,

looking over the people below (whom he keenly refers to as "the masses");
but also increasingly a needy person, far removed from the wealth with
which he was once associated, and, if economic indicators are anything
to go by, soon to be a lone drifter, in search of shelter—of four walls and
a roof?

II. DEFAULT BY DESIGN

Pimlico Secondary School, London, 1970
Architectural Press Archive / RIBA Library Photographs Collection

5

Bloody Fools!

The Story of Pimlico School, 1970–2010

November 1988: unemployment among architects in the Netherlands reaches an all-time high, and like many other new graduates, I try my luck abroad. London is my destination. The practice I hope to join seems a good choice: it can look back on some decent work and enjoys something of a reputation—the firm's founder has been knighted—mainly stemming from public commissions in the 1960s and 1970s. Meanwhile, however, like almost any London practice, its financial well-being has come to rely almost exclusively on private commissions in the Docklands, where a building boom, seemingly without limits, keeps ever-larger segments of London's architectural scene afloat.

My residence is a flat on the upper and lower ground floors of one of the white stucco Georgian terraces on Denbigh Street, Pimlico SW1. The buildings on most of the nearby streets are in the same architectural style, and for a while it is difficult to find the shortest way home from the closest tube station. Every day on my way to work, I pass a concrete and glass building located in a large sunken concrete pit, strangely at odds with the rest of the neighborhood. The effect of the pit is somewhat disorienting: it sets the building apart from its surroundings, but contrary to the most common architectural intervention to achieve this aim, a podium, the pit avoids the suggestion of contextual disdain. Instead, the sunken ground level gives the building a kind of humility.

Although the building is clearly past its prime, its function as a school is still apparent from the classrooms, and most notably their blackboards, that can be seen through large panes of glass. The in situ concrete finish of the building is covered in graffiti, but not entirely. It is as if the abundant presence of exposed concrete has discouraged even the staunchest graffiti artists from finishing their task. Every day before dinnertime, there are people practicing their tennis skills, taking on the concrete walls of the schoolyard as their opponents. The walls of the schoolyard are slightly slanted, causing a kind of delayed, upward bouncing back of the ball that creates the illusion one can actually beat the wall. Still, after trying a few times, one learns that this is a game with no other opponent than oneself.

The London architectural guide credits this building—Pimlico School—to the Greater London Council (GLC) Department of Architecture and Civic Design. The guide makes reference to an individual architect/author only in passing: John Bancroft. Like many of his London contemporaries, Bancroft chose to forgo the pursuit of a private practice and to exercise his profession as a civil servant.

His choice was less unusual than one might think. In the late 1960s and early 1970s it was common for cities like London to have large public works departments that carried impressive portfolios. Career prospects for architects who joined these departments were good to the point that the GLC's Architects Department even became a hotbed for talented young architects, many with close ties to the Architectural Association and Cambridge University. At its height in the 1960s, the department had a staff of over three thousand. Public buildings that carry its signature include works as diverse as the Hayward Gallery, Queen Elizabeth Hall, and the Michael Faraday Memorial. Even today, the built legacy looks refreshingly modern and innovative.

1963: The Greater London Council is established and replaces the London County Council (LCC) as the first strategic planning authority to cover all of the London agglomeration. Its first main task is to provide a development plan for the Greater London Area with the aim of triggering a general modernization of housing, public services, utilities, and road and transport facilities. The GLC's far-reaching ambitions culminated in a proposal for a central London motorway loop coupled with a comprehensive redevelopment of Covent Garden. The public inquiry that follows lasts nearly two years (from July 1970 to May 1972), and—needless to say—much of the plan is derailed by fierce opposition. Nevertheless, the plan prescribes many other modernizations in the city that are carried out, so for almost a decade there is more than enough work to keep a large workforce of civil-servant architects busy.

The experimental nature of the buildings is directly mirrored by the experimental way in which work within the council's Architects Department is carried out. Reportedly, the atmosphere in the workplace is one of "creative inefficiency": a "plan factory" based on the principle of productive anarchy. The department's organization consists of individual groups, each of which has a considerable degree of autonomy and is intended to resemble a small private practice. Supervision and interference by the department head are kept to a minimum in order "to delegate to the groups the freedom to manage the design and execute the work at their own discretion."[1] In his introduction to the book *GLC Architecture 1965/70*, former department head Hubert Bennett describes the philosophy as follows: "Encouragement is given to new ideas; and the exercise of imagination and self-discipline is a predominant feature at all levels."[2] Ironically, it is exactly this internal policy that catches up with him when three years later, during the development of South Bank, he gets wind only at the very last moment of a monolithic concrete building that is being proposed. His all-out attempt to secure a revised proposal in his capacity as department head utterly fails.

The absence of a conventional architect-client relationship—in a municipal architects' department, client and architect are essentially parts of the same body—creates a curious dynamic within the department. The usual oppositions between architectural ambitions and budget limitations are resolved through a simulated dialectic between the architect and what is referred to as "the administrative officer in charge." Since each group is intended to resemble a small private practice, a job architect like John Bancroft essentially becomes the equivalent of the architect-owner of a private practice, the department's prime link to (and confidant of) the client (read: the department). The job architect acts as the overseer of the body of work carried out by the group—a star in his own right. It is striking that most of the architects credited for what today are famous monuments in the city are at very early stages of their careers. When John Bancroft becomes head of the Schools Division at the LCC Architects Department in 1957, he is only twenty-eight years old. He causes amusement by wearing a smock at the drawing board.

In the early 1970s, amid growing criticism of the department's Brutalist concrete monuments, optimism begins to fade. During the economic

John Bancroft
"John Bancroft (1928–2011): Designer of Pimlico School Remembered," *Building Design Magazine*, September 7, 2011

crisis of that decade, Britain faces increasing internal criticism of the welfare state and its built manifestations. With the installation of a new Conservative government in 1979, Britain becomes one of Europe's most passionate advocates of the free market. In a relatively short time its capital city changes from a welfare stronghold to the playground of extreme laissez-faire. Much of London's development now takes place in the name of "small instead of large government." A few years after her ascent to power, Margaret Thatcher abolishes the GLC and, in doing so, dismantles any overriding capacity for the city to steer its own planning efforts. (The chief impetus for development of the Docklands is an ad hoc exemption from a system of central planning.) Critics argue that the abolition of the GLC is politically motivated, given its powerful opposition to Thatcher's government. London-wide government returns only in 2000 in the form of the Greater London Authority (GLA) after a referendum held by Tony Blair's Labour government. However, the structure and powers of the GLA are very different from those of its predecessor. London has changed, and with it, the role of its architects.

Many of the GLC's Architects Department's buildings are controversial from the start. Pimlico School is one of them, and for good reason: the school is the built manifestation of the comprehensive schooling (Labour) policies of the Inner London Education Authority, located on a razed and open block in the heart of Westminster, a staunch Tory borough. A contemporary critic likens it to a battleship, describing it as a "100-odd meter long, turreted, metallic grey thing lying in its own sunken rectangle."[3] Over time Pimlico School earns a reputation, especially in music and drama. Proponents and opponents still debate whether this occurred because of or in spite of the architecture of its building.

The building provokes an ambivalent reading, even for professionals. It reflects both the unscrupulous imposition of architectural Brutalism on its surroundings and a genuine desire to match those surroundings in scale: an awkward compromise between affront and respect. The lowest story of the building is sunk into a pit (the schoolyard) to match the level of the basements of the surrounding town houses. From the pit emerges the school, an odd creature of concrete and glass. Boxy projected classrooms with slanted glazed windows (supposedly self-cleaning) look out on the neighborhood but also allow the neighborhood to peep in, the spatial equivalent of a system of checks and balances between the city's progressive educational policies and onlooking taxpayers.

In a 2008 interview Bancroft argues: "I wanted pupils to feel they were part of a community. So, I divided the place up in the form of glass screens, so you would get views down from the level you were into the other parts of the school. Also I wanted to make sure that from time to time you would catch a glimpse of the great surrounding community that Pimlico is."[4]

2011: I visit the neighborhood again for the first time since leaving in 1991. Even though I have visited London regularly in the years between, I have somehow—perhaps guided by an ominous sense of what I might find—refrained from returning to my initial place of residence. My London work experience has meanwhile taught me that the survival of large public monuments from the 1960s and 1970s is far from guaranteed.

The pit is still there, but the school has gone. It was slated for demolition a year earlier to make place for a new visual- and performing-arts center, commissioned by the Westminster City Council and partially funded through a government program (meanwhile scrapped) to help fund the erection of schools but mostly financed by private sources.[5] In the new scheme, almost half the site is dedicated to luxury flats to provide the development with a sound financial base. The text on the website of the architect's practice responsible for the scheme—Architecture PLB—is a sad mixture of opportunism, groveling hypocrisy, and utter lack of collegiality with the original architect:

> The new Pimlico Academy replaces the existing Pimlico School on the same site to address Westminster City's council's concerns about the existing 1960's building being able to accommodate future requirements of both the school and the local community. Well-designed buildings, we believe, should reflect the lives of the people who use them. Only by listening to these people—to their hopes and concerns—can we create a shared vision that is both pragmatic and inspirational. We develop richer, more meaningful briefs with our clients because at Architecture PLB we understand the difference between hearing and listening.[6]

The scheme proves hard to combat. Bancroft, along with the school's many admirers, fights a long battle to save Pimlico School (even remortgaging his house in the process), firmly believing that the Westminster City Council's decision to demolish it is driven by political, not functional, motives. The main obstacle to saving Pimlico School from demolition proves to be the inability to get the building listed. Ministers take the expedient view that perceived design faults impair the building's architectural value. The excessive use of glass makes the building too hot in the summer and too cold in the winter. (Edith Farnsworth used the same argument in court against Ludwig Mies van der Rohe.) As in so many cases, the tipping point in the battle over preservation of the building is the demolition of a part supposedly of "lesser interest" (a fairly common procedure to pave the way for eventual demolition of "prestigious" buildings that present a financial liability to profitable redevelopment of inner-city sites). In the case of Pimlico School, the first sacrifice is the indoor swimming pool, located in a separate wing. Once the original configuration of the building has been compromised, it is increasingly difficult to argue for preserving what is left. In the words of Bancroft's wife: "The demolition of the swimming pool was the wedge that drove the school's eventual demolition."[7]

August 29, 2011: with the fate of Pimlico School inevitable and demolition work well under way, John Bancroft passes away at the age of eighty-two. When taken to the demolition site shortly before his death by film director Tom Cordell for the shooting of the documentary *Utopia London*, his demeanor is silent and restrained. While watching the demolition, he supposedly mutters, "Bloody fools."

Just as sometimes the essence of an entire era can be encapsulated in a single moment, the essence of a city can be encapsulated in a single building or, more precisely, in the fate that the city bestows on that building. The story of Pimlico School is essentially the story of London since 1970. In the demolition of Pimlico School, one could read the definitive end of a short-lived, fragile period of naïve optimism before the brutal rule of the market economy became the common denominator. It is ironic that the benign ideology of the welfare state chose to be represented by an architectural style known as Brutalism. The market economy, it seems, applies the irony in reverse, using a polished, politically correct architectural language to conceal an essentially brutal rule: survival of the fittest under the guise of good taste.

Especially from today's perspective, the story of John Bancroft's life, as well as that of his most important building, provides an intriguing point of reference. In the age of the star architect, the idea of forgoing the pursuit of a private practice in favor of a shared ideology seems remote and untenable, but what architecture seems to lack most today is exactly the kind of shared purpose that civil servants like John Bancroft and his colleagues worked for. Forty years ago, serving the public cause proved a powerful source of inspiration; given the numbers of architects who made that choice, one might even speak of a common ground.[8]

Pimlico Secondary School, London, 1971
Photograph by Sam Lambert / Architectural Press Archive / RIBA Library Photographs
Collection

Marzahn, 1960s
Photograph from the collection of Lothar Idziak. Courtesy of Michael Idziak. Drehscheibe
Online Forums (http://www.drehscheibe-online.de)

6

Architektur ohne Eigenschaften

April 20, 1945: It is the führer's birthday, but there is little cause for celebration. The Red Army is steadily advancing toward Berlin. Shots can be heard inside the city. In the Führerbunker, the command center of German military operations, confusion ensues. The Russians supposedly hold a railway bridge over the Oder, from which long-range artillery is being fired. A phone call to the front breaks more disturbing news: the shooting is not long-range but short-range fire. The Russians have taken up positions at Marzahn, only twelve kilometers from the center of Berlin. In the days that follow, the Russians move even closer. After a long and piteous rant, Hitler concludes that "it has become impossible to lead and the war is lost."[1]

The devastation is enormous. The cities of the Third Reich, which once stretched from Normandy to Stalingrad and even to parts of North Africa, have been reduced to collections of ruins and streets piled with rubble. Allied bombings and the close-range, urban combat of the last six months of the war have destroyed nearly a quarter of all German homes. In Berlin, more than half of the living space is in ruins. In the Soviet-occupied zone of Germany alone, there is an estimated shortage of about 1.4 million dwellings.[2]

This shortage will shape East German politics for the next four decades as the country embarks on a state housing plan unparalleled in human history, comprising every conceivable aspect of government, industry, culture, science, and technology. In a race against time, design, construction, and manufacturing merge into a single, integrated effort to settle the housing question once and for all. By the mid-1980s East Germany has built more than 2.1 million prefabricated housing units, and more than half of the country's population lives in mass-produced homes. In some East German cities, the proportion is higher still: 65 percent in Rostock, 72 percent in Frankfurt an der Oder, 85 percent in Schwedt.

Marzahn becomes a so-called *Großsiedlung,* (large housing estate) where the share of industrially produced homes reaches virtually 100 percent.[3]

Marzahn was in the news again recently, when a group of neo-Nazis stole a Christmas tree from a newly opened refugee center in town.[4] Ever since a National Democratic Party march got out of hand there in 2013, Marzahn has found itself at the forefront of a debate about the burden of immigration in East German cities. The center, an agglomeration of some two hundred container units—planned as an emergency measure in anticipation of an influx of refugees after a decision of the Berlin Senate—has sparked concerns among local residents. Wary of the negative impact of a large foreign community, they set up the so-called Marzahn Civil Initiative, driven by a desire to reverse the downward spiral of the area since German reunification. However, by focusing on immigration, the initiative also constitutes a curious paradox. In the previous two decades, Marzahn has experienced wholesale urban flight, losing about 30 percent of its population.[5] Since the fall of the Berlin Wall, Marzahn, designed to help solve a housing shortage, has suffered a housing surplus. Its vacant dwellings—over 12 percent of the total—could have easily satisfied the needs of the new arrivals. However, since 2002 a demolition plan has been in motion, which has led to the elimination of nearly a quarter of its apartments. Given the apparent shortage of appropriate homes for new (foreign) inhabitants, the whole course of events seems erratic. Why demolish prefabricated housing units only to hastily replace them with more provisional ones? The new arrivals, the subject of so much controversy, might have been viewed as a means to counter the trend of a shrinking population and a good reason to preserve existing homes. But apparently not everyone sees it that way.

The scenes of neo-Nazis marching through the prefabricated housing blocks of Marzahn look like an uncanny time warp: a reenactment of the twentieth century's most defining chapter, but played in reverse. Nazism should have met its end in the triumph of the Communists' antifascist ideology, but today communism's built legacy, in the form of its prefabricated housing blocks, has become the site of its resurgence. In Marzahn, history has made a U-turn. The fate of Marzahn and other places like it across the former East Germany resembles that of public housing projects in American inner cities, demolished during the 1960s and 1970s.

There, the departure of white middle-class families for the suburbs, so-called white flight, left these projects blighted and desolate, with an embittered, ghettoized, and predominantly black population.[6] Forty years later, in Marzahn, the same thing happens again, but this time it is white bitterness that remains.

East versus West

Under the Yalta and Potsdam agreements of 1945, the city of Berlin is to be governed by the Allied Control Council (ACC). Marzahn—part of greater Berlin since 1920—becomes part of the sector under Soviet occupation. In 1948 the Soviets withdraw from the ACC and proceed to install a separate socialist government in their zone. In 1949 the Deutsche Demokratische Republik (DDR) is founded, and East Berlin (although unrecognized by Western powers) is designated as its official capital. Subsequently, the eastern districts of the city are firmly integrated into the new Communist state. Stalin, in the year before his death, had made an effort at rapprochement in the form of a proposal for German unification (never properly explained in the history books), but this attempt is abruptly aborted when Nikita Khrushchev comes to power in 1953. Khrushchev fervently opposes German unification, which he perceives as capitulation to the West; rather, the East must thrive in its own right by building an economy based on the advancement of science and industry. Owing its existence to the USSR's victory over Nazi Germany, the DDR becomes a trophy, a laboratory where some socialist principles are exercised in extreme form simply to make a point about the defeated country. East Germany is to be a showcase of the blessings of communism: a model state, where every policy formulated in Moscow is executed with an even greater degree of conviction. The DDR has to be exemplary; some countries inevitably have to be more Communist than others.

"We will bury you!" says Khrushchev in 1956, addressing Western ambassadors at a Polish Embassy reception in Moscow.[7] Despite other possible interpretations, the phrase is generally taken to mean that the USSR intends to outlive (that is, outperform) Western nations in an economic sense, as the ultimate proof of superiority of the Communist system. In this competition, East German communism, in particular, cannot afford to fail. Shortly thereafter, announcements from the Socialist Unity Party of Germany (SED) suggest that the DDR economy will overtake that of West Germany (or, as the SED chooses to call it, the Bonn splinter state) by 1961.[8] Ironically, this happens to be the year in which the Berlin Wall is built: not so much the proclaimed antifascist rampart as a way to conceal the failure of such broadly announced ambitions.

Khrushchev differs from his predecessor on more than just German reunification. Like Germany, the USSR is suffering, even ten years after the end of the war, from a substantial shortfall of adequate housing. Stalinist policies toward reconstruction may have boosted the image of Soviet cities, but they fail to supply the required amount of housing. In his famous speech at the National Conference of Builders on the introduction of industrial building methods, Khrushchev explicitly denounces the wasteful manner in which the postwar reconstruction of Soviet cities has unfolded: "The facades of residential buildings are sometimes hung with a multitude of all kinds of superfluous decoration that point to a lack of taste in the architects. Builders sometimes even have difficulty executing these decorations. Architects have mainly been interested in creating a silhouette and have failed to take thought of what the construction and exploitation of these buildings would cost. What people need is apartments. They don't have time to gaze admiringly at silhouettes; they need houses to live in!"[9]

Although this statement can be read as a clear critique of the previous regime, Khrushchev never mentions Stalin's name. In 1954 the time is not yet ripe for an outright political critique of his predecessor, who has died only a year earlier. Such a critique does not appear until two years later in Khrushchev's famous secret speech, which provokes intense political controversy.[10] For the time being, the target is Stalin's architects, who should have known better: "Led on by the example of the great masters, architects want to design nothing but unique buildings and erect monuments to themselves. Such architects are a stumbling block in the way of industrializing construction. If Pushkin created for himself a monument 'not made by human hands,' many architects feel they simply must create a 'handmade' monument to themselves in the form of a building constructed in accordance with a unique design" [laughter, applause].

Is the stumbling block just particular architects, or is it the notion of architecture altogether? Khrushchev's lines curiously resonate with comments made by Chinese president Xi Jinping about "weird buildings" and the "wasteful" contemporary architecture currently blossoming in China.[11] (The role of head of state / architecture critic lives on, it seems.) In both cases, industrial methods are advocated to speed up construction and provide much-needed housing. With the construction industry increasingly developing into a semiautonomous sector, a tempting notion of architecture without architects presents itself.

"Cheaper, Better, and Faster"

It does not take long before Khrushchev's views become official policy in the DDR. In fact, it is the East Germans who are ultimately responsible for the propagandistic title under which Khrushchev's speech later becomes known. In the beginning of 1955, they publish it under the headline "Besser, billiger, und schneller bauen" (Build better, cheaper, and faster—an adaptation of the considerably less catchy Russian title, "On the Introduction of Industrial Methods, Improving the Quality and Reducing the Cost of Construction").[12] In giving Khrushchev's speech the snappy and ultimately enduring catchphrase, the East Germans retroactively coauthor its contents. This mechanism—in which the DDR consistently offers a form of endorsement that surpasses the original—continues to characterize East German–Soviet relations until the fall of the wall.

The conditions for implementing Khrushchev's views are basically already in place. Since the founding of the DDR in 1949, the government has progressively nationalized the building sector in East Germany, bringing various formerly private businesses, such as manufacturers, contractors, and builders, together under central state control. As of 1949, all civil servants (*Bauämter*) have to answer to the Ministry of Reconstruction (Ministerium für Aufbau; after 1958, Ministerium für Bauwesen). Shortly afterward, in 1951, the Deutsche Bauakademie der DDR (DBA) is founded as the ministry's theoretical and scientific research organ, dedicated to the advancement of East German building practice.

Initially both institutions take a conservative view. Their mission is to restore the beauty of the traditional German cities. In line with the Stalinist policies of the 1930s and 1940s, they promote national culture and denounce modernism. Now that important Bauhaus representatives such as Walter Gropius and Ludwig Mies van der Rohe have emigrated to the United States, the style of international modernism (which in part originated from the Bauhaus) is viewed as Western and therefore inappropriate as an expression of the utopian workers' state. The DBA is conceived as an institution in the tradition of architectural academies in Germany and elsewhere as custodians of a national building style. At the opening of the DBA in 1951, DDR chief Walter Ulbricht states its mission as follows: "The Deutsche Bauakademie has the noble task of retrieving the honor of architecture as an art and German architecture as a German art. In the wake of the functionalism and formalism of the so-called Bauhaus style, which—particularly in West Germany, as introduced by the Americans—was perceived to have led architecture to a dead end, it is necessary to base the new German architecture on Germany's classical legacy and on the progressive architectures of all nations, above all: Soviet architecture."[13]

In the context of the DDR's persistent housing shortage, however, this approach soon proves problematic. On June 16, 1953, faced with a demand for a 10 percent increase in production, workers revolt during the construction of the new Stalinallee in East Berlin. Initially a labor protest, the revolt soon draws in the general populace, and on June 17 similar protests occur throughout the DDR, with more than a million people striking in some seven hundred cities. Fearing an anti-Communist counterrevolution, the government enlists Soviet occupation forces to end the riot; some fifty people are killed, and ten thousand more are jailed.

Given an increasingly ambitious and seemingly unrealistic construction program, the new approach to building is timely indeed. Only the use of industrial methods can allow an increase in production without imposing unfeasible working hours on the builders. The simple need to deliver the largest possible number of homes to the DDR population in the shortest time ultimately compels DDR functionaries and architects to follow Khrushchev's example.

The first official acknowledgment of the shift comes from Ulbricht at the First Conference of Builders in the DDR in 1955, in somewhat veiled terms: "The Moscow building conference has given us valuable information. We know that major shortcomings still exist, that more attention must be paid to the economy of urban development. But we also know that under the particular conditions of national and social struggle in Germany, that our way is right. This path leads to a German architecture that serves the interests of the whole people."[14] Since Germany has its own modernist tradition, Ulbricht's desire to "hold on to a typically German architecture" is almost a stroke of luck because it can later be reinterpreted as an endorsement of the style that he initially opposed. Thus in theory, at least, Ulbricht toes the party line. It is clear, however, that something will have to change to avoid a repetition of the events of 1953.

Perhaps the clearest indication of the shift is the appointment of Gerhard Kosel as the new head of the Ministry of Reconstruction (Staatssekretär im Ministerium für Aufbau). Kosel—a former student of Bruno Taut and Hanz Poelzig, two major exponents of modern architecture—replaced Kurt Liebknecht, a promoter of the Stalinist school, who have previously dismissed mass-produced housing projects such as the Hansaviertel in West Berlin as un-German, cosmopolitan, and American. Before returning to Germany, Kosel has worked in the USSR, where he has experimented with industrial construction methods in Magnitogorsk and Novokuznetsk.[15] His task in the DDR is to introduce and promote general and comprehensive industrialization of construction in line with the policies of the Soviet Union.

Still, the expertise Kosel brings back could hardly be qualified as Soviet. Under Kosel's tutelage, a group of architects and city planners occupies key positions in the administrative structure, many of whose roots went back to the Bauhaus. After the Nazis outlaw its existence, the Bauhaus becomes a strangely schizophrenic phenomenon, with half-lives in two parallel universes: East and West. While architects like Walter Gropius and Konrad Wachsmann emigrate to the United States, others, like Hannes Meyer and Ernst May, choose the USSR to further their cause. The expertise Kosel brings is not so much Russian as it is German, or at least the continuation of another, interrupted German tradition.

With Kosel assuming his positions as minister of reconstruction and head of the DBA, both of these institutions become complicit in opposition to their original cause: designed as a defense against modernism, they now began to promote it. Everything the Communist system has sought to expel (Bauhaus, the United States, the West) simply reenters through the back door. This about-face constitutes an interesting historic moment in the sense that it shows that the whole idea of an independent

Communist universe was a fallacy. One could say that the USSR and later the DDR are actually laboratories of all modernisms combined, in which modernism develops from counterculture into official culture, with nothing to stand in its way.

In August 1954, before Khrushchev's famous address, experts are sent to France to study precast systems. After the workers' uprising of 1953, the engineers Raymond Camus and Édouard Fougea, from the French firms Citroen and Coignet, and the Danish engineers Axel Nielsen and R. A. Larson receive international and particularly Eastern European attention when they presented the technology of prefabricated concrete as a panacea for Europe's ongoing housing shortage. These are the countries (France and Denmark) to which Khrushchev referred when he talked about "other countries making extensive use of concrete, rather than brick, in construction."[16] More than any other European nation, France has been experimenting with industrial building; the system Camus patented in 1948 catches Khrushchev's eye in particular as a potential example for the Soviet construction industry.[17] The French systems from Camus and Coignet (also exported to Western countries) lay the foundation of the Soviet concrete factories, which in turn are exported to every corner of the Communist globe.

This is the context in which Gerhard Kosel is active in the USSR, and these are the systems that he imports into the DDR upon his return. Their acceptance is significantly aided by the DDR's various "scientific" building institutions established as part of his rule. Building's status as a science somewhat depoliticizes it, making the foreign origin of any components less of an issue. It is mainly for this reason that the DDR develops into a laboratory for the concrete industry, where ideas from the Eastern and Western Hemispheres can enjoy a perfect testing ground. France, Denmark, and Finland happily contribute to the construction program, and the DDR becomes the world's front-runner in the development of prefabrication systems for mass housing projects. In the DDR, *die Platte,* as it comes to be called, becomes a methodical science.

Building praxis in the DDR is definitively transformed when Kosel delegates a central role to the Institut für Städtebau und Hochbau. The institute oversees the absorption of private architects' practices into so-called *Projektierungsbüros,* which act as the direct executive organs of the ministry and the DBA. Each architect is now an employee of the state. The process-oriented term *Projektierung* ("projecting") is indicative of the desire of the DDR government to merge architecture, urbanism, building design, housing typologies, and industrial production into a single state-controlled effort. The ambition is to streamline the traditional division of professional responsibilities in the design of buildings—between architect and contractor and between design and execution—and make the process a single, integrated whole. This is an uncompromising thrust forward, the final resolution of the Marxist dialectic: the synthesis becomes a real and existing state within the East German construction industry.

An Evolution of Systems

In the decades that follow, this philosophy takes definitive shape in the DDR. Architecture no longer evolves as a succession of styles but becomes a series of typological and technical breakthroughs, void of authors and void of signatures. It is in the DDR that Khrushchev's way toward the future unfolds in its most extreme form. Architects' identities are submerged in favor of systems; decisions on where and how these systems translate into eventual buildings are largely made without ever consulting the architects who design them.

These systems—the names of which sound more like the license plates of cars than like housing designs—become the main architectural legacy of the DDR. Developed as part of a relentless search for a better, cheaper, and faster way forward, successive systems follow in rapid-fire fashion: QA3 (A), P2, WHH 17, WHH-GT 18/21, QP 59/61/64.[18] The main measure of optimization is technical performance, and here an almost Darwinian pattern of evolution emerges. In the 1950s the initial system, known as QA3 (A) (Querwandtyp Nummer 3, Variante A), is still based on the use of smaller elements because of the limited capacity of building cranes. As a consequence, the walls and facades consist of multiple stacked elements, while floorplates have relatively small spans, with limited possibilities for layouts of floor plans. The advent of more powerful cranes at the start of the 1960s enables building with larger elements: five- to nine-ton modules can now be lifted effortlessly, which drastically reduces costs per dwelling. (Whereas in the QA3 (A) system each dwelling consisted of about 150 elements, later systems use a mere 30 elements per dwelling.) The first so-called *Plattenbauten* (buildings entirely composed of prefabricated

P2 system facades, 1964
Graphic from *Deutsche Architektur*, nr. 5/1964. Reproduction courtesy of Leibniz Institute for Research on Society and Space (IRS)

concrete panels) are born. In time, not just facades and wall and floor elements—in other words, the elements of the structural system—are being prefabricated; the 1960s also sees the on-site installation of fully prefabricated kitchens and bathrooms as ready-mades.

The initial systems are based on relatively small spans of 2.40 and 3.60 meters. A major breakthrough occurs with the arrival of a system called P2. Prestrung concrete makes a span of 6 meters possible; in combination with a greater building depth of 12 meters, this eliminates the need for internal partition walls. Apartments can now be designed on a floorplate uninterrupted by structure, which, like a kind of miniature *plan libre,* permits a great degree of flexibility in the layout of apartments. Greater depth allows kitchens and bathrooms to be situated away from the facade, leaving it to be used entirely for living rooms and bedrooms. The famous full-height transparent *Vitrinenschrank* ("glass window cabinet") permits light to penetrate via the living rooms and creates the first open kitchen, allowing living, cooking, and eating to unfold in a single space.

The greater height of the buildings, however, makes it necessary to introduce elevators, which initially interfere with the modular system. As a consequence, the elevators and the staircases are sometimes placed in a separate shaft outside the building and are embraced as a welcome source of articulation within the extruded monotony of the modular system.

The use of industrial building systems has significant consequences for urban planning. It requires a shift from the model of perimeter blocks with a central courtyard, remainders of the earlier socialist realist period, to so-called *Zeilenbau,* essentially an urban pattern made up of parallel rows of slabs. The distance between the blocks, as well as their height, is determined by the radius of building cranes. In short, the industrial mode of building standardizes not only the architecture but also the practice of urban planning: the urban plan becomes a reflection of industrial logistics. The crane is the main architect of the new settlements.[19]

It isn't until the introduction of even higher building types, such as the WHH 17 and later the WHH-GT 18/21 (respectively, seventeen, eighteen, and twenty-one floors), based on a tower plan with a central core, that a certain compositional logic reenters the urban plans. The towers can be placed at strategic locations to mark exceptional points in the city—for example, at the end of axes, creating a kind of industrially produced monumentality. Strangely, this monumentality feels like a Stalinist leftover that has survived both Khrushchev's and the SED's purge of his principles in the mid-1950s. The art of placing buildings in a plausible urban ensemble becomes an important topic in architectural education, producing quasi-formal rules about the interplay among a limited number of building types.[20]

WBS 70

By 1970 the sheer number of different building systems is contradicting the idea of standardization. Myriad systems, each with its own code, stultify the DDR; each type represents a standard in itself, and it is this variegation that causes the entire DDR building effort to fall short of the required quota. Too many specific, tailor-made components and regional variants drive up construction costs; a new system with fewer components is needed, with a smaller catalog of types and a unified system across all regions of the country.

The basis for such a system is provided in a study by Wilfried Stallknecht and Achim Felz for the Ministerium für Bauwesen in 1969. This study culminates in a nationwide standardized system, based on a six-by-six grid, which permits a large number of permutations with the use of only a limited number of elements. This system becomes known under the name WBS 70, short for Wohnungsbauserie 1970. It is the largest and most ambitious industrial production system of dwellings the DDR will produce, and the one on which the country, still faced with a substantial housing shortage, comes to rely over the next two decades. The first building using the WBS 70 system is constructed in 1973 in Neubrandenburg. From there, the system starts its road trip across the DDR, eventually making up most of its built environment. By 1990, 644,900 housing units have been built using the WBS 70 system.

Although WBS 70 has been conceived to homogenize building production across the DDR, it still produces local variants, mostly due to the creative urges of local housing corporations. Over time, the unified system generates an ever-wider range of panel types and other special elements; countless window and facade design variations are developed, many using art. Some buildings have balconies; others feature loggias or bay windows. Even the notion of the single-floor apartment, almost universal until then, is no longer sacrosanct as maisonettes and double-height studio types are increasingly developed. Angles greater or less than ninety degrees emerge (until 1970 these had been a mortal architectural sin). Conic floor elements are developed, capable of producing radial blocks with radial floor plans; in some inner-city locations the WBS 70 system can even be found with mansard roofs.

WBS 70 can be viewed as the culmination of the *Plattenbau* systems, produced and applied in abundance in the Communist hemisphere ever since Khrushchev's famous speech. Complete buildings are supplied to Poland, Yugoslavia, Syria, Egypt, Mozambique, and Vietnam. Supposedly, one can build more crisply in the conditioned environment of a factory than on-site. However, weaknesses in the general assemblage of prefabricated elements invariably reveal themselves on building sites, where the real outdoors takes its revenge on any hypothetical perfection. Despite the indiscriminate application of standardized concrete panels throughout the Communist world, different levels of sophistication of the construction industry in different countries become apparent in the way panels are joined on-site. It is in the size of the joints that evidence of locality appears: in the DDR, two to four centimeters; in the USSR, five to ten centimeters; in North Vietnam, twenty to thirty centimeters.

The universal presence of the WBS 70 system has a major effect on what little is left of traditional building practice. It effectively kills the craft of individual tradespeople such as plasterers, tile layers, and painters. By the time industrialization reaches its peak in the 1970s, the DDR's small building companies and craftsmen have all but disappeared.

Big Changes for a Small Town

At the outset of the 1970s the DDR sees major political changes. First Secretary of the SED Walter Ulbricht is replaced by Erich Honecker, who introduces a policy called "Real and Existing Socialism," which aims to raise consumer wealth as the ultimate proof of the success of the Communist system.[21]

Crucial to the success of Honecker's policies is the resolution of housing problems in the DDR. At the Eighth Party Congress of the SED in 1971, the newly appointed Honecker declares that the East German housing crisis will definitively be resolved by 1990. The issue of housing is key to Communist prestige and has loomed large in Marxist rhetoric since

Friedrich Engels. The availability of the new WBS 70 inspires confidence in the new DDR leadership, and a wave of so-called *Großsiedlungen* is announced in a bid to solve the DDR's housing shortage once and for all. A number of small towns encircling East Berlin are designated for vast new tracts of industrially produced housing blocks.

One of these towns is Marzahn. On March 27, 1973, the Berlin Magistrate, the State Planning Commission, and the Politbüro approve preliminary plans for a settlement of 35,000 people. In subsequent rounds the plan is vastly extended, and the scope of the combined *Großsiedlungen* ultimately embraces 400,000 people and 150,000 apartments. Ironically, Marzahn has also been part of Albert Speer's vision for his new capital, Germania, which included extensive plans to settle 445,000 people in modern housing projects outside the northeast edge of Berlin.[22]

Since the arrival of Soviet troops in 1945, Marzahn has been untouched by most of the DDR's frantic construction programs. Apart from hosting the DDR's first collective farm, Marzahn remains the same somewhat provincial village it had always been, where German traditions and the local Protestant church enjoy relatively uninterrupted rule.

All of this changes on the morning of April 11, 1977. The transformation that follows is swift and total. Over 650 hectares of land are dug up, and almost seven million cubic meters of soil are displaced to make room for nearly 1,300 building foundations. Multiple construction teams, working in three shifts, finish housing blocks with as many as 120 units in as many days.[23] Forty-five combination *Kindergärten / Kinderkrippen* and fifty-one polytechnic high schools are erected, all within about 150 days. Sixteen shopping centers, fifteen local restaurants and pubs, nine senior citizens' homes, five hospitals, eight general service centers, fifty indoor sports arenas, two indoor community swimming pools (with saunas), and nine youth clubs are built in direct coordination with each housing block.[24]

The local river, the Wuhle, which cut a gentle swale between the old villages of Marzahn and Hellersdorf, is redirected to form an artificial lake at the foot of a planned artificial mountain, the Kienberg: a hundred-meter-high, thirty-one-hectare tumulus made of seven million cubic meters of construction debris, demolished old houses, war rubble, and displaced earth. Together, the Kienberg and the Wuhle are to be the center of a new and completely artificially landscaped recreation park, which includes a

Marzahn, 1985
Photograph by Peter Zimmerman / Bundesarchiv, Bild 183-1985-0723-004

ski hill, an all-weather bobsled run, boat rental facilities, an open-air stage, and spaces for picnicking, hiking, and soccer.[25] Neither the lake nor the hill is ever completed.

By 1984 Marzahn has become the largest mass housing project in European history. The area is used as a showcase of East German industrial prestige: a tour of Marzahn is a must for celebrities and guests of honor in the capital of the DDR, including heads of state such as Indira Gandhi and Mikhail and Raisa Gorbachev. For Marzahners themselves, probably the most memorable visit is that of Sigmund Jähn, the first (and only) East German cosmonaut, on September 22, 1978, accompanied by

Soviet cosmonaut Valery Bikovsky. Having just returned from a space mission in Soyuz, they receive the Order of Karl Marx from Honecker at the Palast der Republik; the two men visit Marzahn in the company of an SED entourage and are taken on a guided tour of one of the freshly completed WBS 70 living units.[26]

The DDR had aimed to overtake West Germany in 1961 in the size of its per capita economy.[27] Although in real economic terms that ambition never materialized, the question remains how delusional this ambition was. If one looks at photographs of the 1960s and 1970s, living conditions in Marzahn do not seem all that remote from those of, for instance, Gropiusstadt in West Berlin. Particularly in the face of the asymmetries that exist today, the old imagery of well-populated, lively modern neighborhoods in both East and West suggest that despite ideological oppositions, the differences might have been smaller then than they are now.

Exodus

The East German residential construction program was intended to eliminate the country's housing shortage by 1990. It largely did. It is ironic that its most impressive achievement—solving the housing crisis—coincided with the disappearance of the DDR as a country. Had East Germany withstood the events of 1989–1990, the majority of its population would have lived in an entirely industrially produced urban environment in which all traces of history and tradition had been erased. This, however, is not what came to pass.[28]

After 1989 massive emigration from the East German *Großsiedlungen* ensues. From a population of 15.3 million in 1990, the population of the former East Germany declines to 12.5 million.[29] The same country that has once suffered a severe housing shortage now suffers a housing surplus. The West German media scare of social housing estates spiraling inevitably into decline becomes a self-fulfilling prophecy.[30] Those who can afford to move out do so, either to newly rediscovered central Berlin or to the burgeoning suburbs that seemed to grow overnight on the green pastures of Brandenburg.

Meanwhile, wholesale demolition of East German *Plattenbausiedlungen,* called for by some West German politicians, proves unrealistic. Instead, a more nuanced approach of *Rückbau* is preferred.[31] This demolition process, also referred to as *Normalisierung* (normalization), aims to transform former *Plattenbau* areas into normal residential neighborhoods, which supposedly represent a more humane form, if not an aspirational ideal, of suburban living. *Normalisierung* is an attempt to address two issues at once: the creation of a more consumer-fashionable living environment and the reduction of the now-unwanted housing stock.

The *Rückbau* approach is based on partial demolition, reducing the eleven-story slabs to three- or four-story buildings; these friendlier blocks will consist of terraced housing with ground-floor access for each dwelling, or apartment maisonettes in low slabs. The resulting buildings are further insulated with polystyrene panels and often are given a crisp, pastel render. The *Plattenbauten* in the northern and eastern parts of Marzahn—the outskirts of the outskirts—are the first to go. Some blocks disappear entirely and are replaced by parks and playgrounds. This time, urban planning is about eliminating things, not creating them.

During the years of *Normalisierung* from 2002 to 2007,[32] Marzahn loses 4,500 of its 58,500 dwelling units.[33] The process comes to a halt only when an influx of well-heeled West Germans and well-financed foreigners into central Berlin begins to push poorer residents to the city's edge. Coupled with a wave of migrants from Eastern Europe (invariably used to living in *Plattenbau*), this trend stabilizes the vacancy rate at 3 percent in the mid-2010s,[34] a rate deemed acceptable to the market and, therefore, to politicians.

Ironically, the process of *Normalisierung*, however much it might choose to reject the original ideology of the system that it is trying to normalize, is inevitably based on the properties of that system. The prefabrication that has been a tool for rapid construction turns out to be a tool for rapid demolition: easy to assemble, the buildings also prove easy to disassemble. Built panel by panel, they are dismantled panel by panel; their demolition is the reverse of their construction. Even urbanism itself, based on turning radii and heights of standard cranes, invites this rapid and surgically precise deconstruction. The debris after demolition looks surprisingly ordered: the same parts that have gone into the buildings come out; the demolition sites looks like the construction sites a few decades earlier; only the factories are missing.

The waste (if one can call it that) is conscientiously recycled. Panels are used to create other buildings inside Germany, buildings at odds with

Marzahn, 2004
Photograph by Karlheinz Schindler / Picture-Alliance / © ZB–Fotoreport

the original idea of the *Plattenbau:* single-family homes, even holiday homes. A pitched roof and a layer of *Putz* suffices to erase all traces of the originals. In an almost perverse mirroring of bygone days, when the DDR's Bauakademie obsessively researched and advocated the virtues of large-scale panel housing and urbanism, the Technical University of Brandenburg now professes the same enthusiasm for low-density, low-rise building typologies made of the reused building panels.

If East German prefabrication technology was once proudly exported to friendly socialist regimes, it is now the disassembled panels, the discarded products of a failed state, that attain the same status: they are shipped not only to neighboring countries like the Czech Republic and Poland but also farther away. Since 2005 occasional ships set sail from

Recycled concrete panel home, Wusterwitz, Germany, 2007
Photograph by Adrienne Norman

the German Baltic coast toward St. Petersburg, packed with facade panels gathered from East German demolition sites to be reused in the construction of new microrayons in Russia. There, prefabricated panels are going through a revival, and the superior standard of the German panels makes these neighborhoods feel brand new.[35] Far from becoming obsolete, the concrete WBS 70 panels have proved intrinsically tougher than the political system that begat them, and they now operate as a finite, almost wholly recyclable resource in the context of the market economy.

Marzahn is the largest mass housing project in European history, the ultimate demonstration of the capabilities of a single industrial system, a *Gesamtplanungsprojekt*. The *Großsiedlung* Marzahn is the outcome of a long evolution that arguably started in 1955, when the Fifth SED Congress decided to cautiously embrace Khrushchev's directives on industrialization. But somehow that reading doesn't tell the whole story. The roots go back further, before the founding of the DDR, probably even before communism settled in Russia. The blessings of industrialization had long preoccupied both the political Right and Left, being as much at the center of Henry Ford's doctrines as those of Lenin. (Recall "Communism is Soviet power plus electrification.")[36] Industrialization definitively entered the consciousness of the avant-garde after the Futurist manifesto's celebrations of violence and machinery in 1909; five years later, with the outbreak of World War I, its destructive powers had become unequivocally manifest. Industrialization proved a force for good as well as bad; therefore, it was all the more political. Industrialization became the principal subject of the Bauhaus, developed and cultivated to an almost mystical level. In 1924 Mies famously said, "In the industrialization of building I see the core problem of our time. If we manage to carry through this industrialization, then all social, economic, technical and artistic questions would be easily solved."[37]

In Marzahn, Mies got what he had asked for. However, in fully banking on the power of industry over the skills of the craftsman, he made the architect as a craftsman redundant. What the protagonists of the modern movement failed to recognize was how fundamentally antimodern their profession was, even in the context of their rhetoric: their fascination with industrial progress could (and would) inevitably spell their own demise. The culmination of modern architecture is not the heroic modern architect but ultimately the disappearance of the architect as an author of buildings. One may wonder: Is this disappearance an accidental by-product of forces beyond the architect's control, or is it a moment of supreme and calculated vanity, the modern generation's wish to be the last?

If the history of modern architecture, with its ideals of transforming the world for the masses, is like the unfolding of a Greek tragedy, the forty years of DDR architecture are like the deus ex machina: the sudden unexpected intervention of a new ability that abruptly solves a previously unsolvable problem. The solution comes at a price: a forced choice where, if modern architecture is to deliver on its promises, the modern architect must leave the stage. In true dramatic fashion, the last act of the Greek tragedy—the exodus—ends with the death of its main actor.

But how tragic is this course of events? The value of every invention lies in what it makes redundant, in the elimination of the tiresome and difficult processes that are no longer necessary. Whatever else one may think about it, the automated architecture of the former DDR eliminated a whole regime of painful improvisations and arguable design decisions. (Every architect reading this knows what I am talking about, but few will care to admit it.) Architecture is no longer a matter of individual talent (and therefore the exclusive domain of the happy few blessed with it) but a matter of savoir faire, something you do not inherit but acquire. You progress by studying what is there, what others have invented before you, such as industrial processes and typological variations. Architecture becomes something you can learn. If architects have long struggled whether to view their work as an art or as a science, it seems that the DDR provided a conclusive answer. In 2014 the Venice Architecture Biennale purported to suspend the notion of the contemporary architect (at least for the duration of the biennale) and place architecture's basic elements and their evolution at the center of the exhibition: architecture, not architects. The East German effort went a step further, eliminating the need for the architect as the master builder and turning the whole country into a grand exhibition of what could be achieved in his absence.

Marzahn, viewed in this way, becomes something extremely liberating. Its anonymous buildings, stripped of the presence of authors, feel like a welcome change from the wanton nature of much contemporary architecture. In many ways this extends to the DDR effort as a whole. The succession of anonymously coded building systems resembles an X-ray that reveals genuine progress: a succession of real inventions as opposed to the parade of styles or fashions. Indeed, all notions of style and taste (a bourgeois instrument to perpetuate class distinctions) can be abandoned. The disappearance of the architect, an accessory of the bourgeois, becomes like the removal of the last obstacle to a utopian classless society.

Postscript

I spent the first nineteen years of my life in a two-bedroom flat, in a block made entirely out of prefabricated concrete. The block was surrounded by other blocks, identical in construction and appearance; the only difference was the orientation, either north-south or east-west. Each of the blocks' giant L-shaped formations enclosed a vast lawn about the size of a soccer field. Because the rent was low, my parents could save enough money to put me through university. I remember a happy childhood. Occasionally, relatives from smaller towns would visit us and comment that the anonymous and repetitive buildings were alienating and even inhumane, but for us, the environment fostered a sense of familiarity precisely because the buildings were so similar to one another. To us, the repetitive and repeated message of the architecture was self-evident: the equality of the buildings was a reflection of the equality of their inhabitants.

In 2014 I went back for the first time since 1989. The rough concrete finish of the panels was gone, replaced by brick, presumably covering a cavity filled with a thick blanket of stone wool, allowing these older buildings to meet contemporary thermal standards. The former wooden window frames had been replaced by PVC frames that made them look and feel a bit like refrigerator doors. The vast majority of the loggias had been converted into little storage rooms, many of them equipped with satellite dishes, sometimes accompanied by Turkish flags. Men congregated in a local coffeehouse, which must have changed hands many times since my childhood. The current owner no longer sells alcohol.

Contrary to what this might suggest, I did not grow up in a (former) Communist country but in the Netherlands. In Western Europe, too, prefabricated housing projects were built as part of postwar welfare states and reconstruction programs. The neighborhood I describe here is the Westwijk in Vlaardingen, a town near Rotterdam, where a large majority of people used to find employment in the Rotterdam port—seemingly a far cry from life in the former DDR, but closer than one might assume. The flats I grew up in were constructed in accord with the Dura Coignet system, a Dutch adaptation by the contractor Dura of the French Coignet system, which had also been exported to former Eastern Bloc countries, and which strongly resembles the WBS 70 system used in the former DDR.[38] The technical adaptation of the French system to suit Dutch building regulations had been made possible by large public subsidies to help solve a pressing housing shortage in the Netherlands—such policies being, at least during those years, as common in the West as in the East. It was this type of cheap, mass-produced public housing that in the 1960s and 1970s helped eliminate the shortage. Moreover, it generated the financial space for a whole generation of working-class children, particularly in Western Europe, to acquire a higher education and climb the ladder. Europe's middle class was born and bred in the gray concrete of these anonymous buildings.

Marzahn's typical rectangular buildings feel remarkably familiar, and it is there that the generic nature of my old neighborhood becomes part of a larger story, one that transcends nations and political systems. For a while the East and the West, despite their political differences, seem to have run on parallel tracks. Produced in the millions, abundantly applied in both the Western and Eastern Hemispheres, the prefabricated panels are—at an almost improbably poetic level—an expression of a global bond, a form of consensus in the context of an otherwise deep ideological rift, a universal response to a globally felt urgency.

The demolition of buildings stipulates an ideological cleansing, a foreclosure of historical chapters, even if it leaves major issues unresolved. The East German standardization effort is generally viewed as a radical phenomenon of the past. But how radical was it? It can also be explained as simply the all-out pursuit of a universally available minimum standard. Like communism itself, the whole effort contains a curious paradox. Even though it necessitated "radical" change, its ultimate goal—"normal" conditions for the largest possible number of people—was surprisingly mundane. Today we experience the opposite: a default drive toward the exceptional, where extravagant architecture seems wedded to an unequal distribution of wealth. If the Communist system represents a radical pursuit of the mundane, the market economy exemplifies the inverse: a mundane pursuit of the radical. In this respect, then, the term *Normalisierung* is a curious misnomer. When we talk about "normalizing" the former *Großsiedlungen*, what we actually mean is making them conform to the laws of the market economy and all the inequalities that come in its wake. Normal (East) German workers can barely afford the "normalized" homes. The more we try to make the former *Großsiedlungen* look normal, the more we reduce the availability of normal conditions to normal people. Once again, the normal becomes radical, extreme. Buildings may serve to mark the events of history, but more often than not, history is marked by the narratives of their disappearance. You don't know what you've got until it's gone.

Ernst Neufert
Photograph by Pit Ludwig, from *Darmstädter Echo* (Darmstadt: Echo Newspapers GmbH, March 3, 1960). Stadtarchiv Darmstadt.

7

Neufert

The Exceptional Pursuit of the Norm

His built output—a few industrial complexes, some housing projects, and the Quelle Mail Order headquarters in Nuremberg—is not much to speak of, but his name is known to every practicing architect: Ernst Neufert, author of *Architect's Data,* more commonly referred to as *Neufert.*[1] If the importance of an architect equals the extent to which his work lives on in others, Neufert is the most important of the twentieth century. There is probably no architect who has not used *Neufert,* whether as a didactic tool or as a volume of references. It contains all the necessary information to design and execute works of architecture. *Neufert* is enduringly popular. As of 2016, it is in its forty-first German edition, has been translated into seventeen languages, and has sold over 500,000 copies.[2]

Ernst Neufert's life maps closely to the unfolding of the twentieth century. He was born on March 15, 1900, and his first job, as an apprentice mason at the age of fourteen, coincided with the outbreak of World War I. The year the war ended, he graduated from the School of Construction in Weimar. When the Bauhaus opened in 1919, he enrolled as one of its first students and soon started to work for the architectural practice of Walter Gropius and Adolf Meyer. In 1926, at the height of the Weimar Republic, he was made head of the building department at the State Technical University of Architecture and Civil Engineering (Staatliche Bauhochschule)—"the other Bauhaus."

Emigration to the US after the Nazi takeover in 1933 would have been the logical next step. Neufert's life story might then have echoed many of his colleagues: educated in Germany, ascending to stardom in the United States. Neufert did not emigrate. But even his seemingly nonconformist choice to stay in Germany was a form of conformism—a largely apolitical act. The post he accepted under the regime was that of resident architect at the United Lusatia Glassworks (Vereinigte Lausitzer Glaswerke). Even in terms of his career choices, Neufert exhibited what would become the main paradox of his life: an exceptional pursuit of the norm.

Neufert's collaboration with Albert Speer began in 1938. For Speer, who was then Hitler's general building inspector for the Reich's capital city, he worked on the categorization, standardization, and rationalization of Berlin's residential buildings.[3] The standards he developed and promoted were duly incorporated into the Nazis' building plans, both at home and in occupied territories.[4] By 1944 Neufert was in charge of planning the entire postwar reconstruction of Germany's war-ravaged cities.

Unlike Speer, Neufert was never accused of collaboration with the Nazis or convicted of any wrongdoing. Technically, he did not actively participate in the Nazi war machine, and there is no record of party membership.[5] For Neufert, it was as if the whole episode never happened. After the war, he simply resumed his career as professor of architecture at Darmstadt University, and was appointed emeritus professor in 1965.

Standardization

Neufert's involvement in the standardization of architectural dimensions and building practices, for which he is best known, started in 1926, when he began teaching at the Staatliche Bauhochschule in Weimar. Here, a compulsory module for new students was *Schnellentwerfen* (fast design), which allowed a very limited time to develop architectural solutions to a given brief. The academic catalog from 1929 described the class:

> *The instructor of the course speaks about the class of buildings known as "schools" and develops a series of economic, organizational and spatial questions out of their pedagogical and human meaning that are based on examples of executed buildings from the period. Then the instructor selects a few narrowly focused tasks and develops the following program in collaboration with the audience:*
>
> *A new building for the Bauhochschule is to be designed on a recently visited building site. Training workshops and residential studios are to be attached to it. The spatial requirements are known to the students. Three hours of intensive labor, then, the designs are collected. On the next morning, the instructor proceeds through the reviewed submissions on the*

epidiascope with specific issues in mind, and every designer must discuss
and defend his or her proposal on an impromptu basis. This is followed by
a sharp critique—first from one's classmates, then from the instructor, just
as one will later have to do when one becomes an architect and has to
defend one's ideas before an actual builder. The design is then reworked
during one's free time over the following three weeks.[6]

To make the exercise as efficient as possible—this was, after all, mass higher education—students were provided with the exact same drafting tools. Neufert even insisted that the studio's desks, documents, and storage systems conform to the Deutsches Institut für Normung (DIN) 476 standard.[7]

The DIN 476 standard is better known through the A series of paper formats. Released in 1922 and set out by German engineer Walter Porstmann, the system is based on the metric system (an A0 sheet has a surface area of 1 square meter), with fixed proportions (1:√2). These standard paper sizes allowed for increased efficiency in publishing and were first championed by the German War Ministry during World War I.[8]

Neufert explicitly acknowledged the influence of the DIN 476 standards on his work, in his book's opening pages: "Standard [paper] formats constitute the basis for the dimensions of furniture used for writing and record keeping. These are also constitutive of the dimensions of spaces. Exact knowledge of standard [paper] formats is important for the builder."[9] Neufert's obsessive belief in standard systems even affected his book; unusually, it is the size of an A4 sheet of paper, making production inexpensive and the book easy to store and carry. Furthermore, the book engages with the notion of *Existenzminimum,* variously describing methods of achieving efficient spatial planning and the use of movable, collapsing furniture, such as the Pullman bed.[10] The first edition of the book, published in March 1936, sold out in a matter of weeks.

The Book and the Method

The publication of *Architect's Data* in 1936 was the high point of Neufert's long, uninterrupted career. Its German title, *Bauentwurfslehre,* translates literally as "teachings on building design," more forceful than the neutral *Architect's Data.* The work is simultaneously a handbook, a textbook, and a reference; it is a didactic treatise rather than a mere repository of data. An equivalent of sorts, the *Metric Handbook,* was published in 1968 for a British readership and according to United Kingdom standards, and has sold about 100,000 copies.[11] Possibly this was the impetus for the English-language edition of Neufert's tome, released only in 1970.

Neufert's first edition is divided into five sections: *Arbeitsvorbereitung* (Preparatory work), *Entwurf* (Design), *Bauliche Einzelheiten* (Construction details), *Gestaltung und Bemessung der Umgebung, der Räume und Einrichtungen* (Giving shape and dimension to the environment, spaces, and domestic furnishings), and *Gebäudekunde* (Building types). The book includes organizational diagrams, recommended minimum measurements for spaces, exact measurements of standard-sized furnishings, and treatises on standard building typologies such as dwellings (high-rise and low-rise), factories, schools, and office buildings.[12] The 2015 German edition runs to 594 pages.

In 1943 Neufert published a second book, *Bauordnungslehre,* on behalf of Speer, who, in addition to being Hitler's court architect, was by this time his minister of armaments and war production. Often regarded as a sequel to *Bauentwurfslehre,* it adopts a more urgent tone toward standardization and rationalization, as critical to total war. Speer wrote:

> *Total War requires the concentration of all powers in the construction industry as well. Thoroughgoing centralization, for the purpose of economizing technical powers and building mass production systems, is the prerequisite for improving productivity. . . . With this new order, one can hardly rely on arbitrary measure of building components and the parliamentary deliberations of participating manufacturing organizations. Rather, one must establish a building order in the broadest sense of the word, with a firm hand and with the collaboration of industry, in order to ease the work of the manufacturer, the planner, and the builder in equal measure. And to achieve appropriate integration of building components. Professor Neufert dedicates himself to this important task as my Representative for Standardization in the Building Industry. . . .*

Neufert himself wrote:

> *During the First World War,* Normenlehre *by Porstmann appeared, which is as relevant today as it was then. After the World War, the stan-*

dard numbers were established, which as an overarching proportional system unified the proportions of individual standards. Since then, a very large literature on standards has emerged which actually encompasses all technical areas save that of design and construction.[13]

Although adoption of his ideas was progressing slowly, by the sixth edition of *Introduction to DIN Standards,* Neufert was given a full two and a half pages to discuss his efforts to standardize architecture.[14] He was already exploring new applications of his standardizing principles.

Bricks

During the war, Neufert began to focus on one of the humblest building components: the brick. Like the A-series format for paper, Neufert's ideal brick was based on the metric system: one meter should contain eight bricks, so Neufert named his principle "the Octametric system." Neufert's brick sizes were all multiples of 12.5 centimeters, one-eighth of a meter. "The logical clarity of these brick measurements will help ease difficulties associated with its implementation in annexed countries."[15]

Neufert published his recommendations on Octametric bricks in 1941, a date that suggests sinister motives behind the obsessive drive for standardization. Not only did Hitler and Speer need to rebuild German cities quickly to keep up morale, but a standardized building system was also essential because forced laborers, prisoners, and volunteers had no prior experience in building, and the first two groups were suspected of sabotage and perhaps 30 to 40 percent less productive due to malnutrition, disease, and torture. Furthermore, with prison and slave labor hailing from all lands occupied by the Reich, a standardized building system would eliminate much miscommunication.[16] Neufert hoped that a standard grid of 12.5 centimeters could be set for all architects and builders, in effect standardizing design itself. From 1941 the SS adopted Neufert's Octametric system in Poland and some of its furniture-production facilities.[17] Neufert wrote, "If a building is planned according to the Octametric system, the contractor only needs an Octametric levelling rod in order to organize the entire building, the axial distances, windows, doors, posts, and partitions, on a rapid and mistake-free basis."[18]

Neufert, however exhilarated he might have been by success, was not above self-correction. In the 1944 version of *Bauentwurfslehre*—in a process similar to Le Corbusier's in developing his Modular Man—he retroactively amended measurements relating to the human body to suit his newly developed system of proportions. For instance, the ideal shoulder height was raised from 143 to 150 centimeters even though he kept the height of the human body itself at 175 centimeters.[19]

After the war, the dubious political origin of Neufert's brick system posed no barrier to its adoption. In 1950 his Octametric system became an official DIN standard called "Dimensional Coordination in Building Construction," DIN 4172, which led to the prescription of standard-sized windows, doors, kitchens, bathrooms, and even ceiling heights. In 1952 DIN 152, the updated version, was enshrined in West German law: state subsidies for public housing would be extended only to builders who followed the norm. East Germany followed suit a few years later. The norms were so influential that even a few years after reunification, the only bricks available in Germany adhered to Neufert's Octametric system.[20]

The Importance of Being Ernst

Ernst Neufert worked toward standardization regardless of circumstances or regimes. His work was tied to no political ideology, save for its absolute devotion to the efficiency of industry. He kept a wide network of collaborators throughout his life. His efforts were apolitical and, to some extent, amoral: he was a man who accepted work on plans to resettle the Aryan population in the newly conquered Eastern Europe, and a technocrat who would later argue for standardizing building and the design industry as a whole during the early years of West Germany's *Wirtschaftswunder.*

Tellingly, one product of his Octametric system was the *Z-Möbel,* a mail-order furnishing system developed by a Bavarian wood-carver, Alfred Oskar Zwink (together with prisoners from the Dachau concentration camp), using Neufert's spatial diktat. The cupboards were quite vernacular in style but could be assembled without any knowledge of carpentry. To Neufert, this proved his standards did not impose stylistic or ideological paradigms on those who followed them.[21] This was a man who, over the course of his life, associated with the likes of Gropius, Antoni Gaudí, and Frank Lloyd Wright, as well as Albert Speer. It would seem, for the rational-above-all Ernst Neufert, that the end really did justify the means.

The 1970s: The World Falls Out with Modularity

For Neufert, the modular system was as much about construction as about redefining spatial realities, whether they were idealized or derived from reality. British prime minister Harold Macmillan even described modular coordination as "a way of drawing Britain and the rest of Europe closer together." The European Productivity Agency studied modular systems in 1954, and the United Nations published detailed reports extolling their advantages in 1962 and 1966.[22]

But by the 1970s, with the "death of modern architecture" in the cards, modularity had fallen from grace as a practicality, a mere building "method" for housing the dispossessed or the aspirational upper-middle class. Walter's Way was such an endeavor: an experimental and self-built private housing development in South London, initiated in the 1980s by Walter Segal.[23] Back in 1964, another Walter—Walter Gropius, founder of the Bauhaus—had anticipated this rejection of modular building techniques:

> *Genuine variety without monotony could have been attained if we had taken greater interest and influence in the development and design of . . . standardized, component building parts which could be assembled into a wide diversity of house types. Instead, the idea of prefabrication was seized by manufacturing firms who came up with the stifling project of mass-producing whole house types instead of component parts only. The resulting monotony further deepened the horror of a nostalgic, sentimental, unguided public of a prefabricated future.*[24]

Neufert died in 1986 at the age of eighty-five, simply of old age, having lived roughly a decade longer than the average life expectancy at the time. Only in death did Neufert defy the norm. But even there, maybe he didn't: his age exactly doubled the life expectancy of 1900, the year he was born. The total length of his life constitutes a perfect multiple—almost like the system of standard paper sizes he promoted.

A firm bearing his name, Neufert Consulting GmbH, in the village of Bergisch Gladbach just outside Cologne, carries on his work. In addition to producing updates of *Architect's Data,* the company consults on human resources, organizational structures, and information technology infrastructure.[25]

Neufert is everywhere.

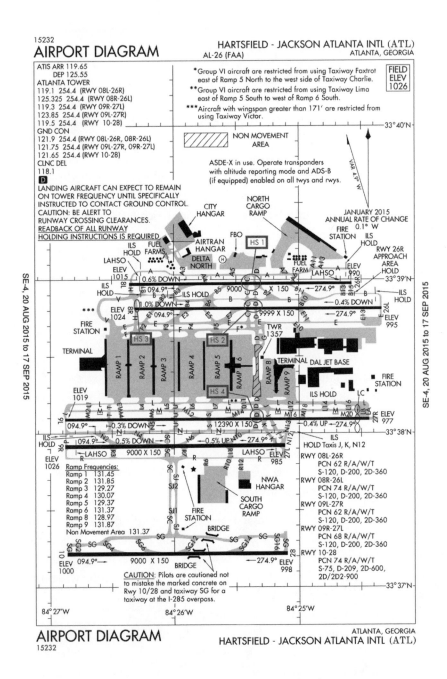

FAA airport diagram for Hartsfield-Jackson Atlanta International Airport (ATL)
National Aeronautical Charting Office (NACO), Federal Aviation Administration (FAA).
Wikimedia Commons.

8

Reference without a Source

The Appeal of Atlanta Airport

Hartsfield-Jackson Atlanta International Airport, more commonly known by its IATA code as ATL, is the largest airport in the world. It is about to get larger: from 96 million passengers today, its capacity is set to swell to roughly 130 million in 2030.[1] By the time it reaches that number, an even larger airport will have opened: Al Maktoum International Airport in Dubai is expected to process 160 million passengers annually.

Size matters. Atlanta's airport was largely responsible for the city's acquisition of the Olympics in 1996; city officials argued that it was one of the few bidding cities that could handle the arrival and departure of the expected number of visitors. The acquisition of the Olympics fueled further development of the airport, with new amenities and the opening of a dedicated international terminal in May 2012.[2] In 2015 Hartsfield-Jackson Atlanta International Airport was ranked the world's busiest airport for the seventeenth consecutive year.

Size equals competence. It becomes a default measure of success, a feature that inspires emulation. The appeal, even the triumph, of Atlanta Airport is simply that it is the largest. As the aftermath of the Atlanta Olympics demonstrated, being the largest allows one to stay the largest— at least for a while. Nothing breeds success like success.

If modernity in architecture was initially predicated on the idea that form should express progress, it is now a rat race subject to the inescapable imperative of the market economy: competition. Only the measurable survives. The ultimate outcome of modernization is not the triumph of an ideal form but form's ultimate irrelevance in the face of figures. Form defers to performance. Atlanta Airport is no exception.

I remember the first time I saw it. It was on paper. I encountered the airport in the role in which most people in my profession do: as a benchmark, a canonical example. The drawings showed a compellingly perpendicular rhythm of five parallel concourses, connected by a people transport system (PTS) running underneath. A terminal stood at each end—one domestic, one international. The whole complex was flanked by a pair of parallel runways on either side. The almost unfeasibly simple composition offered a seductive paradigm. (Al Maktoum, the airport that will overtake Atlanta as the busiest airport in the world, is an exact copy.)

Atlanta Airport is a masterpiece, a sublimely utilitarian creation unburdened by sentimentality and ostensibly a product of the machine age—literally so when mechanical transport takes priority: what the elevator was to the skyscraper, the PTS is to ATL. The elevator opened up the possibility for disjunction between the floors of a building in section; the PTS opens up the possibility of a disjunction of spaces in plan. The airport becomes a collage of disjointed fragments. The skyscraper is a reproduction of the world in the vertical; Atlanta Airport is the same in the horizontal.

Atlanta Airport has a history, too. There were earlier configurations, but nobody remembers them. (Originally the site was a racetrack.) Each new layer has erased not only all previous ones but also any memory of them: Atlanta Airport is the outcome of successive amnesias. Its authors, verifiable only after a long Google search (and even then subject to a considerable amount of confusion), are barely known in the world of architecture.[3] Still, when a sequence of the airport's past incarnations (the result of an intensive archive search) is pinned up on a wall, it somehow manages to look like an evolution: not a gradual growth toward its present state but rather a journey toward the ideal diagram, an evolution in thinking about airports more than an evolution of their physical reality.

Before I first visited the airport, I had proposed ATL's organigram in the context of multiple other airport projects, either for new airports or for airports facing vast expansions. When I finally did visit—like most people, on a layover on my way to another continent—the experience was predominantly one of disbelief. It is not so much that when you get there, there is no there; rather, the "there" that you find in no way constitutes a difference from the reality encountered at other airports. Order from above gives way to chaos on the ground; functionality on paper creates impasse in reality; perfection in two dimensions produces its breakdown in the third. For the average passenger, ATL simply constitutes the familiar experience of long lines, dilapidated fast-food franchises, chaotic schedules, panicky improvisation, and general discomfort. If Atlanta Airport is exemplary of anything, it is of how ultimately even the most perfect diagram falls victim to utter indifference toward its presumed implications. Everyone who has ever used ATL—more than a billion people by now—will confirm this. ATL's best-kept secret is common knowledge.

ATL raises an obvious question: Are diagrams important, or are they just illusionary shields to protect architects from the chaos that inevitably ensues, with or without them? In forever avoiding a finite state, the airport disregards the diagram's main implication. It is chaotic and formless by definition, defying above all the possibility of any definitive configuration.

Like most airports, Atlanta's is in a constant state of conversion. Ever-larger billboards with ever-slicker renderings of an even more promising future conceal the reality of today in exchange for a better one tomorrow, next week, next month, next year. Prolonged expectation—or suspended disbelief—followed by disappointment is the quintessential experience of an airport, like waiting for a flight that is eventually canceled.

There is some official recognition of the airport's shortcomings in *Navigate 2030: The ATL Masterplan* (2014), a report that will dictate the development of Atlanta Airport through 2030. The master plan was assembled over two years through phases of inventory, capacity assessment, proposal of alternatives, and an implementation plan. At this point the study has already announced a need for new gates, a doubling of parking capacity, and the introduction of a sixth runway.[4] To achieve these goals, the airport plans to spend about $779 million on construction in 2017 (other major airports typically spend between $25 million and $75 million annually).[5] Even with this commitment, it remains a question whether any of these measures will change anything—that is, whether it is the airport that should change, or our perception of it. For decades we have viewed airports as purely logistical entities, as machines. More recently, however, it has become increasingly clear that what we thought was the airport's main raison d'être is no more than a pretext.

Over the past twenty years airports have become subject to intensified international competition, which has changed their planning significantly. They need to offer favorable conditions to airlines, particularly their home carriers—Delta Air Lines at ATL—and in order to stay in business, keep landing rights and tariffs within strict limits. As a result, airports are increasingly dependent on revenues from alternative, non-aviation-related sources. They must acquire multiple identities as shopping centers, hotel operators, and real estate ventures. A paradigm shift ensues: instead of regarding the airport as a peripheral inconvenience for the city, cities start to develop around airports. City airports become airport cities.[6]

Currently, 85 percent of all passengers flying in and out of Atlanta Airport are transfer passengers. Given the current growth plans, these numbers are likely to increase. This large number of transfer passengers makes Atlanta Airport virtually an autonomous entity, independent from the city of Atlanta, which most passengers never see. If one counts only the fifteen million passengers per year destined for Atlanta itself, ATL is smaller than ZRH, the airport serving Zurich, Switzerland. The city of Atlanta is not so much the raison d'être for the airport as it is its facilitator, a service provider, mostly as a reservoir of cheap labor. It is the airport that has the upper hand, as a city in its own right which for the vast majority of travelers has replaced Atlanta proper.

The airport's official name is Hartsfield-Jackson Atlanta International Airport. It used to be just Hartsfield, named after a former mayor of Atlanta, but the widow of his successor, Maynard Jackson, successfully petitioned to add the latter's name. (She is rumored to have appeared in court to pursue a greater emphasis on it, too.) Picture its name if the city's current mayor, Kasim Reed, were to add himself to the list: Hartsfield-Jackson-Reed Atlanta International Airport. Somehow, the more successive city officials add their name, the more they drop away in favor of the airport's independent brand: ATL.

Perhaps the relation between Atlanta Airport and the city of Atlanta is conceptual rather than territorial. In the Office of Metropolitan Architecture's famous tome S, M, L, XL (1995), there is an essay about Atlanta as representing the next stage of modernity: the phased explosion of the center into a ubiquitous periphery.[7] In the last instance, a ubiquitous periphery destroys the notion of the periphery: without a center, no periphery. The city becomes atomized. Atomization, described as an essential feature of Atlanta at the scale of the city, is reproduced by its airport at a global level: as a stopover in journeys from elsewhere to elsewhere, the airport is a "nowhere." Its population-in-flux belongs everywhere but there. The airport offers a sneak preview of a future, a space without loyalty to place. We had better learn to like it, cherish it as ours, if only for a few hours.

Is an airport a piece of architecture or an act of urbanism? In architectural terms, the airport represents the successive breakdown of stated intentions. In an urbanistic sense, it represents the opposite: the unleashing of potential. Where architecture insists on a form of behavioral innocence, implied by the purity of its organigrams (it expects them to be followed), urbanism exists only in the knowledge that its blueprints will be ignored. Its true genius resides in recognizing that its diagrams in no way control what happens after they are realized.

In this urbanistic notion lies the relevance of Atlanta Airport's diagram: not as the end but as the beginning of something, accelerating a scenario that otherwise would happen only over centuries. The diagram doesn't prevent complexity; it makes complexity instant, bypassing an excruciating process of evolution. An operation the size of an airport has no time to wait for evolution; evolution is what happens afterward, through an endless process of conversions, corrections, extensions, and diversions, in the search for a perfection that will never come. In an airport, evolution is a retroactive concept: it happens not before but ever after, in the gradual destruction of its own perfection.

The primary function of an airport is to serve movement. Therein lies its true modernity: not progress but progression, even if we have no idea what we progress toward. Jean Baudrillard once described America's highways as places of conformism: "A route that leads nowhere, but keeps one in touch with everyone. Any speculation about the future is pointless. . . . The whole point is to keep thinking about the future, if only as an existential ritual. . . . It is important to suspend any definitive conclusions. . . . We're all going somewhere, even if it doesn't matter where."[8] The airport is an even more radical embodiment of this metaphor: a place to which one goes only in order to leave.

When planes land, they cost the money they could be making; they are meant to be up in the air, preferably in perpetuity. In that sense, the airport is no more than a necessary evil: the last obstacle in the way of constant movement (and constant revenue), an admission of failure in our eternal effort to create the *perpetuum mobile,* a self-effacing and place-erasing final station on the route to real modernity—the last hurdle in a disappearing act.

Hartsfield-Jackson Atlanta International Airport, walkway
Photograph: © Raymond McCrea Jones / Redux Pictures / Hollandse Hoogte

Nothing is wholly obvious without becoming enigmatic.
—Jean Baudrillard, The Perfect Crime

9

The Inevitable Box

Creativity

Can a body of work be built on the basis of one good idea? If so, what makes such an idea? Is the measure of a good idea how much it renders further ideas unnecessary? When something good is invented, what reason can there be against applying it until something better comes along? Once the ideal paradigm is established, we repeat it. Everything unfolds from there; further choices are self-evident.

There are many ideas; there are few good ideas. Good ideas occur infrequently. Technology, the media, and the Internet do nothing to change that. Sometimes centuries pass before the next good idea presents itself. Entire generations are forgotten by history because they didn't have a good idea.

If architecture is both the consequence and the expression of technological breakthroughs, one wonders which technological breakthroughs shape architecture today. The information revolution—*the* revolution of our time—doesn't change buildings; it changes the way we use them. Its effects on architecture are limited. In allowing us to be productive regardless of circumstances or location, it even reduces the demand for buildings. We do whatever, wherever, whenever. Anything can happen in any space. By further disengaging buildings from what goes on inside them, the digital (more about that later) makes architecture less important, not more.

Architecture promotes itself as a creative discipline. Insofar as creativity is predicated on the new, on invention, it is different from logic, which is predicated on deduction. Sometimes creativity and logic meet in perfect sync; more often they clash. The love affair between creativity and logic is at best turbulent, of limited importance for the majority of architectural production. Ever since industrial production began, architecture has followed an ethos of repetition and reduction. Creativity occurs in the margins, if at all.

In the name of creativity, architecture sides with the masterpiece against the cliché, with the unique against the common, with the specific against the generic. Creativity prioritizes the exception over the rule and chooses the margins over the mainstream. In doing so, it leaves a vast territory unaddressed. It forever compels architecture to operate against the odds, confronted with an unbridgeable gap between its pretenses and its legacy. Given that creativity is about ideas, any architecture dependent on it is inevitably a losing proposition. Not only are there too few ideas to cover the number of projects in progress (the same applies to careers), but creativity also bars architecture from using the ideas of others, denying it access to its collective memory.

At least one major revolution in architecture is presented each year. The sheer frequency of revolutions negates their validity. Contemporary architecture is like a dog chasing its tail, reinventing itself every decade, every year, every month, every week, with every new Internet post.

The Internet gives rise to unprecedented individual presence, but it highlights our similarities more than our differences; the great equalizer, it destroys the notion of the unique. There is no point in trying: whatever is designed, a quick Google search inevitably returns similar projects, algorithmically aligned. What we thought was a first has a following even before it is finished; emulation precedes the original. Dates are studied in the desperate hope of reconstructing a chronology that could allow us to preserve the illusion, but this usually proves to be a precarious effort. Google doesn't honor masterpieces; it knows only categories, tags, "search engine operatives." Any hope of being original is instantaneously reduced to a fleeting illusion. Where we thought there was one, there are many. Unwittingly, an old notion in architecture returns: that of style. Our new modernity reinforces old ideas.

Still, originality remains our driver. To be the first, not the best, is what we aspire to. After the first, there is nothing. (This conveniently ensures that the first is also the best.) In our frantic search for newness, progress becomes the first casualty. Architecture becomes instant; evolution impossible.

Where do we go from here?

Rationale

Four walls, a floor, and a ceiling: architecture's ur-space, the room, is inevitably a variation of the same theme. Its most common iteration is based on the use of ninety-degree angles between wall and floor, ceiling and wall, and wall and wall. The ninety-degree angle inevitably leads to its mirrored other, a perpendicular parallel. It becomes the only angle, the one compositional act that leaves an identical residue, where the primary product equals its own waste—two for the price of one.

Any space structured on the ninety-degree angle triggers a chain reaction in which each step implies the next. In its fractal repetition, any series of such spaces creates a theoretically ideal condition: zero waste of space. Any such (series of) space(s) is called "a box."

The box has existed for some time. He who designs a box will not be the first. Originality and the box are incompatible.

The box is the natural outcome of all rational parameters combined, the form in which geometry and economy meet in perfect sync. The box doesn't resist; it complies. It is easy. It suits any use and any size. It offers multiple options to expand in length, height, and width. (It can rely on the same options to shrink.) The box serves no other intent than its intended purpose. The box is architecture liberated from peripheral considerations—not least the obligation to produce masterpieces.

The box is where architecture stops being a matter of individual creation. In allowing comprehensible instructions, it invites the participation of others. Further design work can be delegated; remaining decisions can be conveyed over the phone; the only challenge for the architect is the extent to which he can still credibly consider himself the "author." The box renders real the work of architecture once again. No longer reliant on unpredictable bursts of inspiration, it can be productive, meet quotas, and be delivered on time and on budget.

Henry Ford + architecture = the inevitable box.

Beauty

Some boxes are beautiful; many are ugly. Beauty is not something the world can afford to wait for. We must accept the outcome of our systems and declare whatever occurs as a result beautiful. Beauty can exist only as a retroactive concept, a form of surrender to the inevitable. Like good sportsmanship, beauty is in the graceful admission of defeat.

The box happens both by design and by default. A focus on proportions delayed this inevitable conclusion, at least for a while: slender boxes, boxes based on certain proportional systems, even cubes. But no matter how hard we try to reclaim the default as design, all attempts to appeal to the senses suffer defeat in the face of the box's provable optimum: the outcome of calculation, not of composition. The best box is a box.

Computer programs have been developed to design the box with an ever-increasing degree of sophistication: Microstation, AutoCAD, Rhino, Revit, Bim. Still, the ultimate box is designed in Excel.

Only the aesthetic of chance survives, yet another speculation. Only 1 in 12,487 boxes has a hope of being a beautiful box.

The box is architecture's main achievement. It is also its main trauma— both the result of an extreme effort and of no effort whatsoever. It exists with or without architects. All roads lead to the box.

Didactics

Can the box be taught? The box is a stack of typical plans, which consist of (1) a core of vertical transport surrounded by (2) a ring of lettable space, the depth of which is determined by rules regarding access to daylight (which vary from country to country). Sometimes the permissible length of a dead-end corridor also plays a role (this also varies from country to country). The total required floor space divided by the available space per floor gives the total number of floors. The number of floors checked against fire-department regulations may affect the size of the core, which in turn affects the size of the typical floor plan. The box's proportions are the outcome of these simple equations. To contain building costs, the box must be wrapped in a skin made from the largest possible repetition of standard elements. The structural system? A grid, of course. The logic is the same for offices as it is for residential buildings. Other functions— theaters, libraries, concert halls, museums—because of their introverted nature, only make the box more probable, not less.

The proper mathematical definition of the box is a "rectangular prism": a six-faced volume with each face set at ninety-degree angles to the adjoining ones. Still, when it is referred to as "a box," an important semantic shift occurs. Where the rectangular prism denotes volume and mass as a single entity, the box separates these. The rectangular prism is a finite entity; the box is by definition incomplete: a container, something empty and in need of filling. The box exists only by virtue of what it contains—in a state of anticipation, waiting for content, whatever that may turn out to be. In architectural terms, the box is not a matter of form following function but of form preceding function—a way to capture the largest possible multiplicity of uses.

Block, slab, tower, hall: architecture has multiple names for the box. But since they all describe the same form, their effect on form is limited.

No matter what height, length, or width it is, a box is still a box. Neither a focus on a proportional system nor an insistence on typological purity fundamentally changes the box. In obeying the laws of both art and science, the box is ultimately neither.

The box has two mirror axes, three if you count the horizontal. Yet it is most often as an "off-balance" composition that we encounter the box: an eccentric entrance, an off-axis lift core, an asymmetric juxtaposition of two symmetrical boxes. Paradoxically, the emergence of the box as the ultimate typology has coincided with the denial of its most defining feature: symmetry.

When did the pitched roof stop being a necessity? The dirty secret of modern architecture is that it never did. We stopped using it without any superior solution having presented itself. The omission of the pitched roof is an intentional technological regression, a deliberate forgoing of the best solution in favor of an aesthetic ideal, eschewing function for form—the symbol of a desire for progress instead of progress itself. We choose to endure the inconvenience. After all, architecture and the box have had an inconvenient relation for centuries. The pitched roof helped them avoid seeing eye to eye. It was what stood between architecture and the naked truth, what prevented the box from being a box. In our drift toward the box, the pitched roof was a necessary casualty—no progress without cruelty! With bigger things at stake, the pitched roof had to go.

Freedom

The box allows for the simple translation of regulations; that is, it allows itself to be read as such. Insofar as regulations exist to encourage demonstrations that they are being followed, the box is the penultimate outcome: the architectural equivalent of the model citizen. Allowing for the easy reconstruction of each design decision that goes into it, the box is the ideal subject for bureaucratic scrutiny. (The fact that the vast majority of bureaucrats work in one probably helps.)

Safety is key; the box's fundamental creativity lies in how it allows for the elimination of risk. In the same way in which the computer systems of a car force drivers to remain within certain limits, the box allows the creativity of designers to be contained. It allows the possibility for co-drivers. Whenever we stray beyond its confines, an invisible second hand simply overrules our decisions. The box is a form that effortlessly surrenders to criteria other than our own. Still, it is a form, and as such, it allows us to retain the notion of the architect as its author. The box is the perfect preemptive strike against our own marginalization.

The more prescriptive the functional requirements, the more the box approaches its ideal state. Not in its guise as the office or the industrial warehouse but as the still more anonymous form of the parking garage is the box at its most profound (closely followed by the budget hotel). In the parking garage—a miracle of typological purity—the box acquires the status of a masterpiece. The design of a parking garage, essentially a storage facility, is void of ego: it serves only to accommodate the maximum number of cars. Space is a paradigmatic feature, but only in the sense that there needs to be as little of it as possible.

Designing a parking garage is like solving a mathematical equation, one of the few instances where the architect's brief is unequivocally clear, and where the provision of quality is in perfect tandem with the provision of quantity. It is not his or her peers who pass the verdict, but numbers alone. At last, there is the possibility to be the unequivocal best. (When it comes to the design of a parking garage, any hope to be the first is in vain.)

Despite their strict functional requirements, parking garages have given rise to a surprising number of typological inventions. There are continuous-ramp ones, split-level ones, flat ones with an external spiral, corkscrew ones. The parking garage is a straitjacket that allows multiple solutions, one that inspires creative freedom precisely because there is none.

Flexibility

The box is a flexible typology. Flexibility admits the possibility of the unexpected. The box can be used for anything; the element of surprise is its main delight. Boxes house bowling alleys, shooting ranges, ice rinks, snow ramps, and music concerts requiring earplugs, even if outside there is only deafening silence. Sex happens in boxes. In fact, the best sex happens in boxes in anonymous industrial parks, traceable only via obscure Internet sites. With no visible indication on the outside (apart from the unusually large number of expensive cars parked in front), few would suspect.

In its drive toward ultimate flexibility, the box absorbs an ever-larger number of unlikely typologies: the theater, the opera, the concert hall; it even makes for the ideal football stadium.[1] A simple offset of the rectangular pitch—unburdened of the stadium typology's outdated Roman heritage: no more arena—the box is a direct extension of the game. It involves audiences in a way no other stadium type does. In doing away with the traditional opposition between spectator and spectacle, the box appeals to players and audience alike, propelling the popularity of football to unprecedented heights.

Despite its professed open-endedness, the box exposes flexibility as a zero-sum game: a curious form of full circle, in which full tolerance of activities inside implies complete intolerance of anything in the way of their unfolding. In pursuit of the perfect abstract space, the box no longer endures the presence of its enablers. Columns, beams, pipes, ducts, wiring, and other structural and mechanical necessities are banned to the exterior, like intestines rejected by the body. That which was to have only the most discreet presence becomes a form of exterior decoration by default. *Ornament und Verbrechen*: the box concedes to having broken modern architecture's ground rule. With its perfect, perpendicular skin now riddled by a baroque human-made tangle of services, the box has stopped being a box. The search for flexibility has reached the end.

Modernity

The box is the common manifestation of all modernity's miracles—the idiot box (television), the boom box (the cassette player), the juke box (the juke box), the black box (both a form of experimental theater and the data recorder of an airplane), the magic box (whatever). What God was to the traditional world, the box is to the modern world. Christians worship God; atheists worship the box. (This is why Christian churches in the form of a box never work.) However, that doesn't make the box a pagan symbol. Rather, it makes it a symbol of overcoming the need for a god: the most powerful signal that God is indeed dead, replaced by rational perfection. (Is it a coincidence that the box was so emphatically embraced by the Communist world?)

The box is the perfect antimyth. (Even the box's best known myth, Pandora's box, exists only because of an error in translation.)[2] For defenders of the sacrosanct, the box is a derogatory term. Sanctuaries are often rectangular prisms, but to refer to them as boxes would be disrespectful. The box is appropriate only as a nom de guerre, as a collective name (a container?) for all that is discarded: an object of worship for the disenfranchised.

The box is without identity. That is usually viewed as something negative. Still, it is precisely in its anonymity that the general appeal of the box resides. "Here Rests in Honored Glory, a Soldier, Known but to God."[3] There is no family, no next of kin to pay their last respects. With no possibility for personal remembering, his memory becomes collective, all-powerful, universal. He who is known but to God belongs to all of us.

The box should be photographed only in black and white. This grants even recent boxes an aura of history. In black and white the box approaches its pure state. It is dematerialized: its walls and floors—generally reinforced concrete—can be anything. The difference between concrete and a natural stone—let's say travertine—becomes indistinguishable. Black-and-white photographs reinforce the box's general indifference toward the effort invested in it. Any trace of expenditure is erased; the box becomes the product both of money and of a lack of money. There is no more evidence of rich or poor. The classless society is best represented not through socialist red but through a black-and-white box.

The box is without allegiance. It defies loyalties to any political system. (During the Cold War, both sides built their fair share of boxes, often supplied by the same manufacturers.) The box offers no guarantees other than the predictability of its geometry. It is both the most and the least ideological form of architecture, an expression both of vision and of an utter lack thereof. Neither its unconditional embrace nor its outright rejection will affect the box. Like modernity, the box is inevitable.

The box is the beloved subject of abstract art, the ultimate "nonreference Untitled," referred to only as "specific object."[4] It is displayed as part of a series, produced in factories, with all traceable hand of the artist removed. It is not a symbol, and definitely not minimalism, because those terms would attribute too much intention. The box just is. Only silence is appropriate. Yet the less we say about the box, the more mythical is the aura it acquires. Honoring the box is inescapable and inevitable; it is our origin and our destiny—all there ever was, all there ever will be.

A box is a box is a box.

Consensus

Few admit to liking the box, yet it is the outcome of all consensual processes. Decisions need to be argued, preferably with hard figures. But the triumph of the quantifiable has coincided with a crisis of numbers. The numerical has become promiscuous, supporting multiple hypotheses at once. Any conclusion can be drawn from any set of figures. Conclusions and figures have gone through a divorce, meeting again only by chance. When they do—if they do—it will most likely be in a box.

There are good clients and bad clients. Good clients want boxes; bad clients want boxes. There are those who know about building; there are those who don't. From the ones who do, we expect sympathy; from the ones who don't, we demand trust. The majority offers neither.

Le Corbusier's buildings had voids; Mies's had space; Kahn's had light. It is safe to assume that many of architecture's past triumphs have, at least partially, come about because of the ignorance of its patrons. As soon as those who commission us become educated, they will see through our sophisms. They will find their own ways to optimize buildings, make efficiency gains, and reduce expenditure. From then on, buildings will have just floors and walls; the immaterial in architecture will become immaterial.

Not beauty but profit is architecture's main driver. They are different things, but the equation of the two is the basis of all client-architect relations. Without it, there would be no buildings. Still, how real is this equation? We think we agree, but where we see abstraction, clients see the absence of complication. Where we see consistency, they see repetition. Where we see minimalism, they see minimal effort. Both sides leave the table with a sense of complete victory.

Like any proposition, the box needs to be discussed. But in which terms, and more important, on whose? A language problem ensues. (PR consultants prefer to call it a communication problem.) The services of mediators are called on to help convert economic logic into architectural considerations and vice versa. Occasionally, the help of another architect is sought, directly employed by the client: a special type of architect, accustomed to discerning beauty in the profitable. (The reverse never happens.) He talks at length about the box, even if he is careful never to refer to it as such. Instead, he speaks of a "prismatic volume," a "compact mass," an "efficient machine." It is in language, not drawings, that he and his colleagues find common ground.

There is no evidence like self-evidence.

Asymmetry—modernity's great contribution to architecture— remains only in the relations of power. For every word the client utters, the architect utters at least five; one voice is deep, the other high; one is calm, the other nervous; one operates through reason, the other through association; one demands a suspension of disbelief, the other simply does not believe. Conviction comes with the absence of power; power, in contrast, can be achieved only through the suspension of conviction. Like the ideal box, power is a product of calculation.

Charisma is a last resort. It helps conceal our lack of power. Like a state of hypnosis, it has the capacity to suspend reality, to put off the inevitable. Therefore, charisma doesn't prevent the eventual triumph of the box but delays it, hopefully long enough to pass off its inevitable emergence as deliberate. Charisma takes personal credit for the generic; it allows retroactive attribution in the absence of an identifiable author.

Money

Some boxes are cheap; some are expensive. Mies's Seagram Building was 50 percent over budget; Trump Tower was 50 percent under. Combined, these two buildings prove that the box allows for a 100 percent margin, covering the entire spectrum from full budget compliance to full budget defiance. The two extremes do not so much demonstrate the box's flexibility in the face of money as its ultimate indifference to it.

Architecture, or more precisely real estate, is governed by a simple law: maximizing return while minimizing cost. Money is not an alien subject to architects, but their exposure to it is partial, exclusively determined by a focus on the second half of the mantra. If knowledge equals power, the architect works on the basis of a 50 percent handicap, making the fight for his own reward inevitably a losing battle. With an average fee of 5 percent of construction cost with a 10 percent profit margin, the overall profit of an architect equals 0.5 percent of the total construction budget of a building. The average real estate developer takes home a profit of 10 percent of that budget. Even the real estate agent and the bank, with virtually no labor invested in the process, outrank the architect with respective percentages of 3.5 percent and 2 percent. We get paid; they get rich.

Where other professions operate on a basis of maximizing financial return while minimizing labor, architecture is predicated on the reverse. When it comes to money, architecture has developed its own theory of relativity. Einstein offered the possibility to become younger with time; architecture offers the possibility of becoming poorer by working.

Still, we shouldn't complain. The box is the product of both much and little work. If we can't change the reward for our labor, we can always reconsider how much of our labor we reward it with. We do have a choice.

History

When did the box start to inspire the search for *the* box? When did it become (part of) a deliberate ideology? It is hard to construct a genealogy of the box. There is no manifesto; it never needed one (unless you count cubism). In emphatically standing for something, manifestos are automatically against something else. In its ubiquity, the box has nothing to stand against except itself. A manifesto of the box can be directed only at the futility of any effort to find an alternative: not a manifesto but a declaration of victory.

Does the box originate from the rectangular plan? "Typical Plan is an architecture of the rectangle; any other shape makes it atypical—even the square."[5] The box offers the next evolutionary stage: all shapes predicated on the ninety-degree angle will qualify. The box is all-encompassing.

Still, there must be an ideal box somewhere. The search for the ideal box is in fact the reason that the box exists. From a Platonic ideal to Laugier's enlightened hut, or from Durand's typology to Viollet-le-Duc's box diagrams, the box is most celebrated in its abstract form, linked to neither place nor time but applicable to any situation. The box becomes synonymous with architecture's future. If the traditional city accommodated the box, the ideal city exists because of it. The box becomes the urban planner's obvious first choice (Haussmann thought in boxes despite the Parisian spiral of arrondissements), applicable to various scales, each one triggering the next: from room to house, from building to city block. The box acts like a contract; it allows objects and spaces to coexist without interfering in the other's business. Each new addition hardly limits the space of the next; on the contrary, it provides ever-greater legitimacy. The advent of industrialization meant that mass production, standardization, modularity, and repetition became the reality of architectural production. The more the box can approximate its pure state, the more it becomes an ideological feature. The avant-garde considers industrialized society best represented through its most elemental figures. The box is essential to the syntax of this new language: from Kazimir Malevich's architektons to Walter Gropius's Bauhaus; from Adolf Loos's Raumplan to Le Corbusier's *plan libre*.

And then there was Mies.[6] The evolution of the box ended in 1948 in Plano, Illinois.[7] After Mies, there was no more point in doing a box. The best box had been made. It is unlikely that another burst of inspiration will change this. Mies is where the rest of history begins.[8]

In substituting glass for four of its six faces, Mies's box (in theory) is no longer a box. It dissolves into a single horizontal space sandwiched between a floor and roof, a momentary framing of a continuous outside. Man is one with the cosmos. Despite its seeming dissolution, what this box actually does is expand the ideology of the box beyond its confines. In revealing its inside to the outside, it doesn't so much surrender to the outside as claim the outside as part of its interior. Enjoyed from comfortable conditions inside, the outside becomes domesticated—part of the perfect world of the home. (Who needs privacy in a perfect world?)

The box met its end twice. If the first time it did so as an unappreciated success, the second time it did so as an overblown failure: the Pruitt-Igoe estate in St. Louis, Missouri.[9] After Pruitt-Igoe, there was no more point in doing a box. The worst box had been made. The rest of history must decide whether to give the box another chance.[10]

Pruitt-Igoe has been demolished; Mies has vanished in a forest of clones. Their legacy is ubiquitous, their original untraceable. They simultaneously exist forever and don't exist at all. There is a void at the heart of history, from which the best and the worst have gone missing. Without absolute references, disorientation ensues. Denied its memory, architecture opts for nostalgia. History becomes a new source of inspiration. Sampling, mixing, reconfiguring, and continuously borrowing from its past, architecture induces a strange form of temporal confusion. History is never over; by constantly recycling it, architecture hopes to avenge its fleeting nature, granting itself eternal life.

The box goes undercover. In a momentary lapse of confidence, it becomes apologetic, disguising itself as multiple smaller versions of its former self—atomized, fractal editions of its previous boldness. In abandoning *the* box in favor of many boxes, this plural box doesn't necessarily address the box's perceived crisis. In the name of "the people," people's real needs are being overlooked: a proliferation of corners (one for every user) spells the end of orientation; forests of boxes are turned forty-five degrees to balance on a single point; logic is ignored.

Gradually, the box's first life—as the emergence of the ideal form—is being superseded by a second that celebrates the irrelevance of form in the face of numbers. Only the measurable survives—not form but size. Only in its most extreme form can the box still represent an ideological attitude—in giant, infinite boxes such as those of the Continuous Monument and No-Stop City, both of which were conceived half a century ago. Sometimes a more recent creation comes close, such as Atlanta Airport, a wonder of the utilitarian, the perfect diagram of the machine age: a masterpiece, largely despite (or maybe because of) the lack of awareness on the part of those presiding over its creation.

Lately the box has seen a revival. As a trend in architecture, however, this is misleading. Architecture no longer really proposes the box; it cites it. The twentieth century's love affair between ethics and aesthetics has become no more than a marriage of convenience in the twenty-first. Sobriety, abstraction, simplicity, and other modernist dogmas make their second appearance, but only as folly. From the typology box to the deconstructed box, from the *Großform* box to the Swiss box, from the glass box to the white plastered box, and from the minimalist box to the high-tech box, contemporary architecture is in love with the idea of being in love with the box.

Boxes cannot be remade; they can only be made over. Boldness can give way only to shame: pitched roofs, add-on porticos, portes-cochères, and giant facade paintings all deemphasize the box's Platonic and repetitive nature, only to reinforce it. More reverent attempts at reconstruction have also been made, but no matter how much respect is paid, the original box seems definitively out of reach. Our respect seems only to push it away further. Dilapidated modern buildings restored to their original state invariably transition to tributary pastiche. A restored Le Corbusier feels like a Richard Meier, a restored Mies like a John Pawson. We cannot relive history. There are only memories of memories. Postmodernism, with its tongue firmly in cheek, is the only remaining style, forever.

Simplicity has lost out to Simplicity™.

The Antibox

The box, perhaps predictably, has provoked a reaction. Ever since Vitra and Bilbao, the benefits of another type of architecture have been discovered: a more extravagant architecture, driven by macroeconomic ambitions, tourism, legacy, and city branding. A big global market calls for big thinking. To register on the global radar, one should not propose the norm but rather the exception. Architecture becomes about unsettling the habitual, a form of disruption—not the box but the antibox.

The antibox is accompanied by a new philosophical imperative: "Think outside the box!" The box has come to stand between us and freedom. "We think out of the box, so you don't have to live in one,"[11] Yet at one point it was the box that liberated architecture from outdated straitjackets. Our new visionaries, it seems, lack memory.

Form followed function. Then form followed fiasco.[12] Now form just follows form. Form operates on the basis of escalation: the more you have of it, the more of it you need. Form breeds form. In our eternal quest to be original, each new form becomes a reaction to the previous one. The explanation of each building resides in the building that preceded it. When the logic of each object is deferred to another, architecture becomes a matter of perpetual second-guessing.

In partially delegating the production of form to the computer, the antibox has seemingly boosted the production of extravagant shapes beyond any apparent limits. What started as a deliberate meditation on the notion of form in the early antiboxes has turned into a game of chance. Authorship has become relative: with creation now delegated to algorithms, the antibox's main delight is the surprise it causes to the designers. (The term "autopoesis" is a dead give-away.) In insisting on the digital as just another source of form, the antibox has blinded itself to its implications, which are not formal at all. In describing the compositional logic of an essentially virtual domain, "digital architecture" represents the overcoming of the physical—the definitive triumph of the metaphysical. Therefore, it is the antithesis of architecture.

Digital architecture $\neq$ architecture; digital architecture $=$ the digital.

The antibox celebrates the death of the ninety-degree angle—in fact, of every angle. Only curves remain. Floor, walls, and roof smoothly morph into a single continuous surface that only the most complex geometrical equations can capture. In its attempts to achieve a perfect ergonomic architecture—enveloping the body and its movement like a glove—the antibox falls into an age-old trap, only with more sophistication and virtuosity. The antibox is nothing more than form follows function 2.0, that is, a perfectly executed mistake. Strangely, in celebrating complex geometries, the antibox has highlighted the relevance of simple geometries, the essence of which resides not in the perfect accommodation of a single function but in accommodating the greatest degree of uncertainty: the largest possible array of as-yet-unknown functions.

It is questionable how long the antibox will endure. In time, form will prove to be a finite resource. By further accelerating design production, the antibox will only expedite its inevitable exhaustion. In a context where everything is iconic, ultimately nothing is iconic. Form is set free, only to find itself orphaned. Every exception thrives on the existence of a rule: without a norm, there is no exception. The greatest blow the box could strike against the antibox would be to disappear altogether—without the box, no antibox. The dreamed outcome of the antibox's ideological program would equal its own destruction. This, perhaps unexpectedly, opens an exciting prospect for the box. Boxes have moved from rule to exception. The noniconic has become the new iconic. The box has come full circle. Soon it will appear strikingly exotic again.

Review

We all know him; he has spent the better part of his career defying the box.

He has won numerous awards doing so. Now he is back in school, as a teacher. The university where he teaches? Most likely American (home to both the most extreme embrace of the box and its most vehement rejection). The discussion is about sloping floors, curved walls, absent corners, exploded roofs. There are no criteria and therefore no conclusions. (The antibox doesn't solicit debate, only its simulation.) Marks are limited to pass and fail. Everyone passes, but not before being subjected to the ritual agony of a long review.

He is unhappy: too many of the antiboxes presented still carry the box's DNA. No amount of morphing, animating, or scripting is able conceal that when one traces the various antiboxes' origins, they invariably owe their assaulted, deformed state to the box. Exasperated after reviewing the fifth or even the sixth student team, he exclaims, "Every form need not begin as a box!" His students rebel. More out of annoyance than conviction, they start proposing more straightforward, sometimes even deliberately dull boxes. It works. These boxes prove immune to his feedback. They successfully resist the esoteric comments that more intricate projects typically tend to solicit. There is nothing to discuss beyond the initial premise.

It's a box. Take it or leave it.

Fame

All masters did a box.
Anyone can do a box.
Anyone can be a master.
When everyone is a master, no one is a master.

The Machine Box

Located in places no one has ever heard of, their existence is now vital to ours. Shipping containers are the preferred method of construction. They are in constant danger of overheating, which is why they are generally in a cold climate, preferably near cold water. There is invariably a wind farm next door. These boxes are not for humans but for machines, for "stuff." In a recent iteration, the box's poignancy has become inversely proportional to human presence: it is good where habitation is temporary (the budget hotel), excellent where it is secondary (the parking garage), and outstanding when it is nonexistent (the mechanical storage facility). If information constitutes the main revolution of our time, it is in its main spatial component—the data center or, at another scale, the memory chip—that the box reaches its apotheosis. It would take a surface five times the surface of the earth to store the contents of the machine box in the form of a traditional library. Data centers are giant boxes that house other boxes, which in turn house endless rows of interconnected little boxes. The smaller the replica, the fewer the people who understand what goes on inside. The machine box represents a vanishing point. Its fractal nature is mirrored by its security diagram: progressive rings of evacuation formed by the level of security clearance required to enter. The more central your position, the fewer people there are around you. A journey from edge to center doesn't offer a progression of intimacy but, on the contrary, only an ever-greater alienation. The heart is abandoned as in an emergency fire drill. The interior, although exclusively human made, gives the impression of untarnished nature: a neatly choreographed jungle of wires, cables, and ducts, each coded with a different color to allow reconstruction of their precise role in the system. Somehow this box is both primordial and futuristic, both nature and antinature. There is beauty, that much is certain. Yet one cannot be quite sure whether this is a beauty that has preceded or will outlive us.

Is the machine box the outcome of a Nietzschean prediction, an epistemological journey to the epicenter of civilization, only to find a void? A nihilistic trick? Like a Russian doll, there is only the tautological, fractal reproduction of the container itself, a box in a box in a box. There is no more inhabitation, only intrusion. What parking garages manifested on a more primitive level, the new, humanless boxes manifest in the extreme.

Form follows machine. People and their behavior are unpredictable. The box is better off without them. Man becomes a guest in his own creation, entering only on the condition that he is externalized.

Welcome to the box, the box, the box.

Plot

Imagine a Hollywood film scenario. The main character is a retired police detective. Much of his career has been dedicated to a single murder case, one of those pesky ones that has defied resolution. It still does. Through a flashback, we witness the police investigation some thirty years earlier. It is slow; the methods used are clumsy; communication among police officers is flawed; important clues are overlooked; and wrong suspects are arrested, only to be released again. Then, in an unexpected plot twist, it is revealed that the murder has been committed by the main character. Suddenly, his clumsy, seemingly ineffective detours make perfect sense: not failed attempts to resolve a case but strategic moves to prevent its resolution. He doesn't want to go to prison, but he also doesn't want to frame anybody else. He is trapped between the immorality of his deed and the moral implications of his guilt. His only option is to continue the search. His freedom depends simultaneously on the display of motivation and the absence of results.

Does the character in this script resemble the contemporary architect? To what extent is his work a form of denial, an attempt to delay the truth, possibly forever? Like the detective, the architect lives on borrowed time; his promises of progress, of new and improved versions are only a fragile alibi. Barred from destiny, his work becomes a ritual act. He is like the monk rewriting the holy scripture over and over again. Words are changed, votes are taken on which parts ought to be kept, language is used to change the meaning of words, and moral codes are applied to omit parts considered too vulgar. With each reproduction, he finds himself further removed from the original. As more perfect, celebratory (beautiful?) versions are created, the original meaning recedes further and further away. His only option is to keep working.

End

Osaka, Japan. A crucifix is cut into the concrete wall behind the altar. It is backlit in the morning as it faces east. This box has no material content, only space. It cannot be optimized; it can only be experienced. Its emptiness is an invitation for the spiritual to enter. The implied function—a church—is denoted only through material absence. It is manifested through light entering space; it is immaterial. Zen meets Christ. Does it always take an encounter with "the other" to comprehend the nature of things? Who is the other when it comes to the box? Is it in churches, whose very mission it was meant to replace, that the box ultimately finds refuge?

Amsterdam, the Netherlands, 1975. Black boxes are being stacked in a frame of prefabricated concrete junctions to become an old people's home. It takes an established critic to identify the symbolic implication: crosses and coffins. The building goes on to acquire global fame. It is meanwhile demolished.

The ultimate box is the one we all end up in.

III. FOUND CAUSES

The Air Ocean World Town Plan, 1927

Courtesy of The Estate of R. Buckminster Fuller. Reproduction courtesy of the Department of Special Collections, Stanford University Libraries, from *4D Time Lock* (R. Buckminster Fuller, 1928) in the R. Buckminster Fuller Papers.

10

Spaceship Earth

When I use the word nature, I sometimes mean God.
Do you ever say God and mean Nature?
    —R. Buckminster Fuller, interviewed by *Playboy,* February 1972

The interview is long, stretching across a total of nineteen pages in double columns. Fuller's view of the world, the blessings of science, and the often counterproductive role of existing power structures is elaborate and entertaining, but it is this comical exchange, somewhere in the middle of the interview, that encapsulates the subject, the dilemma of man's relationship with nature, in the most perfect way.

Since the Enlightenment—the formal launch of modernity—our thinking about nature has oscillated between two different attitudes. According to one, man is an actor who engages with malleable nature to further his existential progress (which is viewed as an integral part of nature); the other considers nature an absolute and views man as being outside it. The first portrays nature as an evolving resource that man explores; the second, as an ideal condition that man exploits to its detriment. When he does, nature inevitably turns into an instrument of wrath. There is a long and diverse tradition in romantic and religious art of depicting natural disasters as punishment for man's sins.

History offers compelling arguments for both points of view. Man's scientific and technological progress operates on the principle of escalation. Technology solves problems, but it also gives rise to new ones. The more technology we have at our disposal, the more technology we need to deal with the consequences. We invent ever more sophisticated techniques of food production, only to follow up with ways to contain overpopulation. First comes the baby boom, then the contraceptive pill (1960). The evolution of the hospital is complemented by the incessant perfection of weapons and the casualties of war. The assembly line (1913) leads to mass production, creating the need for mass entertainment in the form of television (1925). Fertilizer (1928) and genetically modified plants (1929) enable the feeding of an ever-larger number of mouths. The demographic surge that follows brings a risk of epidemics. In response, medical innovation gives us penicillin (1931). The internal combustion engine (1860) creates the prospect of depleted fossil-fuel resources, which in turn triggers the search for alternative energy sources like hydroelectric power (1878), wind turbines (1887), solar panels (1941), and, ultimately, nuclear energy (1945).

Just as one can plot man's scientific evolution as linear progress, one can explain it as a series of emergency measures to deal with the disastrous consequences of the previous big invention. Modern history condemns us to a permanent rat race against the consequences of our creativity. We progress, but only toward an ever-larger need for progress. No sooner do we think that we have successfully conquered the forces of nature than we are confronted with our utter dependence. Modern science has not successfully disproved God's existence. We play God, only to suffer God's wrath.

Our attitude to nature is deeply schizophrenic, vacillating between omnipotence and impotence, between determinism and fatalism. In the past three hundred years the world's population has ballooned from six hundred million to seven billion. That simple quantitative evolution allows for utterly contrary readings, as both a technological triumph and an apocalyptic reality. And both interpretations can boast an impressive series of advocates, with Benedict de Spinoza, Albert Einstein, and R. Buckminster Fuller on one side squaring off against Thomas Malthus, Paul Ralph Ehrlich, and James Lovelock on the other.

It can be argued that this dialectic between a belief in technological progress and worries about its fatal potential reaches its apex in the second half of the twentieth century. Nuclear fission offers man the prospect both of abundant energy and of eradication, simultaneously feeding moods of technohubris and impending doom. The late 1960s see the first man on the moon coincide with daunting predictions about the future of the earth.

In the run-up to Neil Armstrong's small step, a group of scientists, economists, and planners concerned about the imminent exhaustion of the world's resources at the then-current rate of economic growth gather in Rome for the first meeting of what would become known as the Club of Rome. Their aim is to alert government leaders to the prospect of imminent disaster in the hope of inspiring worldwide action. When it comes to the role of science and technology, the words spoken by the club's founder, Aurelio Peccei, bring an unexpected denouement:

> *The modern scientific technology brings forces under control that rival those of nature itself: employing them, man can invent his own future. It is now in his power to create a world substantially without want, drudgery and disease. It is also possible to fashion a perfect tyranny or eliminate life completely. The direction taken depends on man's effectiveness in putting scientific and technical capacity in the control of reason, and directing it to good ends.*[1]

No longer are science and technology viewed in either / or terms—as a blessing or a curse—but as potential and choice: man's last chance to control his destiny. The depletion of resources—presumed imminent—is interpreted as an impetus for technology to reach greater heights, to the benefit, not the detriment, of man. The world becomes the site of a technological project to protect man from man, finally offering the prospect of a resolution between man's accelerating technological development and the apocalypse.

This attitude is echoed in Fuller's *Operating Manual for Spaceship Earth,* in which he described the planet as a spaceship in orbit, with a finite amount of resources; once depleted, these cannot be replenished. This small manuscript, published shortly after Fuller's address at the fiftieth annual convention of the American Planners Association in Washington, D.C., builds on many of his earlier ideas, such as a reallocation of U.S. Army resources and a global energy grid. The metaphor of a spaceship—reflecting space travel as the apex of technological prestige at the time—is by no means coincidental and has also been used in Adlai Stevenson's speech to the United Nations three years earlier.

While the Club of Rome goes on to publish its findings in the report *The Limits to Growth,*[2] Fuller bares all in the American men's magazine *Playboy,* outlining the ideological pursuits of his career. The report and the interview appear almost simultaneously in 1972, four years after the meeting in Rome. The tone is remarkably similar: both texts want us to recognize the relationship between phenomena previously considered mutually exclusive. Fuller talks about nature as the manifestation of a nonanthropomorphic god, without the usual implication of human submissiveness. The Club of Rome talks about the imminent depletion of resources, not as a form of divine punishment but as a call to human action. The underlying concerns are the same, but one looks for the answer in a form of global engineering, while the other issues a global warning about the earth's resources. Interestingly, a kind of symbiosis emerges, where the creativity and inventiveness of one carries the potential to avert the apocalyptic conclusions of the other. According to Fuller, a reconciliation of the forces of nature and those of technology was within reach if one was prepared to think (and act) big. "Science now finds there can be ample for all, but only if the sovereign fences are completely removed" is one of the key phrases of his operating manual, emphasizing the inevitable link between the scale of the problem and that of the action required.[3]

By the mid-1970s, however, that prospect seems increasingly unlikely. A different intellectual and political momentum is beginning to take hold, and the call for a smarter use of resources collides with a bold reemergence of laissez-faire liberalism. In 1976 Milton Friedman is the sole recipient of the Nobel Memorial Prize in Economic Sciences. A few years later, the near-simultaneous election victories of Ronald Reagan and Margaret Thatcher pave the way for the global rollout of the neoliberal market economy. The Club of Rome's and Fuller's calls to act on a global scale, after first running into the constraints of national borders, now run into the limitations posed by private interests, leaving only global awareness of the problem, without the possibility of a global answer.

The term "sustainability" doesn't appear until well into the next decade, in the Brundtland report commissioned by the United Nations in 1987. This report hopes "to unite countries to pursue sustainable development together to address a heavy deterioration of the human environment and natural resources." (Interestingly, the term finds its roots in forest management, developed in the context of a feudal system of private landownership in the seventeenth and eighteenth centuries in response to declining timber reserves.) The Brundtland report describes sustainable development as "a process for meeting human development goals while sustaining the ability of natural systems to continue to provide the natural resources and ecosystem services upon which the economy and society depend."[4]

In insisting on this definition, the report presents humans' relation to the environment exclusively as something that needs to be managed and kept under control. The issue is narrowed to moderating human behavior. The report is very much a product of its time. In the context of the market economy, which has firmly taken hold in the United States and Western Europe, any hopes of a large-scale mobilization of scientific resources have become obsolete. Government intervention is to be kept to a minimum, and by the late 1980s Fuller's propositions seem an exotic possibility at best.

The term "sustainable development" constitutes an interesting contradiction in terms. Derived from the Latin verb *sustinere*, "to sustain" literally means to "underhold" (*tenere*, to hold; *sub*, under), that is, "to carry, maintain, or preserve." New development, by definition, is the opposite of preservation. Therefore, the term embodies a fundamental discrepancy among its stated purpose, the applied methods, and the results achieved. Just as the notion of "safe sex" had to be changed to "safer sex" to acknowledge the mismatch between aims and means, sustainable development might be renamed "development that is somewhat less damaging to the environment" or "slightly less wasteful."

The first manifestations of sustainable architecture mark an aggressive return to tradition. In the United States there is the rehabilitation of the conventional city plan by the New Urbanists; in Europe there is the advance of the "neo" neoclassical architecture of Leon Krier. More recently, sustainable architecture has taken the form of increasingly literal demonstrations: green roofs, green walls, tree houses, shelters covered in earth. Being green has come to equal looking green. Increasingly, sustainable architecture seems to advocate a return to a primordial condition, manifesting itself in so-called Hobbit Houses, after J. R. R. Tolkien's children's novel.[5]

Dug into hillside for low visual impact and shelter, the house uses stone and mud from local diggings and spare wood from surrounding woodland. Windows, the burner and the plumbing and wiring, are retrieved from rubbish piles. Straw bales in floor, walls and roof provide insulation.

The fridge is cooled by air coming underground through foundations. Water is provided by gravity from a nearby spring.[6]

In the final instance, in the special-niche "earth-covered architecture," sustainable architecture takes the form of an apology for architecture's supposed former crimes, literally hiding itself under the ground:

Covered in earth, the house returns to nature a good part of what constructional encroachment takes away—counteracting the fraying of our landscape by urban sprawl.[7]

"Green is good" appears to be the new global consensus. Green architects and their critics meet in perfect concurrence, making the language of self-promotion and criticality forever indistinguishable. Manifest failings are concealed by clever marketing, as in the case of the "sustainable" city of Masdar, Abu Dhabi, which has been forced repeatedly to lower its performance targets. Meanwhile, one can hardly imagine any new development without the necessary sustainability paragraph, even if we know that it often means little more than lip service. "Greenwash," or "the retroactive disinformation disseminated by an organization so as to present an environmentally responsible public image," has become an official tributary stream of the English language.[8] But even the fact that we now see through it all in no way undermines our undivided conviction to the cause.

That consensus, however, is partially artificial: it is possible only because a very significant (and politically contentious) aspect is intentionally left undiscussed. The ethos of a moderate use of resources used to be inextricably linked to their fair distribution. This double awareness formed the basis of the marriage between environmental consciousness and socialist policies, manifested in multiple Green Parties being founded across Europe in the late 1970s.

It is on the question of distribution, or rather the willingness to engage with it, that the narrative of sustainability differs from that of modernity. The economy of means—an integral part of modernism—serves both aims: saving and sharing. In the case of sustainability, it implies only the first.

The metaphor of the earth as a spaceship (and before that, as a ship) with a fixed amount of supplies is an essential part of modern discourse precisely because of this double implication: finite supplies and a crew whom these supplies should support, as becomes apparent from this quote by George Orwell:

> The world is a raft sailing through space with, potentially, plenty of provisions for everybody; the idea that we must all cooperate and see to it that everyone does his fair share of the work and gets his fair share of the provisions seems so blatantly obvious that one would say that no one could possibly fail to accept it unless he had some corrupt motive for clinging to the present system.[9]

Orwell's words echo those of the nineteenth-century American political economist and philosopher Henry George, who argues that natural resources and common opportunities, most important, the revenues of the land, should be jointly owned:

> It is a well-provisioned ship, this on which we sail through space. If the bread and beef above decks seem to grow scarce, we but open a hatch and there is a new supply, of which before we never dreamed. And very great command over the services of others comes to those who as the hatches are opened are permitted to say, "This is mine!"[10]

Both authors make an explicit link between scarcity and distribution, which they view as inseparable. Using the metaphor of a ship, they argue that there is no point in discussing a person's relation to resources without also discussing the individual's relation to society. Our survival depends on both. The question is ultimately political, as was also revealed in the Club of Rome's later publication, *The First Global Revolution*,[11] in which it states that its earlier apocalyptic predictions had been partially intended to inspire unity among men.

They didn't. More than forty years after the initial publication of *The Limits of Growth*, the predicted depletion of resources has become an argument against their fair distribution. No longer are sharing and saving part of the same cause; they have become opponents. The argument goes as follows: if developing nations adopt the standards and the associated behavior of developed nations, the planet will perish. The West plays a very ambiguous role here, denying new economies the standards it enjoys in the name of the preservation of the collective. "If per capita pollution were as high in China as it is in the United States . . ."

In the current discourse, the threat of depletion becomes something that promotes the cause of inequality. Today, it is the world's most affluent countries, not the most populated, that represent the largest claim on the earth's resources per capita. To argue that it is in our collective interest that the industrial condition remain a privileged, that is, Western condition is hardly a tenable position.

The friction between population growth and the idea of a fair distribution—a minimum standard of living for all—is nothing new. Modernity emerged precisely from this friction, caused by the increase in the need for resources in conjunction with the limited capacity of the earth to generate them. Modernism responded with a twofold agenda: it embraced the blessings of science and technology as a way of enhancing this capacity while at the same time promoting an ethos of equality over excess to keep escalating demand in check. In that respect, there is a direct line between Mies's "less is more" and Buckminster Fuller's anticipatory comprehensive design slogan: "Doing more with less."

In focusing only on the ethos of less, the contemporary notion of sustainability represents an abortive concept. Urging only the curbing of excess without the promise of collective progress, it lacks a political narrative, demanding that we settle for what we end up with for the sake of self-preservation.

In contrast to the creative avalanche triggered by modernity, the current preoccupation with sustainability suffers from a profound lack of imagination. No longer are science and technology challenged to come up with unexpected solutions; they are forged into a moral straitjacket and preemptively made to subscribe to foregone conclusions. In sanctifying only the politically correct and demanding the crucifixion of everyone who dares to question its hypotheses, sustainability seems to spell the end of creative freedom.

When Freeman Dyson suggested the mass cultivation of specially bred "carbon-eating trees to underline the productive relation between CO_2 emissions and plant life,"[12] he was dismissed as a mad scientist. The idea that global warming could help retrieve vast tracts of Russian territory from permafrost and convert them into agricultural land has similarly been dismissed as phantasmagoria. Half a century ago, the idea of Siberian river reversal was aborted because of fears of an eventual cooling of the Arctic atmosphere. Today, the same idea could hold the key to averting the much-feared melting of Arctic ice caps.

Somehow, the rhetoric of sustainability marks a strange return of religion over reason. Once again nature is an absolute to be idealized and feared. Large-scale human interventions in nature, even for our own benefit, have become taboo. Yet when it comes to lifting us out of the current impasse, these types of interventions should by no means be discounted. The alternative—the insistence on moderate consumption in the face of an ever-larger group with whom we must share—means that there will be proportionally less all around. This leaves us with two options: a continuous lowering of the minimum standard or preserving the same standard, but for a limited number of people. Neither is an appealing prospect.

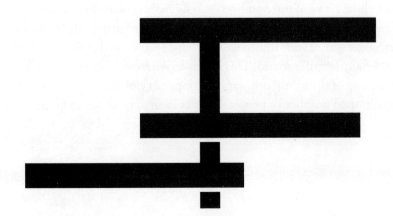

Farnsworth House logo
© Farnsworth House, a site of the National Trust for Historic Preservation

11

Mies en Scène

Plano, Illinois, 2015. Even seventy years after its inception, the house inspires awe, and not just among architects. The tour of which I am part includes writers, artists, scientists, and tech entrepreneurs. Somehow, this elegant glass and steel house in its natural setting transcends the usual mixed views on modern architecture, invoking, against overwhelming odds, the possibility of a universal sense of beauty.

Our guide recites his lines without a single pause: "In the summer, yellow and white daffodils along with Virginia bluebells wrapped across the property; in the spring, the dark lush green of the Fox River Valley; in the fall, on the original nine acres alone, ninety different specimen trees planted for their fall foliage and in the winter, a stark white outline of snow on the ferry against the stark white outline of the home." The house was designed to coexist with the nature that surrounds it, but, as the description makes clear, that nature was equally designed to coexist with the house.

"Beinahe nichts" was how Mies described his creation: almost nothing—barely a house. On closer inspection, there is hardly any nature either. In the same way in which everything about the Farnsworth House is controlled, everything around the Farnsworth House is also controlled. The surrounding landscape was designed by Mies, who manipulated the natural setting to the extent that it may essentially be considered domestic. The property was originally cornfield and meadow. When the house was constructed, trees were planted along the original eastern property boundary to shield the site from view, and the tall native grasses on the site were replaced with high-mown grass. Later, when Lord Peter Palumbo purchased the house, the landscape was enhanced by Lanning Roper, and the gardens were resodded as the owner's collection of Serra, Calder, Oldenburg, Goldsworthy, and Kelly sculptures found homes in the "natural" setting.[1]

All evocations of a hovering human-made object amid unspoiled nature aside, this is essentially a house with a garden, just like any traditional country mansion before it. The surrounding grounds—and this is key—are large. They constitute the only "nature" one sees, tempting the viewer to take it for "real" nature and creating the illusion that the rest of the world is just like the immediate vicinity: all there is, and even if we know it's not, all there ever should be.

It is hard to catch the house in a lie. Its fully glazed perimeter leaves no element of the outside obscured from view. With no evidence of any attempt to hide even part of the context, we presume candor: the context is as we see it, and therefore, it must be authentic. The dirty secret is that the architecture does not stop at the walls of the house; it stretches out across all nine acres of the property. The house isn't so much a mastery of industrial control offsetting the wilderness of nature as it is an insertion of one human-made creation (the house) into another (the surrounding grounds). The coexistence with nature is a myth, nothing but a beautifully conceived Mies en scène.

The house's real relation to nature is complex, to say the least. Unequivocally, according to contemporary environmental standards, the house would constitute an ecological crime. Structure and window frames make a continuous row of thermal bridges; the uninsulated concrete roof and floor slabs do not allow for heat or cold absorption, making the house too cold in the winter and too hot in the summer; the positioning of the house means that there is minimal cooling from the shade of the nearby trees; track-mounted shantung drapery does little to mitigate solar heat gain; the elevated floor is based on a proportional system, not on a calculation of rising water levels in case of a flood. And flooded the house has been, three times, most recently in 2008 after Hurricane Ike. It is as though its creator secretly welcomed the flood as a tumultuous spoilsport, an uncomfortable reminder that the forces of nature are not altogether benign.

In fact, on the official website of the Farnsworth House, there is a header titled "Flood Mitigation Project"; since in 1954, it cites, the house has been at risk of flooding because of the higher water level of the nearby Fox River, as well as ever more frequent climate-related "incidents."[2] Currently, proposed solutions include elevating the house, putting it on hydraulic lifts, or moving it to a "safer" location. Ironically, it was the idea of moving the house that persuaded preservationists to purchase it in the first place: in 2003 the National Trust for Historic Preservation paid $7.5 million in an auction at Sotheby's to keep it out of the hands of developers.[3] Now, a mere fourteen years later, the same group is considering moving the building from its original site.

The Farnsworth House is a perfect paradox, celebrating both man's industrial command over nature and nature itself as an absolute and independent ideal. From within the house, one simultaneously enjoys the most immediate proximity to nature and the largest possible distance from it. Man is close, but man is an observer, not a part. As Mies claimed, "If you view nature through the glass walls of the Farnsworth House, it gains a more profound significance than if viewed from the outside. That way more is said about nature—it becomes part of a larger whole."[4]

The house is a reflection of our deeply ambiguous relationship with nature: on the one hand, an instrument for our benefit; on the other, something that exists beyond us and that we idealize. Most likely, the Farnsworth House is universally appreciated because it can be interpreted as a manifestation of both. The house does not so much resolve the contradiction as engage both views in a temporary cease-fire.

The tour is coming to an end. We leave the same way we came: through the gift shop at the grounds' entrance. The items sold there invariably carry the same illustration: three simple horizontal lines, representing the roof, the floor, and the podium in front of the house. There is no evidence of all the work done on the landscape, not even in the many books for sale. To defy exposure, the lie must be complete. Still, even with all its secrets revealed and all its myths debunked, the house constitutes an undeniable aesthetic experience. In the end, it is rigor we value, not truth.

Farnsworth House
Photograph by Reinier de Graaf

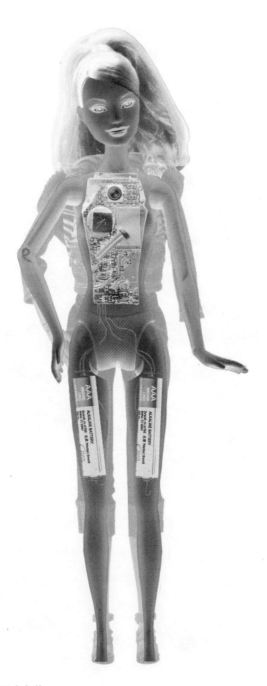

Barbie Video Girl doll
Barbie Video Girl doll by Mattel. As published in "Lights, Camera, Barbie?" by Warren Buckleitner, *New York Times*, July 23, 2010.

12

Intruders

How Smart Technology Infiltrates Architecture

In February 2015 the New York Toy Fair introduced the "Hello Barbie," a prototype of the first conversation-ready Barbie doll. Fitted with a microchip, Barbie had become the world's first smart doll, complete with wireless connection and speech-recognition software. Sales pitch: You talk, she answers. The iconic girls' toy, first launched in 1959, had been given her first real twenty-first-century upgrade. Able to play interactive games, tell jokes, adapt to personal preferences, and "learn continuously," the doll was designed to develop a unique relationship with her owner: "Smart Barbie will remember all of your likes and dislikes; you will become the best of friends."[1]

Barbie's incarnation as a smart doll, even if somewhat comical in its presentation, is symptomatic of the digital revolution's increasing impact on our lives. Notwithstanding the privacy dispute that surrounded the Barbie launch, Cisco, one of the largest tech companies in the world, anticipates that by 2020 up to fifty billion objects will be connected to the Internet, from children's toys to remote-controlled cars and from advanced medical equipment to basic home appliances, leisure accessories, clothing, and even pet collars. Equipped with sensors, transmitters, and receivers, these objects will gather and act on information ranging from your body temperature to your bank balance, from your eating habits to your breathing rhythm, from your sleeping pattern to your sex life, from your refrigerator's contents to your relationship status, and from your choice of coffee to its corresponding hipster level.

Things have come a long way. When in 1982 a soft-drink vending machine at Carnegie Mellon University was the first device to be connected to a computer network, it was able to report on the amount and temperature of its contents. Today, thanks to the miniaturization of microprocessors, the prevalence of wireless networks, and the extension of battery life, the modest vending machine treats us to a hot or cold drink depending on the weather, knows our favorite snacks, provides vital information about allergens, alarms employees when bored teenagers sabotage the supply system, and never runs out of stock.

Connected devices have come to anticipate and cater to our every need, so it must come as no surprise that we turn to them even—or especially—in our most private circumstances: our home. By far the largest market for smart devices conceived for our "comfort" is the "streamlining" of our domestic existence. Nest, a tech company formerly owned by Google and now by Alphabet, markets the Learning Thermostat, which allows users to remotely control the temperature in their homes from their smartphones. The thermostat learns to anticipate their patterns over long periods, so it can eventually regulate the temperature on its owners' behalf. Future-Shape, a German company pursuing "large-area contactless sensor systems," has developed a textile floor surface with thirty-two sensors per square meter, which tracks movement to switch on lights and open doors for us. TOTO, a Japanese manufacturer specializing in bathroom technology, can now boast the Intelligence Toilet II, featuring a urine-sample catcher that measures glucose, urine temperature, and hormone levels and records the data to wirelessly transmit a health report to your computer. Samsung has revealed a transparent touch screen at the International Consumer Electronics Show to replace window glass, which it claims will be available within ten years.

The complex tangle of smart technologies that can be integrated into our homes is seemingly endless. In 2015 British Gas announced a range of "smart home" products aimed at the British market, developed by industrial designer Yves Behar. Behar predicts: "In the future, everything will be smart, connected and make my life easier in some way. More importantly, the technology is invisible—I never have to pull out my phone, hide my face in a screen or even push a button, for the product to work. I think this is the shape of things to come: invisible design, where things magically happen around me."[2]

The interesting or alarming thing (depending on how you look at it) in all these developments is the displacement of the notion of control. In each case—the thermostat, the toilet, the floor, the window, and on a larger scale the traffic and weather sensors—devices are designed both to react to and trigger changes in circumstances. In doing so, they introduce a fundamental ambiguity about who is in charge. They analyze our behaviors over time to build up an automated pattern that regulates the world around us until eventually this world, continuously doctored and perfected, fits us like a glove. The patterns we leave, however incidental or random, become automated, eternal. They are our new truths. (Is it a coincidence that there is an acute resemblance between smart-city marketing-speak and biblical language?) The more our patterns are ingrained as systems, the more they become a straitjacket. Our unique identity, our behavioral DNA, becomes a form of solitary confinement from which there is no escape.

Thus far, the exchange of data in the realm of smart architecture has primarily been between humans and the individual objects they own. Various smart utensils collect information and relay it back to us so that we can monitor and potentially modify our behavior. However, the pivotal position of humans in the exchange of information is by no means a given. The theoretical incorporation of all devices, institutional as well as private, into the Internet of Everything will also further the increasingly autonomous exchange of data among objects themselves. Objects will directly transmit information to other objects without the intercession of humans. Our devices will act independently on whatever information is available at any given moment.

Imagine the following scenario: You and your family have gone away for the weekend. Your house is empty; the doors are locked. You have let the neighbors know, but ever since the neighborhood-wide introduction of a smart surveillance system, the old neighborly task of keeping an eye open has become outsourced. Before your departure, your smart toilet has taken a urine sample (part of a daily routine of smart health checkups). It indicates that you have a cold. In your absence, the information is relayed to your smart thermostat, which proceeds to raise the temperature in your home to the point where your smart windows decide to open themselves. This is caught on one of the neighborhood smart surveillance cameras, which, besides spotting suspicious behavior, are also programmed to pick up on the more reassuring signs of occupancy, such as the opening of windows from inside. The camera's observations (all good) are transmitted to the computers of the local police; because you are evidently home, your house is no longer a priority for police attention, and patrol patterns are adjusted accordingly. Police computers also feed the info on your supposed whereabouts back to the intelligent security system in your home: a courtesy service to the public in case one forgets to deactivate the system, but also intended to prevent police response to false alarms. The smart alarm system is informed that you are home and goes into standby mode.

Meanwhile, through the injection of malware into the police IT system, a group of burglars has gained access to real-time information on the adjusted police patrols. Your smart home is now fair game for a break-in. The open windows provide the burglars easy access. The touch-screen facility fitted on the inside of the glass allows them to further deactivate the house's internal security system (insofar as the electronic all-clear from police computers hasn't already done so). The burglars' footsteps, traced by the sensor-packed floors, help open whatever doors have remained closed inside. As an unexpected side effect—at times, smart technology takes even its criminal users by surprise—the clear deviation from your usual pattern of footsteps is reported as a medical emergency to the computers of the local ambulance service, which arrives on the scene within minutes. Fully in accordance with protocol, they escort one of the burglars to the local hospital, where he is treated for injuries sustained during a previous break-in. The same malware that has allowed the burglars access to police communications has also provided them with your personal details: your CPR number, your bank details, your tax records, and your medical history. In the hospital, staff are under the assumption that they are dealing with the homeowner. Treatment is fully covered by and billed to your medical insurance.

The rise of smart devices and the vast amounts of data that are being gathered and processed from individuals have already raised concerns. The United States' National Security Agency and the United Kingdom's Government Communication Headquarters, among many other national governmental bodies and agencies, were embroiled in the mass surveillance scandal Edward Snowden revealed to the world in 2013. Over many years, data were gathered globally and indiscriminately under the guise of national security. Smart buildings, and smart devices embedded in their elements, could provide an endless stream of data for governments and corporations to access continuously, effectively monitoring minute aspects of people's lives and over time learning about each individual's habits. In 2013 a Silicon Valley entrepreneur, Tom Coates, connected his home's smart devices to Twitter. House of Coates (@houseofcoates) reports its everyday activities: "Someone just activated the Sitting Room Sensor so I'm pretty sure someone's at home," and "Looks like Tom's gone out. I saw him check in at Four Barrel Coffee."

If the house is turning into an automated, responsive cell, the city is becoming an increasingly comprehensive surveillance system. Smart devices need not be under a malicious cyberattack but could be quietly mined for information by either corporate or governmental interests using built-in "back doors." For instance, in 2014 Jim Farley, a senior executive at Ford, announced, "We know everyone who breaks the law, we know when you're doing it. We have GPS in your car, so we know what you're doing. By the way, we don't supply that data to anyone."[3]

But even with back doors supposedly secured, the potential hacking of a connected built environment poses a major security threat. Today, when an average person's personal computer is infected with malware, the worst possible outcome is a loss of money and dignity. In the future, individuals, smart buildings, and even smart cities, for all their intelligence, could become large-scale targets of sabotage. In early 2014 a University of Michigan researcher was able to gain control over the signal colors of nearly one hundred wirelessly networked traffic lights. As early as 2011, security researcher Jay Radcliffe demonstrated that implanted medical devices could be caused to malfunction; an automatic insulin pump used by diabetics could be hacked and its functions stopped. The *Economist* magazine raised a similar concern for our dwellings in 2014: what if boilers could be hacked and made to explode? As security expert Joshua Corman said, "If my PC is hit by a cyber-attack, it is a nuisance; if my car is attacked; it could kill me."[4] The same can be said of buildings.

In the 1970s Peter Eisenman designed a series of experimental houses as a demonstration of the autonomous logic of (architectural) form over function—of the inescapable separation of man and object. Architecture, in Eisenman's experiment, was to be fundamentally liberated from the anthropocentrism that dominated it. Function, considered by many the primary purpose of architecture, was only an accessory to its deeper cause: the manifestation of meaning, of the idea. At the time, Eisenman provocatively referred to the inhabitants of his house as "intruders" to emphasize the feeling of estrangement that ensued from architecture's autonomy.

In the smart house it is not so much the separation of form and function—of man and object—as it is the separation of man and function that comes into play. The object is equated to its function in the extreme, automated and sublimated to the point where a new alienation ensues: a separation of man from the functioning of his own home, even when that functioning is tailored to his personal behavioral pattern. As the elements of our home acquire increasingly independent lives, we become the estranged visitors in the world we have created in our mirror image. In that sense, smart technology makes us *all* intruders.

13

"Public" Space

"Are you a member of the World Federalist Party?"

"Yes!"

"Who is the other member?"

The trick question, posed by a seemingly random spectator, makes any further continuation of the oration pointless; people have already burst out in laughter. World federalism, the grandest of political ambitions, has just been rendered a joke.

This is Speakers' Corner in Hyde Park in London, the routine happening that takes place every Sunday afternoon in a small corner of the park, just opposite the Marble Arch tube station. The event is a free-for-all: whoever feels that he or she has something worth delivering to the crowd of mostly foreign tourists can do so by getting up on a soapbox and launching into a monologue.

Some come prepared, delivering clearly prewritten speeches; others rely on spontaneous improvisation. In most cases the speaker's level of preparation is inversely proportional to his or her success. Interruptions from the audience routinely throw the orators off. Public speaking is one thing, but dealing with hecklers is quite another; heckling is an art that rivals and perhaps surpasses the art of public speaking. What catenaccio is to football, heckling is to speech.[1]

A gay rights activist addresses a small crowd: "It is important that we speak out about our sexual identity and openly manifest ourselves. If we don't, we will be pushed back to the margins. The odds are stacked against us. Did you know that only last week, a gay couple was attacked on Edgware Road simply because they were kissing in public?" The speaker doesn't specify of the attackers ethnicity, but the location of the attack implies it. There have been incidents in the park recently, too. His words are guarded. Advocating one minority's rights risks infringing on another's. After decades of happily accommodating the eccentric, the heretical, the unwelcome, and the provocative, Speakers' Corner is once again a place of tensions, to be protected and preserved as a beacon for Britain as a free society: a symbol of "the tolerance which is both extended by the law to opinion of every kind and expected by the law in the conduct of those who disagree, even strongly, with what they hear."[2]

The wall seems endless, interrupted only by double doors roughly every fifty meters, about twice the width of a tennis court. And that is exactly what people use the wall for: tennis practice. Like the wall, the line of people practicing their strokes is endless. The wall never gives up, returning the ball as it is hit, defying any attempt to beat it. Well-angled serves produce even better angled returns; players chase their own shots until they inevitably infringe on the imaginary courts of their neighbors.

Farther away from the wall, people are roller-skating. Others use the area as a skateboard circuit. Not everyone is into sports; some sit on the ground munching food they brought. The vast, even surface in front of the wall is large enough to accommodate all these activities simultaneously. The location is a textbook example of public space—or, at least, of what we have come to understand as such over the past decades. The space is public property; it is open and accessible to everyone regardless of gender, race, ethnicity, age, or income.[3] It is car free (a very important criterion for those American academics who have theorized the notion of public space); it is regulated through nothing more than subtle spatial negotiations among users. Activities that unfold in the space do so bottom-up. The location conforms to every politically correct definition that has been applied to public space in recent memory.

This wasn't always the case. This is the Zeppelin Field, part of the Reichsparteitagsgelände in Nuremberg, Germany, one of Albert Speer's first works for the Third Reich. It was here that Adolf Hitler addressed the Nazi Party's massive rallies, the ideal space to condition the masses to embrace his evil cause. During Hitler's rule, the complex served as a self-portrayal of the Nazi state, with no other functional purpose than to demonstrate the unity of the nation: *Ein Volk, ein Reich, ein Führer.* Since 1945 it has been used both for American football practice by the U.S. Army and to host the heavy-metal festival Monsters of Rock. In 1973 the Zeppelin Field and the nearby Kongresshalle and Grosse Strasse were placed under monument protection, securing their existence as modern ruins.

The innocence of current activities at Zeppelin Field stands in stark contrast to its history. The unofficial annexation by skateboarders and roller skaters shows that even the most politically incorrect architecture can somehow evolve into public space. Still, how reassuring is that? The Zeppelin Field's current incarnation suggests that a key to successful public space is a certain loss of memory. There is a laundry list of less obvious examples. Plaza Mayor in Madrid was a place for public executions during the Spanish Inquisition; the Piazza San Marco hosted violent clashes over the sovereignty of the Venetian state. Even Speakers' Corner at Hyde Park has a more turbulent history than the current parade of quasi-comical orations suggests. Its status as a place for free speech, protected by law, was secured only after violent workers' protests in the nineteenth century, during which it was frequented by Marx and Lenin. Not history but ignorance of it seems to account for successful public space.

After the third instance of eye contact, I am suspicious. There is something strange about the area. The natural setting with ample trees and bushes is peaceful—a welcome relief from the city, on a hot day—but something about the body language of its visitors has me wondering. There aren't many of them, but given that the only restaurant in the park has already closed its doors, the place still seems busy. Even the number of cars in the lot at the park's entrance seems excessive—hard to match to the number of visitors I encounter on my walk.

This is my first reconnaissance mission for a major planning project we have secured. One by one, I am exploring areas adjacent to the site we will plan. Increasingly, these field trips seem like anthropological research, bringing me into contact with phenomena that, although officially of little relevance to the task we are expected to carry out as architects, are difficult to ignore. Life is unquestionably more interesting than architecture and only becomes more so as society grows more complex.

Contrary to my expectations, the first person to speak to me is not a man—so far, it has been only men seeking eye contact—but a woman. She asks how I am doing. I reply that I'm fine and inquire about the nature of her visit. She is forthright and tells me she is not here scouting for sex. She is past that age. She assures me, unsolicited, that she has had her fair share in her days, but now she visits the park purely for relaxation, to briefly escape the hassle of living with teenage kids. The whole scene, she confides, makes her laugh. Around her neck hang binoculars. "To observe the wild-life," she explains. Allegedly, some rare birds have been spotted in the park, resettled from warmer climates; much to the delight of nature watchers, global warming has wrought a subtle transformation in the park's flora and fauna—a good reason for her to come here more often.

As I continue my walk, I discover that the park's main transformation is in the nature of man's presence—apparently an all-out mission to reap-propriate this idyllic setting as his natural habitat. The evidence is scat-tered wherever I look: empty tissue packets, aluminum pill strips, used condoms, and even small plastic bags (makeshift prophylactics?). Just as I am about to leave the park, I catch a glimpse of the woman who spoke to me using her binoculars. It is not birds she is watching. The wildlife she is observing is of an altogether different kind. It also turns out that she is more than a casual observer. It is the movements of one man in particular (her husband?) that she is following. He regularly returns to report to her, presumably on the results of his chase. After his third incursion into the woods, he brings back two other men. The four of them walk to the parking lot, get into a large station wagon, and leave. Their teenage kids are off having fun with friends. They are about to do the same.

The park's secondary use as a free zone for sexual recreation, I read later, posed problems for the local authorities who preside over it. Con-fronted with an avalanche of complaints from families eager to use the park in more conventional ways, they tried to curtail the activity. Their first approach was an indirect attempt at repression, unleashing an-other form of wildlife in the park—a benign species of buffalo—in the hope that a fear of bovine disturbance would discourage people from having sex.

That ploy hardly improved matters. In fact, it caused sexual activities, previously confined to a particular zone, to spread across the entire park. In addition, there were sightings of people allegedly trying to involve the animals in their sexual practices. In the end, the authorities opted for a compromise. They officially split the park into zones and placed informa-tion boards with maps indicating which zones of the park could be used for what, including sex. A special park force was created to sweep sexual activity out of unsanctioned zones and to keep all parts of the park equally tidy. The approach worked. Sexual activity retreated to its original con-fines, and the complaints diminished. As is often the case, a dispute about the nature of the public realm was resolved by simply splitting it among the feuding parties.

What is the nature of public space in modern society? Public space—and I challenge anyone to come up with a better definition—is space accessible to all, subject only to common law. The immediate implication of that definition is that public space is a product of the law and not of architecture or urban planning. Public space—even successful public space—has nothing to do with either.

The right to public space exists on the sole condition of not violating public order. Public space can thus be defined only in the negative: through what is not allowed, not through what could or should happen. It is the essence of public space that it defies any other intention than that of simply being public. Like justice, true public space is blind.

This basically means that every notion that architects have developed about public space since the 1960s has been deeply misguided. What's worse, our notions have probably only contributed to the demise of public space. It is tempting to blame the new urbanists—Andrés Duany gave the notion of public space a near-evangelical dimension—but that only partially explains the problem, the root of which runs deeper, and which perhaps started the moment at which public space became synonymous with good intentions. In *The Death and Life of Great American Cities*, Jane Jacobs blamed the demise of American inner-city neighborhoods on the unnecessarily reductionist practices of modern planning.[4] Diversity—in the form of mixed uses, pedestrian permeability, informality, buildings of various ages and differing degrees of urban density—held the key to turning the trend. In seeking design solutions to a political problem in American society at the time—a mass urban exodus by white middle-class families to avoid racial integration—Jacobs inadvertently advocated a type of symptomatic treatment, necessarily doomed from the outset. Jacobs had successfully identified a question, only to provide it with the wrong answer.

The paradox of Jacobs's work continues to haunt the discipline of urban planning today. In identifying her "four generators of diversity," Jacobs essentially elevated an accidental condition—largely the result of an absence of planning—to the status of a planning paradigm. The ensuing conundrum is predictable: once the accidental outcome becomes the target of planning policy—a product of intentions—it stops being accidental, organic, or truly public. Ever since Jacobs's well-intended book, the discipline of urban planning has been like a cat chasing its tail, trying to control the uncontrollable, script the unpredictable, invariably insisting on making space where it should leave it be. In identifying public space as a panacea, *The Death and Life of Great American Cities* proved to be the kiss of death for urbanism.

Once its salutary effects had been established, public space was inevitably held to its promise, with an ever-larger number of indicators serving as proof of its usefulness. In 2011 UN-Habitat adopted a resolution stating that good public space enhances community cohesion and promotes health, happiness, and well-being for all citizens. The same document highlights the economic significance of public space: it increases property values, multiplies retail activity, enhances safety, fosters social cohesion and equality, improves health, well-being, and the environment, promotes effective transportation, and generally makes the city more attractive.[5]

Even if these criteria are essentially uncontentious, there is something fundamentally wrong with the idea of subjecting public space to set criteria. Criteria imply measurable performance, but it is the essence of public space that it constitutes a break from the need to perform, a liberation from any other purpose than just to exist as such. The obligation to effectively fulfill other purposes inevitably throws public space into an existential crisis. Many of the criteria—fostering investment, increasing property values, and multiplying retail activity—represent not common but private interests. To allow public space to be measured against them is the first step in surrendering public space to the private.

Public space is often equated with tourism. Successful public space increases visitor numbers; conversely, increased visitor numbers are an indication of the success of public space. Again, tourism is not a public but a private activity: the temporary relocation of one's private sphere in pursuit of an even greater degree of privacy. Tourism constitutes the least public state of mind. In this context, public space is experienced as part of a private holiday; it backgrounds a leisure condition, in which the city takes the form of a resort, its history featuring only as a distraction—no longer what anchors us but what allows us to escape.

It is not only the conflict between the public and private sector but also the shift from real to virtual realms that affects the nature of public space. The distinction between the public and the private used to be a matter of numbers: the more private the considerations, the smaller the number of people one would share them with. In public, we shared what we knew we had in common; public space was the space of our common denominator, that which defined us as a collective. The Internet changed all that. Facebook makes everyone into a public persona; Twitter makes everyone a public commentator; and Instagram exposes every intimately private moment to the public eye. Mass followings have become instantaneous. The expectations placed on physical space have changed and continue to change accordingly: just like the virtual space of the Internet before, public space is no longer the other side of our private realm but an extension of it.

It is worth questioning whether much of what we regard as public space actually qualifies as such. The glut of good intentions, together with an increase in supervision and surveillance, sometimes masquerading in the form of public art and design initiatives, has transformed spaces of spontaneity into preprogrammed, overdetermined areas. The ever more complex legislation on public space serves as proof: Dutch law on public space contains 4,317 articles and 367,829 subparagraphs. To compile a similar list of what is allowed requires a huge power of imagination. The law no longer prohibits but prescribes.

Public space used to be synonymous with the right to protest (thereby forever sealing the fate of shopping malls as nonpublic spaces). A product of the law, true public space allowed for an arena to oppose that same law. It is interesting that each of the three examples earlier in this chapter—public speech at Speakers' Corner, the informal annexation of the Zeppelin Field, and the outdoor sex in an Amsterdam park—started out in defiance of the laws that later incorporated them.

The activities did not change: speech remained speech; sports remained sports; sex remained sex. At the same time, everything changed. The subversive aura that once surrounded these activities became sanctified parts of mainstream culture, staged evidence of our society's tolerance. With recognition came regulation; with regulation came reversal. The adventurous gave way to the predictable, controversy to consensus, polemics to politeness, rebellion to recreation, the eccentric to entertainment. Public space used to accommodate a defiance of prevailing powers; today it defies the notion of "the public" itself. First, rights are fought for; then they are consumed. History repeats itself, first as tragedy, then as farce.

Public space has been in trouble ever since we identified it as such.

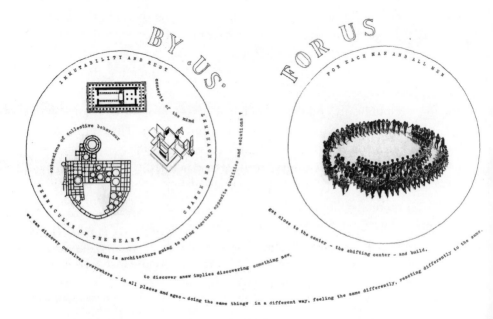

Otterlo Circles, 1962
© Aldo van Eyck / Aldo van Eyck Archive

14

From CIAM to Cyberspace

Architecture and the Community

July 1953: An international group breaks away from the Congrès Inter-nationaux d'Architecture Moderne (CIAM), until then the prevailing coalition of modern architects.[1] Critical of what they see as CIAM's dogmatic functionalist approach, the members of this new group—eventually known as Team 10—believe in reestablishing the relationship between architecture and the human habitat. With the formation of Team 10, "the community" becomes a central concern within modern architecture's discourse.[2]

The group meets regularly, generally in the garden of one of their homes in France, England, or the Netherlands.[3] There is ample photographic record of these meetings—the same cast of characters arranged in different compositions—and the scene is always the same: a circle of people, seated on chairs on semimanicured lawns.[4] In every picture there is a tree, always slightly off center. The intentionally domestic setting is as much a manifesto as any outcome of the meetings, written or otherwise. The wives attend—either that, or we've been looking at a vast reservoir of female architects who have failed to make it into the history books.

It is unclear to what extent the meetings are meant to promote an exchange of views, or whether they are just a form of primordial bonding. Mantras such as "By us, for us," as seen in Aldo van Eyck's Otterlo Circles, feel equally ambiguous: an architecture for the people from the people.[5] Yet if one studies the photos of the group more closely and observes the eerie, almost tribal consensus among its members, one is left with the impression of a strange hubris, a sense of the self-inflated significance of the architectural profession and those practicing it. As one looks at this isolated, exclusive club, "the people" seem far away, and one wonders to what extent "By us, for us" ultimately means architecture for architects.

Some of the meetings produce written documents. In 1954 "The Doorn Manifesto," credited to Alison and Peter Smithson, argues that each local situation calls for its own specific concept of habitat.[6] In the last sentence, architecture, and not sociology, is cited as the prime source of expertise to solve societal issues: "The appropriateness of any solution may lie in the field of architectural invention rather than social anthropology."[7] Building on this, Jaap Bakema writes *From Chair to City; A Story of People and Space* in 1964, in which he goes further to equate the history of mankind with the history of "place-making": buildings are supposed to represent the relations of people living in them.[8] This is taken literally by the book's cover, which depicts a mix of high-rise and low-rise buildings as parents with children.

For Team 10, the built environment both deserves blame and offers a panacea for social problems. However, despite the confidence of its manifestos, Team 10 does little to change the way in which residential neighborhoods continue to be built over much of the 1950s and 1960s. The arrangement of residential slabs changes into somewhat more varied patterns, no longer exclusively dictated by equal quotas of sunlight but now also arranged to create "a sense of place." (In the Netherlands at least, these places are often the size of a football field. One might wonder whether there is a correlation between the successes of Dutch soccer in the 1970s and the type of neighborhoods in which most of the players grew up.)

The community becomes the paradigmatic feature of the 1950s and 1960s, not only in the architecture of Team 10 but also in academia, where the discipline of sociology becomes popular. It is a time of sociological experiments. With the emergence of the middle class as the new majority post–World War II, the notion of class struggle, the dominating ideological feature in social and political theory at the beginning of the century, increasingly fades into the background. The focus shifts to a theorization of human relationships. The main driver of the economic system—individual consumption—comes under increased scrutiny. With this come new, albeit frail, attempts at "alternative forms of collectivity."

In 1950 sociologist George A. Hillery Jr. publishes *A Research Odyssey: Developing and Testing a Community Theory.*[9] The title is painfully appropriate because the book is a journey across every conceivable definition of community, ending with ninety-four in total. Unwittingly, the book is an early indication of how prominent the search for a new collectivity in postwar society will continue to be in the following decades.

Over the next decade, that search becomes increasingly experimental. This is the age of the commune. While the community looks at existing, latent sources of cohesion within society—neighborhood, ethnicity, religion—the commune's raison d'être is that its ideals cannot be realized in the context of society as a whole. The commune has a radical political dimension, viewing society as nothing but the source of unwelcome compromises. Only in isolation—a start from scratch—can a new, "ideal" set of relationships among people be formed.

In the late 1960s various communes crop up across the United States and Europe. The commune eventually known as Drop City takes shape in 1965 in Trinidad, Colorado. Drop City is an initiative by three artists to celebrate a minimalist lifestyle, privileging creative work in an age of materialism. There is an interesting relationship with architecture. Given their limited building experience, the artists look for efficient structures that are quick and easy to build. They settle on structures based on the geodesic dome designed by R. Buckminster Fuller, constructed with reclaimed materials, such as culled lumber, bottle caps, and chopped-out car tops.[10] Documentary filmmaker Joan Grossman later writes: "Drop City has become a lab for experimental building, and in 1966 Fuller himself honors Drop City with his Dymaxion Award for 'poetically economic structural accomplishments'; the commune attracts international attention and inspires a generation of alternative communities, but the flood of attention leads to overcrowding, and the community is eventually abandoned to transients. By 1973, Drop City has become the world's first geodesic ghost town."[11]

In Europe, the political dimension of the commune is less comical. In Berlin, ten men and women segregate from society, living under the name Kommune 1.[12] Their main credo—"Das Private ist politisch" (The private is political)—makes living in a commune essentially a political statement against the family, viewed as a bourgeois tool designed to further consumption and to reaffirm class segregation.[13] Kommune 1's manifesto is largely a form of agitation. It calls on people to raid warehouses and department stores as bastions of consumerism, which, like the family, Kommune 1 sees as the holdover from the former National Socialist government of Germany, with the same people still in power and the same mechanisms still in place.

To the extent that Kommune 1 constitutes a community, it is no longer a reflection or product of the shared values of society but the exact opposite, a protest against society; rejection of particular mainstream values becomes the primary source of bonding. Apparently, at this point in history, the notion of "the community" can exist only on the condition of a seemingly inevitable deescalation of the scale of consensus.

In the context of this realization, it interesting to note that the moment at which "community architect" surfaces as an official term is in the mid-1970s. In 1974 Rod Hackney, together with the residents of Black Road, Macclesfield, devises a pilot scheme to renovate a working-class neighborhood facing imminent demolition.[14] The ensuing press campaign brands the effort: "It's only Working Class conservation!"[15] With the extensive proliferation of this slogan in the media, community architecture is born in combination with an early form of residents' participation, that other great 1970s phenomenon. Paradoxically, it emerges from an unlikely alliance of protest and preservation—against, rather than with, the prevailing dogmas of society as a whole.

Community and society constitute in these examples an interesting dichotomy, although the words are more related than one might expect. In German, community and society branch from the same tree: *Gemeinschaft* (community) and *Gesellschaft* (society).[16] *Gemeinschaft* precedes *Gesellschaft* in scale and level of organization. Society is the institutionalized version of the community. The moment society becomes the predominant form of organizing human relationships, however, the community also becomes a tool of rejection. In the face of a larger society that seemingly fails to deliver on its promises, the community supersedes society.[17]

"Who is society? There is no such thing! There are individuals, men and women, and there are families."[18] These words, spoken by Margaret Thatcher in 1987, seem to mark a strange full circle to the Kommune 1 manifesto, which, albeit for different reasons, contains an equally fierce assault on society. Twenty years later, the notion of a society that can be entrusted with any collective task—a society that acts for the greater good—

appears to be rejected by supporters and opponents of "the family" alike. The result is an ideological vacuum in which "the community" has become ideological property claimed by both the Left and the Right.

In the context of this ideological disarray, something interesting happens in architecture as well. Throughout the 1980s, "the community" dominates architectural discourse; however, it becomes less and less clear who its protagonists really are. In the early 1990s a manifesto is published arguing for "the restoration of existing urban centers and towns within coherent metropolitan regions, the reconfiguration of sprawling suburbs into communities of real neighborhoods and diverse districts, the conservation of natural environments, and the preservation of our built legacy."[19] Although this statement evidently takes a cue from the Team 10 theorists, it is an excerpt from a very different type of manifesto, the "Charter of the New Urbanism. While their rhetoric is similar, New Urbanism is an almost antidotal movement to Team 10; its actors have very different political associations, and it ultimately realizes (or at least represents) a very different style of architecture. The architects from Team 10 were primarily agents of a large public sector, while the architects of the New Urbanism are mostly agents of the private sector. Their most notorious achievement—Celebration—is a town commissioned and managed by the Disney Corporation, with Disney performing tasks previously performed by the state.[20]

To what extent can an urbanism that puts itself at the service of private, at times gated, communities such as Celebration make credible moral claims about society? It is clear that "the community" of the New Urbanists is very different from the community of Team 10: a product not of society at large but of a society of parts and partial interests. In the New Urbanism movement, "the community" is a concept of division, thus ensuring the breakdown of any possibility of a broader community.

Still, there is one important thing that Team 10 and the New Urbanists have in common: they see the community as a product of spatial parameters. Throughout their discourse, "the community" remains a fairly straightforward notion, defined through spatial proximity in an orderly progression of scales: the neighborhood, the city, and the nation.

The decade that follows turns everything upside down. In a globalized economy, where cities increasingly compete in economic terms, "the community" is defined not by territory but by economic interdependence. Employers present themselves as substitutes for or sponsors of urban communities. McDonald's, for instance, creates local training programs,[21] youth sports, and community charity funds in many American cities.

As a consequence, the idea that communities can and should be shaped through and beyond the built environment they inhabit starts to acquire traction in the late 1990s. "Community planning" expands from architecture and urbanism to a multidisciplinary approach, an exclusive type of expertise simultaneously embraced by technology firms, management consultants, and even public institutions, all claiming unique knowledge of the subject. Vancouver, consistently at the top of lists of so-called livable cities,[22] is as much a form of knowledge as it is a city in Canada. In a state of near bankruptcy as recently as the 1970s,[23] the city makes a remarkable turnaround during the 1990s, largely thanks to one man. With few conventional planning options left at his disposal, the head of the Vancouver Municipal Planning Department practically invents "community planning." The term becomes synonymous with everything that is good for the city—a vibrant public realm, integrated (green) public space, sustainable infrastructure, and so on—albeit more as a perpetual announcement of things to come than as real urban transformation. It becomes hype: the first real evidence of a merger between urbanism and marketing. Even if Vancouver does not change that much, the perception of Vancouver does. In the 1990s real estate prices escalate dramatically,[24] and Vancouver becomes a success story, almost irrespective of any real physical change. "Vancouverism" is a model, soon to be exported to cities as diverse as Abu Dhabi, Rotterdam, and Dallas.

Others soon join municipal planners to create their own versions of future communities. This is evident in the emergence of "community-planning" or grassroots movements defined by broad neighborhood participation. At the extreme this amounts to overall surrender to local powers. In Rio's favelas the relevant power is the gang—the only remaining form of efficient organization—which runs the systems of justice and order. Community is what emerges when society turns its back.

More and more, community formation relies on exclusion and voluntary isolation. In the United States, the public sector has increasingly relegated the management of cities to corporations. Communism (the only ideology to elevate "the community" to a global political doctrine) once spanned a third of the globe; currently it is contained to insular states like North Korea. Religion, the cement that held society together, is more and more a means to secede from a society no longer under its spell, turning religious communities into "believers," diversely defined. Sects build consensus on a shared rejection of all that refuses to conform to their spiritual truths. Others find their answers through silence and mystery: Scientology, Freemasons, the Omertà. Their bond is shared knowledge of what cannot be said.

The public introduction of the Internet and World Wide Web in the 1990s signals an important possibility to resurrect the community as a mainstream, even global, notion.[25] In the new virtual domain even the most marginal preoccupations can (and do) acquire mass followings. An array of "online communities" emerges and it is in on the Internet that "the community" is frequently invoked. Still, that promise proves double edged. The unprecedented online exposure of anything and everything doesn't so much elevate them to mainstream status as it tends to destroy the notion of the mainstream altogether. The mainstream and the marginal become interchangeable. When everything seems important, ultimately nothing is. If once the community was a vehicle of meaning, defined in opposition to a dominant culture or to the anonymous masses of society, the Internet leaves nothing to oppose.

Community exists not as antidote to anonymity, but because of it. We can augment our persona, fix our shortcomings, and renegotiate our relationships at will. Milan Kundera wrote that we cannot know if our decisions are the best ones, because the first rehearsal of life is life itself.[26] But the creators of virtual communities such as Second Life make that no longer true: their "Metaverse" offers endless trial and error, where humans—or rather, avatars—can free themselves from the limitations of reality.[27] Property and services are traded for virtual currency that every now and then— in a strange intersection of virtual and real—can be exchanged for hard cash. Products are granted a first life in virtual communities before they emerge in the real world. Second Life's virtual schizophrenia clinic serves as an ironic climax.[28]

The virtual used to be as an extension of the real, but increasingly it precedes the real, as a test bed where every fact of life is preemptively augmented before it sees the light of day. It seems that the first rehearsal for life is no longer life itself but acted out in cyberspace.

Tokyo, December 2013, the Akihabara district: The shops, selling Japanese video games, appear to be doing well.[29] But the games are no longer limited to the shops. Fetishes in the games have found their way into the streets. Electric wires above the railroad overpass cut into the vagina of a mammoth young girl in school uniform, sitting on top. A passing train seems to emerge like a giant penis.

An Otaku—a local resident named after a game character—shares his meal with a two-dimensional print of his virtual girlfriend. In Akihabara, games and the virtual community built around them have become reality. "The community" has come full circle.

Postscript

Thirty years ago, as a student at the TU Delft, I witnessed the slow death of sociology as a subject taught within architecture. Strangely, the abandonment of that subject, which approached "the community" as an object of scientific study, based on empirical research, gave rise to the term's unprecedented popularity in the architectural profession, allowing its rhetoric about "the community" to go unchecked.

"The community" became the most frequently invoked concept in architectural and urban discourse, endowing even the most mediocre designs with an aura of good intentions and implicitly condemning designers who declined to use the word. It legitimized everything from Team X to New Urbanism, from Pendrecht to Celebration, from Aldo van Eyck to Larry Beasley, evolving from a physical (Team 10) to a virtual construct, either as marketing (Vancouver) or as online phenomenon. If Vancouver marks the point where community architecture is abandoned as something physical, the Akihabara district, in all its absurdity, marks an odd return to the community as a physical phenomenon or, at least, as proof of the need thereof, with all the associated relevance for form, style, design, and maybe even architecture.

Perhaps it is time to revisit "the community" in the complexity it deserves. Architecture's preoccupation with its relevance for the community has prevented it from acquiring real knowledge of the community. Similarly, "the community" is the subject of business, religion, politics, and the Internet, each seeking answers while clouded by ulterior motives. What is needed is open and integrated discourse on how the community is manifested and manipulated within all these domains.

Akihabara train station
Photomontage by Yoshinobu Kimura (Tamaki), 2004. Incorporated PVC figure,
Shinyokohama Arina in Akihabara, by Ooshima Yuuki (Sculptor) / Kaiyodo
(Manufacturer).

Paul de Ley and Joke van den Bout, Bickerseiland, 1973
Collectie Het Nieuwe Instituut, LEYP, f20-1

15

With the Masses

The Architecture of Participation

December 5, 1986: Residents of De Afrikaanderwijk, a nineteenth-century quarter of Rotterdam, have been invited to a public meeting to express their views on a future housing project. The session will start in a few minutes, but the main room of the local community center is already heavy with smoke from hand-rolled cigarettes. Most of the locals are employed in Rotterdam's nearby port. "Organized" gatherings usually serve as sites of protest against the erosion of workers' rights. To the people in the room, meetings are by definition a form of resistance. It is the only kind they have come to know in recent times.

The projection screen is barely visible; the stale air is a literal smoke-screen, preempting the arguments designed to convince the residents of "good" and "necessary" changes to their neighborhood. The municipal official chairing the session has trouble making himself heard, even with a microphone. The architect, he announces, will start a few minutes late. The crowd is not amused and demands an apology as a sign of goodwill. The chair doesn't know how to react. As far as he is concerned, this session is a simple back-and-forth between the architect of the project and its future users. Unsure how to appease the crowd, he points to the crates of beer in the back of the room, intended for the end of the evening.

His concession does the trick. The noise subsides, and the architect begins. His story is well rehearsed and progresses smoothly, punctuated by the pops of opening beer bottles. With the exception of a few squabbling teenagers, everybody listens politely, and when it is time for questions, there is a hush. A bulky man in a leather jacket in the front row raises his hand. Scanning the room for tacit approval, he kicks off: "I would like to ask the architect. . . . In my current home, when my neighbor above me flushes his shit, I can hear it. Will that also be the case in your building?" The architect raises his eyebrows—not a question he had expected. He starts on a technical explanation of modern insulation standards, abruptly curtailed when the whole room erupts in laughter. "Don't be so serious, we're just fuckin' with ya!"

In an apparent effort to mediate, a woman addresses her fellow residents: "I prefer a kitchen on the facade, with a window: that's the best way to get rid of the cooking smells—but the architect has clearly explained to me that this is simply not an option in such a large building." She is keen to show off her recently and personally acquired knowledge. Meanwhile, the architect, equally keen to avoid having his bluffs called publicly, quickly points to another raised finger.

"What are these doors made of?" asks another resident, referring to the sliding partitions that close off the kitchens from the living rooms. The project is deliberately presented at an early stage, so this question cannot be definitively answered: the architect proceeds to list various options, using the kitchen doors as a welcome opportunity to show his eagerness to engage. "We are keen to make decisions in close consultation with you. We just propose; you choose. It can be anything: wood, plastic . . ."

"Glass! That would seem the most elegant option to me," someone interjects. "Mmm, to me, too . . . but we are working with a limited budget," the architect replies. "Glass!" somebody else chimes in: "Glass!" The preference is quickly adopted by the rest of the room, building to a fervent chant: "Glass, GLASS, GLASS!" The architect smiles. In reality, the issue is of little concern to him: when it comes to kitchen doors, he is willing to concede, happy with the distraction from more contentious issues, which indeed remain undiscussed for the rest of the evening.

And the issues are many. First, his building has nothing to do with the neighborhood. The architect has taken his inspiration from Oscar Niemeyer's Copan building in Brazil, transposing its sensuous concrete curves to Rotterdam South's nineteenth-century urban fabric—a historic part of the city that is lucky to have survived the onslaught of the Luftwaffe intact. A month before the consultation, one of the city officials gently points out what he considers the project's main weakness: while differentiating new buildings from their context is not a cardinal sin—contrast can even be a form of contextual respect—it is nevertheless well known that the architect has proposed this same design in about a dozen other locations, without success. To the official, the architect's arguments seem fueled by desperation rather than considered reflection.

The architect, however, won't stand for it. He has been on television recently as one of a new and promising generation. For most architects, youth is a relative notion: he has turned forty and is in a hurry, viewing clashes with local authorities or evenings like this as little more than speed bumps in the path of his career. After the TV appearance, the ultimate goal is international fame. The conversation is finally freed from apologies for new urban interventions; newness is once again believed to have legitimacy in its own right. In the prevailing discourse of the late 1980s, there is a consensus that Architecture (invariably capitalized) is an autonomous discipline, independent of any context—material, societal, or otherwise. Rather, context must be recognized as being as unstable as architecture itself.

Initially part of a critical effort to cleanse the discourse of improper arguments, this thinking quickly becomes a tool in the hands of up-and-coming architects to do exactly as they please: proposing whatever, whenever, wherever. Fed up with the stultifying moral code and crippling humanism of the generation before them, they are determined to emulate their predecessors on their own terms. Perhaps autonomy from context equates to immunity from criticism.

In Tom Wolfe's *Bonfire of the Vanities,* a wealthy New York City trader finds his gilded life disrupted; accidentally entering the Bronx, he and his mistress are suddenly confronted with a world that has been blocked from their lives thus far. In many ways, the evening in Rotterdam could be a parallel: a sociological mismatch as the ambitious architect meets his Waterloo or, at least, a battle that dents his ego. But it doesn't. The evening is only a necessary distraction from the pursuit of his real goals. A community meeting is never going to change them.

I remember the first time I saw the idea of resident participation carried to something approaching a full conclusion. The year before the Afrikaanderwijk meeting, I was taken to see a student housing project on the outskirts of Brussels. Although the building, commissioned by the Catholic University of Louvain, had been controversial in the 1970s, its trials

La MéMé, Woluwe-Saint-Lambert, 2016
Photograph by Maarten Lambrechts

seemed a distant memory to us fifteen years later—we visited from curiosity rather than reverence.

1968: Increasing tensions between Belgium's Flemish- and French-speaking factions turn the University of Louvain (or Leuven)—formerly an integrated language community—into a scene of violent conflict, propelling the expansion of the Francophone medical campus at an alternative location.[1]

The conflict merges in 1968 with a more general revolt against the university authorities. The architect selected by the university has proposed a sort of nineteenth-century classical pastiche, inspired by the typical American Ivy League campus. In character with the political climate of their time, the students protest against what they perceive to be a bourgeois imposition and demand a new selection process. Remarkably, the university agrees to the formation of a student committee, taking a seat but forgoing the right to vote.

The student committee produces a counterproposal by Lucien Kroll, just over forty and known for his cooperative manner of practicing architecture. Kroll is already a notorious figure among students, and his reputation features tales of secret nightly sessions coaching students to prepare for reviews at La Cambre, where he had studied. The university is perplexed by the students' choice. Kroll has no prior history with the university; having practiced mainly in Belgium's African colonies, he is an unknown quantity. Still, happy to put an end to student unrest, they concede, and Kroll set to work. His appointment is clearly a trade-off; by acquiescing to the demand for Kroll, the authorities hope to mitigate the underlying language conflict, which is potentially the greater source of political unrest.

With Kroll as their guide, students start focusing on the Maison Médicale—La MéMé, as it is nicknamed—even participating in the building's construction. Kroll organizes collaborators and students into groups, encouraging the use of models over drawings. This method becomes manifest in the building's facade, which reflects the coexistence of disparate political factions: here shaped by the fascists, there by the Communists, and so on. Having defused the conflict between the students and their university, the production of architecture provides a vehicle to transcend differences within the student body itself.

Kroll works intimately with the students for two years. Weekly sessions are organized at his studio (also his house) at Auderghem, on the outskirts of Brussels, with about thirty to thirty-five students at a time. They work long hours. Kroll's wife, Simone, prepares dinner; when there are more people than chairs, they eat collectively on the floor. These are happy days.

The location of the meetings—in the privacy of Kroll's home—is intentional. Distance from the institution, which had previously forgone any participation, would allow the process to unfold with more freedom. The location, however, does not discourage the university's committee members from dropping by (and enjoying pleasant picnics in the garden). In an attempt to fend off "institutional involvement," the meetings are pushed later and later into the evenings and ultimately into the weekends. This has the desired effect. Belgian civil servants observe strict hours, and the university can scarcely afford overtime rates.

Kroll takes the idea of collaboration between architect and user to an intimate extreme, a kind of architectural method acting. During one of the legendary meetings, Kroll learns that the group has collectively purchased a small house for the sole purpose of rebuilding it: ripping up floors, demolishing walls and stairs, the whole nine yards. Kroll turns this into a core method: building a shell house and allowing inhabitants to transform it. The mock-house method is a live demonstration of the design process he envisions for the project as a whole, enabling future inhabitants to discover untold needs. Kroll accepts every outcome, even if it defies all prevailing architecture conventions. A tall American student designs for himself a very small room seven meters high; Kroll remains silent, although the room's next inhabitant might have very different wishes. The building's future popularity proved him right: when the student leaves, three others argue over his room.

Louis Le Roy, a self-professed "ecotect," is Kroll's preferred gardener for the project. Central to his philosophy is that people should work with nature to reach the highest degree of complexity. But the university refuses to engage him, and no one else is appointed. The project has a large landscape component, and Kroll's ambitions are not limited to the official boundaries of the site. In his vision, La MéMé's social zone should be integrated with the adjacent neighborhood. The students initially balk at the idea; having recently gained autonomy from the university, they are reluctant to engage with the townsfolk.

Kroll gets his way in a typically unconventional manner: halfway through construction, he throws a summer party at the site, and the festivities alert the neighbors. Curious more than alarmed, they enter the site; after hearing Kroll's explanation, they returned home to bring back plants from their gardens. The project succeeds in soliciting participation beyond its boundaries without intending to do so.

The first two years are happy ones. The collaboration with students is harmonious, and even relations with the university are not altogether bad. All of that changes when the representatives of the university come to visit the project in the fall of 1972. Confronted with a result that does not seem to represent their "values," the university demands drastic action. In addition, the building is substantially over budget. Kroll is fired from the project.

Kroll's response is unexpected: seeking alternative suppliers, he lowers the projections for material costs so dramatically as to bring the project on budget without making a single alteration to the community-led design. Kroll effectively exposes the main contractor as guilty of cartel pricing—a common practice at the time and rarely questioned, especially by architects. The contractor, seeing his (illegitimate) hopes dashed, is furious and seeks compensation. The dispute is fought all the way to the federal minister of finance, who eventually decides in Kroll's favor.

In response, the university decides to cut his honorarium, arguing that the previous year's summer party had vandalized the building site and the associated costs have to come out of Kroll's fee. Kroll takes the matter to trial again. The eventual hearing demonstrates little sympathy for Kroll or his ideological struggle. Representatives from the order of Belgian architects are conspicuously absent, officially declaring a neutral stance. In reality, there is no little schadenfreude for a traitor who had, in their view, attempted to undermine the authority of the architect.

These same views are echoed ten years later by the professors showing our group around La MéMé. Why voluntarily surrender when the powers of the architect are already so eroded? What use is a project where only first-generation users have the opportunity to adapt their space? Participation, they argue, reduces architecture to a game of chance. Descriptions vary from "failed experiment" to "Frankenstein's monster" and "less than the sum of its parts." We are encouraged to take stock, forget, and move on to more serious business.

Roughly thirty years after that visit to La MéMé, I manage to get an appointment with Lucien Kroll. Recent discourse has made me curious about his views on the past, on La MéMé and the ensuing controversy, and on the present, in which participation has acquired a new relevance, a new tang.[2] Ironically, like "community" before it, the term "participation" has come to reinforce convictions on both ends of the political spectrum. For the Right, the term allows for a seemingly benign rollback of the welfare state, reducing public spending. For the Left, the idea relates to equal opportunities for democratic agency.

Located in an inconspicuous small apartment block, Kroll's residence is apparently indistinguishable from that of his neighbors. There are two doorbells, one for his home, the other for his atelier, which still goes by the initialism AUAI (Atelier d'Urbanisme d'Architecture et d'Informatique).[3] I ring, but no one answers. A passing neighbor advises me to just keep ringing both bells. I decide to sneak past him instead, descending into the complex, where I find a door—unlocked—marked AUAI. I enter. The place is overrun by old-school drawing boards, but there is nobody inside. I am undoubtedly trespassing; still, I take my chances and proceed. Have I missed my last chance to catch Lucien Kroll alive? But then, I hear voices in the garden, people finishing lunch.

This must be the ambiance in which Kroll met his students in the mid-1970s: a wooden table set with food and drink amid the garden, all made by Simone. Kroll is at the head of the table, a tall figure with his back to me. My main purpose is to reconstruct the events surrounding La MéMé, but at eighty-nine, Kroll does not remember much. His anecdotes are at best atmospheric, recalling emotional exchanges with various nameless and ageless actors. His spotty memory has an interesting effect: the lack of precise memories forces him to reflect on past efforts in grandiose terms. "According to Vitruvius, the Roman master builder, architecture was the combination of three virtues: Utilitas, Firmitas, and Venustas. He forgot Humanitas. . . . That, I felt, needed changing." Architecture's historic dimension is invariably a product of exaggeration; to the extent that Kroll's work is about breaking traditions, this isn't one of them. The student clashes at La MéMé are compared to women's suffrage, the early granting of which, according to Kroll, could have prevented industrialized warfare, potentially lessening the tremendous loss of life. (I assume that he is referring to the trenches of World War I; although odd, the comparison isn't entirely implausible, given most European countries' late adoption of women's voting rights.)

Moreover, without rapid industrialization, the Bauhaus—in Kroll's opinion, the ultimate source of evil—might not have opened. Visiting Germany after the war, he has witnessed the dangers of rooting architectural consensus within the benediction of the building industry. Anonymous housing is the antithesis of what Kroll hoped to achieve; if industrial building methods are indeed an inescapable reality, then the only possible approach for diversity is to pursue a tailored, case-by-case application. Only in the individual wishes of users can an authentic source of diversity be found.

Still, it remains an open question whether Kroll, in inverting the principles of the Bauhaus, is nevertheless indebted to those principles. His method—a rigorous prioritization of process over outcome, accepting whatever emerges as a result—is oddly reminiscent of the Bauhaus's revolt against the tradition of the Beaux-Arts. The style of his Auderghem residence, his home for more than forty years, gives the conflicting impression of a personal taste that is distinctly more "modern" in style than many of his projects, making one speculate on the extent to which his methods involve a personal sacrifice.

Our conversation is coming to an end. Kroll escorts me to the taxi, and we share a few last thoughts. Participation is enjoying renewed attention today, and Kroll's legacy has moved back into the limelight; he gives interviews, features in publications, and appears in videos on the Internet. The appetite for user involvement seems to go through cycles: *en vogue* in the 1970s, frowned on in the 1980s, ignored in the 1990s, forgotten in the first years of the twenty-first century, only to make a comeback in the postrecession chill of the past five years. There is an almost surreal contrast between Kroll's earnest idealism and the near-pathological narcissism that appeared to drive architects a short decade later. Strangely, the legacy of each period is inversely proportional to the extent to which its architects would seem to seek personal recognition. La MéMé has earned its place in history: petitions against its gradual demolition are met with massive support, while much of the 1980s statement architecture barely registers in our conscience.

What explains the architecture profession's drastic mood shifts on an issue so central to its legitimacy? Is there a correlation between architecture's role within the prevailing power structures and its readiness to listen to users? Traditionally, the commissioner of a building is also its user, and participation is guaranteed through the dependence of the architect on his or her patron. The advent of the welfare state and the introduction of mass housing changed things fundamentally. Commissioners were no longer users. User participation became a matter of choice, either actively sought by enlightened architects, such as Lucien Kroll, or through the overly determined instruction of commissioning parties, suddenly eager to ensure an apparently humanist legacy. The urban renewal processes of the 1970s reintroduced certain aspects of traditional practice—the user could express his or her wishes directly—but the architect was bound only to the extent that the client (and not the user) agreed. This half-baked involvement—a suggestion of power—discredited the whole notion of user participation and was dismissed as a frustrating process for users and architects alike. The atmosphere of mistrust and resistance during meetings, as seen in Afrikaanderwijk, finds its roots here.

In the questioning of larger structures, the power of a project like La MéMé is apparent. By allowing the students agency, the university could go where society as a whole would not dare tread. The same political experiment, transplanted into a regular part of the city, such as working-class Afrikaanderwijk, could have had consequences beyond our wildest imagination.

I revisited the Afrikaanderwijk project recently. Most of the social rental apartments in the project had been sold on the market as private residences. The area had been transformed after a property boom radiating from the center of Rotterdam. Residents now exist in the abstract as "prospective buyers"; new projects are no longer subjected to painful interrogations in smoke-filled rooms. Projects either sell or they don't. Only the market passes judgment.

The 1960s catered to a largely anonymous population of tenants, categorized by the similarity of their needs. In the 1970s user participation served as a tool against the uniformity created by the welfare state. A prevailing form of housing production—the renewal of old inner-city neighborhoods—helped. The anonymous masses of the 1960s became the neighborhood communities of the 1970s, the scale of which allowed for the consultation of users on the future of their living environment, or for protest if they weren't consulted.

The triumph of the market economy in the 1990s caused a breakdown of this logic. In the context of property markets, buildings are tradable assets on balance sheets. Users and their demands are irrelevant; the decisive factor becomes the elimination of financial risk. Paradoxically, the market's celebration of diversity—"consumer choice"—has largely achieved monotony, made not by standardized industrial production but by an invented virtual consensus.

Few architects have embraced the idea of user participation; fewer still have carried it to an extended conclusion. Users as cocreators have steadily gained traction in other creative domains, but any notion of "the people" as a participatory force—one that helps determine the outcome of a design process—finds architecture well outside its comfort zone. Such ideals are still considered naïve and irreverent; many champions remain largely unsung. Segal, Hundertwasser, Kroll, Habraken, and de Carlo are among the names we know, but the identities of those behind today's *Baugruppen*, for example, remain undisclosed. In the context of the paradoxical mechanics of a free-market economy, it is increasingly unclear for what, for whom, and why buildings are produced. As a result, architecture routinely loses itself in overwrought mental constructions to justify the physical ones. It seems that a new revisionist movement is needed. After making a convincing case of being *for* the masses in the twentieth century, architecture will have to be *with* the masses in the twenty-first.

IV. TRIAL AND ERROR

2005

Tony Blair is elected to serve a third term as UK prime minister. Over four million people travel to the Vatican to mourn Pope John Paul II.

16

Ex Nihilo Nihil Fit: Part One

January 17

After a limited competition in the fall of 2004, involving three other parties, we have been appointed as master planner for a fifty-acre site in West London—not quite the West London one usually thinks of, but farther west, where the level of wealth begins to drop again. Here, property prices aren't (yet) quite as inflated as in the neighboring (royal) borough, but it is expected that they will soon get there. We are meant to take on an underused industrial piece of land that, despite numerous previous planning attempts, has refused to come to life. Given its location right against the edge of Kensington and Chelsea, its potential is supposed to be enormous, representing one of the biggest development opportunities in London, but so far investors have been shy about coming forward, and thus the site has remained somewhat of an anomaly: a collection of car-repair workshops, small chemical facilities, and secondhand-furniture shops—not quite what one would expect in the middle of a booming property market.

The site's immediate problem as a prospective development location is that it is cut off from its surroundings, locked in by heavy rail and road infrastructure. Trying to enter, even by foot, proves to be a testing experience. Any small roads that appear to provide access invariably lead to dead ends. The fences one typically runs into are familiar: Procter palisade fences, manufactured by an expert supplier to the fencing industry for over fifty years, are the ultimate burglarproof fences available on the market, and also the ugliest: a series of connected vertical steel strips, forking out into a trident at the top, ready to spit-roast anyone trying to climb over.

There is one road that provides access, but it requires searching. Like a secret passage, it casually extends from behind a local petrol station into the site, bending to go behind the neighboring tube station, where it leads to a barrier watched from a security cabin, which on the day we visit is unmanned. There is only a phone number to call. A dog barks from the other side. Visitors are discouraged.

The site is owned by six parties who have come together to form a consortium, somewhat comically referred to as the Landowners. The official name, Development Partnership, cannot yet be used. The drafting of a contract among the six parties has proven considerably more time consuming than anticipated, and until a signed agreement is in place, the group cannot legally be referred to as a partnership. Nevertheless, the opportunities are attractive, and thus the parties have decided to proceed in good faith, taking for granted the feudal connotations of the name under which they must operate.

This coming together of parties is also viewed favorably by the Greater London Authority (GLA), the city's overriding administrative body. Since its reinstatement in 2000, the GLA has become a force to be reckoned with, to the point that its known or presumed preferences are preemptively incorporated into local initiatives such as this one. I well remember London in the absence of such an authority during the late 1980s after Margaret Thatcher had dismantled the equivalent Greater London Council (GLC), viewing the powerful body as unwelcome political competition; the city operated instead as a collection of thirty-three largely individual townships. With the exception of the Docklands, a deliberately engineered free-for-all, larger ambitions were generally dismissed as inappropriate socialist interventions, and the city as a whole was left reliant on piecemeal developments. Not today. In singling out areas such as this one, labeling them "key opportunity areas," and providing the accompanying incentives, it is the GLA that now provokes the initiative. The pecking order has been reversed. Even if twenty-first-century London continues to be a tapestry of individual developments, the new / old administrative body has found a clever way to suggest a coherent course of action.

Pleasing the GLA however, isn't the only motivation behind the landowners' pact. This becomes apparent when we further examine the task we have been given. So far we have studied the site as a single plot of land. However, superimposing the individual ownership boundaries reveals an unexpectedly complex topography, not unlike the post-Tito fragmentation of the Balkans. It is virtually impossible to imagine development along the lines of individual ownerships. Some plots are thin slivers of land, too narrow to hold buildings; other sites are landlocked, relying on the goodwill of neighbors for access; still others are hampered by immovable infrastructure, located partly under the overpass of the highway and the overground tube line that cross the site. It is clear that the area stands a chance only if it is developed as a whole so that its cumulative advantages can cancel out the disadvantages of each individual parcel. Still, the absence of a binding contract that would make the parties truly one will prove to significantly increase the difficulty of our mission.

It is the GLA that has pushed for our appointment. Sensitive to international reputations and impressed by our ability to deal with similar cases involving the integration of urban development and infrastructure, it feels that we are the party best equipped to cope with the complexity—in both an urban and a political sense—of this particular piece of land. The GLA, however, will participate only as a reviewer, on the other side of the table. Our client will be the landowners. It is through them that we will have to conduct our business on a daily basis. Their views of us are mixed: half of them seem to be impressed (in London you never really know), the other half suitably skeptical about the abilities of a foreign firm to deal with local intricacies. Still, given the GLA's emphatic endorsement, we have been given the benefit of the doubt.

February 14

Our first major setback occurs when the landowners choose the party most skeptical of our involvement to act as a point of contact. This is a London development firm that owns the large landlocked parcel in the middle of the site. It is a clever move on the part of the landowners to appoint the party that stands to gain most from the development but can't move an inch without the consent of the other landowners. In carefully matching power and dependency, the group of landowners has essentially opted to remain leaderless. There is nothing we can do but work with the party they chose to represent them in a constructive way and hope that they will do the same with us.

This may not be as easy as it sounds. London's ostensibly progressive mood hardly means that short-term greed has been weeded out. Far from it. Upon introduction, it immediately becomes clear that as far as our client reps are concerned, the ambitions stated by the GLA—to bring jobs, affordable housing, and community provisions into the area—are no more than a front. This is a scheme that is to "hit the ground running" (developer slang for financial returns kicking in immediately upon delivery). Any other discussion is inappropriate, particularly discussions of design and long-term visions. They downplay the work we have done to date. The group has chosen an architect, not a scheme. We have to start fresh, this time with their input. This is the London I got to know in the 1980s, during my first job as an architect: staunchly conservative and downright hostile to modernism. Yet, in typical English fashion, all oppositions are deferred, preferably forever, allowing business to progress as usual, whatever the nature of the business is. In an earlier meeting, shortly before awarding the contract, Mayor Ken Livingstone has indicated that in regard to this West London site, he "wants the maximum!" For our client reps, the clarity of his brief leaves nothing to be desired: the largest possible amount of development for the lowest possible cost. It is the financial returns that must be maximized. The mayor's remarks have actually put them at ease. They know how to go about this. Their approach works. The walls of their Mayfair offices are hung with paintings by Holbein, and the driveway is littered with expensive sports cars, making us feel like we are part of an edition of Top Gear. Their general views on society complete that picture.

It proves hard to gain our client reps' trust. My English accent, acquired during my initial years of London employment, helps only to a limited extent. They set the ground rules: before engaging with any of the public authorities overviewing the effort, all presentations will have to be vetted in advance. They ask that we rehearse any voice-over accompanying our slides in their presence first. We are not to deviate from the script. I feel hampered by the apparent lack of mandate. The public authorities have appointed us, so presumably it is our views on the site they want to hear, not the landowners'. We have a bit of a track record in getting large development projects approved; our client rep's desire to reduce us to a ventriloquist's dummy seems in no one's interest, least of all theirs.

April 25

"That's crap!" The crass comment stands in stark contrast to the posh accent with which it is delivered. Or perhaps not. I guess this is how the headmaster of an average English "public" (that is, private) school sets pupils straight who are out of line. The sudden, unexpected abandonment of politeness proves a powerful tactic: aggression coupled with the element of surprise. We are suitably intimidated, unaware of any bad behavior on our part. The comment pertains to a foam model we brought to a previous meeting, which is now proudly displayed on the middle of our meeting table as evidence of our incompetence. Last week, during a session of the combined landowners, our client reps have been pressured to come up with results, or else.

I guess this is their way of passing on the message. The same model that had been received with enthusiasm the week before is now subject to vilification. Too abstract, too little detail, too unrealistic. If there isn't evidence of progress before the next landowners' meeting (in less than a month), there will be a major problem. "It's not working at the moment, I'm afraid," is the understated conclusion of our client reps. Only a week ago we had been asked to leave the model behind. Given what has just happened, that now feels like a nasty setup. It is not until much later, after multiple other jobs in Britain, that I realize that every consultant—as we are referred to here—has to confront threats of being fired at least once in the course of a project. It is part of a routine, an initiation ritual that helps establish the pecking order, allowing new participants to become part of the herd. Only when the threat isn't made should one be worried. Our meeting is coming to an end. Their unequivocal position leaves little room for argumentation. We decide to cave and promise to do better at the next meeting. As soon as we do, things go back to normal. We shake hands. It is as though the exchange hasn't taken place. We have passed the test.

April 26

We wonder what to do. How do we turn around the apparent dissatisfaction? We really don't think that we have done a bad job so far. In fact, quite the opposite. We are convinced that we have laid the groundwork for a masterpiece. It is just that our large one-size-fits-all solution happens to be at odds with prevailing market conditions, which require a development in small increments. The master plan must accommodate multiple phasing scenarios, allowing the landowners to take things one step at a time, backtrack, or even prematurely abort in case of disappointing financial revenues. When it comes to failure, it is best to think small.

We decide to start over, turn things around, and make the criticism of our plan into the point of departure. We propose a layout with three clusters of urban development, separated by two parks. (Our site has a linear shape.) Each cluster is a reflection of its existing surroundings and mimics the typology of neighboring areas: low-rise single-family units in the north; high-rise buildings on either side of the highway overpass; nine-story perimeter blocks in the center, providing urban density close to the area's tube station; and a number of large circular buildings to accompany the curvilinear formal language of a large shopping mall under construction immediately south of our site.

In theory, our approach allows for six different phasing scenarios. Given the fact that each phase is composed of multiple smaller parts, it even permits phasing of the phases. Only the parks will have to be constructed in one go. They also constitute the lion's share of our design work. It is the parks that add value and will prove crucial in winning the argument for the enormous density we have packed into the clusters. On the whole, our proposition embodies twice the density the public authorities have been willing to consider so far. The approach constitutes a major gamble. If the authorities go for it, we will double our client's profit; if not, we will ruin their chances to transform this site for some time to come.

But then again, that is the nature of their game. If it weren't for a tragic loss every now and then, real estate speculation would have no aesthetic dimension.

May 23

"That was an extraordinary presentation!" Our client rep has followed us outside, where we are waiting for a taxi to take us back to the airport. "The landowners are very happy now!" We have just presented our plan. The inexplicable crisis of a month ago has been followed by an equally inexplicable recovery. This time we have refrained from bringing foam models; we have stuck to drawings, focusing on the detail of streets, squares, parks, little courtyards, and other nonbuilt spaces. Judging from these drawings, one would think that we have just proposed a resort in the middle of London, not a hyperdense urban development. After our presentation, in order to win an early popular endorsement, the landowners decide to take this plan to public consultation. We receive our last instructions. We must continue to focus on the nature and character of the public spaces; talking about the quantity of buildings—of no interest to the general public—is to be avoided.

"Ah . . . I see your taxi has arrived. Have a safe trip home."

September 1

The public consultation takes place in a local bingo hall. The setting reminds me of those typical resident-participation events that I witnessed my employers being subjected to as an intern in the 1980s, although here the crowd seems less philistine. Class war in contemporary London, even in its last iteration—the war between the lay and the professional class—seems almost a thing of the past. Again, the presentation takes place without a model, only this time it isn't by choice. Our model was confiscated at Rotterdam Airport for the simple reason that it resembled a self-made explosive device. We tried to persuade customs officials, but the conceptual nature of our model—resin blocks for buildings, springs for trees, nails for light posts, screws and cogwheels for street furniture, all held together by electricity wires—was wasted on them. These are tense times. Only last week a major terror attack occurred in the London Underground. Airport security is in no mood for chances.

But the public consultation itself has been amply prepared. The services of an agency named Good Relations have been called on to "manage" public opinion. This, as it turns out, consists of an extreme editing of our presentation, reducing it to about a third of its original length. Only commonplaces are left, evidence of intentions absolutely nobody can disagree with. The approach backfires. Somehow the rigorous editing has the opposite effect, creating mistrust among the audience and whetting its appetite for more information, for detail, for numbers. Quizzed on the exact scale of the proposed development, one of our client reps is overcome with panic and reaches in his bag for papers, which soon flurry across the table and onto the floor. "Forgive me. I do not know the exact numbers off the top of my head and I'm afraid I haven't got them at hand at the moment. . . . I will get back to you at the nearest opportunity." The next public consultation is in three months.

September 19

With the support of the public ensured—it isn't, but the system makes it impossible to tell the difference—it is time to direct the energy to the market. A branding campaign is initiated to market the development to potential investors, starting with the search for a name. The branding team, essentially composed of the client reps' chairman, comes up with the idea to name the development after the area's postal code. It is short and pithy and considerably different in speech than in writing, which somewhat adds to its flair. In addition, the same code has been used in television broadcasts. The offices of a media corporation are located just down the road; by alluding to an old TV program, the brand cleverly suggests that it is part of the new development.

The chairman of the client reps' firm, it turns out, is a genius—a walking PR machine, an inexhaustible well of ideas on how to spin almost any approach. He seems strangely out of place in his conservative Mayfair setting. With his long patrician locks—he is only just beginning to turn gray—he personifies the ultimate hippie-made-good, with no other choice but to defect to the other side. Who could possibly blame him? He reminds me of Howard Kirk in Malcolm Bradbury's *The History Man:* a university lecturer in the permissive early 1970s, living a life of free sex as a way to promote the Marxist revolution, only to vote Conservative at the end of the decade. Such personality changes can exist in any Western society, but nowhere are they manifested more extremely than in Britain. Its two-party system, with its absolute nature of political victories and defeats, is unforgiving. Convictions, however radical, are condemned to be a matter of role play. Political affiliations must allow for abandonment, much like a character that can be written out of the script. The possibility to claim that one has only been acting one's part gives everyone a way out—an insurance policy against victory of the other side. He asks where we're from (I'm sure he knows), and without waiting for the answer, he proceeds to recount memories of his time in Amsterdam, about its unique system to prevent squatting by having the same squatters keep vacant buildings occupied legally. "So progressive, we don't have any of that forward thinking here."

November 30

A workshop is held to coordinate with the neighboring shopping center. Its construction is nearly finished, while we have only just begun designing: hardly a battle of equals. Traffic is an issue. The shopping center has located its car-park entrance just opposite our southern cluster, fully consuming whatever traffic capacity was previously available for our site. The matter needs to be resolved, even if nobody sees how. The shopping center will open in less than three months.

For the purpose of this workshop, the shopping center has retained the services of an experienced landscape architect from the London scene. He goes to great lengths to explain that he has nothing to do with the design of the shopping center. He has been called on only to help the design of the public space around it. He can be of no assistance in crafting an alternative traffic arrangement.

Much to our surprise, he presents an alternative design for the southernmost part of our site. His proposals are clearly uninformed by any of the work we have carried out on that part of the site, but that doesn't stop him from putting forward his ideas with great conviction. I am somewhat puzzled because his presentation hasn't been listed as an item on the agenda. I inquire whether by any chance this means that the shopping center intends to buy that part of the site. Are secret negotiations going on with one of the landowners? Clearly, the landscape architect won't perform these services on his own initiative. My question is naïve. As the moderator delicately points out, even if that were the case, no one in the room would tell me. There is, however, one nagging detail that remains unresolved. What is the point of this workshop?

December 14

The year is coming to an end. Further workshops with the shopping center have been put on hold. We are to proceed as if the southern site is up to us to plan and propose as we see fit. The work we have conducted falls well short of a planning application, but it was never the idea to get that far by year's end. Local elections are coming up in May, and before the political campaigns begin, the landowners would like some preliminary assurances that if an application is submitted, it will eventually be viewed favorably by the local authorities. For that reason, it is agreed to submit an interim plan with roughly half the deliverables required for a proper planning application and gauge the borough's reaction. Our contact person at the borough thanks us for all the hard work put in, promises to study our submission with great interest, and agrees to get back to us in the first months of the next year.

2006

Saddam Hussein is found guilty of crimes against humanity and is sentenced to death by hanging. President Bush vetoes legislation expanding stem-cell research.

February 28

"Nobody cancels Dame Selma Powers." The planning officer to whom we communicate our unavailability is in deep shock, not so much about our manifest lack of organization—the cancellation concerns one of our own proposed dates—as about our blatant lack of respect. Dame Selma Powers has been a borough councilor for the Labour Party for nearly twenty years. She is influential, as is apparent from the long list of positions she has held: chair of the Environment Committee, vice chair of the Association of London Government, member of the London Development Agency, chair of Greater London Enterprise, deputy chair of Business Link for London, vice chair of the Improvement and Development Agency, United Kingdom representative on the Committee of the Regions. She was awarded damehood for services to London and to local government in 1991. She is not someone to mess with, let alone cancel a meeting with.

Still, that is what we have done. According to our client rep, the consequences could be catastrophic enough to undo an entire year of hard work, lobbying, and painstakingly trying to win the support of the general public. The councilor is of the same political color as the mayor, meaning that the support of the GLA, so far unwavering, could also be in jeopardy. We hear terrible stories about the councilor, from habitual temper fits and public shouting matches to uninhibited abuse of her powers whenever she feels like it. Allegedly, her long time in power has made her lose all sense of proportion. We don't really know how to remedy the situation other than to apologize and propose a new date.

Once we meet the councilor in person, she is surprisingly pleasant, taking ample time to listen to our explanation of the project. She nods to indicate that she understands whenever we look at her for a reaction, but she stops short of endorsing the plan. When our client rep explicitly asks whether she will, she doesn't reply. Instead, she helps herself to one of the apples that for some inexplicable reason have been put in a bowl in the middle of our meeting table. Mao liked pork; the dame likes apples. There is probably no clearer manifestation of power than that of a leader's personal taste acquiring the status of a national tradition—well, a local tradition in the dame's case. She pauses for a moment, takes a bite, and then, with a full mouth, responds, "Don't look for an endorsement; you are not going to get one." She proceeds: "It is not in your interest to receive an endorsement from this council." When we ask why, she simply states, "We are going to lose the upcoming elections." We are surprised. Sure, we have seen the polls indicating a firm lead for the Conservatives, but with the elections more than two months away, how can she be so certain? She just is: "The writing is on the wall. People are tired of Labour's rule. This is not going to be a poor borough for much longer. People like you are making sure of that." "How have you been faring so far?" the dame inquires. Our client rep reports on our progress, stating that we appear to have been doing well with the general public. The consultation sessions, he thinks, have been a success, to the point that there even seems to be mild enthusiasm that something may finally be happening to the site. His response meets the dame's cynical grin: "You haven't even started yet. Things will be very different once you go for planning approval. You haven't really met the people of our borough yet: retired judges with too much time on their hands, opportunistic solicitors looking to score a quick legal win, aspiring local politicians in search of a following, neighborhood activists looking for a cause, whatever that cause may be, and other professional objectors. These people don't generally attend public consultations, but once you submit a planning application, they will all come out of the woodwork." She senses the scare her words instill in us, but she is happy to provide further advice: "Your only chance is to speak to the Conservatives, seeking their early endorsement. Don't say you have been at this for more than a year, pretend it is new, make the idea feel like it's theirs. Once it is something they will be able to champion, they will be all too happy to ignore the nagging crowds. In this respect, there will be no difference between a Labour or a Conservative council."

May 4

Local elections indeed prove disastrous for Labour. In London alone, Labour loses 177 seats, many of them to the Conservatives, who go from controlling eight to controlling fourteen boroughs. The borough of our master plan is one of the most extreme cases: a former Labour stronghold turning Conservative after nearly twenty years of uninterrupted Labour rule. The explanations we hear are manifold, both in the media and in the corridors of our project. The popularity of political parties, even at a local level, tends to follow the general popularity of their leaders. Tony Blair is at the start of his third term as prime minister, but after nine years in power the past is catching up with him. He is reviled on the party's left for dragging Britain into war in Iraq. His longtime chancellor of the Exchequer, Gordon Brown, believes that it is now his turn to lead. And Labour finally faces a serious rival from the Conservatives as the Tories' new leader, David Cameron, tries to push his party from the right toward the center. The air of change hovering over national politics directly affects voting at the local level.

June 14

The presentation to the newly elected local council takes place at the borough's town hall, an architectural masterpiece in the form of a large concrete box hovering over a public plaza like an extraterrestrial spaceship about to pay humankind its first visit. The only way to enter is from underneath, via an escalator, which feels like an improvised slide. The town hall dates back to the late 1960s and was designed by one of the GLC's much-acclaimed civil service architects at a time when the department still possessed a certain glamour. Once one is inside, the glamour seems long gone. The ubiquitous gray carpets stretch out ad infinitum. If there is such a thing as the smell of bureaucracy, it is probably the smell of carpet in need of cleaning. People carrying large ring binders drag themselves across the floor seemingly in slow motion, as if participating in a piece of performance art representing the antithesis of inspiration. The paperless office, it seems, has yet to arrive. Ample filing cabinets divide the space into small parcels in what seems a determined attempt to bury the concept of the open office plan.

The new council proves to be a diverse group of people, at first sight not that different from the council it has replaced. The leader is the owner of a small business who has made his way up the hierarchy of the local political scene by doing a lot of grassroots political work. Elected to public office for the first time, he has delegated the running of his business to his oldest son, who has just come of age. "It will be a while before he'll follow in my footsteps." The leader is an outgoing man, clearly pleased with his recent political success and apparently so overwhelmed by it that he fails to realize that his son has just done exactly that.

The other members of the council are less forthcoming. Somewhat subdued, each member comes forward to shake our hands, mumbling under his or her breath what we presume is an introduction. The group's composition is fully in line with contemporary political standards. The number of nonwhite councilors equals the number of whites; the number of female councilors equals the number of males. In that sense, differences between Conservative and Labour have become nonexistent. In regard to issues of race or gender equality, every party these days is progressive, or, as Cameron would put it, socially inclusive. They have to be. If the last election is anything to go by, party loyalty among voters is a thing of the past. Votes can be won (and lost) across all layers of society.

There is, however, one disturbing element of gender affirmation that haunts me throughout the entire presentation. One of the female councilors has brought her knitting to the meeting. It is not so much her knitting as the suggestion that she is distracted that kills my ability to concentrate. My male mind has a hard time fathoming anybody doing two things at the same time. Knitting while observing a presentation definitely crosses the limit. That, however, proves wrong. "Did you really think you could just come here with your European examples, simply assuming we will all turn around to your ways eventually? No sir! Thank you very much." Having made her point, she stoically proceeds with her knitting work. A male member then takes the floor. He is wearing a long, home-knit, woolen jumper, which makes me think that he might be the previous speaker's husband. He candidly admits that he hasn't understood a word of what we said. Perhaps that also isn't necessary. If one looks at our drawings, it doesn't take a specialist to discern that we have designed "a mugger's paradise." He concludes by stating that he would be happy, however, to conform to majority opinion should other members of the council view the matter differently. After the previous speaker's eloquent plea to preserve British ways, that seems a remote possibility at best.

It looks like we may have to start from scratch—not exactly an uplifting prospect. In advance of the presentation, our client reps have already indicated that they will not consider any new design work resulting from this meeting as subject to additional fees. We may be condemned to designing two master plans for the price of one—that is, if we are lucky and the new council views our work more favorably the next time. Given that its members seem principally to dislike us rather than our work, that seems unlikely. We could well be working until the next election without ever receiving an endorsement, let alone planning approval. We are beginning to think that under the current circumstances, our client might be better off without us.

After every council member has had a chance to comment—everyone broadly agrees with the first two speakers—the leader declares the meeting closed and promises a written report with conclusions within a week. To us, that seems redundant at this point. The conclusions are abundantly clear.

Just as I'm about to collect my coat from the wardrobe, I feel a hand on my shoulder. It is the leader. He would like to talk to me alone briefly. He tells me not to worry too much about what just happened. The members of the new council just want to assert their presence. They're playing for the gallery. Given the fact that no audience has been present, I presume that largely means one another. Our next meeting, he assures me, will be considerably milder. He doesn't have the feeling that councilors dislike the plan. It is just that our references are all a bit foreign to them, which doesn't help give them the sense of comfort they are looking for. The former Labour government is associated with—as he puts it—opening up London to the forces of internationalization, which has given a lot of ordinary Londoners the feeling that their city has been snatched away from them. It is those Londoners, he emphasizes, who have voted for the borough's new administration. Maybe we should present something that feels a little more British next time.

June 15–July 17

Over the next month our master plan undergoes an extreme makeover. We abandon the previous mode of representation. No longer do we aggressively insert new white blocks into aerial photographs of the context. Instead, we use Photoshop to superimpose roof plans of existing buildings of similar size, illustrating what our work could end up looking like. Even if the master plan remains essentially unchanged, the frame of reference is now radically altered, as is the language. "Perimeter blocks" become "mansion houses," patio dwellings become "terraced homes," our circular buildings in the southern part of the site are relabeled "crescents"—the council's new leader is originally from Bath—and the two high-rise buildings on either side of the highway overpass become "the gateway to London." The next presentation is a resounding success. The leader compliments us on our flexibility and turns to our client to say that whatever he's paying us, it isn't enough. We have just demonstrated a rare ability to work with both sides of the political spectrum.

We feel invincible.

17

London

To anyone working in the field of architecture, London represents a rude awakening, not least because of the city's barely recognized but quite blatant indifference to it. Concepts, logic, and narratives (mainly narratives) are readily embraced but just as easily relinquished in the face of more mundane considerations. This process in itself is nothing unusual, but what makes London different is the perfect simulation it manages to enact around a subject that it ultimately considers completely irrelevant.

London's tradition of architectural controversies acted out in public (Paternoster Square, Chelsea Barracks) is long and manifold. Rarely is the intensity of the debate warranted by the quality of what is debated. More often, the debated serves as promotion of proposals that would otherwise receive little exposure. One often wonders whether the staged run-ins between "modern architects" (spokesman: usually Richard Rogers) and their opponents (spokesman: usually Prince Charles) serve any other purpose than the embellishment of the two prevailing establishments that the two men have come to represent.

When London is asked whether it is prepared to commit to modernity, it perpetually defers the answer. With many of its modern icons at odds with a prevailing aesthetic regime, London thrives as much on the existence of that regime as it does on breaking its rules. Paradoxically, London's modern buildings have a vested interest in the rest of the city perpetuating the status quo: designed to be different, modern buildings are intended to remain different.

Every new modern building suggests the possibility that it could be the last. If there is a modern London, it is not the result of conviction but of slowly conceding ground. London engages modernity on its own terms, hosting modernity without ever really entering into the obligation to modernize as a city. Even though the city is now an almost permanent construction site of new and ever more modern projects, one cannot help feeling that the modernization of London itself will always be officially on hold.

London constitutes a definitive rebuke to architecture's main mission: while architecture acts to change things, London (most of the time) adapts to the change of things. Its genius resides in a regime of permanent improvisation. Maybe the city has such a long tradition of accommodating change without really having to change its physical substance that its people will never truly believe the reasons architects cite for their interventions.

Successive photographs of places like Piccadilly Circus taken in the course of the twentieth century show only the most marginal incremental changes. True modernization (progress?) now takes place in domains other than architecture: domains removed from the physical. Maybe London is the ultimate demonstration that being modern and practicing modern architecture have become distinctly different things.

London frequently quotes the "arrested development" of its city fabric with a sense of pride. It even goes to great lengths to undo modernizations that have already taken effect. Many architectural icons from the 1960s and 1970s are now up for demolition to make space for new buildings more favorable to the "city's history" (which apparently ends in 1960). In this respect, even London's costly efforts to cleanse its streets of single-decker buses in favor of "a worthy successor" to its old double-decker buses serve as an illustration.

Over the past twenty years, it appears that in the name of a safer and cleaner living environment, London has witnessed the gradual disappearance of its charmingly irresponsible character (the one that so lovingly embraced the punk scene and other countercultures of the 1980s) once so crucial to its identity. Today the city's "culture" is uncritically equated with success, affluence, with doing well, with "the good." Ambitious "urban regeneration" coupled with an excessive focus on the public realm promotes an urban condition void of accident, coincidence, and surprise. Will this approach last? Or will any attempt to eliminate the bad lead only to its even more triumphant return?

18

How Is Denmark?

March 4

The first thing I recall is the warm blanket that engulfs you upon leaving the arrivals hall of the airport. We have just passed through a long regime of air conditioning, escalators, and travelators from the gate to the hotel pickup desk. Finally, we're outside. It's March. If there is such a thing as an ideal climate, it is probably the Middle East outside the summer months. We will be coming back every month for at least a year, and I realize that the pleasant sensation of entering a mild summer day in midwinter is the sensation we will be experiencing on most of our visits.

I was here about fifteen years ago, on a stopover in a trip to Thailand. Except for people in the oil business, Dubai was not really a destination then. At that time, the departure lounges served mainly as a tax-free shopping haven for those passing through. I remember the endless display windows with jewelry and a heavily discounted car displayed on a podium in the transfer hall. Both are still there, only the Bentley has been replaced by a Lamborghini, and the display windows have evolved to contain a whole range of contemporary designer products. The heavy discounts have gone; the airport is different. The percentage split of transfer and arrival passengers has reversed. Once a quick stopover on a journey elsewhere, Dubai has become the end of the road; it is no longer a passing stage but a city here to stay.

April 12

Much has been written about the building frenzy in this small emirate. "A bubble built on debt"; "Albert Speer meets Walt Disney on the shores of Arabia."[1] Dubai is supposed to be a badly planned city with an ill-equipped infrastructure that has not managed to keep up with the city's prolific developments. But when we arrive at approximately 11 p.m., the city is a far cry from these apocalyptic descriptions. At this time of night, the generously sized roads carry almost no traffic. The journey from the airport to our hotel (almost from one end of Dubai to the other) takes less than half an hour. On our way we pass the concrete skeleton of the Burj Dubai (as it is still known). Its dark concrete structure fades almost seamlessly into the dark of night, leaving only the building lamps lit on each floor as a discreet indication of its presence. Towering over the giant billboards in front, the half-finished illuminated building looks just like another announcement of itself—virtual reality, there but not quite there.

Albeit exclusively from photographs and maps, the area is all too familiar. Next door we hope to build the world's largest rotating structure—an effort to outdo Dubai in being Dubai, a project we have been intensively working on over the past months. But at this point, all of that is still highly confidential.

April 14

"How is Denmark?" is the first question fired at us. We are seated on a sofa in the quarters of the ruler of a nearby emirate in what we are told is his "working palace" (supposedly designed by his wife, who is an avid interior decorator).

After a slight correction to note that we are from Holland, a polite introduction session ensues, in which we describe our office and he explains his vision for the city we are supposed to design. He comments on the increasingly cluttered infrastructure and traffic congestion elsewhere in the UAE and recalls memories of the fort as the ideal symbiosis of working, living, and playing, involving all its inhabitants.

For somebody who thinks that we are from Denmark, his discourse holds a remarkable number of familiar terms: generic city, critical mass, density, the culture of congestion. His oration continues uninterrupted for about fifty minutes, even as he feverishly shakes his empty coffee cup at one of the servants for a refill (he is served instantly). Less than an hour later we are outside. His Highness did not wish to see examples of our work; he will await the results.

"That went well . . . very well!" comments our contact. "Sheikh was happy."

June 26

12:15 p.m. Our projects are beginning to feel like Teflon efforts: we have established enough contact to deliver our work, but almost all our endeavors lack real engagement with the local situation. We want to recruit people with knowledge of the UAE and a command of the language. This takes us to the American University of Sharjah.

For the first time in all our trips to the Middle East, we manage to get lost. The campus of the university isn't hard to find, but once we have passed the main entrance, the whole system of navigation breaks down or, rather, folds in on itself. Like a religious mantra, each road sign is a mere repetition of the university's name. We are being guided in all directions: north east south west. It is as though the American University of Sharjah has taken its mission to the extreme in an effort to spread its brand across the globe.

1 p.m. We finally make it to the Architecture Department. The building is a large monumental structure built in a neoclassical, vaguely Orientalist palace style. The campus is almost a welcome relief after the random exuberance of Dubai, where the technology of the curtain wall now seems exclusively dedicated to creating ever more bizarre forms of high-rise. The Architecture Department of the University of Sharjah has opted for the full implementation of Robert Venturi's "decorated shed." Inside the impressive exterior resides an extremely utilitarian interior: exposed steel and concrete and (occasionally) timber are the only materials that serve as backdrops to large rectangular tables with computer screens. Interior design is virtually absent. We instantly feel at home.

1:15 p.m. So far in the UAE, we have been able to travel without our reputation preceding us; here our entrance provokes a collective stop and stare. The gap between our respective statuses in the worlds of business and academia seems to have reached its climax in the Middle East.

The Architecture Department is mainly populated by young women. Architecture, we are told, is not considered a serious profession in the Arab world: as a form of design it ranks among the "softer" subjects. Young men are dissuaded from pursuing the subject and are encouraged to become engineers.

The students we meet are all from the Middle East, but locals are a small minority. Interesting hybrid backgrounds emerge: Ukrainian-Palestinian,

Turkish-Jordanian. Most students we talk to are informed and sharp; they appear immune to the stereotypical descriptions of the Gulf's development proclaimed by their (mostly American) teachers. One wonders who is educating whom.

July 27

Evenings in Dubai are weird. It is impossible to get away from the fundamental experiment that Dubai is. Even "a night on the town" incites conceptual speculation, albeit different one from that during the day.

A bar, described by a fellow hotel guest as "very democratic," reveals an instant X-ray of Dubai's ethnic diversity: half of the clientele are male, over forty, and white; the other half are female, under twenty-one, and Chinese, Ethiopian, Sudanese, Moroccan, Turkish, Iranian, Uzbek, Turkmen, Chechnian, Tadjik, Kazakh, Kirghiz, or from other former Soviet republics we hardly knew existed.

Dubai's nightlife represents the city's operating principle in its most blatant form: an orchestrated match of complementary needs among different kinds of expats. It is here that the world's most pressing asymmetries are converted into economic exchange and the basic underlying principle of globalization is presented in the raw. In Dubai, Michel Houellebecq's novel *Platform* is acted out on a daily basis.

In 2002 AMO, in an attempt to identify the most pressing issues for the next twenty years, produced *The Atlas of Globalization,* which identified the existence of an A-world and a Z-world. The A-world was the part of the world that was secure and rich but old and stagnant; the Z-world was the part that was hazardous and poor but young and vibrant. The basic principle of a global market, much like the flow of electricity, seems to be driven by the energy generated between opposite poles where the specific properties of one automatically generate a demand for the opposite properties of the other.

September 25

We have been invited to take part in an obscure urban planning project. The main feature is a mysterious Russian professor who claims that he can make rain in the desert. He presents news flashes of recent and very unusual flooding in the UAE as proof. All of this is made possible through the use of "Magnetic Technologies" the remnants of an aborted science program for climate control from Soviet times, which the professor has now patented. His portfolio includes a credential letter signed by Leonid Brezhnev.

Weird antenna-like equipment is loaded onto pickup trucks (much like the infamous SS-20 nuclear missiles) and driven into the desert. The antennas shoot ions into the atmosphere that provoke clouds to burst and cause rain. The professor's presentation continues to show pyramids of snow, sphinxes of ice, and photographs of himself and various high-ranking government officials in the burning desert sun, testing the hardness of freshly fallen hail.

A question about the possible undesirable side effects is rebutted with the confident statement that the only real problem of the technology is keeping count of the many positive things that occur in its wake. Among the many blessings of the artificial rain are increased human fertility rates, cured cases of skin cancer, and the mass return of animal species until recently considered extinct.

2007

The Burj Dubai surpasses Toronto's CN Tower as the world's tallest free-standing structure. The Bank of England bails out mortgage company Northern Rock.

January 30

Final presentation of our design for a new city. Suddenly we are summoned. A Dutch minister, accompanied by a delegation of businessmen, is visiting the emirate—an opportunity not to be wasted. But who is the minister? One of the local delegate members politely offers a young blond woman from the foreign delegation directions to the bathroom so she can freshen up and fix her appearance. She is the minister.

We get to attend the talks that take place on the same sofa that was used at our first introduction. The talks largely amount to an overall promotion of the emirate as *the* place in the Gulf to do business and to invest. The emirate contains a large free zone, where foreign companies that choose to settle there are exempt from taxes. The emirate's annual economic growth amounts to almost 20 percent.

The lunch that follows is animated and constructive. His Highness and the minister talk about the latest developments in communication technology; the conversation leads to a comparison of their personal mobile phones and the exchange of numbers.

In the evening of the same day I browse the Internet to find pictures of Madeleine Albright and Condoleezza Rice entertained on the same palace sofa, leaving me to wonder just how extensive His Highness's phone directory might be.

February 2

Friday, our day off. The desert looks almost verdant. Some of the valleys even begin to show a strange resemblance to the luscious greens on the omnipresent billboards of future urban quarters. At times, from the right angle, one could completely forget that one is in the desert. At regular intervals, empty bottles and paper wraps—the leftovers of picnics?—litter the thin crust of green.

We are told that this is the result of an uninterrupted two-week period of rain during the beginning of January. The morning edition of *Gulf News* featured a long article on climate change and who would stand to gain or lose from it. This emirate appears to be among the winners. But as we drive on and the valleys continue to become greener, a strange feeling of discomfort enters our minds. It has been more than four months since we encountered our mysterious Russian professor; meanwhile, what advanced state could his experiments have reached?

February 10

"Welcome to this mad part of the world." We are received with what soon turns out to be the standard greeting of the many consultants in the peer review of a large urban project. Apart from a few locals, the overwhelming majority of the participants are of Western origin. Initial presentations include dissertations on examples of "timeless urbanism" in Brisbane, East Perth, and Sydney. Panel members bicker over the appropriate style for the new city: should it be Islamic, neo-Mediterranean, hybrid, or contemporary?

But in one respect all members of the peer-review panel find themselves in complete agreement: to make a good master plan, there are "many hands required." With consultancy now a self-propelling, multibillion-dollar business, one wonders what other conclusion they could reach.

The main problem of the whole operation seems to be the reviews themselves. It is disheartening to see how each new version of the plan is essentially weaker than the one it replaces. The "plan" is the result of a random sequence of subjective interventions. The logic of each is virtually impossible to reconstruct. In the discussions—as in the initial greeting—there is much talk about the supposed madness of this part of the world. But if the peer review is anything to go by, one wonders who the real authors of the madness are. To what extent is the madness that almost all consultants refer to a madness of their own making?

February 11

We hear of a large variety of decoy techniques to simulate site activity in the face of impatient decision makers, ranging from visual presentations showing construction activity on projects other than the one at hand to pointlessly having trucks move sand from one corner of a site to the other. At one point we are told that at tremendous expense, one of the boats that sucks sand from the Gulf and sprays it over the land (a technique called "rainbowing") was instructed to turn on its pumps. Only this time, it wasn't sand, it was just water. It was nothing other than a performance to get people to say, "It is happening, fantastic, it is happening."

February 13

"Live your dream. . . . Imagination becomes reality. . . . History rising. . . . A place that lives. . . . Delivering distinction. . . . Real estate with real deadlines. . . . Call it home by calling. . . . We think out of the box so you don't have to live in one."

To what extent have the disciplines of urbanism and marketing merged? Once urban plans were designed to accommodate the masses; today the masses have to be seduced. If twenty-five years ago urban plans were still produced to cater to an actual demographic necessity—a more or less delayed response to a more or less urgent need—today urban plans are designed to attract the population they are planning for.

During the past thirty years, almost anywhere in the world, the initiative to build the city has been transferred to the private sector. The discipline of urbanism now must give shape to developments while at the same time it finds itself entirely at the mercy of the market to make those developments happen.

Rather than organizing and giving form to a known quantity of clearly defined uses, the task at hand becomes the accommodation of an imagined future: to preempt an urban experience while the precise substance of that experience remains undefined. The primary challenge is to be vague and explicit at the same time.

The consequences of this shift have largely left the profession of urbanism in limbo. It is as though the ethic of thorough analysis and accurate planning has become worthless overnight. Advertising slogans and questions of marketability have taken its place. Renderings precede plans; the sale of land precedes the planning of infrastructure; the image precedes the substance. For every engineer, there are a hundred salesmen.

February 14

Even if the predominant experience of Dubai is one of hospitality, power in Dubai is absolute and without concession. Like Singapore, that other great champion of globalization, Dubai's negligible size coincides with an impressive global footprint. It has the economy of a nation run with the efficiency of a business. Where in larger nations political power has become an increasingly abstract notion, in Dubai it uninhibitedly manifests itself in almost all layers of society. Dubai's seemingly free enterprise is tightly orchestrated and controlled. This is a free-market economy where nothing is left to chance. Separation between the public and private sectors, common in Western free markets, does not exist. Instead, business interests are a prerequisite to holding public office, and captains of industry simultaneously occupy key government positions. The seemingly individual property businesses advertised on Dubai's many billboards are all part of a well-disguised monopoly, and the ruler is invariably their majority shareholder. The extravagance of Dubai's urban developments is manageable precisely because these developments ultimately originate from the same source. The diversity of Dubai's urban landscape is simulated; the country's particular form of governance ensures coexistence without conflict.

February 15

Well, almost. Events with respect to a recent urban development indicate that not all is perfect. Apparently the sale of plots had preceded the planning of utilities and amenities. By the time the need was identified, the sale of land had already been completed, resulting in a community of 200,000 people without schools, fire stations, electricity, or even a mosque. The money involved in buying back enough land to accommodate these amenities allegedly consumed the entire profit of the development.

March 5

Project feedback: Please go for the New York grid, but make it radial. . . . We love the idea of the square but would like it to be less square. . . . In proximity to the development's tallest building there should be a large number of other tall buildings. . . . The tallest building should have a view in all directions. . . . Furthermore, we want geometric forms that are organic, and basically lots of water everywhere.

Hausmannian patterns emerge on the flip-over board, accompanied by numbers that are the outcome of incomprehensible formulas. Apparently we (they) are all going to get rich.

We are keen to participate but not entirely sure which recommendations to follow.

April 8

Even after monthly visits for nearly a year, it is difficult to discover a single logic to Dubai. As a place, it remains profoundly ambiguous: both global and local, both futuristic and primordial, both modern and traditional. At times its massive highway network makes it feel American; at other times it feels surprisingly European—a metro is under construction—but whenever such foreign impressions tend to dominate, the city unequivocally asserts itself as Middle Eastern.

Dubai is like a petri dish of different urban models in which a single model is never allowed to become dominant. Its "authenticity" is born out of careful curation of familiar experiences. An array of urban patterns is applied to support its multiplicity: circular patterns, organic patterns, morphed patterns, nonpatterns, and, shockingly, even the grid.

When it comes to urbanism, Dubai signals the next phase of the agnostic. Phenomena observed in Rem Koolhaas's *Delirious New York* are taken to an extreme in Dubai. With an 85 percent expatriate population, Dubai isn't so much a "culture of the congestion" as it is a congestion of culture(s). In Koolhaas's *City of the Captive Globe*, it was the grid that held together the various architectural expressions that inhabited it. In Dubai, any notion of a singular pattern as the carrier of its diversity is an utter folly. Visions of the ideal "carrier" of the city are as exchangeable as the buildings that inhabit it. After architecture, it is urbanism that turns into multiple choice. What New York was to architecture, Dubai is to urbanism.

April 9

Like Manhattan, Dubai is limited in size. Its options for expansion are restricted: upward, into the sky, or outward, into the sea. Dubai eagerly uses both. The proportions of its skyscrapers defy all engineering conventions;

its large inhabited waterworks exceed imagination. Dubai's waterworks reproduce Manhattan's skyscrapers in the horizontal: the infinite reproduction of a given plot becomes the infinite multiplication of the coastline. Like Manhattan, Dubai is a triumph of the artificial. Possibly worth another book: Delirious Dubai.

May 3

Fourteen months have passed since our first visit. We are inundated with work, and our future here looks bright. Nevertheless, we cannot help but feel overwhelmed. For all its rampant activity, the region still appears volatile and at times temperamental. Will we be able to consolidate our status as a serious player, or will our involvement prove temporary—no more than a quick stopover on a journey elsewhere?

Ex Nihilo Nihil Fit: Part Two

May 10

Back in London. Nearly a year has passed since our triumphant presentation to the new council. Slowly but steadily we have been working out the details required for a planning application, but despite our progress, no prospective date for a submission has been set. The landowners are becoming nervous, financial markets have begun to show their first signs of instability, and everyone wants to get planning permission before all hell breaks loose. Somehow, everyone is convinced that it will. The turbulence that is about to ensue in the financial markets is presumed to be as certain as Labour's election defeat the year before. London seems to breed a form of insider knowledge, making certain events, supposedly determined by chance, highly predictable.

That, however, does not apply to the British planning system, which, notorious for its vagueness, is a constant source of worry. London has a rich history of applications unraveling at the last minute, even if the full scope of requirements has been observed, feedback has been taken into account, and all comments have been addressed. All it takes is a local councilor bumping into a local resident at the local shopping center and informally discussing the plans over a cup of coffee. The proverbial cup of coffee is a serious danger to any presumed certainty. "One of the local residents would like slightly more comfort." Eighteen months of work can easily be thrown out the window.

Members of the landowners' group are increasingly beginning to lose faith in the collective approach. It is too time consuming, too risky, too much a case of "loser loses all." Frictions are becoming apparent. Some openly wonder how things would have gone if they had individually submitted planning permissions for their sites. There are also worries about what might happen if the agreement among the landowners—still not signed—falls through. So far, we have planned the site without taking the individual landholdings into account. If the deal were to fall through and the site were carved up into individual planning applications, some land-owners would be a lot better off than others. Some have gotten abundant density on their site (the clusters), others exclusively parkland, and still others are stuck with public provisions, which in financial terms represent an obligation to invest rather than an opportunity to reap the rewards of a profitable real estate venture.

For the first time, we realize that we do not have one site to plan but six. Our client rep seems to have an ever-smaller mandate to act on behalf of the group as a whole. Representatives of the other landowners are now beginning to attend our design meetings, offering, in what seems a desperate case of a collective effort at micromanaging, seemingly well-intended design suggestions. We receive suggestions to move blocks, re-distribute parklands, and move public provisions to ever more remote parts of the site (where they make no sense whatsoever), invariably with the same goal: more profitable development on the land of the party offering the suggestion. For the time being, we manage to keep everyone calm. If landowners did go in with individual applications, things might be quicker, but one wouldn't be able to achieve anywhere near the densities we are currently proposing. Risk would be lower, but so would reward. Given that financial chaos has not yet arrived on London's doorstep, they agree, at least for the moment.

June 11

I have a missed call. One of our client reps has been trying to get in touch with me, but obligations on another project have prevented me from answering, so he has sent an e-mail—probably his preferred option in any case. Bad news is invariably easier to deliver in writing than in person. E-mail is a wonderful invention in that respect: it allows the same instantaneous delivery as the phone, but without the embarrassment of an uneasy conversation. In fact, e-mail is the perfect excuse not to speak at all, and as a result of its existence, fewer and fewer people do. Still, the method of transmittal does not fundamentally change the news itself, which is indeed bad. Predictably, the southernmost part of our site, so enthusiastically planned by the landscape architect participating in the workshop, has been sold to the neighboring shopping center. The question I had asked in that workshop had been naïve. That much I was told. I now know why: not because of the hypothetical case that a sale was being considered and no one would tell me, but simply because everyone in the room already knew. The sale had been factored in from the beginning. A set of parallel development figures had long been drafted. Simulation is an integral part of the British planning system, but it is not so much a way to preempt the form and function of future development as it is ultimately a game to affect land values. In that respect, planning becomes a process about the probability of building rather than about building itself. Building is a possibility, a fundamentally tentative and therefore unstable act.

I pick up the phone and ask our client rep what can be done to undo this. His answer is as short as it is dispiriting: "Nothing." I instinctively know that he is right. "But how does this affect our master plan?" I try asking. It doesn't. "We will just not build the southern cluster, that's all; elaboration of the remaining master plan is business as usual. That is the way we see it, and we hope you do too." Well, yes, but . . . The composition of three clusters separated by two parks had been intentional, meant to be realized in full, even if that entailed a number of consecutive phases. For the first time, I am beginning to realize that our whole phasing approach—supposedly a clever trick on our part—can just as easily be used against us: not the incremental realization of an ambition to defy potentially adversarial forces but precisely a means for those adversarial forces to get the better of our ambition, a way to dress down rather than dress up. The point of phasing is not to realize ambitions incrementally but never to finish them. The nature of a compromise is that it is made afterward, in the face of the inevitable, to everyone's disappointment; here compromise is the essential point of conceptual departure. Overnight, roughly a quarter of the master plan has gone up in smoke. Six sites have become five.

July 9

A media corporation approaches us. It already owns a slice of land on the site, so technically it is part of the landowners' group that is our client. The land it owns within the site is unsuited for development, but it does hold a key position in allowing access to other sites that are suited for development. All other sites are unusable unless there is general access to this site, and thus the corporation stands to receive substantial sums from developments on neighboring sites.

Even though it owns only a small portion of the master plan's site, the media corporation is a large landholder in the area. Most of the land immediately west of our site is in its possession. It includes the bulk of the corporation's office space and a historic building dating back to the early 1960s and under consideration for listing by English Heritage.

Given looming budget cuts, the corporation is considering selling these assets on the market and curious about the extent to which a visionary plan for the future of the area as a whole could affect their value. Clearly, its land will be worth a lot more if it is part of one of London's future hot spots than it would if it were simply one of London's many gentrification areas. Unlike our client reps and most of the other landowners, the corporation finds our master plan lacking in ambition, overly compromised, and simply too considerate of the often conflicting demands of the other landowners. It asks us to work in parallel to the existing arrangement with the landowners' group on a separate version of the master plan. This commission includes a vision for all its assets across the road that forms the western edge of our site.

August 22

The commission proves paradoxical, however. During our first brainstorming session, it becomes clear that we can by no means assume that any of the development we plan will actually be built. The purpose is to make what the corporation calls "an illustrative master plan" demonstrating everything that could happen if the vibe in the area would indeed take off. In short, our assignment is to create hype and, it is hoped, a self-fulfilling prophecy. We get carte blanche to develop ideas. The two towers straddling the highway overpass, which we conceived as the gateway to London, are to triple in height, and we also are simply to assume that the site that has recently been sold to the shopping center is part of our site again. The corporation is convinced that once the neighboring shopping center sees our plans, it will simply join in. We are paired with one of Britain's most prominent real estate agent firms, which acts as an adviser to the corporation in property matters. Together we are to develop a strategy that would allow for a "controlled sale" of the corporation's holdings on its site. The vision for the area as a whole is intended to capitalize on the area's legacy without necessarily maintaining the individual buildings that make up that legacy. We should have a redevelopment plan ready as soon as possible so it can go through approval procedures before the heritage committee has a chance to list the building. We should not be overly worried about the building's history. Preemptive demolition, or at least partial demolition, is the preferred strategy.

September 14

The British bank Northern Rock has borrowed large sums of money to fund mortgages for customers and needs to pay off its debt by reselling those mortgages in the international capital markets. Falling demand for mortgages means that Northern Rock faces a liquidity crisis and needs a loan from the British government. Fears of a bankruptcy prompt customers to queue to withdraw their savings. It is the first run on a British bank in 150 years.

September 26

"Too detailed!" I have always thought that I am a decent presenter, but evidently not. The verdict of the corporation's media trainers is unequivocal. Fair enough; this is their core business. In no instance are we to deviate from the script, which basically amounts to "This part of London will be a wonderful place; the presence of the corporation will attract media and creative businesses from all over the world—a future potential which will greatly enhance the value of corporation land in case of an eventual sale." Any statement beyond this constitutes an unwelcome and potentially fatal distraction.

We are being subjected to media training because in a few days we will confront the corporation's leadership to present our vision. We have one chance to get the leadership on board. If we blow this, it won't be just our vision but the whole idea of a vision that is likely to be axed. The slightest off-the-cuff remark could trigger this scenario. I'm not sure whether making presenters nervous in advance is an established media training doctrine, but if it is, they are good at their job.

We will meet the leadership during a weekend retreat in the countryside, where they will have to reach consensus on a number of difficult issues. Budget cuts are inevitable; even the amount is fixed. What remains to be decided is where and how, and most important, who will bear the brunt. During a weekend of painful decisions, we will be the only ones with a vaguely uplifting message. Profits from the sale of the corporation's assets might help avoid further cuts in the future, even if they won't prevent this round.

"Don't say you have been working on the site for four years! People are going to wonder what they spent their money on." We still do not manage to strike the right tone. "By all means, *look* like you improvise, but never improvise. Please, start again, from the beginning."

October 10

"Past the fourth cattle grill, to your left." The person kind enough to give us our last directions is wearing Wellington boots and carrying a double-barreled rifle (and probably surname). He is out goose hunting, or, in his words, "gathering raw material for the last politically incorrect dish on the estate's dinner menu."

The corporation has been very particular about its choice of location. In front of us looms a castle that evokes memories of an epic TV production about an aristocratic family symbolizing the atmosphere of a better age. The setting perfectly captures the prevailing mood of the corporation, which has also seen better days. Still, the lavishness of the venue leaves us wondering whether it has decided to go out with a bang, or whether budget constraints might be less severe than portrayed.

I feel nervous. These feelings were meant to have evaporated in the course of preparatory sessions, but they still prevail throughout my entire presentation. The script drafted by the media instructors has left little of substance. I feel embarrassed by the meaningless phrases I hear myself uttering. Improvising is out of the question, but when it comes to simply repeating the scripted sentences accompanying each slide, my memory increasingly fails me. I resort to clicking from slide to slide without further explanation, assuming that the images speak for themselves. The presentation has been reduced to a mere five minutes, but they seem to last a lifetime.

It has been agreed in advance that corporation officials will answer questions. They will be eager to do so. Back in their office's war room, every question that could possibly be asked was paired with an answer. When the time comes, there are none. We are simply thanked for our presentation and politely asked to leave the room. They are ready to move to the next item on the agenda.

October 29

"Corporation Funding Slashed!" The *Evening Standard*'s headline leaves little doubt. In the days that follow, the news of corporation budget cuts goes viral, even on the many media outlets of the corporation. Its official position is that the quality of its programming will not need to suffer, but between the lines the real message is all too clear. Its immediate future can be summed up in one word: austerity.

In this context it is hardly opportune to launch an ambitious redevelopment vision of its lands. This would send the wrong signal. (The location of its hideout a week earlier—a luxury retreat—is to remain a closely guarded secret, protected by a confidentiality agreement signed by those attending.) The corporation's real estate department, responsible for the idea of a vision, has received a slap on the wrist. It was naïve to think that one could simply ride the waves of a neighboring development to push the value of corporation lands. The organization is simply too high profile to operate by stealth. It should have known that.

November 14

"Say it to them!" The moderator urges the person making the statement to start over, this time facing the people in the room. Given the room's sparse population, there is something comical about the moderator's request, further reinforced by his eager use of the microphone. We are in a large meeting room on the fourth floor of the corporation's offices, where a session has been organized to solicit the views of potential stakeholders. This is now the approach favored over an ambitious master plan. If there is going to be a vision, it can't be the corporation's alone. It must organically be distilled out of the interests of those affected. Given the vagueness of the corporation's new brief, that amounts to pretty much anybody. Still, despite many invitations, the turnout is disappointing. The meeting is attended mostly by members of the landowners' group and corporation officials.

The session has been announced as a "visioning day," but if the ambiance is anything to go by, no great visions are likely to be produced. The room has no daylight, its suspended ceiling carries remnants of days before the smoking ban, and the carpeted floor, like that of the borough town hall, desperately needs cleaning. Only instant coffee is served. (Actually, people have to help themselves.) Lunch will be sandwiches, so we don't have to leave the room. Guests are meant to sit at round tables casually positioned across the room, a setting that somehow reinforces the animosity among the many warring factions formed during the process.

The moderator, a former corporation talk-show host brought back from retirement, is funny. He was prime-time material once, we are told, but something about his dress sense—corduroy trousers and a black polo-neck sweater—tells us that must have been some time ago. As the event progresses, we get glimpses of his old flair as he refers with an apt sense of irony to the people in the audience as visionaries.

The moderator isn't the only form of human infrastructure to support the day. Artists from the local community have been recruited to "register the meeting's mood," which they do by producing a form of real-time graffiti on the room's walls, clad in white paper for the occasion. Their "document" is to serve as the session's testament: a shared larger vision for the area. In a single day, the room is expected to deliver what three years of urban planning couldn't.

As a last resort, the corporation has opted for the workshop format, modern management's ultimate tool, the physical manifestation of its prevailing theory that any problem, no matter how complex or contentious, is solvable by putting people together in a room. The more deplorable the conditions in that room, the greater the expectations of the outcome.

But the tool fails to deliver. As the session progresses, it becomes ever more futile. Statements absolutely no one can disagree with are the only shared conclusions. By the end of the afternoon, the artists have decorated the room exclusively with clichés, inscribed on the walls as if they are century-old wisdoms

As charming as this ritual may have been, the day was doomed from the start. The most important stakeholder, the shopping center, declined the invitation. Its absence is a blow to the corporation's intentions. Despite lofty rhetoric about a "bottom-up" process, this visioning day was primarily conceived to bring the shopping center back to the table in the hope of reintegrating its land into the larger plan. At the end of the day, the only real vision that emerges is that of a well-deserved drink at the pub.

2008

The world is hit by the worst financial crisis since 1929. Barack Obama is elected forty-fourth president of the United States of America.

March 12

Major turbulence hits the U.S. financial markets. Some of Wall Street's biggest names have all but gone under. The U.S. Federal Reserve has injected $236 billion into the American banking system; the price of gold has reached a record at $1,000 an ounce; and Venezuela, in a canny investment strategy, has decided to open oil contracts in euros to hedge against the dollar.

In his first budget speech, Chancellor of the Exchequer Alistair Darling maintains that the United Kingdom is well positioned to withstand these events. No one believes him. Bad news from the United States trickles in daily, shattering any illusion that his proposals—an adjustment of growth forecasts offset by a simple increase in taxes—are going to weather the storm. Darling's insular reading of the situation is almost admirable: the UK economy faces its biggest slowdown since Labour came to power; the world, the biggest financial crisis since 1929.

April 7

The shopping center formally gives notice that it has decided to pursue its own course. It sees no point in further dialogue. The main subject of disagreement is one of the master plan's two parks. The parks are a much smaller source of revenue than the built-up areas. A proposal to share the park land equally is rejected. The shopping center's reasoning is simple. No dialogue means no master plan; no master plan means no park; no park means that the shopping center can develop its site in full. In the short term, a standoff simply offers better financial prospects. With the stock markets in turmoil, any long-term view is a luxury at best.

April 16

More bad news. The corporation informally tells us that it is considering the sale of its narrow strip of land on the original master-plan site. This strip, by allowing access to the remaining part of the site, was key to the corporation's leverage over the other landowners. After the sale, the corporation will no longer be in a position to strong-arm them into complying with its vision. Neither will we. Because we have defected to the corporation, our loyalty is seriously in question, and with it, our plans for the site. Like the shopping center, the remaining landowners intend to plan as they please.

The opportunistic mood of the different parties is understandable given London's upcoming mayoral elections. Acting Labour mayor Ken Livingstone is involved in a tight race with his Conservative opponent, but among most Londoners the expectation is that the local borough elections two years earlier are but a premonition of the shift in political direction that awaits London as a whole.

May 1

Expectations are confirmed: Alexander Boris de Pfeffel Johnson, Conservative MP for Henley, popular, a former journalist and a cycle fanatic, is elected London's new mayor, in charge of the Greater London Authority.

May 15

Two weeks after Johnson's victory, English Heritage announces its intention to have the 1960s building on corporation land listed as part of Grade II preservation measures, ending hope of any redevelopment plans, including (partial) demolition. Another important ingredient of the vision has just been eliminated. The vision will now merely address the corporation's offices farther up the road.

September 15

An early morning corporation TV broadcast, not about its own problems this time. We see London staff of the American bank Lehman Brothers leaving its Docklands headquarters, carrying their belongings in boxes. Earlier that morning they had arrived for work, only to find administrators from PricewaterhouseCoopers handing out leaflets announcing their employer's bankruptcy. Heavily exposed, Lehman New York has sucked the money back to base, cutting London adrift.

Contrary to its earlier mood, the UK government is acutely aware that its economy is not isolated from international events. It knows that the Lehman effect will ripple far and wide. The same day Prime Minister

Gordon Brown decides to waive competition rules to allow Lloyds to take over the United Kingdom's biggest mortgage seller, HBOS, after a huge drop in its share price.

September 21

The corporation reverses its interest in revamping its offices, feeling that under the current financial circumstances, redeveloping its newest buildings first would send the wrong signal. It officially tells us that the project is dead, and that the sales of its assets will now take place under normal market conditions. It has been a pleasure working with us.

October 2

In a final effort to make the most of what is left of the site, we reengage with the original landowners' group, now reduced to four members. We are welcomed back, but only on condition that we limit our work to their specific requests and agree to be paid by the hour. Work on the parks has been suspended, and only the central cluster is left as a project. The area we are to plan is now about a tenth of its original size.

October 8

Gordon Brown and Alistair Darling announce a £50 billion bank bailout. In an internationally coordinated move with central banks, it is agreed to cut interest rates by half a percentage point. The move marks the beginning of an unprecedented period of reductions, bringing interest rates down to 2 percent, with a budget-cutting spree expected in the new year. The scale of the internationally coordinated cut is unprecedented. Still, the financial markets plunge.

October 2008

We go for what we suspect will be our last meeting. We traverse the square that we have crossed for the past four years on our way to their Mayfair office, grab our habitual sandwich at the nearby EAT—catering has never been their forte—wallow in our usual admiration of their car collection, pass the Holbein paintings in the hallway, and climb up the narrow steps up to the meeting room in the attic.

Our suspicions are confirmed. The landowners—still not a partnership—have decided to pass. Having agreed to disagree, they will no longer submit a planning application for their combined lands; instead, they will draft a more general document outlining the potential of the site. This document will serve as input for the Greater London Authority in producing a renewed planning framework. It will be drafted by a newly appointed planning agency specializing in the more intricate policy requirements. Our services will no longer be needed, and our contract will be terminated.

There is, however, one small favor they ask of us, and that is to give the agency a report of our work to date. We frown. The document in the making sounds suspiciously like the document we were given as a brief when we started four years ago. Our last task, it seems, is formulating our successor's brief.

A Year Later

A magazine publishes the new mayor's plans to redevelop the area as an "inspiring new hub for creative and high-tech industries with 4,500 new homes, public realm and community and leisure facilities." The article almost literally echoes the words of his predecessor published six years earlier in the same magazine, outlining "regeneration plans with 4000 new homes putting the area on the map as an economically vibrant area."

At the time of the article, the site stands as we found it: isolated from its surroundings and underused. Visitors are discouraged. The security cabin at the barrier still carries the same phone number. The dog, we meanwhile know, barks but does not bite.

20

Facing the Facts

In September 2008 the world began to face the largest economic crisis since the Great Depression of the 1930s. This crisis was particularly felt in the construction industry because the preceding years had given rise to an unprecedented construction boom. From 2000 to 2007, probably more square meters worldwide were developed than in the entire post–World War II boom.[1] However, it is estimated that in 2008 the rapid decline in real estate values wiped out $28.8 trillion of global wealth, bringing this boom to an abrupt halt.[2]

The architectural remnants of this boom are well known: taller, ever more extravagant structures conjuring up ever more extravagant skylines, individual buildings burdened with the expectation of changing the fate of entire cities, and "the iconic" as the one "shared value" of an otherwise divided architectural profession. As architecture was consistently driven into a mode of excess, inevitably a need for a more objective and abstract organizing device emerged. Casually, almost as an accidental by-product of the drive for growth, the urban plan reemerged as *the* vehicle to deal with an increasing demand for large quantities of built substance.

This rehabilitation of urbanism as the other product of the construction boom has largely gone unnoticed. Architects have been happy to leave the domain of urban planning to large engineering firms, and as a result, common practices or theories to explain the urban plans of the past ten years for the most part do not exist. As an office, we have been both witness and participant in this silent revolution. At close range we experienced cities imagining and conceiving (and drafting) futures of a boldness not seen since the days of Le Corbusier. In 2007 a substantial part of our office's revenue was generated by commissions for the design of large urban master plans. The 2008 crisis caused many of these planning operations to be suspended, put on hold for undefined periods of time, stuck between premature abortions and anticipated restarts.

What remains is a body of work primarily known through its imagery: visions of the future planned in a time of immense demand and market prosperity. Even if the precrisis boom was propelled exclusively by the forces of the market, it allowed, for the first time in fifty years, a strange and unexpected peek into a new and uncompromised modernity. The sheer scale of many of the operations provides extraordinary snapshots of how certain contemporary architects think entire cities ought to be built. The city has been turned into an imaginary universe, in which idea(l)s are taken to their ultimate conclusion, executed without contradiction. In this sense, it is through the imagery of unrealized urban visions, and not through the built architectural icons, that the real significance of the past decade is most clearly revealed.

What will be next? The current moment is mainly one of questions. Will the precrisis boom go into the history books as an aberration, or will it prove only a precursor of things to come? Is the term "on hold," applied to so many enterprises, merely a convenient euphemism to keep hope alive, a shared inability to face the facts (for clients and architects alike), or does it signify only the pause it seems to insist on, a coma from which one day these enterprises will awaken?

2009

Russia shuts off all gas supplies to Europe through Ukraine.
Copenhagen climate summit fails to produce results.

21

Naukograd

January

We are approached to design a science campus in a former Soviet republic, about 100 kilometers from the Chinese border. The brief describes a business park that will be the location of a newly founded technical university, as well as the new headquarters for the republic's Institute for Oil and Gas, which is also our client on this job. The aim is to create a "Technopolis"; translated into Russian, it is "Naukograd": an old Soviet concept to denote cities especially built for the pursuit of science in the former USSR. This reference in particular persuades us to proceed; we begin to make preparations for our first visit.

February

On the plane I'm seated next to the dean of a well-known American school of architecture. It turns out that it was he who suggested us for this job. He had been approached by one of his students, an admirer of our work who happened to be the daughter of a trusted adviser to the republic's president (and allegedly very beautiful). Through her father, she had broached the idea of having the new science campus designed by a well-known Western architect.

It is midwinter when we arrive. Covered in snow, the site looks devastatingly beautiful, almost too beautiful to be disturbed by buildings. We immediately imagine a campus of long, hovering buildings, leaving a virtually uninterrupted ground plane, invoking former constructivist (Soviet?) architectural experiments. Given the use of the word "Naukograd," we assume that there is an appetite for such ideas. But upon further inquiry, it becomes apparent that the term "Technopolis," contrary to our beliefs, should not be read as an indication of a wish to resurrect the idea of the Naukograd, but was inspired by a visit of our client to modern science parks in Japan.

Ample preparations appear to have been made in advance of our arrival; a daunting schedule with various unfeasibly close milestones is presented to us. Also, we are introduced to the contractor who will build our design. He has apparently been selected without any form of tendering. Still, having constructed the president's palace and currently building the new ski resort next door, he has an excellent track record and is already mobilized on-site.

March

Second visit: during a presentation in which we unveil some preliminary directions, we allow ourselves to get carried away in ranting against recent architecture in the republic, showing ample examples of the pastiche that has been built on the back of the recent oil boom. The prime object of our polemic turns out to be our client's current headquarters.

April

We continue to work and produce various options. Our client communicates with us via Skype (the chat version) to share preferences and direction. Suddenly, we get the message that time has run out, and without any further reasons being given, we are instructed to pursue only the "middle" of our three remaining options from now on. When we inquire about the arguments that drove this choice, we are told to "give up our resistance" on penalty of being reported to a senior officer.

June

Interim presentation at the institute's headquarters. Before we enter these maximum-security premises, the underside of our vehicle is inspected with what look like brooms with mirrors at the end. We are cleared and allowed to proceed toward the building that only a month ago we had so eloquently vilified. (We now think that it is a masterpiece.) We are escorted into a large elevator and taken up to the boardroom, where we set up our presentation. After some twenty minutes the president of the company enters the boardroom from the opposite end through a hidden door that appears to give access to an elevator exclusively for his personal use.

We show slides, and our commentary consists of short sentences to give the translators enough time to follow. After we explain that circulation in our plan should be read as "an egalitarian system based on democratic principles," the translation stops, and the translator gently asks us to proceed to the next slide. His English is impeccable.

September

After nine months of work we conclude our master plan. Two days before the final presentation we are asked not to present in person but to send the drawings by e-mail. An offer to pay up front serves as a financial incentive for our absence. We proceed and get paid within a week. Silence ensues.

November

We are alerted to a short video on the Internet of long buildings hovering above an uninterrupted ground plane. The sky above appears to have been retouched and seems just a shade too blue. The overall compositional resemblance is striking, except that the buildings seem clad in a curious mix of aluminum and marble; moreover, they seem to have been covered by the same pitched roofs as an adjacent ski resort. An animated Russian voice talks over the images. "Naukograd" is the only word we can make out.

December

An unexpected fax arrives: the same client is requesting another science campus, based on the same design principles but designed for a different location. One had not managed to acquire the land for the previous iteration. The skiing resort next door had made a better offer and is currently expanding its operations to include the campus site.

We decline.

2010

Russia wins its bid as host for the 2018 World Cup. The arrest of WikiLeaks founder Julian Assange sparks a web war.

22

A Spanish Tender

August 28

"Donne," "Signori." The two red doors are identical, but the length of the queues in front varies considerably. Especially for women, the wait is agonizingly long. The sun is out in full force, but for some reason the shadow cast by the abundant trees on the festival terrain never covers the waiting area outside the lavatories. It is burning hot. With each passing year, the peak of summer seems to occur later in the season. To make matters worse, the Mediterranean coast is without its usual breeze this year.

Someone in the male queue suggests mixing the two so that equal waiting times can be introduced for men and women. Notwithstanding the gallantry of the suggestion, a discussion ensues, partly in Italian, partly in English, about whether to adopt the idea. Does the time gain warrant the breach of convention? After some negotiation, in which the signori pledge to act discreetly and aim carefully—we are dealing with a civilized audience here—the two queues merge. The first in line will enter the first door that opens, regardless of gender. The average waiting time is reduced by 40 percent.

We are in the Giardini, at the opening of the twelfth edition of the Venice Architecture Biennial, where queues are not uncommon. Once every two years, everyone in attendance, regardless of status, is subjected to the exact same treatment. The biennial's most essential experience is its democratic distribution of inconveniences—the lavatories' gender distinction might be the last barrier to breaking down the usual pecking order in the world of architecture—at least for a few days.

The only spoilsport is the monstrously large motorized yacht moored in front of the Giardini's entrance. It supposedly belongs to a Russian oligarch whose wife—or girlfriend, no one really knows—has a passion for art and in its wake also for architecture. Russians are plentiful at this edition of the biennial. Our office is partly responsible. The biennial serves as the launching pad for a recently founded Russian school, the curriculum and program of which we have helped design. The launch is planned in conjunction with a public discussion between us and the school's founders on how this all came about. This will be a final moment of self-reflection in public before the school officially comes into existence. Later in the evening, a large, invitation-only party will take place in a palazzo especially rented (or bought, I don't remember exactly) for the occasion. Even though we have initially advised against the biennial as the occasion for the school's first public announcement—we feel that this century-old institution hardly provides the setting for something new and fresh—our Russian counterpart has decided to press on. To him, our reservations are like wisps of fog looming in front of the runway on which he is about to land his Gulfstream. It is too late to divert to another airport.

I get word that a young Russian architect wants to talk to me. I assume that it is to inquire about a teaching position at the school, but when we eventually meet for coffee in the restaurant of the Italian pavilion, the subject he has in mind turns out to be altogether different. He presents a long list of people he has either spoken to or is about to speak to during this biennial. The list is impressive. Among others, it features two directors of the biennial, two award-winning Swiss architects, the dean of the Department of Architecture at an American Ivy League university, an Italian architect who is also an aspiring politician, a well-known Russian architect involved in our school, and a few prominent Russian architecture critics. The last name on the list is the young Russian architect himself.

He introduces himself as Sasha. Although I have never heard of him, he apparently is a rising star in Russian architecture. Sasha would like to add my name to the list. His description of what that means is as elaborate as it is vague—a trait even my relatively short experience makes me think is common among Russians. First of all, it is not clear whether he would like me to sign up in a private capacity, or whether he solicits my signature as a way of signing up our office. When I ask him, he looks bewildered. "Of course, of course," he replies. I am not sure whether it is because of a sudden lapse in his command of English, or whether he truly doesn't understand the difference. His further explanation doesn't make things clearer: "It will be good, all good. You, or anybody from your office. It would be nice!"

He refers to the people on the list as "the council," whose task amounts to acting as the jury for an international competition in Moscow. I'm intrigued by his language. His use of the word "council" is a direct translation of the Russian word *soviet,* which suggests rather more extensive powers than those typically attributed to an architectural jury.

Just as I'm about to become interested—we have been talking for over an hour—he reveals the name of the competition. I realize that this is the same competition that we retrieved from the office trash can a month earlier, after our legal department had initially dismissed the terms as not favorable (they never are). We reconsidered only because of our Russian contact, a former colleague who had returned home to Russia to set up practice. Describing the project as "big money, big names, and big government backing"—three indispensable ingredients without which nothing in Russia moved—she persuaded us to simply submit the request for quotation and for the time being swallow all legal sticking points. Everything would be negotiable further down the line. This was Russia. Her office was too small to participate, but for us it would be the ideal opportunity. After setting up a foothold in Moscow academically, we could now also have a chance to engage on a big scale professionally.

I tell Sasha that because of our participation in the competition, we would have to pass as jury members. The two roles are incompatible. He looks unconvinced and insists that a council is something altogether different from an architectural jury. In his view there is no problem working on two parallel strands of this "extremely important project." Even if a problem occurs, we can always abort participation in the design competition. I feel slightly thrown off balance. Surely the rewards of winning must outweigh the prestige of being part of a jury for a competition, however important? He smiles mysteriously, as if he is in possession of some privileged knowledge that cannot be spoken. "Believe me, it is better to be part of the council. The road is long, and this competition is only the first short stage of a long and possibly much more rewarding process later on." He insists that in Russia things are different. Our language is not as rich; in Russian a single English word has many translations and many meanings. He repeats that a council is not the same as a jury; there is a subtle but important difference. Reluctant to exchange the certainty of participation for some vague promise further down the line, I decline his offer. We exchange some further pleasantries, get up from our seats, and leave for the award ceremony, which is about to take place next door. Our office's founder is about to receive the Golden Lion from the hands of the biennial's director, who, in turn, became the latest Pritzker Prize laureate a month earlier. August in Venice is wonderful.

The possibility of a big Russian project has been brought to our attention during a visit to Geneva a few months earlier (March), in a meeting with a former aide to Mikhail Gorbachev in the context of exploring a potential renewable-energy project for Russia. The aide alerts us to a Russian oligarch who, after negotiating a major joint venture between a Russian and a British oil company, has risen to national prominence and is now believed to be the richest man in Russia. He is amiably referred to as Nr. 1 in the circles of rich Russians. Nr. 1 has been charged by the Russian authorities with setting up a special foundation to build a new city on the outskirts of Moscow. Our host is discreet about further information and limits himself to a mere hint that this could provide an occasion to put into practice some of our fascinations. Since he knows Nr. 1 personally, he promises to put a good word in for us.

Shortly after the visit, seemingly out of the blue, I receive a call from a former colleague who has learned that we may be invited to join a group of foreign architects who are to help oversee a major urban development in Russia. He starts quoting names and mentions the name of a French architect who will be the chair of the supervising group. A Google search reveals a French firm with a respectable portfolio of commercial projects and what seems to be some limited experience in Russia. The name is conspicuously absent from the list later presented by young Sasha in Venice. When asked, he raises his eyebrows but declines to comment further.

Russian plans to build the new city on the outskirts of Moscow register on the international scene only in late July, in the form of an international call for tender. The magnitude of the effort becomes apparent. The city is to be the Russian equivalent of Silicon Valley, a showcase of Russia's new modernity, a way for Russia to claim its place among the most advanced nations on earth. The project is to bring together various technology sectors vital to the Russian economy, such as information technology, telecommunications, biomedicine, and nuclear power. Foreign companies active in the same sectors will enjoy significant tax breaks if they set up there. The estimated cost of constructing the city is $2 billion over the next three years. So far, the Russian government has committed $132 million. In addition to the Russian government, several U.S. companies have pledged investments totaling over $1 billion. A series of memorandums of understanding is in the process of being signed. The new city is described as "a prototype of the Russian city of the future"—a national project in the strictest sense of the word. Twenty-seven consortia, mostly Western, reacted to the call for tender. Five will eventually be selected to proceed to the next round, which will take the form of a competition to design the layout of the new city. Firms will be notified of their selection by mid-October.

The Western press is predictably scathing. "Innovation, by Order of the Kremlin" is the headline of a major American newspaper. The analogy with Silicon Valley is improbable if not impossible. Silicon Valley cannot be reproduced. Its vibrancy and entrepreneurial spirit are a result of the right conditions, not of any top-down instructions. The implication is clear: Silicon Valley is unequivocally tied to Western freedoms. Only under these conditions is the spontaneous outburst of creativity and innovation thinkable. If Russia wants to follow suit, it will have to copy these political conditions, not the physical model of Silicon Valley.

Still, that is only a half-truth. The Western press collectively chooses to ignore that there is another type of environment dedicated to scientific pursuit, rooted in the very absence of "freedom." Much of that tradition is rooted in modern Russia's predecessor, the USSR. The isolated science cities in the Soviet Union, the *naukograds,* catered for much of Russia's rich and adventurous scientific tradition. But the concept of science pursued in isolation is by no means Russia's alone. The same concept underlies Los Alamos and Bletchley Park. In these instances, too, the effort is not spontaneous but carefully orchestrated from the top and clouded in secrecy. Perhaps it is good to remember that it was Bletchley Park that gave us the computer, and not Silicon Valley.

October 9

We receive a letter. Contrary to what was suggested earlier, we see not one but two lists of five competitors. The first lists consortia that have been selected to proceed to the next round straightaway; the second lists another five companies that, if they want to proceed to the next round, will have to agree to an additional tender. A total of six companies will be allowed to take part in the design competition; only one of the five companies on the second list will proceed to the next round.

We wonder what prompted this sudden change in procedure. The first list contains only engineering firms; the second, mostly architecture firms. The existence of two lists suggests some disagreement on the side of the organizer that is now thrown back to the candidates to resolve. The interest of architects in the competition seems to have come as somewhat of a surprise. In Russia, the design of a city is apparently still firmly considered a job for engineers, one where the emotive arguments of architects have little place. However, given the apparent interest of architects, it looks like the organizers are willing to give it a go.

The deliverables are modest: three Ao drawing pads demonstrating town-planning and architectural ideas, town-planning strategy, environment and landscape strategy, transport/pedestrian flows, and energy strategy; a 3D visualization; and a three-page explanatory note. The fee arrangement seems fair: a third of the total fee for participation in the competition as a whole will be paid for participation in the additional tender, even to those firms that do not make it to the second round. We agree to take part.

November 13

Only a few days after we submit the documents for the additional tender, we are notified that we have made it to the next round. We are confirmed as the sixth participant in the competition. Strangely, the note that conveys the news is written in Spanish. We wonder whether the note is really intended for us. Is it all a mistake? Have we failed after all? Or is the correspondence perhaps handled by a new Spanish employee? This can by no means be ruled out. The foundation's staff is becoming ever more numerous and international. Still, the name below the note is unmistakably Russian. As it turns out, the note is intended as a funny gesture to our project leader, who is American. The Russian author is an old hand in the development business who has spent part of his professional life in Cuba. Writing a note in Spanish is his idea of a joke. Never waste a good opportunity to stick it to the Americans.

Siemens's Moscow office sends us a note of congratulation and inquires about the possibility of collaborating on the city's infrastructure. News travels fast. If only a week ago we were still the runner-up, we are now apparently tipped to win by multiple stakeholders. There is little time to enjoy this, however. The submission, due December 15, is less than a month away.

December 10

We have developed something of a fascination with Russia's (or rather the USSR's) old science cities. We know that we have to tread carefully, acutely aware that any message about science pursued in isolation is as controversial in Russia as it is anywhere else. After all, it is Russia's idea to reproduce Silicon Valley on its territory and not some imperial notion on behalf of Silicon Valley itself. In 2010 Russia seems to love America more than America loves itself. (Nr. 1's cochair at this point is a former CEO of a large American corporation.) Taking the American route is likely to offend the Russians far less than harking back to a tradition and a system they are all too keen to forget.

Still, pressing questions persist. What compelled scientists to leave Russia at the beginning of the 1990s? Was it the lure of a better life elsewhere? Or was it the collapse of a system that until then had managed to create the conditions that had emerged outside that system only by chance? Although both reasons may have been important, it is important to know which of the two came first. Had the infrastructure not collapsed, would the exodus have happened on a more modest scale? In terms of urban design, do we emulate the original environment, no longer there in any tangible form, or do we emulate the environment where those who left ended up?

We decide to go for a combination of the two and divide our design into two parts: a controlled environment dedicated to the pursuit of science and a residential environment that works with the forces of the market to take shape. These days, utopian approaches will have to fund themselves, even in Russia. Our design is a careful mix of compliance and resistance, an arranged marriage between the rigid planning system that underlay the former science cities and the looseness of a (Western) real estate venture.

Thus, we have embarked on creating an urban environment which is both practical and utopian: one which can thrive under the forces of the market economy, while remaining open and flexible enough to allow the innovation required to foster significant scientific research. The design proposal aims to perpetuate a tradition of modern architecture and planning in which infrastructure and landscape form a deliberate part of the collective and of collective interests rather than their dedication to private enclaves.

The language of our competition-entry text is a little grandiose, but its intentions are earnest. Our proposal is endowed with a certain idealism, even if at this point we have no idea whether there is any real appetite for it. Like any competition entry, this is a shot in the dark. We engage in a last discussion about details: the order of drawings, the font size of the text, perhaps the inclusion of an extra diagram. There is not much freedom in the composition of the panels. Nearly twenty years after the collapse of the USSR and Russia's subsequent embrace of places like Silicon Valley, Russian bureaucracy is still deeply ingrained in every official procedure. Even though standardization and prescriptions are no longer legitimized by an overriding ideology, they stubbornly survive as habits. We spray-glue our printed panels onto foam boards, which we pack in a foam box. The box is sealed with duct tape, which we also use to make two handles so it can be carried. That's that. Fingers crossed. It's 4:00 a.m. We have to board a plane to Moscow the next day to deliver our submission in person. We'd better get some sleep.

December 12

It is shortly after midnight when we arrive at Sheremetyevo Airport. We have taken the evening flight to recover from the nearly all-nighter the previous day. A customs official catches our eye, or rather, we catch his. Our journey from the luggage conveyor belt to the exit is filled with suspense. Will he stop us? If so, when? If he stops us before we have firmly committed to the green "No Goods to Declare" lane, we can maintain that we had every intention to "declare." His eyes follow our trajectory. He is aware of what we're trying to do. I duck into the men's room, halfway toward the exit, well before committing to either lane. When I come back out, he is still there, motionless, his eyes fixed on our packed-to-the-max trolley. We have done the proper paperwork. At least, we think we have. In Russia, one can never be quite sure. Following one rule almost invariably implies the violation of another. Russia's bureaucracy isn't so much about providing certainty for those who follow its rules as it is about the deliberate creation of uncertainty about the extent of its rules, their totality remaining forever obscured from view. The sanctioning of each action becomes a matter of negotiation. Approval or denial can be granted on the spot, depending on which rule is invoked. Asking for approval in advance is a definite kiss of death, a 100 percent guarantee that whatever is asked will be denied. One has to proceed even in the absence of any certainty that one can. The prime product of Russia's bureaucracy is the tentative nature of everything, even the massive fortunes of its oligarchs.

"Vhat is zis?" The customs official points to the two large rolled-up rugs that stick out of our trolley. Literally seconds after we have decided to take our chances and go for the green lane, he stops us. We explain and show the Cyrillic documents we have obtained as a result of our attempts to acquire prior approval. Apparently, the documents cover only what is within a theoretical maximum envelope around the trolley, which our rugs apparently violate.

The rugs are a bit of a story. In addition to six A0 panels, the competition requires the submission of an extremely large model, the size of which seems carefully determined so as to infringe on as many maximum-baggage-size regulations as possible. In the course of the competition, we long debated how to get around this requirement. Our solution was to print an aerial photograph of the site on a rug, which would serve as a base for the model. The buildings would be made individually as separate Perspex blocks and placed on the rug once it was rolled out, allowing for separate transportation of the buildings and the base. The unconventional approach considerably reduced the production time of the model. The only thing we had to do in addition was to produce a series of IKEA-like instructions on how to assemble the components. When we simulated this assembly in the office, the result was surprisingly beautiful. Placed on the printed carpet, the blocks worked like lenses, magnifying the floor plans underneath and seemingly lifting them up to the roof level of each block. What started as a two-dimensional shortcut to comply with competition requirements turned into a remarkably three-dimensional deliverable—one that could become part of our standard repertoire. However, still afraid that our unconventional take on the notion of a model will be interpreted as a cop-out—a way to get out of the obligation to make a real model—we decide to produce two models of the extravagant size required. Transport is no longer an issue, so why not? One of the rugs showed the site in summer, the other in winter. Identical in size, they are meant to be displayed only in tandem. We have not verified the legality of this approach. If all goes well, we will have twice as much display size as our opponents. If not, we possibly face disqualification. We decide to take our chances.

As we listen to the deep sighs of the border guard, it appears that we may not even get to that stage. He looks mutely at us. His English is insufficient to explain all that should have happened; our Russian is insufficient to explain all that has. I think that he mistakes the rugs for illegal contraband—expensive Afghan or Persian pieces—but that hardly makes sense given the origin stated on our boarding passes (it is lucky that we held on to them). Our point of departure, Amsterdam, is generally associated with an altogether different type of contraband. "Maquette, maquette": I try the Dutch word, hoping that its French origins might resonate. They do. The guard repeats my words and indicates that he understands. Still, how does a rug pass as a model? And what about the little white boxes on our trolley? What do they contain? Given the abundance of our apparently official paperwork, he is visibly eager to let us pass—he too, could end up in trouble—but he needs a minimum of convincing that what we carry remotely corresponds to its description on paper. In this respect, the odds are clearly against us. There is no way around it. I call the hotel driver to get himself a coffee and be patient. We take one of the rugs from the trolley—we opt for the "summer rug" because we think that it has a better chance of sparking recognition—and unroll it on the white tiles of the airport floor. The guard takes a moment to study it. Then, presumably after he has worked out which part of Moscow he is looking at, he nods. There is no need to unpack any of the boxes. We can proceed.

December 18

Again, we are traveling on a Saturday. We have taken the later of the two morning flights, which gets us in a little after 6 p.m. local time. As our experience with traveling to Russia grows, we know which flight to pick. The choice between the two is a matter of priorities, depending on the purpose of each visit. The earlier KL 907 is a smaller plane, and its business class—if one can call it that—suffers from typically Dutch "service" standards, but it gets in at the relatively quiet Terminal D. If one is in a hurry, the time saved in avoiding queues for Russian passport control can be paramount. The later flight, the SU 230, has a more comfortable business class but gets in at the far busier Terminal F. Waiting times for immigration can take up to two hours, but today we are not in a hurry. The final presentation of the competition isn't until the next day. We feel that the efforts of the last month have earned us a comfortable plane journey. On arrival, we pick the line that says "Diplomats" to save some time, but that is only partially successful. Flights coming into this terminal appear to carry an unusually large number of "diplomats."

We arrive at the venue a little after 8:30 p.m. It feels much later. It is December, and in Moscow it has already been dark for hours. We have to set up our material for display during the presentations, which will take place the following two days. Our panels and rugs have been delivered earlier in the afternoon and have been neatly placed in the space we have been allocated: a spot on the concrete floor of the building marked with tape. All our material seems to be there. Because we have two rugs, we need roughly twice the allocated space. Luckily we are one of the first teams to arrive, so we can take the liberty to infringe slightly on the terrain of our neighbors. We place the rugs in such a way that they hide the taped demarcation lines on the floor of the exhibition hall. That way, our infringement can remain unnoticed. Thanks to the clarity of our IKEA user manual, we finish quickly. For the first time that evening we get a chance to look at the building, a center for contemporary arts, originally designed as a fire station by a famous constructivist architect. Its current owner (the wife / girlfriend of the owner of the large yacht in front of the Giardini)—has been kind enough to make the space available for exhibiting the competition entries.

The spot next to us has been allocated to another Dutch architect who has entered the competition as a subconsultant of a big Dutch engineering firm. We are surprised to see her here because we thought that our victory in the additional tender had put an end to its aspirations. However, one of the competitors on the first list had dropped out, leaving an extra spot for another firm on the second list. She immediately notices what we have been up to and contests the legality of our territorial ambitions. Luckily we manage to negotiate a settlement. Our winter carpet is allowed to slide slightly under the lifted base of her model. We seal our truce with a drink.

One by one, our competitors trickle in and begin to set up. A reading of the name tags on the models tells us where they come from: apart from the Dutch firm, there is a Swedish, a Singaporean, a British, and a large publicly held French engineering firm. We are the only architects. We catch a first glimpse of their proposals. If what has been produced for this competition is indicative of the current state of urban planning, the signs are hardly encouraging. The Dutch have produced a zigzag version of Central Park flanked by "Dutch" perimeter blocks; the Swedes, a radial plan with an imaginary focal point in the middle of an adjacent golf course; the Singaporeans, a series of lobes linked by a circular road, half of which fall outside the official perimeter; the British, a plan so nondescript that it defies description; and the French, a series of "urban villages" as the ultimate contradiction in terms. We, for our part, have opted for the revival of a discarded twentieth-century prototype, possibly against our better judgment.

Meanwhile, various members of the council that will serve as the competition jury have also made their entrance, taking the opportunity to familiarize themselves with what has been submitted in advance of tomorrow's presentations. Young Sasha is there too. A Russian council member compliments the French entry. The French plan allows for phasing and thus piecemeal development over time, a global dogma that ultimately neutralizes even the most megalomaniacal ambitions. (Even the most authoritarian states now use it.) He tells us that, on the whole, opinion is favorable toward the French entry. Our Dutch competitor confirms this and remarks that this competition, like all competitions east of the former Berlin Wall, is most likely rigged.

With a two-day presentation marathon in store, that is hardly an encouraging statement. Even if it is true, I'm keen to suspend the thought that the competition is over for at least another forty-eight hours. Only naïveté will pull us through at this point. We finish our drinks and decide to call it a day.

December 19

We arrive shortly before noon. We will be the fourth team to present, immediately before lunch—after the Singaporeans and before the Dutch. The order of presentation is alphabetic, just as the order of the next day will be inversely alphabetic. (If this competition is indeed rigged, it goes to great length to preserve at least the illusion of fairness.) We are called in about twenty minutes after our scheduled time. For the first time, I see the council in its entirety, assembled in a single room, seated around a large U-shaped table that faces the projection screen. I feel nervous. I have never met most of the members in person before, and given the varied nature of this crowd, there is no way of telling how our story will land. It is the first time I have seen the French chairman—*le président de conseil*—in real life, seated at the short end of the table, directly facing the screen, flanked by his Russian cochair to his left and another jury member to his right. There is an even number of seats at this end of the table. The absence of a middle chair causes the jury chairman and his jury member colleague to occupy equal positions. This somewhat curious seating arrangement, in combination with his colleague's significantly greater height, creates confusion about who is actually chairing this meeting. In this group of mostly renowned architects, the council's chairman is a bit of an unknown quantity. He is rumored to have a certain history with Russia through earlier projects, through which he allegedly also knows the acting "city manager" for the foundation. At the same time, he is firmly embedded in the Western architectural scene, making him the perfect middleman between the Russian and the international side of this venture. There is one problem: the chairman speaks only French. For this session, there are no simultaneous translation facilities. After each sentence, his assistant, a young Russian woman, repeats what he has just said in both Russian and English. His lack of proficiency in other languages allows the chairman to claim triple the regular speaking time, giving a peculiar weight to his otherwise mundane statements.

I transfer our presentation from our USB stick to the desktop of the computer on the lectern—luckily it supports the same version of Power-Point—and begin. Our argument is based on the limited value of Silicon Valley as an urban model. As a planning paradigm, we argue, Silicon Valley is a contradiction in terms. Its success is the result not of planning but of favorable conditions. The term "valley" instead of "city" is indicative. Attempting to apply the outcome of a spontaneous process retroactively as an intentional model would be wrong. Our proposal proposes a moderate reincarnation of the old science cities as "a planned antithesis."

The Q&A session is mostly consumed by questions about what made us decide to split our master plan into two different quarters (a residential and a research cluster). The move seems relatively unexpected, especially from an office—as one council member puts it—that has spent the better part of its existence arguing for mixing functions. We will have to appear in front of the council again tomorrow; it is left up to the teams whether to answer questions immediately or dwell on them for twenty-four hours and come back with an answer the next day. The questions are expected, so we answer promptly: By keeping the two clusters separate, we hope to be able to optimize each in its own right. Given the limited size of the site, the two quarters are still relatively close to each other. I realize that the answer sounds rehearsed, but still, we are seriously convinced this is the right approach—the split is an integral part of our deliberately schizophrenic proposition (a word we refrain from using). We don't really get the time to read the facial expression of the various council members to gauge a reaction. The council's secretary thanks us for our presentation and asks that we vacate the room for the next candidate.

That evening we have dinner at the Kalina Bar on the twenty-first floor of the Lotte Plaza complex at Novinsky Bulvar. The bar enjoys a nice view over Moscow, but before we are allowed to enjoy it, we must go through an elaborate security check. First, there are the detection gates at the bar's entrance; then we are also frisked by the security staff: imposing, all-dressed-in-black types in constant communication via headsets. (We have no idea with whom and why.) The elaborate security procedure gives the bar a simultaneous aura of exclusivity and seediness. Its clientele apparently consists of Moscow's new elites: wealthy businessmen with their entourage and Mafiosi accompanied by hookers. It is hard to tell the difference. In modern-day Russia, the old Soviet idea of classlessness finds its equivalent in the indiscriminate display of money, regardless of how it's made.

On the way to our table, we bump into a man who is just leaving. He greets us. His face looks familiar, but we can't remember from where. Politely, we greet him back and want to move on, but before we can, he grabs my arm and starts a conversation. His English is poor, but his message is clear. He says that he is impressed with our work and thinks that we have done well today. It must have been during the day's deliberations that we have seen him. We thank him for his kind words; the waitress points to our seats, but by now the man's speech is unstoppable. He gives us an unsolicited tip. There is a potential sticking point: the flexibility of our plan. Do we really intend to insist on the division between the residential and the research quarter? If we do, we will get the same questions tomorrow and will be perceived as being "difficult to work with." His advice is that we draw a backup plan in which the research quarter is infiltrated with a certain amount of housing, if only to demonstrate our flexibility and show the council that we can listen. Assuming that his suggestion must be based on something that has eluded us, we decide to take his remarks seriously. After dessert we head back to the hotel to draw up a plan B.

December 20

Each team has five minutes to show its animation (another compulsory deliverable that has been added a week before the deadline) and then another fifteen minutes to elaborate on questions posed during the session the day before. We proceed to show plans in which both quarters are mixed use. The members of the council are surprised. This was not what they had expected or intended to initiate when they asked the question. The question had been informative, merely to hear our arguments. Our apparent willingness to abandon overnight what we had defended so adamantly the day before raises far bigger concerns. How strong was our conviction? Indeed, how strong is our conviction on any point of the plan? I try to catch the eye of the man we met the evening before, but he is busy checking messages on his mobile and pretends not to be following the discussion. I try to respond in general terms, stating that in my view at this stage any conviction is premature and that convictions will undoubtedly be softened or strengthened by an encounter with the local situation, which we won't know until we go to work. Because this is a competition, there is the inevitable disadvantage of the absence of any dialogue during the process. They don't buy it: yesterday we appeared convinced, but now we have simply abandoned one of the most important conceptual features of our plan, if not the most important. Just when the discussion promises to become lively, our man receives a call and leaves the room with the phone to his ear.

"And what about the central empty zone between our two quarters?" a (Russian) council member asks. Regardless of whether the quarters are mixed use, a development like this needs a center. We have left the most important spot, the area directly opposite the train station—rebranded for the purposes of this project as "the hub"—unbuilt to preserve a view toward the lower valley directly adjacent to the development: the future golf course. At this point, young Sasha, who has been quiet so far, intervenes: "Is the other council member unaware that the use of the unbuilt, of the void, is part of the standard repertoire of modern Russian town planning?" A discussion ensues on what in terms of Russian history should be labeled modern, which then turns into a heated dispute over the legacy of the Soviet Union. (At this point, our intentions appear to have been understood.) The chairman intervenes (in French) and asks the two gentlemen to have their discussion elsewhere, at a later time. The USSR is not up for judgment these two days. We are grateful for young Sasha's support but not entirely sure whether it has helped or hurt our chances.

Our time is up. The Singaporean firm, seven letters earlier in the Latin alphabet, is next. We can wait outside where coffee and tea are served. If yesterday the majority of our time was spent in anticipation, today the majority is spent reflecting. We are not sure how we have performed these two days and even less sure whether our efforts will result in any follow-up.

It is early in the evening by the time the jury wraps up; their deliberations have far exceeded the scheduled time. When we are finally called in to hear its verdict, it announces not one but two winners, the French firm and us. The order, we are assured, is only alphabetic. No further details on the evaluation that led to this decision are shared. We receive congratulations from our colleagues and in turn extend our congratulations to our French cowinners.

At the reception afterward, we raise toast glasses with the council chairman. Even though we now both converse in French, he has trouble explaining what just happened. "Normally, the winner is known in advance here, but so far the foundation has not mingled." He thinks that we have a fair shot. It was the clear opinion of the council that we had the best proposal, but the representatives of the foundation who were present insisted that not one but two winners be nominated, suggesting that the French firm be selected as well. He assures us that we need not be overly worried. It is just so the Russian president is not confronted with a fait accompli and can feel that he has a choice.

The chairman is scheduled to make a presentation of the two plans to Medvedev on December 26. He asks that we give him all the material and tips us that the main discussion will indeed be about the center. If we would like to produce new or revised material, that is fine. If we slightly enhance the notion of a center in our plan, it might help him help us. We agree to submit new material to him before the 26th. As we are about to leave, somebody taps me on the shoulder. It is the man from the Kalina Bar. Enthusiastically, he shakes both our hands. "See . . . ? What did I tell you?"

The council's chairman will miss his Christmas. For Russians, December 26 is a regular working day. Russia switched to the Gregorian calendar only in 1918; Christmas is still celebrated according to the Julian calendar, which is thirteen days behind. Christmas isn't due until January 7, just as the October 25 revolution actually happened on November 7. A lot can change in thirteen days.

December 21

It is Friday, the last working day of the year. We learn that the council's chairman won't be presenting after all. The results will first be internally discussed by representatives of the foundation. On the basis of that discussion, the plan will be presented to Medvedev's advisers, who will then present it to the president.

Now that the chairman is no longer giving the presentation in person, he suggests that we make a small booklet with our presentation and send it to the foundation. It should be the exact same sequence of images as in the PowerPoint presentation, with a single, brutally simple sentence for each slide to serve as a voice-over in our absence. We proceed and write a letter to Nr. 1, expressing our gratitude for the opportunity.

December 24

The Russia media announce that two firms—the French firm and us—have won the competition for the master plan. That same day, our Dutch colleague tweets that she is very happy to have placed third in this very important competition.

December 31

New Year's Eve. The rest of the year has passed without further developments. The first decade of the twenty-first-century has come to an end.

Happy New Year.

2011

US forces kill Osama bin Laden. President Ben Ali flees Tunisia, sparking copycat protests that become the Arab Spring.

January 3

Back in the office. No news of a meeting with Medvedev. If such a meeting has taken place, it is a well-kept secret. We decide to use the time to write letters to representatives of the various interest groups and draft a press release for immediate posting in case we receive news of a victory.

Late in the afternoon we get a phone call. Apparently a meeting did take place, but the only decision was to not make a decision. The organizers would like to consider public opinion before making the choice—let "the people" decide which plan they think is best. I instinctively know that we are going to lose. The same qualities that made our plan the preferred plan for the jury will make it hard for outsiders to stomach. A contest between the abstract and the picturesque is rarely decided in favor of the abstract—not when it is up to the people, whoever they may be.

January 5

We receive a request to prepare a summary listing of "the advantages of our concept." The summary must be short and concise, max one A4 page, and sent to the foundation before the end of the week. The e-mail comes from a new e-mail address that now is used in tandem with the old. In its short existence, the foundation has not only rapidly expanded its organization but also undergone a series of extreme makeovers of its brand identity. We know from our experience at the school that the Russians have something of a passion for rebranding. In that sense, the new e-mail address doesn't come as a surprise. Still, we decide to call the phone number at the bottom of the e-mail just to be sure. We are answered in impeccable English (part of the new brand concept?) that the summary is to allow an objective, fact-based comparison of the two plans for a jury meeting the following week. The French firm has been asked to prepare the exact same document.

"Let me call you back!" the council's chairman replies when we ask him whether he knows anything about a jury meeting in the next week. When he does, a few hours later, he is exasperated. None of his contacts at the foundation, not even the foundation's city manager, seem to know of this request. He is extremely alarmed by what he perceives as a major procedural aberration. It is the council that should make this comparison.

It actually has, in the form of an elaborate five-hundred-page jury report that is in possession of the foundation. "Quelle est cette merde!" He will get to the bottom of this.

January 6

An American council member publishes an article about the project in an American architecture magazine, stating that the Russians are moving ahead with their high-tech city and that we will probably design it.

January 14

Less than a week after submitting our summary, we receive the comparison document the Russians have drafted on the basis of our summary. Not entirely happy about how our summary list has been translated into a visual document, we issue a number of comments that are all incorporated into the revised document, which is again sent to us for review. My personal assistant, a native Russian, is surprised by the degree of transparency.

Later in the day we are formally notified that the foundation has indeed decided to involve future users of the innovation center in evaluating the master plan's concepts. A total of sixteen companies viewed as prospective settlers have been explicitly invited to express their views. To this effect, a public forum will be held in the same art center as the final presentation on January 20. The meeting format: ten-minute presentations plus five-minute video clips by both short-listed contenders, followed by a Q&A session.

January 19

"Look what's going on!" A wave of indignation sweeps across the office. The Internet poll, set up as part of the new website asking people to vote for either of the two schemes, apparently displays a malfunction, although given what follows, "malfunction" may not be the right word. We have asked everyone in our office and their friends to vote for our scheme, a call that has been enthusiastically answered—only the French have abstained—and given us a comfortable lead. Now, suddenly, the score of the French proposal has shot past us again. This has become a recurring pattern since the poll has been online. Every time we acquire a lead, it quickly evaporates, sometimes in the space of just fifteen minutes. It seems strange that, even if the French have persuaded their employees to do the same, the waves of voters would be so in sync. One of our IT staff voices his doubts. He suspects the introduction of malware in order to guarantee the results of the voting in advance.

January 19

It is a little past six o'clock when our flight (Aeroflot this time) gently touches down. Passengers begin to clap as if a miracle has just taken place. Not exactly a reassuring thought, but we join in just the same, hoping that our clapping might expedite the plane's journey to the gate. We are in a rush to get to the hotel because we still have a lot of preparation to do for the next day. We think that we have a smart strategy. Rather than aiming for "the people" in a general sense, we have opted to target prospective corporate stakeholders who we know are among the sixteen invited respondents. Our city—this is our story—is a reflection of the tech innovation it will house, a smart city before the word has properly caught on. We hope that this approach will help counter the undoubtedly larger emotional appeal of our competitor's proposal: villages in green. We have branded our master plan a "project of projects." The idea is simple: each high-tech company in the master plan develops and supplies the technology for part of the master plan. In engaging these companies as cocreators or, better still, as partners, we hope to galvanize their support and lobbying power.

January 20

"What made you decide to re-create the Soviet Union? Who are you foreigners to mock our history, our hardships, the eradication of our culture and stripping of our human dignity? Have you even the remotest idea what life in the Soviet Union was like?" The voice of the translator, simultaneous through headphones this time, is calm and typically monotonous, but that hardly diminishes the ferocity of the words. The statement in Russian is delivered with such volume that the translator is barely audible at times. The only thing more prominent than the speaker's voice is his odor: the strong smell of cigarette smoke and vodka. It seems that a few more than just the sixteen invited stakeholders have turned up. This public forum is one in the true sense of the word. The man asking the question has introduced himself as one of Moscow's senior citizens, who seem present in large numbers today, eager to see what these foreign architects are up to. They insist that they have their say and that whatever they say is heard. For the first time, I witness firsthand the cocktail of patriotism and hurt pride triggered by the combination of foreign capital and foreign architects. (It will not be until a few years later that the world will be confronted with the full depth of these sentiments.) I see the face of the Siemens representative in the back of the audience. He is clearly intimidated by the apparent rage of the general public. I feel his support withering as the rant goes on. What keeps me going is the fact that the old man's reaction to our competitor has been equally ferocious. "In two centuries of Russian-French relationship, all the French have ever done is screw us over!" The new year that has just started is the year of Russian-French friendship; it is only January.

The overall mood in the space is hostile, a far cry from the mood that prevailed in the same space a month before. Somebody in the audience proposes to hold a vote on the spot and simply pick one of the two plans so we can all go home. He states his preference for the French plan and encourages others to follow suit. At this point, the organizer intervenes and states that we are running out of time. An army of Russian journalists has turned up for the presentation, and their questions also need to be answered.

January 21

The next day, at his request, we meet the foundation's chief executive of design and construction. The foundation occupies an office in a large multitenant office building in Moscow City that also includes a hotel. Given our potential long-term relation, it might be a good idea to change hotels and spend future visits here. In a city renowned for its monumental traffic jams—we have just spent the better part of our journey here looking at the same church tower from a car window—staying at the place of work would make a lot of sense. Yet something in the bland atmosphere of the building holds me back. Even the buildings in Moscow City that are occupied have a strange atmosphere of desertion. Just like the part of Moscow in which it is located, the building complex exudes a scent of failure—of a project that never really happened, even if it was built and occupied.

The atmosphere of the building seems to have no bearing on the chief executive's mood, which is excellent. He tells us not to take anything that happened the day before seriously. Decisions of this magnitude are not going be made at a public forum. That is not the way things work in Russia. We have nothing to worry about. He voices his preference for our project, citing that it would likely be less expensive and more feasible to build. Our project is rational, and he is struck by its density. He wanted to meet us because there is a serious chance that we may be working together soon. In the airport lounge I play back the last two days in my head. There is something about the chaos that increasingly surrounds the project that leaves me wondering how much of it is deliberate—part of a well-conceived smoke screen to conceal an utterly scripted course of events. I am reminded of a chess match between Karpov and Kasparov I once studied. None of the opening moves made any sense. They seemed cowardly, even dilettante, like those of two children playing, until I discovered that these men were thinking not three or four but rather forty moves ahead, setting their eyes further than I could ever follow.

January 22

Layover in Frankfurt. It is becoming increasingly difficult to report back to the office on the status of the effort. The public forum has made me miss our office's quarterly meeting of partners, which I enter via speakerphone. "Proceed as necessary" is the advice.

January 24

The first account of the public forum appears on the foundation's website. No images of our project appear. The French are listed first in all documentation and are given twice as long to explain their proposal in the PR video. I find it difficult to believe that the competition would be decided without some sort of formal announcement. Through the chief executive's secretary, we manage to get a slot in his schedule, two weeks later, on February 9.

February 9

"One hour!" the customs official tells me when I inquire when I might be released from quarantine and legitimately enter the territory of the Russian Federation. Either that or be sent back on the next plane. I have been detained because of a problem with my Russian visa. In the lead-up to this trip, I have had to renew my passport, but my Russian visa, valid for another ten months, is in my old passport. This problem, which is not uncommon, is usually solved by carrying the two passports until a new visa is granted. However, the official at Amsterdam City Hall failed to provide the required cross-reference to the visa from the old passport in the new one. The absence of this reference makes me guilty of attempting to enter the Russian Federation under false pretenses, the penalty for which is immediate deportation. In allowing me to stay in the international zone just before customs, the guards have displayed exceptional clemency. I wait. My mobile phone is running out of battery power, and I can't discern a single socket in any of the white walls. After an hour I ask again and get the same answer: "One hour!" He holds up his finger to create absolute clarity, but I'm confused. Suspecting that he is trying to string me along, I lose my temper. "One hour!" is the answer once again, but this time he points to his watch to clarify. In what can only be described as a bizarre case of language confusion, "one hour" turns out to mean one o'clock in the afternoon. He intends to send me to the Alitalia desk for a return flight to Rome, from which I have traveled. The Italians are notorious for never showing up before 1 p.m., so I will have to be patient. It's 8 a.m. I feel desperate and frustrated. Yelling has made me thirsty. I ask for water. The request is denied.

Before my battery definitively runs out, I decide to call the Dutch embassy:

"Hello?"

"Hello!"

"Who is this?"

I state my name and the name of my company and report my problem. I am put through.

"Hello?"

"Hello!"

"Who is this?"

I state my name and the name of my company and report my problem.

"Ah . . ."

Silence.

"You are here on business?"

"Yes."

"With a Russian firm?"

"Yes."

"Perhaps it is better if you contact them. They can generally do a lot more for people than we can, even if it concerns Dutch nationals. I'm sorry to say this, but that's the way it is."

"Ah . . ."

Silence.

"Did you say Koolhaas?" (I have not.) "If you speak to him, could you please convey that the Dutch embassy would be delighted to include him as part of our Friday afternoon drinks whenever he is in Moscow next? That would be a great honor."

I hang up.

By now it is late enough for a call to the foundation. I call the chief executive's assistant and tell her my problem. "Let me work something out. Stay put!" she replies.

Fifteen minutes later the head of Airport Border Security of the Russian Federation, a short but decisive woman, turns up with scissors and glue. She takes my two passports, which have been confiscated by the guards, rips out the page with the visa from the old passports and glues it into the new. "C'est ça!" I hand over my passport to the guard again for renewed inspection. He proceeds to study my passport as if nothing happened. I receive a series of impressive stamps, which leave an imprint because of the still-wet glue. I can now enter the country. Welcome to Russia.

The quick fix at the airport allows me to make it just in time for the meeting with the chief executive, albeit without any sleep—not exactly the best state to absorb bad news. After a long introduction praising our commitment to the project, he comes clean, but his words are guarded: "You should prepare to lose." He discourages us from presenting any further comparison documents because this would be perceived as "a slap in the face" and urges us to invest our energy in obtaining "the largest possible slice of the pie." The French master plan is going to be divided into parts that will be given to individual architects to be designed further. There is a serious interest from the foundation in retaining our involvement, if not as urbanists, then as architects.

February 10

From: Dutch Embassy, Moscow
  Date: 10 / 02 / 11
  XXXXXX,
  Yesterday my French colleague told me the French have won the competition. This report is still unconfirmed, but she had no doubt the information was correct. Apparently French Prime Minister Fillon had broached the subject during his visit to Moscow last December.
  Regards, XXXX

The news is nothing new, but it does contribute to the increasingly official status the French victory is beginning to acquire. The Dutch Embassy does not doubt the authenticity of a French victory, which appears to have been crafted at the highest diplomatic and political levels.

In what context did Fillon raise the issue? His Russian counterpart is Vladimir Putin, still prime minister at the time. We know that there have been French-Russian conversations about a project for a highway from Moscow to St. Petersburg that has been canceled because of allegations of illegal land speculation by former mayor Luzkow's wife, Tatiana. As a result, a major French contracting firm that is part of a winning consortium that also includes a firm owned by one of Putin's former judo mates, has suffered a major blow to projected work and income. Would the project have been given to another state firm as compensation? It would be a great gesture of friendship in the year dedicated to exactly that. Is it a coincidence that the next council meeting, in which the winner will be publicly announced, is scheduled in Paris?

It appears that the jury's chairman is not aware of any French victory, the legality of which he contests because it must be the council that decides on a winner. He intends to find out what is going on and will call me back once he has a clearer picture. When he does, he sounds resigned.

He has worked in Russia long enough to realize that no matter how large or international the bureaucratic structures that have been put in place, decisions are made ultimately by a small circle of Russians unilaterally and without explanation. He advises us to be philosophical about the whole thing. There will be a further round in which architects of the individual buildings will be selected. Doing a building without all the hassle of coordination that comes with realizing a master plan may be a good thing. He certainly thinks that the new city would benefit from a building by us.

February 15

The foundation's city manager asks to meet us at the bar of the school that we have helped establish. He is aware that we are in Russia and attending the school that day. He begins by saying that he hopes we are not so disappointed as to turn our back on the project. He is eager to discuss a continuation of our involvement, even if he has no specific ideas about what we might do. Instead, he bounces the ball back to us. How would we like to be involved? He suggests that we make a wish list in advance of the council meeting in Paris, during which the French will officially be announced as the winner. He cordially invites us to attend. He converses in staccato Russian sentences, consuming a glass of vodka between each. He is translated by a younger man who introduces himself as Igor. Igor will be the contact person to whom we can address further communication with the foundation.

Igor, as we quickly find, is very bright. He speaks four languages fluently and is representative of a younger generation of Russians who, after spending a long time abroad—in his case, Canada—have decided to pursue their careers in Russia. He is the type we have also encountered at the school: well spoken, funny, supremely intelligent, and keen to view Russia as part of a global community of modern nations. It is exactly twenty years since the USSR was dismantled. As we listen to him talk, that seems ages ago.

February 26

An e-mail from the Dutch Embassy informs us that after consultation with their Russian colleagues, they have been assured that no winner has been appointed. The French Embassy spoke prematurely. It is the last time we ever engage with our national representative. From here, we are on our own—and probably no worse off.

February 28

The first 2011 meeting of the urban council takes place in Paris. The council is to meet four times a year. In principle, meetings are supposed to take place in Moscow, but for the announcement of the French winner, an exception has been made. We do not attend. In a last-minute e-mail we have been notified that discussions will be limited to the elaboration of the master plan itself; a discussion of future work for architects is not on the agenda. Such a discussion is considered more appropriate for the next council meeting, which will take place in Moscow in three months. At the time of the Paris council meeting, we are in Moscow teaching at the school. Rumors are rife. The first rumors that Putin will run for a (constitutionally questionable) third term in Russia's 2012 presidential elections have entered the public sphere. Putin is said to regard Medvedev's notion of a high-tech, digital, Western-style Russian economy as little more than his successor's plaything. The change in power will happen in early May 2012, soon enough to shelve plans for the new high-tech city before they have come to fruition. At the same time, there is increasing public discontent with the United Russia Party as a whole, putting Putin and Medvedev equally on the spot. Alexander Navalny has just denounced the United Russia Party in a radio broadcast earlier this month as "a party of crooks and thieves." His words have resonated with an attentive public, particularly in Moscow, that views the party as the prime exponent of Russia's deeply flawed political system. Under these conditions nothing is certain.

March 14

We are contacted by Igor, the city manager's deputy. He confirms the intention to have us work among "other great architects." We are asked to focus on one of the "landmark objects in the Visitors' district." We assume that this is the project's much-discussed center. It is becoming increasingly clear that the project runs on two parallel tracks: that of the official council, with its regular but infrequent meetings, and that of the foundation, which appears to operate in a more hands-on manner but haphazardly. Information obtained from both tracks is distinctly out of sync and often contradictory. We opt for the Russian track and engage with Igor's request.

March 29

Nr. 1 looks like his pictures on the Internet. He is a bulky man with a bald head and a gray beard. It has been a while since he rose to prominence, but in that time his appearance has barely changed. He is fifty-three years old, much younger than he looks. His consistent looks are not so much the product of a well-preserved youth as of his age slowly catching up with his appearance. He is dressed unassumingly: with the exception of a "1" sewn into his shirt, there are few outward signs of his $13 billion fortune. He offers us seats at the small round table in his organization's headquarters, a nondescript building in Moscow's old business district. His English is adequate, so there is no need for translation. Every now and then he turns to Igor, who has accompanied us to this meeting, to converse briefly in Russian, as if to make sure he is acting in accordance with his briefing. He asks whether we would be willing to produce three options for the central zone. Next month the project must be presented at the highest political level. Fast-tracking work on the center will allow the foundation to make a big impression fast. He stresses the importance of visualizations over technical detail. He has been impressed by the quality of our competition images and even more by the speed with which they have been produced. The possibility of choosing from multiple options will make the president the de facto author of the scheme. It strikes me how little difference there is between working in Russia and working in a place like Dubai.

Planning as a multiple-choice game of images seems universal practice by now, particularly in autocratic states, where images play a key role in allowing leaders to preserve the illusion of absolute control and achievement. All must be well at all times. Those who deliver bad news are hung out to dry. We are given three weeks to complete our work.

Back in our hotel, we see Nr. 1 appear on the Russian news. An international court of arbitration has just blocked an Anglo-Russian deal to form a strategic partnership on Arctic development. The deal, the court has ruled, breaches the terms of Nr. 1's Anglo-Russian deal already in place. The ruling adds another major victory to Nr. 1's already long list of business triumphs.

April 25

Same office, same table. On it is a laptop, hooked to a small projection monitor on one of the walls. If we want, we can show a PowerPoint presentation. We have brought panels as well: three for each of the three options. The foundation's city manager, who we only ever refer to by his job title—we have trouble remembering his real name—is also present at the meeting. He quickly browses through the panels, using the short window before Nr. 1's arrival to familiarize himself with the material. One week earlier we were asked to share these panels by the council's chair who has gotten wind of our conversations with Nr. 1 and is worried that our proposals will interfere with other parts of the master plan, most notably with the quarters that he and his taller colleague have meanwhile claimed as commissions for their own practices. Eight months ago, young Sasha clearly spelled it out: a council was something very different from a jury.

Our proposals for the central zones are simple and straightforward. After our presentation Igor once again summarizes the ideas in a kind of Russian shorthand, using a mere three words to explain each scheme. Nr. 1 nods approvingly, closes his eyes, and repeats the words—no doubt a rehearsal for more important meetings ahead, outside our presence.

That evening we have dinner with Igor and City Manager at the Meat Club. We eat meat—lots of it. The restaurant is an extreme case of brand consistency, exuding its theme on every level, including the dress code of the waitresses. The terms of our further involvement come up. We are asked to proceed as "district curator"—one of many. The term manifests an interesting ambiguity: "curators" will be architect-designers without formally being so. The concept of the French master plan—urban villages—lends itself par excellence to execution by multiple architects, and as it turns out, the council's chair and his taller Colleague are not the only ones who have claimed a slice of the pie. In exchange for participation in the council, each member has been promised a district. As former competition participants, we are the last to come to the party. Certain border issues may have to be resolved with neighboring district curators. At this point it is not certain whether the French will even be invited to the next council meeting. Once the various district curators take over, the services of the French may no longer be required at all. After all, they are not members of the council. One of the waitresses asks whether I need a refill. I do.

May 16

The second council meeting of the year. (There will be a total of four.) We will have ten minutes to present our proposals for the center, the exact status of which is a matter of guesswork. It is not clear what weight, if any, the visuals shown to the Russian president carry in this room. The French authors of the master plan present first, showing the evolution of their master plan since they won the competition. Most of their work has gone into adapting the master plan to ongoing construction activity on the site, which has meanwhile started and for some reason has willfully ignored the master plan. There is a building by young Sasha called the Cube, for which apparently he received an individual commission some time ago, which has led to the revision of the entire road system as envisioned in the master plan.

The French have carried out their work in the same sort of isolation as we have. The result is predictable. With every change they present, our work, entirely based on a previous version, becomes more obsolete. Once we present, we encounter outrage. Having lost the competition, we should be the last people giving shape to the city's further evolution. It is difficult to imagine that the Russian request to present our proposals here today has come without any form of prior coordination with this council, but that appears to be the case. The international and Russian sections of the foundation operate independently. This project is not one but two efforts.

As long as these run in parallel, everything is fine. Both sides can keep up appearances. Our work has exposed the schism; its quality is irrelevant.

Dinner reservations in the evening are for council members only, but in good collegial spirit both the French and we are invited along. At dinner the full extent of the story becomes clear. Apparently, the so-called guest zone has been promised to another member of the council, who unfortunately has so far failed to show up for any council meetings. Between the main course and dessert, Taller Colleague tries to broker a deal among the individual council members or, as they are now called, district curators. He has drawn a bubble diagram on the back of a napkin, dividing the territory of the master plan among the various district curators and us. He goes around each table asking everyone's approval. His diagram is ingenious: the bubbles overlap to indicate "zones of collaboration" among district curators. There are two central bubbles with a tiny overlap. The one closest to the nearby railway station, which covers a hilltop and is called the hub, is to be handled by another office; the other bubble, covering the lower valley farther from the station, by us. The site we are offered is different from the one we have been working on so far. Agreeing to Taller Colleague's proposition will make our design work of the last three weeks obsolete. We will have to start over. On the other hand, the arrangement seems to have general support from most tables, which would allow a way forward without a repetition of the painful events earlier that day. Our bubble is considerably larger than that of the other office engaged in the center. That seems a sign of generosity, but there is a catch. Two sides of our bubble, on the northeast and the southwest, overlap with the council chair's plot and the plot to be designed by Taller Colleague. It is in these "zones of collaboration" that most buildings are located. The remaining part, exclusively under our design control, is cut by a wide utility corridor, making large parts of the territory allocated to us unsuitable for building. The short conclusion is that the appointed landscape architect, also from France, is the de facto designer of our site. We agree on the spot, worried that if we don't, we'll end up with nothing. The lack of Russian support during the official part of the council meeting hasn't made us very hopeful. This agreement preserves for us a seat at the table. At some point the chaos may start to work in our favor.

May 18

Presentation to Russian president Dmitry Medvedev. The venue is Digital October, around the corner from our school, a refurbished chocolate factory that now houses Russian IT start-ups. The queue to get in is long. Elaborate security precautions have been taken; all those who might come within twenty meters of the Russian president are screened for metal objects and liquids. All bags and overcoats must be handed in. Even though our hotel is quite near, it has taken us ages to get here. We have walked the last kilometer because all roads leading to the venue have been blocked off to allow the presidential convoy clear passage. Medvedev will be presented with the same material that we presented to Nr. 1 three weeks earlier. Neither the discussion we had with the council nor the dinner afterward has had a bearing on what will be shown. The only request that has reached our office in the meantime is to replace the Russian *matruschkas* in our renderings with bright young people. By far the largest part of the exhibition, if one can call it that, is taken up by a model of young Sasha's cube, which so far seems to enjoy the largest prestige of all the ongoing efforts. It is the first item Medvedev passes by after he has entered the building. They seem to know each other; there is a certain familiarity in their greetings. Young Sasha is the only relaxed person in the building. Even Nr. 1 is uncharacteristically nervous. When the president passes our stand, he briefly stops to look at the projection screen. His eyes light up as he sees our slides and murmurs "Krasiva" (beautiful), clearly unaware that what he is looking at has already been overtaken by other events.

June 1

The wheeling and dealing at the council meeting have landed us in a bit of a mess. The change of site implies that the terms of our previous contract, already accepted by both parties, will have to be renegotiated in exchange for much vaguer guarantees with respect to future building commissions. The cultural program—a library, cinema, theater, exhibition space, and art gallery, previously reserved for the guest zone, to be designed by us—is now to be spread across the entire development. The exact distribution across each district is to be negotiated among the district curators, a scenario that will likely only intensify the bickering seen at the last council meeting. It is as though the Russians take a perverse joy in letting the architects fight among themselves and are using this particular project as proof that those who always considered themselves morally superior are no better than the country they love to criticize.

The new contract leaves us with a business center and a hotel. Payment for work performed under the old contract, already submitted and approved, is made contingent on acceptance of the new terms. Without agreement on these terms, the money cannot be released. The Russians with whom we were previously able to reach quick agreements increasingly seem to have their hands tied. Where previously they acted on behalf of the foundation, they now refer to the foundation as an anonymous third entity outside themselves, whose actions even they have a hard time understanding. The project has come under increased state scrutiny, and the support of the state is no longer unconditional.

August 28

We have been involved in the project for a year and have good reasons to wonder whether it has led us anywhere. Yet despite the many difficulties, it proves difficult to let go or even distance ourselves. Our experience, if not rewarding in terms of progress, has certainly given us insight into machinations that we are slowly beginning to discover. Russia has become a form of addiction, fueling a desire to see where and how things will end even though we suspect that they may not end well.

September 2

The third of the four annual council meetings takes place at the Radisson Royal Hotel in Moscow, formerly the Hotel Ukraine. It was the first hotel I stayed at when I started visiting Russia in the early twenty-first century. At the time, it wasn't part of any major hotel chain. The whole interior still breathed the spirit of Soviet times: the rooms were simple, and, as was the case with most hotels then, the reception area doubled as a brothel. Not today. The ground floor has been turned into a shopping gallery for luxury brands, and the bar has become a lavish stakeout for businessmen and their female companions. If money still changes hands in exchange for sex, the price is surely beyond my budget.

The council meeting progresses at its usual pace. Each district curator presents two options, after which the council takes ample time to comment. The U-shaped table that we first encountered when we presented our competition entry has meanwhile acquired epic proportions. The council's chairman is still seated in the middle of the short end. This time there is an odd number of seats, so that he, as head of the council, is clearly placed at the center. There is simultaneous translation, and headphones are placed at each seat. Each place at the table is marked with a name tag. It is the first time we get to see what other district curators have been up to. It soon becomes clear that we haven't been the only ones to take liberties with the French master plan. Every curator presents a design proposal that adheres to the master plan only in honoring the boundaries of his district.

The two French representatives watch the individual presentations with increasing horror. Surely the intentions of their master plan went beyond simply fixing the boundaries of other people's work. One of them tries to claim speaking time to remind the council once more of their underlying intentions. For some reason his microphone malfunctions halfway through his first sentence. The rest of his statement goes unheard. After the last district curator has presented his two options, there is a pause. Where do we take things from here? I suggest that we simply do a test. There is a large model of the whole site in the middle of the U-shaped table. I suggest that each district curator simply put in his preferred option and that we see what the cumulative result ends up looking like. If it is convincing, we might even be able to wrap up this whole thing before lunch.

Each district curator proceeds to put his favorite option in the large model. Given that these council meetings are usually carefully scripted, there is something wryly funny about this impromptu act. Still, the end result is surprisingly compelling. Where the French plan had been a kind of simulated organic growth at the hands of a single designer, this embodies real diversity: different urban villages—what's in a name?—that appear to have emerged over time. The French firm's own rhetoric facilitates its exit as the author.

Over lunch we agree that this is as far as we are going to get today. It might be best simply to spend the afternoon on bilateral conversations to resolve certain border issues among the districts. In essence, each curator ought to be given the mandate to take his preferred option further, to the status of a full-fledged design proposal. That is the agreement. I get an offer to become a full member of the council and accept.

September 19

Nr. 1, who has not been briefed so far on the new division of districts in Taller Colleague's napkin drawing, is finally given a presentation. He does not like the results and wonders why the plans for the guest zone that he was initially shown have not been taken further. Images of these plans have been shown to the Russian president and have met with his consent (the approving nod in front of the projection screen). As the prime person responsible, Nr. 1 now faces the embarrassment of having to inform the president of this sudden change. He is not happy. We are asked to come up with a way to amend our plans that makes it possible to explain them as being an elaboration of our previous scheme. Given the fact that we have a different site, we see no way to do this. Why not just inform the higher political level of what has actually happened? This, we are assured, is not possible. Just find a way, it doesn't matter how far-fetched, as long as it allows the interpretation of being a continuation of the previous scheme. Use your creativity!

It is often suggested that authoritarian systems are more efficient than our consensus-driven processes. They get things done, while we forever debate the prudence of our actions. But my experience in Russia suggests that every system breeds its own type of inefficiency. The impossibility of questioning the leader's positions, however uninformed, can lead to tiresome rituals to undo wrong decisions while appearing to implement them. Trying to handle Nr. 1's feedback has just given us a first taste. Fraught plans, having entered through the front door, disappear by the back. It is an open question which is more time consuming: our lengthy procedures to arrive at decisions or their lengthy procedures to undo them.

September 24

Big news. At the United Russia Congress in Moscow, after a constitutional change extending the presidential term from four years to six, Medvedev proposes that his predecessor, Vladimir Putin, stand for a third, nonconsecutive term as president in the 2012 presidential election. Putin accepts. In return, Putin offers Medvedev the opportunity to stand on the United Russia ticket in the parliamentary elections in December and become prime minister of Russia at the end of his presidential term. Putin could now be in power until 2024. The rightness of the decision, as well as its legality, is questioned by many Russians, particularly in Moscow, where people see their country sliding slowly but surely back into autocratic rule. The matter is debated at the school. Almost immediately, seemingly unrelated complaints about noise from the school start trickling in from the Russian Orthodox church across the river.

October 12

Public hearing at the Russian University of Theatre Arts. The audience: a mix of trade and industry professionals, potential investors, architects, architecture students, and members of the general public, as well as the press. The hearing is a good opportunity to create a positive vibe about the project. We are given fifteen minutes to present. This time we have received detailed instructions on how to act and need to keep in mind that this hearing should not affect the course of the project. The costs (we have no idea) should remain confidential; the buildings we have visualized are concepts, not designs; we should avoid minutiae and focus on the big picture (never a problem). If questions are raised during our presentation, we should avoid jumping prematurely into a Q&A and finish our presentation first. As soon as our presentation is over, we should defer to the foundation's newly appointed director of marketing and PR. The excessive preparations prove unnecessary. The hearing is a nonevent.

December 2

The fourth and last urban council meeting of the year. It is the first time I attend as a member. The associated privileges are clear as soon as I disembark from the plane. At the gate a woman carrying a sign with my name awaits us and guides us to a special waiting area. We are, as she puts it, a "special delegation." She takes our passports and asks us to wait. We can sit on one of the sofas and help ourselves to drinks and snacks. Various televisions play Russian news broadcasts, which for more than a month now have been dominated by the coverage of protests over Putin's prospective third presidential term. After a minute she returns and asks us to follow her past customs. She takes us to a limousine, which drives us straight to our hotel. Whenever traffic jams loom in front, the driver turns on a blue police light on the roof. With screaming sirens, less than thirty minutes after leaving the airport, we arrive at our hotel.

The council meeting takes place at the Maly Theatre. The venue is chosen for the entertainment—some obscure folk-dance performance—provided afterward. For these meetings, it seems, there is money in abundance. The council meeting proceeds according to its usual protocol. We present our progress. With the exception of young Sasha, who displays an unexpected hostility toward what he calls our megalomaniacal object—we are about half a meter taller than his cube—we meet with approval. There is one problem: we haven't really changed our design to reconcile it with the version shown earlier to the president.

December 10

I receive a call from Igor, asking whether I'm looking forward to Christmas. I don't know what prompts his sudden personal interest, but in the course of the conversation that soon becomes clear. That morning Nr. 1 has been briefed on the results of the last council meeting, which apparently have left him speechless. Not knowing how to explain this situation to the president, he dreads confronting him. The idea is to have one of the council members brief the president himself—a highly unusual course of events, but the Russians see no other way out. The council's chairman has already indicated his unavailability; he already sacrificed last year's Christmas. This time it has to be me. Whatever plans I may have had for December 26th, I am politely asked to shelve them.

December 19

We have been invited to the foundation's Christmas party, held in Club Rai on Bolotnaya Naberezhnaya, two streets away from our school. Members only. We're curious. The interior is like a cave, with a peculiar labyrinth of passages that all return to the bar, clad in black metal and lit by black light. In the main space—or should I say cavity?—there is a podium with a single microphone stand. Slowly, the foundation's employees trickle in. A long lineup of Russian artists has been invited to entertain the foundation's staff; each of them is met with enthusiastic cheers. At the end of the evening, there will be a surprise act. We are asked to be patient. The surprise act is Boney M, whose most famous song, ironically, is the 1970s hit "Ra-Ra-Rasputin."

December 26

Christmas. I have been able to reschedule the timing of the presentation to Medvedev for the afternoon of the 27th. A private plane has been organized to take me from Rotterdam Airport; because of the late arrangement, all slots at Amsterdam Airport have been taken.

December 27

The flight takes longer than usual. The small plane, more susceptible to wind, does not reach the same speed as regular civil aircraft, so the journey from Rotterdam Airport to Vnukovo lasts roughly four and a half hours, about an hour more than normal. Once we land, procedures are quick. I wave my passport at the custom officials who await me at the bottom of the aircraft's steps and am through. Igor is there to pick me up. He is worried about time. We have about two hours to get to our destination, but the journey is long. There has been a last-minute change of plans, and we're not going to the Kremlin but to Gorki 9, the president's country residence on the western edge of Moscow. Today the M-Kad, Moscow's ring road, is absolutely clogged, and we may struggle to arrive on time. One doesn't keep the president waiting. We have real-time info on Moscow's traffic situation on the iPad and regularly alter our route. The indication of the quickest route changes almost every ten minutes, as does the indicated time of arrival, invariably for the worse.

Once we leave the M-Kad, traffic improves and Igor relaxes, putting his iPad aside. Our journey takes us through Rublyovka. I witness a wealth that, despite my frequent travels to Russia, I have never seen in this country before. The neighborhood looks like a Russian version of Beverly Hills, covered in snow. Igor points to a tastefully designed—apparently by our Russian friend on the council—shopping mall for luxury brands. We have some time, so we stop for something to eat. We might be in for a long wait at the president's residence without any supply of food. We order two sandwiches each and two large Americanos. After rehearsing our presentation one last time, we finish our coffee, get up, and continue the last part of our journey.

The large villas that straddle the road give way to barbed wire, which in turn gives way to a seemingly endless wall, finally interrupted by a gate marked with the emblem of the Russian Federation. As we approach, the doors open automatically. Our arrival is expected. The guards on the inside greet us with a smile, making our reception feel like the welcome of a much-expected guest. The abundant presence of the Russian flag, a re-arrangement of my own national colors, only serves to reinforce the impression.

That impression quickly fades once we enter the residence, a large Palladian-style villa with an entrance portico, curiously supported by four pairs of Doric columns. The sheer weight of power wielded from within, so it seems, requires extra structural support. We enter and are escorted to the waiting room. The president's appointments are running slightly behind schedule. In the room is a large group of people who look like they could have been there for some time, waiting for their private audience with the president. According to Igor, the combined fortunes of those in the room, a collection of well- and less well-known billionaires, exceeds the GDPs of many countries. Still, every billionaire must wait his turn. I'm a little surprised to see that young Sasha is also present, which is probably naïve, considering that he has attended every defining moment of the project. He is engaged in a deep conversation with Nr. 1, who has arrived before us. Igor encourages me to mingle as well. It might be good for future business, but frankly, I just wouldn't know where to start a conversation. I am happy to wait.

Just as in the VIP waiting area at the airport, there are TV screens in the room with Russian news broadcasts—apparently the favorite pastime of Russia's elite—being shown in an endless loop. The protests, which started moderately three months ago, are continuing in full force. For days now, Academician Sakharov Avenue has been the scene of the "For Fair Elections" protests by the "Orange Protesters," demanding that Medvedev's and Putin's United Russia Party start abiding by proper democratic rules. Sitting in the room with us is the first deputy chief of staff of the Russian Presidential Administration, the main ideologist of the Kremlin for the past twelve years and the architect of Russia's so-called sovereign democracy, a special political doctrine used to legitimize Russia's virtually unopposed one-party rule. Today he has been let go from Medvedev's cabinet. For the past several days he has been the target of the street protests, and the news of his resignation is celebrated as a major victory. What the protesters don't know is that his resignation has coincided with his appointment to the cabinet of Vladimir Putin, still Russia's prime minister at this moment. Officially the job change is a demotion, but given Putin's and Medvedev's imminent job swap, the demotion is in fact a promotion that will ultimately allow him to return to the Presidential Executive Office in an even more powerful capacity. To the people in the room, this is no surprise. I witness the billionaires in the room get up one by one to congratulate him, while on the TV screens an excited crowd celebrates its presumed victory. The whole occurrence lasts no longer than thirty seconds, but it reveals in no uncertain terms how in Russia nothing is what it seems. We in the West can only guess; all our foreign policy doctrines are inevitably one step behind. History is written here, inside this waiting room; the crowds on the TV screens—global headline news—are no more than a backdrop.

Three hours after our appointment's scheduled time, we are called in. It has gotten dark. We take the set of books, which have been sent for the president's viewing in advance of the meeting, and proceed toward the president's office. The idea is that we go will through the books page by page and give a simple explanation. Nr. 1 intends to speak only when asked. Igor, we agree, will give a simple introduction in Russian and then hand the presentation over to me. I am urged to limit my usual verbosity to one sentence per page. Igor will then translate each sentence into Russian. This format has proved effective in earlier confrontations with Nr. 1, so why not try it on the president too? As it turns out, young Sasha is here for the same meeting. He has been commissioned to undertake another building in the project, unforeseen in the master plan, which will somehow have to be amended to accommodate it. Young Sasha and Medvedev seem well at ease in each other's company and appear to be longtime friends. By far the largest part of the meeting is spent discussing the exact location of young Sasha's new building. When it is our turn, about ten minutes are left. The presentation seems to go well. The reaction of the president to this presentation is the same as to the last: "Krasiva!" When the discussion moves to finances, Medvedev defers to his aide, who seems aware of every detail and has been whispering continually in the president's ear. The conclusion is that somehow they are going to find a way to make things work. Some further funds will be diverted to this project; Vladi, as they refer to Putin, has been made aware and has given his blessing. It is important, however, that both buildings be ready and in operation for the G8 summit scheduled to take place in Moscow in the summer of 2014, for which the project is being considered as the location. (Details about the construction schedule are left undiscussed.) After the meeting, Nr. 1 shakes my hand a little longer than usual. The year has ended well for him.

It is too late to catch a flight back. The delayed start of our meeting means that I will have to spend the night in Moscow. I book a hotel room and head toward the center. Igor reports to City Manager by phone. The conversation seems friendly until he informs him of the 2014 completion deadline. An impossible task. The voice on the other end of the line is audible throughout the car: not the definition of a successful meeting but rather that of suicide.

December 31

Back in the Netherlands, another year over. If last year's ending was larded with great expectations, this year provided a great deal of insight into why these expectations may have been premature. We have to be patient. That, it seems, is Russia's quintessential mantra.

Happy 2012.

2012

Vladimir Putin is elected president of Russia. The United Nations calls on the Syrian government to begin a transition to a democratic political system.

January 15

Once the initial euphoria about our meeting has died down, the consequences of Medvedev's request become clear: if indeed the two primary buildings of the guest zone have to be ready for the G8 summit, their structural skeleton has to be up in a year and a half. That leaves only another year to complete both buildings, or to at least make them look finished in front of the TV cameras covering the event. The suggestion of completeness, the erection of a Potemkin Village, is all there is time for.

The buildings' fast-track schedule soon runs into trouble with standard Russian procurement procedures, which still need to be followed. The first official reaction to our December 2011 submission contains no fewer than 1,346 comments. The main part of this submission had been a 1:500 drawing set that incorporated a number of important design changes but otherwise was mostly a blowup of a 1:1,000 drawing set submitted a few months earlier. In doing that, we had thought to make clever use of the Russian system, which prescribes design stages almost exclusively by the scale of the drawings. In the age of computer drawings such a system is highly redundant, largely allowing progression to the next stage by simply entering a different print scale in the print command—a bit like changing the font size of a text.

Still, despite our cutting corners like this, the level of detail of our drawings is about the only element of our submission that is not questioned. Everything else is: the size of buildings, their position, and above all, their contents. Everything is up in the air again. In addition, it becomes clear that our proposal, which contains predominantly public uses—and thus may rely on public funding—will almost certainly have to go through a public tender process. Hence it is by no means certain that we will be the architect of any of the buildings we have put forward. Our official capacity, that of "district curator," grants us no rights in this respect. Our draft contract with the foundation had stipulated the intention of commissioning us to design certain buildings, but because of unresolved differences over legal fine print, that contract had never been signed.

The fate of the French master planners is not much better. The overall coordination of the plan has been transferred to a Russian firm that is also one of the district curators. Because the title "district curator" doesn't exist within the Russian system, there is no conflict of interest. Where the vagueness of the term "district curator" is a liability for us, it presents them with an opportunity. Deeply familiar with the local context, the Russian firm seems a perfect choice. If at first the French were informally sidelined by their colleagues on the jury, they are now also officially sidelined by the Russians. Whatever happened to the French can just as easily happen to us if it hasn't already.

January 20

Another opportunity in Russia presents itself in the form of a new project. In November 2011 Medvedev announced the government's intention to expand the borders of Moscow, effectively making the city twice its current size. On top of that, part of the federal government is being considered for relocation to the new territories out of town. Speculations are rife. Will the Kremlin lose its current function and finally become a museum open to the public? As with the initial stages of our ongoing project, no scenario seems too radical or far-fetched. Are these serious intentions, or are they the final whims of a government on its last legs? No one knows. It seems unlikely that Putin—if the ploy works and he becomes the new (old) president—will endorse such a move. Still, with an international call for tender on behalf of the Moscow administration to private firms to help conceptualize the whole effort, no cost or effort is spared. The scale of the operation alone makes it a compelling subject, reminiscent of the "Grand Paris" effort, on which the operation is also modeled. We express interest. The involvement in an additional project, even if it is a competition, will give us eyes and ears on the ground and, if possible, allow us to react quickly should there be a change of fortune.

February 13

Igor visits our office in Rotterdam. We have asked for this visit in the hope of creating clarity about our eligibility for future work. Perhaps "clarity" is the wrong word. There is perfect clarity—our status is nil—but that is not the clarity we welcome. He sympathizes. Having given multiple guarantees about our further involvement or at least having alluded to the likelihood thereof, he is clearly embarrassed about the harshness and seeming inescapability of the current situation. He comes up with a construction that, in an interesting choice of words, he describes as a "Spanish tender," a tender whose outcome is known in advance.

His idea is simple. There will be a short, six-week exercise for a fee below the official tender limit, so it can be granted as a direct commission. This concept phase will produce a number of requirements for the eventual building that the tender will then impose on contenders. These requirements will be so specific and so tied to the preliminary design of the building already on the table that only the party who authored them— that is, we—will be able to meet them. Thus we will inevitably emerge victorious in any public tender that will follow.

The venue is Rotterdam's only two Michelin stars restaurant. (We pay.) A panoramic window offers a view over the ships that pass by. There are not many because the Rotterdam port has long since relocated much closer to the sea. This part of the Rotterdam port is largely folklore, home to new residential projects close to the city center. While we are still deciding how to react, Igor proceeds to make small talk, inquiring about real estate prices in Rotterdam and comparing them to those in Moscow. Then, suddenly, he smiles, as if the whole thing has been a joke. If we choose such a venue for lunch every time we meet, he assures us, more Spanish tender offers might follow.

February 19

We receive an early-morning phone call. The foundation has rejected the idea of a concept phase and will proceed only with a public tender. This public tender will be open to all international firms wishing to participate and includes the further design of all individual buildings in our district. The same people who alluded to the possibility of a deal in Rotterdam are at the core of its rejection.

February 23

Putin makes his famous Borodino speech. Addressing 100,000 people at the Luzhniki Stadium, he calls on those present "not to betray Russia, but to love her, to unite around the motherland and to work together to overcome its problems." Citing Mikhail Lermontov's poem *Borodino,* Putin reminds his audience that exactly two hundred years ago today the battle of Borodino took place, decisive in the outcome of the Napoleonic War of 1812, fought to rid Russia of the influence of foreign powers. Today is Russia's annual Day of the Defenders of the Fatherland. To Putin, the parallel with the present is obvious. In his mind there is little doubt that the ever-larger protests engulfing Russia's capital are being instigated by foreign powers trying to interfere in Russian affairs. "Such interference is unacceptable. Russia should be allowed to follow its own free will." He ends his speech with Molotov's famous Great Patriotic War slogan "The victory shall be ours!"

February 29

The possibility of our project hosting the 2014 G8 summit goes public. A Russian Newspaper features an article practically announcing the fact. The foundation's chief spokesman is quoted: "We have heard that there might be such an option." He stops short of admitting knowledge of any official decision: "The opportunity to hold the summit in the project will be an additional impetus for its development. If indeed such a decision is made, it will be a serious challenge for those in charge of the project." Thoughts go back to City Manager's rant in reaction to the report of our meeting with Medvedev; suicide is now an official probability.

March 4

Russian voters overwhelmingly grant Vladimir Putin a six-year term as president. With 80 percent of ballots counted, Putin has won 64.7 percent of the vote, comfortably above the 50 percent needed to avoid a runoff and extending his claim on power to eighteen years, equaling the rule of Soviet leader Leonid Brezhnev.

Tens of thousands of Putin's supporters gather on Manezh Square just outside the walls of the Kremlin to celebrate. "We have won!" Putin tells them as tears stream down his right cheek. "We have won a clean victory. Glory to Russia!" Immediately next to Putin is Medvedev, as of today the outgoing president. He has been promised the post of prime minister in Putin's cabinet. His presence symbolizes both victory and defeat. In Russia, it seems, these are interchangeable; there is life after both.

MIPIM, the annual gathering of the elite of the property world in Cannes—an event that brings together investors, local authorities, corporate industrialists, and real estate developers. Spring hits Cannes earlier than it does most of Europe. The better weather helps bring about a feel-good factor essential to the real estate trade—some argue that it is its sole driver—and makes the event something people generally look forward to, if only as a change of scenery. MIPIM is the location of the first council meeting this year, for good reason. With funding all but secured, MIPIM represents the perfect opportunity for the project to become a reality.

For the occasion, an entire stand—a modern circus tent, generally used for catering—has been transformed into something that is supposed to resemble a modern gallery, in which the planned city is featured like a piece of contemporary art. The design of the exhibition has been outsourced to the council chairman's son. The individual projects are represented as plaster models in pristine white, displayed on pedestals like Brancusi sculptures. Any further detail of their realization as buildings is avoided. These are artworks; the exhibition is designed to preemptively discourage specific questions as much as possible. In case one's interest might extend beyond aesthetic delight, there are abundant iPads lying about for those wanting additional information. After all, this is a technology hub. The iPad is a clever exhibition device that provides investors with the more banal details needed to make sound decisions while allowing architectural peers the superficial illusion of mastery over form. It is as if in the context of this exhibition, architecture and real estate have gone through a consensual separation, allowing each one to flourish in its own right without being hampered by the preoccupations of the other. This is not one but two exhibitions, where aesthetic abstraction and market conditions coexist perfectly on either side of the iPad's screen. The irony is that it is the virtual reality of the iPad that provides the most telling insight into the real, while the reality of the exhibition represents a complete fiction. Even if they are in the same room, architects and property developers can continue to dismiss each other as merely a footnote.

The council meeting, organized in one of the city's major hotels, is pretty much a formality. There is little point in a discussion among peers. Here it is the engagement with the world at large, not the efforts of the architects or engineers, that will decide the project's viability. Foundation officials, if they even attend the meetings, are mainly interacting with their smartphones. The breaks between the official sessions (dedicated to "architectural cohesion," "the responsible integration of infrastructure," and other kinds of nonsense) turn out to be of primary importance. During these breaks, the real deals are clinched through which the project, more than through the involvement of an international company of architects, will ultimately acquire its international dimension.

During one of these breaks, the council chairman signs what appears to be a contract with the foundation. The presence of the project at MIPIM has proved effective in consolidating private finance for his quarter. No public tender—not even a Spanish one—is necessary anymore. The chairman's firm receives the design of his quarter as a direct commission. Only the residential part of his district will be tendered in the form of an open competition to help further the careers of upcoming young architects.

A kink in the cable occurs at the last minute. Literally seconds before signing, an American foundation official tries to make the fee fully inclusive of VAT, effectively reducing fees by 20 percent. The council chairman drops his pen. The angry look on his face, however, suffices. The official backs down, and the contract is signed.

March 11

Huge protests occur in Novy Arbat over perceived election fraud. One week after Putin's victory, protests have not gone away. On the contrary, in anticipation of Putin's official inauguration in early May, protesters intend to build up a crescendo of demonstrations to, as one of their leaders puts it, "be the government's constant nightmare."

May 7

Putin is officially inaugurated as president of the Russian Federation. One of his first actions in office is to speculate publicly on the introduction of new laws that will make further protests criminal offenses against the state, or worse, treason. The contours of his future policies become clear: he intends to be the opposition's nightmare every bit as much as they intend to be his.

May 25

As a result of the project's going public at MIPIM and the related media campaign, the project, including our contribution to it, gains notoriety not only in the property world but also in the architectural world. The first evidence is the publication of our work on an architecture website in the form of an opera house proposed in South Korea.

We alert our clients to the plagiarism. They welcome our attentiveness but refrain from further action. In architecture, plagiarism is a tricky thing. There are no laws to curb it, and some would argue that the art of copying is an integral part of the art of architecture, a discipline based on evolution more than on invention. Anyhow, if we cannot prevent plagiarism, we should at least make sure that the original is erected before the copy. We use the case to encourage our clients to expedite the process: set milestones, start scheduling meetings, and so on. Nothing of the kind happens.

June 14

The second council meeting of the year takes place in Suzdal, one of Russia's oldest towns and a major tourist attraction. It is not clear why Suzdal has been chosen as the location for this meeting. Perhaps it is to reverse the usual dynamics, have council members take in rather than exude, be educated rather than—as they have been doing—constantly trying to educate the Russians. The more plausible explanation is that there is simply nothing to talk about. Not much has changed since MIPIM. At present, the overall progress of the projects seems to reside more in its ever more emphatic presence in the media than in actual developments on the ground. With the exception of massive billboards depicting the various projects—including ours—nothing much seems to be happening on-site.

There is some news, however. Young Sasha has completed the design of his second building, the one we first discussed during our meeting with Medvedev in December. In its proposed form, the building would be the tallest building in the project and partially obstruct views from Taller Colleague's quarter. Because the building was not foreseen in the original master plan, which has already been adjusted to accommodate it, its current size and position lead to discussion. It is also starting to affect ongoing developments, and many council members object to what they view as a rogue action. Taller Colleague, in particular, is not happy. Young Sasha, however, is not impressed. Russia's recent regime change, apart from having a clear effect on his architecture—more nationalistic—seems to have also vastly boosted his confidence. He is a "made man"—untouchable by his colleagues.

August 23

We receive the definitive program for our project. The public program has been entirely replaced by a commercial program. We are faced with a catch-22: the more we advocate the public program, the more we undermine the certainty of an eventual commission. The public program requires public funding; public funding requires strict observance of tendering rules. The commercial program pays for the buildings, making public funding unnecessary, but it also annuls our stated goals.

August 26–29

Vernissage of the 2012 Venice Biennale. Two years have passed since we first became acquainted with the project. With the passage of time, the project seems increasingly dubious. There is perpetual uncertainty whether financing is even remotely in place. Interestingly, however, the more uncertain the project becomes, the more grandiose are the settings in which the meetings of the urban council take place. This time the venue for our meetings is the Palazzo Ducale, probably the most expensive place to organize a meeting in Venice.

Like every council meeting so far, the meeting contains one major surprise: out of the blue, a large shopping center is presented, located right next to the train station. The mall is designed by a British firm. It will help create the commercial revenue necessary to make the project a plausible venture. The mall is a surprise to everyone on the council, including its Russian members, normally more privy to confidential information. We know that the shopping mall is a reality from the first moment we see it. Our reluctance to accommodate a commercial program in our project may have significantly contributed to its emergence. Young Sasha's second building meanwhile has become a fait accompli, obstruction of views or not.

The general mood of the gathering is strangely optimistic. During one of the breaks, we ask the council's chairman how he views the project's chances under the new political leadership. He doesn't seem the slightest bit worried: Putin is a man of action, and that is always preferable to a man of mere words (it is unclear whether he is referring to Medvedev). We go back in for the last session.

The Russian Biennale pavilion is dedicated to the theme of science cities in Russia, both old and new. On the top floor there is an exhibition about the project. There is no physical content; the whole concept of MIPIM has been taken a step further. The pavilion's walls and ceiling are decorated exclusively with bar codes. When one scans them with one's phone or one of the many iPads lying about, information about the project becomes viewable. Our project barely features. The alleged costs of the exhibition: one million U.S. dollars. We are not sure whether this is money invested in revealing or in hiding the project.

The ground floor is dedicated to former science cities in the USSR, so-called *naukograds*. This part of the exhibition is designed as a sort of peep show, where glimpses of old photographs of these cities can be caught through little viewing holes, supposedly to convey the notion of secrecy that surrounded such cities in former days, when either they were off-limits to regular citizens or their existence was denied altogether. Ironically, the insipid use of information technology on the top floor suggests a similar form of secrecy, making what was intended to be a contrast between the old and new days into a bizarre echo.

Outside the Russian pavilion, there is a demonstration against the sentences received on August 17 by Nadezhda Tolokonnikova, Maria Alyokhina, and Yekaterina Samutsevich, three members of the group Pussy Riot who were convicted of "hooliganism motivated by religious hatred" after staging a performance against the Russian Orthodox Church's support for Vladimir Putin. The Russian pavilion is intended to celebrate the blessings of modern technology as a victory over old times. The irony is more than palpable.

September 5

We are not selected as a winner in any of the three categories of the Big Moscow competition, our other project for the Russian public sector. The jury evaluating the final submission was haphazardly assembled shortly before the end of the competition and replaced the panel of international experts who had reviewed the work during the course of the competition. The recommendations of this panel, widely broadcast and in which we scored well, have been declared null and void. The new jury, consisting of Moscow's deputy mayor, the chief curator of the Grand Paris, and the dean of Moscow's Higher School of Economics (and a member of the winning team), has made its own decision.

At the same time, the news breaks that the new Russian president has no intention whatsoever to relocate the Kremlin. In fact, the whole idea of a new federal center out of town will be revisited. The new territories will be studied as future housing locations.

October 15

Phone call from Igor: all our work on the science city has "officially" been refused. He is sorry to be conveying this news, but there is nothing we can do. If we are interested, we are invited to be involved in further meetings related to reprogramming of the central zone for potential new projects.

October 26

A letter arrives, bearing no date or letterhead, "officially" informing us. The same day our project comes under heavy attack in the media. In various news feeds high government representatives publicly criticize its monumentality. These objects are incompatible with the atmosphere supposed to make scientists and other residents of the new city feel at ease.

November 16

The fourth and final council meeting of the year, this time on-site in young Sasha's cube, the only building of the project completed so far. As things stand, the second building to be completed will most likely also be a Sasha building. From the large windows on the top floor, we can see that next door, site preparations have commenced. It is odd that in this eminent company of internationally renowned architects, the only realized work is by a young Russian who seems to have operated largely outside the council.

We are asked to participate in workshops, but it is difficult to imagine how we can continue to be a constructive part of the whole operation. We are about to embark on the same trajectory that we started in the beginning of 2011—translating someone else's master plan for the central district into architecture—with no guarantee of a different outcome.

It will be the last council meeting we attend.

December 4

Participants in the Big Moscow competition are asked to present and publicly discuss their proposals at the Moscow Urban Forum. The discussion panel consists of Moscow's deputy mayor, the winners of each of the three competition award categories, and us. The municipal authorities have asked the school to organize this forum, and this request largely accounts for our presence. In advance of the forum, it is via the school that we are asked to omit certain slides from our presentation, most notably one showing Moscow's mayor Sobyanin and then-president Medvedev swapping seats at a table, indicating the relative power of Moscow in the Russian political system. We refuse, stating that we will decline participation if restrictions are placed on the content of our presentation. The authorities consent, and we are allowed to show our presentation unchanged. When it is my turn, the deputy mayor receives an apparently urgent phone call and disappears from the stage. The call lasts as long as my speech. The whole event passes without further incidents.

When the event goes online, our presentation is not featured. Apparently, our refusal to remove slides from our presentation has led to the removal of our presentation as a whole. As we watch the online footage, it is as though we were never there.

December 28

In a rare move, Putin vetoes amendments to the federal law that would allow that "the management company of the project Innovation Center [be granted] the right to approve urban planning and design standards and identify the list of necessary planning permits and authorizations and construction phases" because under Russian law, these functions are "the responsibility of the state." A Russian news site quotes "a source familiar with the issues" stating: "Having returned to the presidency this past spring, Putin acknowledges the need to continue the innovation-friendly policies of former president Dmitry Medvedev. But the president is increasingly critical of certain of the government-sponsored organizations that represent the fruit of these policies and is considering reshaping them to better match his own views."

The Russia of 2012 is considerably different from that of 2010.

2013

Xi Jinping becomes president of China. The United States and five other world powers conclude a historic accord with Iran to cap its nuclear program.

May 20

News trickles in about Nr. 1 being questioned by the Investigative Committee over an alleged misuse of funds to support the opposition. Embezzlement allegations involve a parliamentary deputy who was a consultant of the science-city project until he became a leader of the anti-Kremlin opposition movement in December 2011. The science-city project is a public-private partnership where the private half is now suspected of double-crossing the public half, or at least frustrating the political agenda of those presiding over it. In the witch hunt that ensues, nobody seems safe.

June 19

It is not just personal fortunes that are changing. A month later, Putin officially announces that the 2014 G8 summit will take place not at the project but in Sochi. With its construction schedules delayed ever further, the project is too much of a liability. In preparing for the next Winter Olympics, Sochi has the required infrastructure largely in place. At first glance, the choice of Sochi seems pragmatic. However, like any political decision in Russia, it is also very much a signal—a condemnation of the mixture of hubris and political insensitivity that underlay the idea of a Russian Silicon Valley. Putin doesn't fall for pervasive trends the way Medvedev did. The choice of Sochi over the project to host the G8 serves as a repudiation of all those who thought that something as whimsical as a technology hub might create an independent momentum: "Forget it!"

June 20

We get Igor on the phone and casually inquire how things are. He sounds ill at ease, a far cry from his usual demeanor. We think that the embarrassment of not having spoken to us for so long may serve as an explanation until we hear the sound of sirens in the background. In the middle of our phone call, he quickly apologizes and hangs up. The police have arrived.

The next day Russian news feeds tell us what happened. There has been another raid by agents investigating potential fraud in relation to the technology hub. Such raids have become a common occurrence ever since Russian agents first stormed the foundation's offices on April 18. Although the initial raid was intended to be kept from the public eye, it caused a bit of a storm when an American executive was caught up in it and was forced to surrender his mobile phone. Reports, exclusively from anonymous sources, stated that he was allowed to leave only after foundation officials had repeatedly appealed to investigators, and that he flew directly back to the United States without having his scheduled meeting with Nr. 1.

Even though Putin is denying that the foundation is being targeted for political reasons, it seems increasingly likely that the project has become the subject of a turf war between opposing camps within the Russian government: those who back Prime Minister Medvedev, who made the project the cornerstone of his presidency, and the allies of President Putin, who see Medvedev as a rival. It is our last season at the school, and there we hear increasing rumors that some influential people are doing what they can to accelerate a decision to dismiss Medvedev because he has encroached on their interests. Medvedev, according to general opinion, will not make it to the end of the year.

November 13

Further allegations of fraud. After an across-the-board investigation into the foundation, the Prosecutor General's Office has released a report, according to which 50 billion rubles (around 1.6 billion U.S. dollars) was allocated to the project's development between 2010 and 2012 "in the absence of budget control and approved performance indicators." Nr. 1 is cited by name in the report as being responsible.

2014

President Obama announces that the United States will restore diplomatic relations with Cuba. ISIS declares an Islamic caliphate.

February 28

Armed men of uncertain allegiance appear at Simferopol Airport in the Crimea, Ukraine. Article 4 of the Geneva Convention says that members of the military must wear symbols recognizable at a distance, but they do not need to indicate national origin. The point is to enforce the principle of distinction between civilians and military combatants so civilians are not targeted. Russia denies the presence of its military, but we know instantly what happened. Our thoughts go back to the presidential aide being congratulated on his promotion, while the rest of the world thought that he had been ousted. Sometimes the experiences lived in the context of a single project can provide a key to reading the behavior of an entire state. All one needs to do is magnify them.

March 24

News breaks that Sochi has been bypassed as the G8 summit's host city. This time it is not the Russians but the international community that denies the city the opportunity. Over the past year, East-West relations have soured substantially over Russia's alleged intervention in Ukraine. Following their earlier suspension of participation in summit preparations, the G8 leaders (minus one) announce that they will not travel to Sochi. Instead, they will hold a G7 meeting in Brussels on June 4–5.

July 17

Malaysia Airlines Flight 17 (MH17 / MAS17) is a scheduled international passenger flight from Amsterdam to Kuala Lumpur. About 50 kilometers from the Ukraine-Russia border, the Boeing 777–200ER airliner loses contact. A few moments later the plane crashes near Torez in Donetsk Oblast, Ukraine, killing all 283 passengers and 15 crew on board. The crash occurs during the battle in Shakhtarsk Raion, part of the ongoing war in Donbass, in an area controlled by the Donbass People's Militia. According to American and German intelligence sources, the plane was mistakenly shot down by pro-Russian insurgents using a Buk surface-to-air missile fired from the territory that they control. They base their judgment on sensors that traced the path of the missile, analysis of fragment patterns in the wreckage, voice-print analysis of conversations in which separatist militants claim credit for the strike, and photos and other data from social media sites. On October 13, 2015, the Dutch Safety Board confirms this scenario in a final report on its investigation of the incident, concluding that the airliner was downed by a Buk surface-to-air 9M38-series missile with a 9N314M warhead launched from eastern Ukraine.

We expect a message from Russia. Even though our project has been aborted, that is hardly relevant to what has just happened. We hope for a sign, not an admission of guilt nor an apology but just some small expression of sympathy. Because we are a Dutch firm, it is not improbable that we know some of the people on board. Some of the deceased could have been friends or relatives. Given that we have gotten to know many of the Russians personally, our expectation seems reasonable. We wait for that single phone call, that simple e-mail . . .

23

On Hold

Have you seen the other Iraq?
It's spectacular.
It's peaceful.
It's joyful.
Fewer than 200 US troops are stationed here.
Arabs, Kurds and Westerners all vacation together.
Welcome to Iraqi-Kurdistan![1]

After the death of the great Persian king Jamshid, the tyrant Zahhak usurped the throne and established a reign of terror. Besides being cruel by natural inclination, he suffered from a strange disease that made him even more of an oppressor. Two snakes grew out of his shoulders and caused him severe pain, which could only be alleviated by feeding the snakes human brains each day. So every day Zahhak had two young persons killed and their brains fed to the snakes. The man charged with slaughtering the two young people taken to the palace each day took pity on them and thought up a ruse. He killed only one person a day, replacing the other with a sheep and mixing the two brains. One young person's life was thus saved every day; he was told to leave the country and to stay hidden in distant, inaccessible mountains. The young people thus saved gradually came to constitute a large community; they married among themselves and brought forth offspring. These people were named Kurds. Because during many years they evaded other human company and stayed away from the towns, they developed a language of their own. In the forests and the mountains, they built houses and tilled soil. Some of them came to own property and flocks, and spread themselves over the steppes and deserts.[2]

April 15, 2014

Erbil, northern Iraq. The reason for our presence? A potential project, let's leave it at that. The locals here don't like it if we refer to them or their land as Iraqi. They are Kurds, a people in their own right, and—if it is up to them—soon with a country to match. They deserve it, they feel. Since the U.S. invasion in 2003, their region has been the only one to establish a degree of stability. With safety and security in reach, the region considers itself ready for integration into the international community. No effort is spared in promoting this plan. New, liberal foreign investment laws are to attract foreign capital, and rapidly (re)built infrastructure—two new airports, five new universities—is to generate further favorable conditions. The approach seems to be succeeding. More than two thousand foreign companies have registered in Iraqi Kurdistan since 2003. Around fifty foreign companies from twenty-three different countries are working in the oil and gas sector, with investments nearing $20 billion. Emirates already provides direct passenger service from Dubai six times daily, and even Dutch budget carrier Transavia has recently established two daily flights from Amsterdam.

Success calls for reward. Given the volatility of the rest of Iraq, the Kurds negotiated de facto autonomy from Baghdad in 2006, using their accomplishments as leverage. Currently, the Kurdistan Regional Government exercises executive power granted by the democratically elected Kurdistan National Assembly. The Kurdish government is a coalition both of political parties and of the region's peoples: Chaldeans, Assyrians, Turkmen, Yazidis, and Kurds. It boasts a typically modern political agenda with all the usual contradictions: balancing economic competitiveness with wealth from natural resources and coupling a focus on modern urban development to the preservation of cultural heritage. And naturally, the government is strongly in favor of women's empowerment, educational reform, and political transparency.

Things sound almost too good to be true. Our first acquaintance with Erbil evokes other places in the grip of rapid transformation, like Dubai or Kazakhstan, all of which share a desire to project an image of instant wealth. We stay in the Divan Hotel, located exactly midway between the airport and the old city, in what is called New Downtown Erbil. The marble-clad lobby has ample sofas; the air is stale with cigar smoke that lingers despite the more pervasive smell of frankincense.[3] In the vicinity of the hotel, high-rise developments have sprung up like mushrooms. As in any recovering war zone, Dubai's property company Emaar has been first on the scene. War damage combined with oil wealth constitutes the perfect development opportunity. With twenty-seven-story apartment towers, three five-star hotels, and, in supreme irony, twin towers to dominate the skyline, "Downtown Erbil provides all the key elements that will create a world-class landmark center for Erbil."[4] There is more to come, as we have seen in announcements on the large billboards that straddle the road to our hotel: a new mall with eight thousand shops and stalls is going up. So is an apartment complex known as "Dream City," in which some of the units sell for $1 million. A giant bowling alley is almost finished, and an opera house is not far behind. A recent edition of CBS's *60 Minutes* summed up present-day Erbil perfectly when it stated, "There are more cranes here than minarets."[5] Nothing around us can be much more than five years old, but the vibe is that of a district that has been conducting business as usual for decades. Considering the drastic upheavals of not too long ago, it is almost shocking how normal the whole scene is.

April 16

Our hosts have arranged a tour of the larger Kurdish region. Our official destination is the Roman-era Delal Bridge in the town of Zakho, some two hundred kilometers from Erbil, close to the Turkish-Syrian border. The Kurdish name of the bridge is Pira Delal, which translates as "the beautiful bridge." It is a popular hangout for locals. Legend says that the hands of the builders were amputated to ensure that it would remain unique. Like most Kurdish legends, the narrative has an element of extreme cruelty. One is never sure whether to take this as a form of dark humor or as an earnest reflection of the unspeakable hardships the Kurds have suffered.

The bridge is largely a pretext because going there will give us an overall impression of the larger Kurdish territory, the extent of which turns out to be subject to a considerable degree of vagueness. Iraqi Kurdistan covers about 40,000 square kilometers—four times the area of Lebanon and larger than the Netherlands—and holds a population of nearly 5 million. The Kurdish territory as a whole is variably represented as having an area between 190,000 and 390,000 square kilometers, with an estimated population between 34 and 40 million. Before our trip we are shown maps with complex legends indicating borders that are diffuse at best. Other maps define the size of Kurdish territory as a set of ever-larger concentric circles that seem designed to support whatever level of exaggeration the person explaining them wishes to communicate. The largest circle claims vast parts of Syria, Turkey, Iran, and even Armenia.

Our trip takes us to the outskirts of Mosul, but we do not enter this officially Arab city. It is as though our hosts have read the preceding paragraph and are keen to avoid any impression of overblown Kurdish territorial ambitions. We travel in a convoy of black SUVs with tinted windows. For the first time, the Iraq we know from television presents itself. We encounter roadblocks with checkpoints. Evidently not all is secure. As we continue via the city of Dohuk to finally reach our bridge in Zakho, the scenes become calmer again. The Beautiful Bridge, early Roman, is a relatively young monument. In this part of the world it is not uncommon to find much earlier traces of civilization. The ancient citadel of Erbil, supposedly the world's longest-inhabited human settlement, is more than six thousand years old. Even on a relatively short trip like ours, the cultural and historic diversity of this region is overwhelming. We are shown evidence of Assyrian, Aramaic, Jewish, and Christian presence. Depictions of Santa Claus are lined with Arabic—or Kurdish; we can't tell the difference—script. The Kurdistan presented to us is an almost surrealist cocktail.

April 17

The last day of our stay includes a visit to the Kurdish region's parliament. The Kurds are clearly proud of their new democracy, a giant leap forward, given their immediate past, which they insist on referring to as communism. That, on closer inspection, may be a matter of opinion. Iraq, like Syria, was a Soviet ally, but it was never formally integrated into the Warsaw Pact, probably quite deliberately. Like the United States, the USSR maintained a string of loyal dictators on its fringes as a low-cost insurance policy against influence from the other side. The United States had Pinochet; the USSR, Saddam Hussein. Nevertheless, it remains debatable that that made Iraq any more a Communist country than it made Pinochet's Chile a Western democracy.

Still, if the architectural style of the parliament building is anything to go by, the external signs are most definitely there. The building is a symmetrically organized concrete box, exemplifying the typically Communist mix of modernist economy and token respect for classical order. The entrance canopy doubles as a balcony; columns are expressed in the facade to suggest more vertical proportions; an arcade at the ground floor encircles the building 360 degrees (mainly to harbor loading docks); and its flat roof slightly cantilevers to evoke the association of a cornice. Apparently, Saddam commissioned the building in the 1980s as a luxury hotel to entertain guests from friendly nations (the hotel stood empty most of the time), with a basement that doubled as an underground bunker, big enough to hold an entire tank battalion. The room where currently the parliament sessions take place previously served as one of the hotel's conference rooms. The room is too small, the ceiling is too low, and the seats are too crammed, making the daily work of the young Kurdish democracy feel like little more than improvised motions.

Inside the building there are portraits of eminent representatives of the Kurdish region's new political representation. Most of Saddam's former body doubles seem to have found new careers as front-runners of various political parties. There are portraits of women too, invariably without headscarves—not quite in equal numbers, but enough to leave us with the impression of a functioning secular democracy.

June 16

Another meeting to discuss the project, this time not in Erbil but in London. Because the situation in the north of Iraq is becoming more and more unstable, meeting locations now alternate between Dubai and London. In early June ISIS seized control of Mosul, the second most populous city in Iraq, eighty kilometers west of Erbil, and controls the surrounding province of Nineveh. The Mosul Dam is within its reach, and the world fears an imminent humanitarian and environmental disaster. So far the dam has remained under the control of the Iraqi security forces, but there are other problems. ISIS has also taken control of Fallujah and Tikrit, and it might be only a matter of time before it takes Baghdad, too. Even if Baghdad no longer wields the same influence, Kurdish autonomy has not yet reached a point where Baghdad's fall could pass without consequences.

In all our communications, our contact has played down the number of ISIS fighters, estimating their numbers at a mere two to three thousand and maintaining that it will be only a matter of time before it will be defeated (and thus our project will materialize). After the Mosul campaign, however, these reassurances are hard to sustain. There are reports that Iraqi Sunnis, opposed to the predominantly Shia government, have joined ISIS, bolstering the group's numbers. The Kurds, initially reluctant to be drawn into the conflict, are being forced to defend their territory. The ambiguity of their borders no longer inspires optimistic territorial speculations but works against them. Certain hatched parts of the map have already been lost. The arc of our idyllic trip two months ago is now a front line that must be defended by the Peshmerga.

August 7

We receive word that we have definitively been awarded the job and are invited to make a contract proposal. Meanwhile, ISIS has announced the establishment of the caliphate and has formally changed its name to the Islamic State. The world learns that thousands of Yazidis, taking refuge on Mount Sinjar, are facing enslavement or genocide by IS militants. The Americans announce their intervention, and an aerial bombing campaign begins the following day. Our commission, understandably no longer a priority, is put on hold.

2015

Russia begins conducting air strikes in Syria.

195 countries commit to the Paris Climate Accord.

V. POWERS THAT BE

Brandenburg Gate, Berlin, 1989
Photograph by Klaus Lehnartz / Bundesregierung, Bundesarchiv, B 145 Bild-00100901

24

After the End of History

My career as an architect started when history ended: the summer of 1989. Bad timing. Among the intellectual vanguard the idea pervaded that we had entered some terminal stage of civilization. That summer Francis Fukuyama published his essay "The End of History?" The title ended with a question mark, an open interrogation. Less than three years later he expanded the essay into a best-selling book, this time with a less ambiguous title: *The End of History and the Last Man.* The message was clear:

"The end of the Cold War marks the end of mankind's ideological evolution, the universal recognition of Western liberal democracy makes it the final form of human government. This triumph of the West, or rather of the Western *idea* (more about that later) is rooted in the exhaustion of viable alternatives and in its power to resolve all major contradictions within the confines of its system. In the universal homogeneous state, all human needs are satisfied. There is no more conflict over "large" issues and consequently no more need for generals or statesmen (this part of the observation has definitely materialized); economic activity is all what remains."[1]

"The end of history will be a sad time. The ideological struggles of the past that called for courage, imagination, and idealism will be replaced by economic calculation, the endless solving of technical problems, environmental concerns, and the satisfying of consumer demands. After the end of history, there will be neither art nor philosophy, just the perpetual caretaking of the museum of human history—no exhilarating prospects, merely centuries of boredom."[2]

For a while, Fukuyama's prediction seemed to be coming true. For much of the 1990s, the world of politics was an abstract affair: an age of anonymous international institutions negotiating long, complex treaties. The devil—to the extent that he still featured—was invariably in the details. Few understood the intricacies of what was being discussed, let alone the implications of what was agreed. Still, as long as we—or at least most of us—seemed to be doing well for the moment, nobody much cared. The buildings in which those meetings were held—beige carbuncles with brown mirror-glass windows, designed and executed by anonymous contractors—might have been an indication of what the future had in store for us architects, but at the time, no one seemed particularly worried.

I remember an exhibition we designed some years later for the European Union: *The Image of Europe,* an attempt to address the iconographic deficit of this introverted political entity. The exhibition celebrated the EU's lack of glamour and absence of strong leaders as something positive. (Jean Monet was portrayed as a five-meter-high polystyrene statue, clad in a thin veneer of gold.) The EU's genius lay in the banishing of heroism; that was the main reason to celebrate its success. In less than fifty years it had brought about what centuries of struggle and bloody wars had been unable to accomplish: a single Europe. The only condition was that the unified Europe had to be leaderless. History's resolution was an anticlimax, void of heroes and melodrama. Politics had become a technocratic affair run by bureaucrats. It is no coincidence that Alexandre Kojève, Fukuyama's main muse, served as one himself.

The absence of heroes takes a certain getting used to, and not just in politics. Most of my education had concentrated on modern architecture's heroic period—the focus of my training in both history and design. Now, suddenly, there was no longer a need for such architecture or its heroic impulses. Rooted in intellectual oppositions—in a belief in the possibility of viable alternatives to capitalism—this type of architecture had become outmoded. The battles it had chosen to fight had been resolved; the accomplishment of its mission had made it redundant. History had ruled in its favor, and because of that, history had dismissed it. My education had become irrelevant before I ever had a proper shot at putting it into practice.

I have been in search of a heroic dimension ever since. I think that this goes for most architects my age, and perhaps also for those born in the postheroic age. Perhaps all contemporary professional endeavors can simply be explained as frantic attempts to rediscover this dimension—a romantic longing for the time when architecture made a difference (or thought that it did). "The post-historical period will be characterized by a powerful nostalgia for the time when history did exist."[3] (In this respect, even star architects may have a streak of sincerity.) Still, after the end of history, any hope that one's work can become part of that history must be surrendered. We conduct our work in "extra time," just for the hell of it. From here on, architecture is not important. Let's enjoy it.

It has been a quarter century since Fukuyama's book was first published, and it takes a stretch of the imagination to interpret the current state of the world as "the end of history." If anything, the world seems like a testimony to the inevitability of conflict rather than its resolution. But Fukuyama never said exactly when the end of history would materialize. Like Hegel, whose philosophical inheritance he channels, he categorically separates the realm of ideas from that of the material world. Even if things have clearly crystallized in the former, that doesn't necessarily mean that they are manifest in the latter. Ideas take time to become reality. When Fukuyama writes about "the end of history," he means not mankind's material evolution but its ideological evolution. The end of history arrives not when all material needs are met, but when the whole of humanity comes to the same conclusion about how it ought to be governed—not when we all have the same, but when we all want the same. Fukuyama acknowledges that even when ideological conflicts are overcome, this doesn't mean the end of conflict. In the real world, the synchronization of wills simply creates a situation in which contradictions are replaced by a form of enhanced competition. We overcome our existential struggle, only to see our material struggles intensify.

Still, it is hard to interpret the turmoil of the past two decades as merely the result of enhanced competition. In this respect, Fukuyama distinguishes between "events," on the one hand, and the inevitable course of history, on the other. History is subject to a larger process that operates according to its own laws, independent of daily concerns or "current events." It is precisely here that the essay and the book are as convincing as they are meaningless. The distinction between incidental events, on the one hand, and the inevitable course of history, on the other, creates a convenient format to dismiss as "temporary setbacks" any evidence that contradicts Fukuyama's perceived "end." It seems illogical to think of history as somehow separate from events, particularly since both of Fukuyama's publications were directly fueled by two monumental ones: the fall of the Berlin Wall (the essay) and the collapse of the Soviet Union (the book).

There is a short reference to the material world at the beginning of the essay, but it is hardly convincing. One of the essay's major misconceptions is that despite its dismissal of the material world as a reflection of historic truths, it interprets outward signs of consumerism as the sign of the victory of Western liberal democracy. As evidence, Fukuyama cites color television sets in China, shopping malls in Moscow, and rock music in Tehran. But these phenomena can just as easily be read as evidence of the contrary. The use of modern "Western" gadgets says nothing about the ideology of the people who use them. With the exception of North Korea, a caricature firmly stuck in the 1980s, authoritarian regimes no longer manifest themselves through marching hordes, demagogic speeches, and ruthless propaganda. Instead, they rely on the systematic perversion of consumerist entertainment, fully confident in their command of the repertoire of subtle manipulation that comes with it. Al-Qaeda and ISIS use laptops and smartphones with just as much sophistication as the forces fighting them. Modern technology is simply what it has always been: agnostic, neither for nor against any conviction, just a means to an end. If the universal use of modern technology symbolizes the end of history, it certainly isn't the "happily ever after" Fukuyama would have had us believe it is.

Fukuyama portrays Western liberal democracy as the ideology that triumphed over all others. How accurate is that? To what extent does Western liberal democracy even qualify as an ideology? Liberal democracy, above all, regulates the coexistence of ideologies. Its whole point is to ensure that no single ideology can make a permanent claim to power. Ideology exists only in the plural, ensuring that each ideology cancels out the totalizing implications of the next, and thus, in passing, also its own. All power becomes temporary, subject to regular checks and bureaucratically administered change if needed. For the system to function, democracy has to be agnostic, void of ideology. Liberal democracy is what keeps ideology in check; it is the antithesis of ideology. The entity that presides over the rules of the game cannot also become its content. (In that sense, I have never understood the notion of a "Liberal Democratic Party"—one that quotes the rules of the political process as its end goal.) The only answer to the question of ideology is a tautology: "More democracy."

The idea of liberal democracy described by Fukuyama is different from, for instance, that of the ancient Greek democracy. No longer is politics the space in which ideas are exchanged (by the polis); rather, it becomes a technocratic activity aimed at the neutralization of ideas. After 1945 the main unifying creed of democracy is "Never again!" After the collapse of the Soviet Union in 1991, this creed is accompanied by a sigh of relief. The last major threat had disappeared. In terms of ideology, Fukuyama's liberal democracy is a parasite: it draws from what it would like to dispense. It is defined in the negative, through what it has conquered and now dismisses. Democracy equates itself to freedom, but with the passing of time and the fading of memories, it becomes ever harder to name freedom as a source of legitimacy: freedom from what? The longer one is free, the less freedom constitutes an ideological program. An existential crisis looms around every corner. Democracy becomes a matter of nostalgia for the times when it could not be taken for granted.

In the absence of a clear vision for the future—remember: visions are the domain of ideology, which liberal democracy has now neutralized—the only legitimacy resides in the present moment. Things are good when they work here and now. But how do we know? Only the economy gives daily, measurable updates on how well the system is performing. The economy becomes the de facto measure of political success. Insofar as "liberal" refers to the economic and "democracy" to the political, the pecking order between the two is clear, given the simple sequence of words. It is no coincidence that Fukuyama's ideas, however much he has tried to distance himself, have served to endorse virtually every single neoliberal economic policy since.

To what extent does the term "liberal democracy" constitute a contradiction in terms? Democracy puts power in the hands of the largest number of people; the liberal economy increasingly amounts to the concentration of power in the holders of the largest sums of capital. The equation of democracy and the liberal economy exposes a fundamental friction. When differences increase beyond a certain point—when too much capital is in the hands of too few people—one inevitably turns against the other. Liberal democracy, as advocated by Fukuyama, can function only if at the same time it guarantees a fair distribution of wealth. However, it is precisely the distribution of wealth that the system, given its agnostic nature, has left to chance. It is questionable whether this contradiction can ever be resolved within the confines of liberal democracy.

During the 1990s and the early twenty-first century, in the context of a global economic upturn, it all worked—at least, for a while. Unwittingly and to our amusement, the (then) global currencies spelled the word ¥€$, as if to symbolize a global consensus and collective embrace of liberal democracy and its economic values. Democracy presented itself as a credible ticket to rapid material progress, and no one seriously worried about its ideological foundations.

Problems begin to surface when economic downturn occurs. In the absence of growth, liberal democracy becomes like a sailboat without wind: paralyzed. To stimulate growth or at least control debt, it demands austerity, but in doing that, it can easily fall out of favor with the majority. Its track record from better times doesn't always help. The more democracy claims credit for cyclical economic upturns, the more it is expected to have the answer to the equally cyclical downturns, leaving governments scrambling to implement a trial-and-error policy and hope for the best (witness the Bank of Japan's recent adoption of negative interest rates; who knows what will happen?). Even claiming that democracy creates the conditions for prosperity is risky. Democracy is about fair governance, not about creating wealth. Fairness and wealth are not the same. At some point we may have to choose.

There are periods when the contradiction fades into the background, almost to the point of disappearance, but in no way does this signal its resolution. Even if such a period lasts an entire century, it could still be temporary. Fukuyama interpreted the second half of the twentieth century as the outcome of history's inevitable course, but it could (to retain his terminology) have been merely an "event," a short anomaly in the inevitable historic determinism of capital, which favors the concentration of means over their distribution. The twenty-first century so far, with all its looming asymmetries, once again is demonstrating the real workings of capital. Increasingly, also again, inherited wealth is playing a role in setting people's prospects. After the supposed resolution of class struggle in the twentieth century, a new class distinction is presenting itself in the twenty-first.

In recent years the regimes of Communist countries, as well as those of inherited rule, have operated particularly successfully in the global economy. Not only countries like China and Vietnam but also small city-states such as Dubai and Singapore have systematically outwitted their Western (democratic) competitors. There is increasing evidence that democracy and wealth are separable. Authoritarian rule can deliver what freedom apparently can't. These regimes face little or no opposition, not because their citizens live their lives in the knowledge that any opposition will be fiercely crushed (there is little doubt that it will), but in part because their leaders are perceived to be in control of economic events, which have become a game of chance pretty much everywhere else. Democracy was considered to be the world's ticket to prosperity, but now it appears that there are other tickets that offer shortcuts at a reduced price.

Fukuyama's end of history may largely depend on the course of China, the world's most populous nation. China is no liberal democracy. The Confucian notion of "one country, two systems" doesn't just summarize the country's views regarding free enterprise but reflects its larger conceptual disposition toward ideology as a whole. The past twenty-five years have seen the almost total dismantling of communism as China's principal economic system, starting with the Third Plenum of the Eleventh Central Committee in 1978, followed by Deng Xiaoping's open-door policy, and culminating in China's key role in today's heightened globalized economy. Marxism as an ideological principle has become basically irrelevant, and consumerism is as much a daily reality in China as it is in the West. Still, from Deng onward, Chinese leaders have been much more circumspect in distancing themselves from Communist ideology than, for instance, their Russian colleagues. Today's China may look like a liberal democracy, but even with all the outward symptoms—consumerism, a modern media landscape, metropolitan conditions—firmly in place, power ultimately remains in the hand of a regime whose legitimacy resides in the rejection of liberal democracy's core values. China's attitude is one of conditional approval: the free market is there, but legitimization of its formal status is forever pending. There is the right to consume, but not the regime of political rights that we assume goes with it. In fact, to a large extent, the right to consume replaces political rights, and the market economy serves as the ultimate buyout. The evidence can be seen every day: from currency manipulation to the use of covert import tariffs; from controls on capital outflow to temporary closures of the stock market. Capitalism in China is provisional; all associated rights are indefinitely tentative.

If the validation of Fukuyama's end of history depends on China, the jury will forever remain out. Maybe that's exactly the point: China's position on liberal democracy is one of infinite deferral, an à la carte reading of what is supposed to be an integral concept. Stability is the ideological value that overrides all others, even truth. In regard to the end of history, China exercises its right to remain silent. It neither agrees nor disagrees with Fukuyama. In the absence of a definitive answer, it manages just fine. The end of history can loom, but it must never arrive.

Democratic leaders in the West have been quick to contest the legitimacy of colleagues whose ascent to power has not passed through the "proper" procedures. Many states do not hold elections; more and more states that hold them know the outcome in advance. Just like the free market, democracy has, in many places, become a simulacrum. During the early days of Russian democracy, an array of political parties sprang up. An interesting confusion of language occurred in the naming of these parties. The political mission of the Liberal Democratic Party of Vladimir Zhirinovsky, the restoration of Russian pride through use of military force (including the reannexation of East Germany), was neither liberal nor democratic: a perfect example of the ironic twist Russia tends to give to Western values. Still, it is too simplistic to assume that the absence of the vote alone, or even the rigging of votes—why do we condemn the second more than the first?—is what puts unwanted people in power. In Dubai, if elections were held, the country's ruler would win by a comfortable, if not overwhelming, majority. Even with all election fraud retroactively undone, Putin would still be Russia's legitimate president; China's leaders are endorsed by more people than live in the whole of Germany.

This type of simulated or "managed" democracy is a tempting alternative, not only for authoritarian states that need a fig leaf to allow them to participate on the global stage but also for established democracies to embrace, sliding back into authoritarian mode at the first sign of trouble.[4] Curbing free media and infiltrating and ultimately eliminating opposition: these are now part of everyday practice even in states considered respectable democracies until recently. Italy managed to get rid of Berlusconi (only just), but Putin still serves as a role model for Erdogan's Turkey, Duda's Poland, Orban's Hungary, Netanyahu's Israel, and possibly Trump's United States.

The disastrous Arab Spring was a lesson in failure for peoples still contemplating ousting their authoritarian leaders in hope of a better, more democratic future. The next big political battle will be fought over the question whether the pursuit of democracy is really worth the trouble. Cumulatively, the Arab Spring has produced a degree of instability that now threatens even established democracies outside the Middle East. If bloodshed is the inverse measure of success, a large part of the world is worse off for following the promise of democracy. Ultimately, the ousting of dictators in the name of freedom has only enhanced the nostalgia for the stability of dictatorial rule.

More than fifteen years into the new millennium, the end of the Cold War and its two competing ideologies has not led to the world's adherence to a single idea. Rather, it has led to the reemergence of long-forgotten feuds. Since the fall of the Berlin Wall and the drawing back of the Iron Curtain, the world has seen a proliferation of new walls, both real and intangible: between Israel and Palestine, between the United States and Mexico, between East and West, between rich and poor. In 2016, in response to the Syrian refugee crisis, certain EU member states announced their intention to reinstate border controls, which had been abolished since 1992 (the year Fukuyama's book was published). Within the EU and even inside its member states, secession movements have become rife: the United Kingdom has voted to leave the EU, Marine Le Pen wants France to follow, many Scots want to leave the United Kingdom, and Catalonia is led by a party that wants to leave Spain. Today, the world seems very different from the one Fukuyama had predicted: not a single homogeneous state but a globalized Balkans.

The only universal consensus seems to be the collective embrace of bad taste by those who have done well because of globalization. Whether it is the new rich of Russia, China, India, the Middle East, or the United States, they all seem united in their embrace of lavish marble, chandeliers, and ironmongery clad in twenty-four-karat gold. Contrary to what might be expected, this embrace has not spelled the end of modernism as a style. Quite the opposite: even if the language of big money is the style of Donald Trump, modern architecture remains the flavor of choice of the intellectual elite. Since 1991 it has made a resurgence, sweeping away the more historical focus of the postmodernist 1980s, led by figures such as Aldo

Rossi and Léon Krier. Modern architecture's popularity seems to be strangely at odds with the supposed irrelevance of its earlier mission. Is this the extra lap of victory, permitted after achieving its goals? The ultimate sign that modern architecture is now consigned to a recyclable history? Another form of postmodernism?

During the 1990s and the early twenty-first century, our office expanded from 35 people to its current size of 350. From a single office in Rotterdam, we opened offices in New York, Hong Kong, Beijing, Doha, and Dubai, working on over a hundred projects concurrently in over thirty-five countries. Our office globalized both its portfolio and the composition of our staff: more than forty-five nationalities at any given time. The Dutch are a minority in Rotterdam, as are Americans in New York, the Chinese in Hong Kong, and Arabs in Dubai. We work in the whole world, and the whole world works in our office. We are globalization. Our collective language is (bad) English.

Fukuyama's prediction suggested that after global expansion it would be only a matter of time before the same conditions applied universally. An office like ours, which made the conscious decision to become a global practice in the 1990s, did so partly under the assumption that we could compete on a level playing field in different countries. Today it finds itself having to reconcile a global presence with the absence of globally applicable truths. We find ourselves stuck in highly diverse conditions. As architects, we once thought that we could simply export out knowledge and tell the rest of the world how to proceed; we now find our knowledge of limited value. A profession accustomed to operate with authority no longer encounters conditions where it can operate with authority. Its truths, which it thought were universal, encounter a discordant world that at best agrees to disagree. Twenty-five years ago the apparent truth of Fukuyama's position rendered the implementation of architectural ideology useless; today his misgivings ironically do the same thing.

Fukuyama is still out there. During the past two decades he has spent the better part of his time repudiating events that contradict his predicted "end of history." His position has shifted since the early 1990s, but the subject of his search has remained unchanged. His current preoccupation is Denmark, a small country in northern Europe, which he elevates to the status of a global blueprint.

In January 2016, amidst the Syrian refugee crisis, there was an article in the *Guardian* about Denmark: its government had secured a parliamentary majority in favor of legislation curbing the rights of refugees.[5] Upon arrival, refugees would be forced to give up their valuables in order to pay for their accommodation while applying for asylum. If Fukuyama is right this time, and Denmark is where the end of history can be found—the ideal, homogeneous state in which all human needs have been met—perhaps it is worth noting that it arrived there not through a resolution of mankind's struggles, but by carefully keeping them at bay.

West Berliners peering through the Berlin Wall, 1986
Keystone / Hulton Archive Collection / Getty Images

25

The Other Truth

History is written by those who emerge victorious. The legacy of those who don't is dependent on the goodwill of the ones left standing and whatever eulogies they are prepared to deliver.

A quarter century after the fall of the Berlin Wall, it is as though a large part of the twentieth century never happened. An entire period has been erased from public consciousness, almost like a blank frame in a film. The dissolution of the former Eastern Bloc has been entirely attributed to forces in the West, while the role of the East has largely been forgotten. The free-market economy was and is presumed to be history's inevitable course—our collective manifest destiny. After the rollback of postwar constraints on the free market in the West in the 1980s, it was only a matter of time before it would engulf the East too.

How accurate is this account of events? Those of us old enough to have witnessed the fall of the wall mostly remember the overwhelming sense of surprise, the worries that the West was not quite ready for this. After all, Reagan's call for Gorbachev to "tear down this wall" a few years earlier had been uttered in the firm conviction that he never would. When he did, the act was largely met with disbelief.

Those who had built the wall now demolished it. There was no denying the fact that the dissolution of the East was at least partially fomented by the East—not just through the removal of the wall but also through pressure for reform from within, coupled with crucial proposals for disarmament. It was predominantly this reform that triggered that famous moment of November 1989. Decades later, this historical telling—one the remaining powers have never been particularly keen to emphasize—has almost completely faded into the background. Even the official historical terminology embodies a curious misnomer: the wall did not "fall"; it was torn down.

Today the construction and the demolition of the Berlin Wall feel like events contained within parentheses: whatever is written in between can be removed without fundamentally altering the course of the narrative. The twenty-eight years leading up to 1989 are now widely perceived as time that passed between one pointless act and another. (If you don't build walls, you don't have to tear them down, the logic goes.) But how much historic license can be claimed in viewing recent history as expendable subtext? What other periods should we pretend never happened and dismiss as undesirable deviations from the politically correct outcome? The Berlin Wall was constructed in 1961; the Red Army took Berlin in 1945; the USSR declared war on Nazi Germany in 1941; the October Revolution took place in 1917; Karl Marx and Friedrich Engels launched *The Communist Manifesto* in 1848. How far back do we need to go? How much of history can we regard as an aberration? Where do we insert the opening parenthesis? Twenty-five years ago? Half a century? A century? More?

Before the "fall" of the Berlin Wall, the East had been the home of a parallel narrative that spanned half the globe, with its own interpretation of history, a different philosophical disposition from "economic inevitability," and its own version of the truth. In the East, the wall was portrayed not as a symbol of oppression but as a form of protection—an "antifascist protection rampart" to defend a real democratic system, one acting on behalf of the people, against outside aggression. As a teenager growing up in Western Europe, surfing FM frequencies on the radio, I would sometimes hear the broadcasts of Radio Moscow, transmitted from East Berlin. I remember being mesmerized by its creative interpretations of the truth—or at least the truth as I had come to view it through the Western media. I would hear the same news facts, the same events with the same cast of characters, but they were all embedded in a completely different discourse, invariably relaying the opposing view with an entirely different and almost always inverse notion of victims and perpetrators.

My life so far can be divided into roughly equal halves: half with the wall, half without. I am old enough to remember the ideological context of its existence but young enough to have a vested interest in its absence. For me, it remains an open question whether the existence of two parallel systems may have served a real purpose beyond leading to the eventual disappearance of one of them. Despite the ongoing threat of an all-out confrontation between the two blocs, the West seemed a less harsh, more humane place than it does today, particularly to those struggling to keep up in an ever more intense economic rat race. In retrospect, it is not far-fetched to interpret the welfare state, as it historically existed in Western Europe during the 1960s and 1970s—with labor movements, minimum wages, and social provisions—as a kind of preemptive action against this "other truth," a way of preventing it, indeed, from becoming the only truth.

Today, even though the wall is gone, the divide between East and West persists, only this time the divide is not strictly ideological but between rich and poor, between opportunity and its absence. This is often explained as the economic legacy of forty years of Communist rule, a scar that will heal with time, but as time passes, that position seems increasingly untenable. It appears that the asymmetries produced by an uncontested and unchallenged capitalist system are as significant as the asymmetry created by the former ideological conventions of West and East. The physical wall that once separated the German people seems to have been replaced by an intangible wall (and one that isn't limited to Germany): a default inequality that is no longer subject to any political will, either of the Left or the Right, to remedy its effects.

Much of the twentieth century was dominated by ideological oppositions rooted in highly politicized historical determinism. But if the course of history is dialectic, what follows? Does the twenty-first century mark the absence of ideology, of the political? Consensus by way of amnesia? We no longer hold a regard for the grand social experiments of the last century; we recognize their failure and move on. Through forgetting, we hope to avoid repeating the past and with it, the chance of new failures. Yet in dismissing these experiments as aberrations, we also forgo the nature of their deeper quest—the issues that they, for better or for worse, tried to address.

Somehow the unification of Berlin and the end of the wall granted history a premature sense of closure—the demolition of built structures tends to do that—a happily ever after that may not materialize any time soon. Historical narratives crave a degree of definitiveness that history can never acquire, a desire that condemns us to proceed on the basis of half-truths that we take for the whole truth, so help us God.

In a campaign speech during the 2008 U.S. presidential primaries, candidate Barack Obama quoted William Faulkner: "The past is never dead; in fact, it isn't even past." At the time he was talking about the history of racial relations in the United States. Today, over twenty-five years after the momentous events of 1989, the sentiment seems every bit as true for global relations. In November 2014, ironically coinciding with celebrations in Berlin to mark the quarter century since 1989, the Russian Ministry of Defense voiced its intention to resume patrols of long-range bombers in the Gulf of Mexico. As the West proceeds on the basis of its half-truths, the East seems increasingly set on claiming its own half-truths. We eradicate the time before 1989; it eradicates the time since. It seems that in the end nothing is unilateral, not even the erasure of history.

26

Socialist in Content, Realist in Form

"You like it?"

"Thank you, it means a lot to me!"

The commissar is clearly pleased. The Russian pavilion at the Venice Architecture Biennale is a work of great care and ambition. It is dedicated to the 1935–1939 VDNKh, the Stalin-commissioned open-air exhibition park in Moscow, intended for Soviet republics and regions to show off their latest advances in agriculture, technology, and culture.

In the context of the 2016 Architecture Biennale's theme—*Reporting from the Front*, largely an ostentatious attempt to prove that architects may have a social conscience after all—the Russian show is a bit of an oddity. In rehabilitating the architectural ambitions of Russia's most vilified leader, it reports from a different, somewhat less politically correct front. The exhibition's commissar is one of the few Russian intellectuals to have spoken out in favor of Russia's policy on Ukraine, and thus he has replaced the previous commissar whose active journalistic work (against) prevented him from fully devoting himself to the project.

The exhibition in no uncertain terms serves to embellish Russia's former (and, by implication, current) greatness. Modern Russia, it seems, wastes no opportunity, not even one as superficial as the Venice Architecture Biennale, to make its point, which can be summarized as "Don't look for apologies—not for Russia's past, nor for its present actions." Russia is where it belongs: as a major player on the global stage. Love it or leave it.

The gathering inside the pavilion is a curious reunion of characters encountered while executing projects in Russia: a mix of foreigners insistently in search of opportunities in Russia and Russians eager to salvage international relations against ever-increasing odds. The Architecture Biennale presents the perfect occasion to patch things up. Representatives of the British pavilion, located next door, make their entry. Bewildered by the pavilion's impressively charged content, they are eager to receive an explanation—an eagerness happily satisfied by the commissar, who enthusiastically embarks on a meticulous explanation of architecture in the former USSR.

1931–1932: Forces marshaled by Stalin ensure that Boris Lofan's Palace of the Soviets wins the state-sponsored design competition, beating Le Corbusier, Mendelsohn, and Gropius. Stalin himself leads the competition's jury. His preferences regarding the architectural style of the proposals are given top priority.[1]

The battle between the avant-garde constructivists and the so-called academic architects has been raging since the founding of the Soviet Union: the architect of Lenin's mausoleum, built in 1924 on Red Square, is none other than Aleksey Shchusev, the architect also of the ornate pavilion built by tsarist Russia in Venice's Giardini di Biennale 1914. The search for a national style isn't a simple process, but it had a singular outcome, a singular policy that lasts until Stalin's death. Under Stalin's economic policy of "Socialism in One Country," the USSR becomes more inward looking; the internationalist avant-garde comes to be regarded not only with suspicion but also as a threat to the revolution. In 1930 the Central Executive Committee of the Communist Party releases the following criticism of the avant-garde.

> *It is impossible suddenly to overcome obstacles that are centuries old, the fruit of the cultural and economic backwardness of society. Yet this is the system implicit in these unrealizable and Utopian plans for the construction, at state expense, of new cities based on the total collectivization of living, including collective provisioning, collective care of children, the prohibition of private kitchens. The hasty realization of such schemes, Utopian and doctrinaire, which take no account of the material resources of our country and of the limits within which the people, with their set habits and preferences, can be prepared for them, could easily result in considerable losses and could also discredit the basic principles of the Socialist reconstruction of society.*[2]

In 1932 the Seventeenth Conference of the Communist Party sets out "that within five years, socialism must be achieved within every sphere of Soviet life." Rather than a material goal, what this means is that all artistic and aesthetic content, as well as all stages of architectural production, is to come under complete state control and direction.[3] In the same year, the famed OSA (Association of Contemporary Architects, which counts among its members Moysey Ginzburg and the brothers Aleksandr, Leonid, and Viktor Vesnin), ASNOVA (Association of New Architects), and all other architectural and artistic associations are disbanded. The architects' only choice is to become members of the Stalin-approved Union of Soviet Architects, founded that same year.[4]

The period that follows can be defined only as a search for style or, rather, for stylistic parameters in which architecture can operate across the vast Soviet empire. In 1933 *Architektura SSSR*, the state's architecture journal, states that "Soviet architecture must strive for realistic criteria—for clarity and precision of its images, which must be easily comprehensible and accessible to the masses."[5] It isn't until 1934, however, that the official arts policy to be carried out under Stalin is formulated by the politician and general Andrei Zhdanov at a literary convention:

> *In our country the main heroes of works of literature are the active builders of a new life—working men and women, men and women collective farmers, Party members, business managers, engineers, members of the Young Communist League, Pioneers. Such are the chief types and the chief heroes of our Soviet literature. . . . Our Soviet literature is strong by virtue of the fact that it serves a new cause—the cause of socialist construction.[6]*

Another frequently cited quote, often falsely attributed to Stalin but in fact uttered by the painter Aleksandr Gerasimov in 1939, is probably the most succinct and also the most bewildering on the topic of a national style: "Socialist realism is what is Socialist in content and national in form."[7]

The application of this style to architecture implied the return of decoration to buildings—with sculptures, reliefs, and paintings—together with the production of a built form that is monumental, axial, classically composed, and therefore legible. All architectural output during Stalin's era is conducted under this banner, from metro stations to Moscow's 1935 master plan, with its wide ring roads and monumental radial avenues, and to the district of the 1935–1939 VDNKh Exhibition of Achievements of the National Economy. Originally established as the All-Union Agricultural Exhibition, the exhibition grounds provide space for the various architects favored by the party to demonstrate the different modes of architectural representation for each region of the USSR within a cohesive, self-contained, and monumental urban ensemble.

This architecture is easily compared to the methods of late nineteenth-century Beaux-Arts eclectics. The pavilions are always symmetrical and classically laid out. Then, a certain genre of style is chosen, preferably one that has a historic resonance with what it represents (an Islamic dome for the Kazakhstani pavilion; a stripped neoclassicism for the Leningrad pavilion; a heavily decorated Russian-style encampment for the Ukraine pavilion). Other desirable appliqués, such as statues of miners, kolkhoz women and other agricultural workers, cornucopias, hammers and sickles, and heavy machinery, appear wherever appropriate. Nikita Khrushchev is one of the commissars entrusted with overseeing the execution of Stalin's proletarian fairground.

After the heavy devastation suffered by the USSR during World War II, and with urbanization reaching ever-higher levels, the necessarily slow pace of the ornate Stalinist style of construction can no longer keep up with the needs of an aspiring superpower. Stylistic change from Stalinist parameters, however, does not occur wholly peacefully. Although research groups within the architectural establishment are already investigating the possibilities of prefabrication, it is impossible to align these with the prevailing aesthetic guidelines laid down by Stalin. Until his death in March 1953, everything remains business as usual.

On December 7, 1954, Nikita Khrushchev, the new leader of the Soviet Union, gives a speech at the All-Union Congress of Builders in which he outlines measures meant to increase the productivity of the Soviet building industry.

> A common feature of construction in this country is wastage of resources, and for this a large part of the blame rests with the many architects who use architectural superfluities to decorate buildings built to one-off designs. Such architects are a stumbling block in the way of industrializing construction. In order to build quickly and successfully, we must use standard designs in our building, but this is evidently not to the taste of certain architects. . . .
>
> If an architect wants to be in step with life, he must know and be able to employ not only architectural forms, ornaments, and various decorative elements, but also new progressive materials, reinforced-concrete struc-

*tures and parts, and, above all, must be an expert in cost-saving in con-
struction. And this is what comrade Mordvinov and many of his colleagues have been criticized for at the conference—for forgetting about
the main thing, i.e. the cost of a square meter of floor area, when designing a building and for, in their fascination with unnecessary embellishment of facades, allowing a great number of superfluities.*

*The facades of residential buildings are sometimes hung with a
multitude of all kinds of superfluous decoration that point to a lack of
taste in the architects. Builders sometimes even have difficulty executing
these decorations.*[8]

From that day onward, Soviet and Soviet-bloc architecture will be
dominated by the principles of prefabricated modernism. Later in his
speech, Khrushchev even praises East Germany's facing tiles and Czecho-
slovakia's fine construction materials and suggests that Soviet architects
and engineers can learn from the experts of other countries if necessary—a break with Stalinist rhetoric, which ended international influ-
ences on Soviet architecture. The old-style avant-garde—a contradiction
in terms—is back in charge. From the mid-1950s to the early 1990s, the
USSR and its allies develop and refine a catalog of prefabricated parts and
typologically standardized buildings suited to every imaginable purpose,
which can be built everywhere within its borders.

With intentions similar to those of Stalin's wedding-cake architectural
ensemble at the VDNKh, Khrushchev masterminds his own grand
project, Novy Arbat Avenue, which starts in 1962. The six-lane road cuts
through the older, denser tissue of the Arbat district, west of Moscow's
inner city. In Khrushchev's approved scheme, tall, repetitive, and un-
adorned office towers flank the wide thoroughfare, reminiscent of the
high modernism of Le Corbusier or Hilberseimer. The Khrushchev era
sees its own additions to the VDNKh park, celebrating technological optimism, which is enshrined in pavilions to geology, medical science, the
chemical industry (which extolled the virtues of polyethylene), and,
memorably, atomic energy for peaceful purposes. Notable for their stylistic difference, many of Khrushchev's modifications to the VDNKh see
the defacement of former ornaments—shearing off decorative friezes,
baubles, and entranceways and replacing them with a mechanistic, if not
brutal, use of concrete, steel scaffolding, and even aluminum—continuing

an early twentieth-century enthusiasm for progress and industrialized efficiency.

It is perhaps telling that with the rise of authoritarian and conservative tendencies in today's Russia, the VDNKh is made the subject of the Russian pavilion at the 2016 Venice Architecture Biennale. More telling still is the complete omission of buildings from the Khrushchev and later eras from the presentation of the VDNKh's narrative as it is told in Venice. Stalin-sanctioned exuberance is the curators' exclusive focus of celebration; it is as if there have been literally no interruptions to service between then and now. The exhibition's rhetoric manages to elide the overt politicization of architecture, but it nevertheless presents the old Soviet ornaments and trinkets in a thoroughly choreographed and bombastic way. If history is anything to go by, Novy Arbat might need to wait only a few decades for its own redacted rehabilitation.

It is late in the evening. The commissar has managed to get himself invited to the dinner in honor of the British pavilion's opening (a clumsy attempt at restoring Russian-UK relations?). Seated at a remote end of the table, he makes an effort to engage in animated conversation with his only neighbor, continuing the explanation of Soviet architecture he started in the pavilion. He is cautiously tolerated but otherwise politely ignored.

When it is time to pay, guests notice his empty seat and unfinished dessert. The waiter indicates to the host that there is no need to hand over her credit card. The bill has been taken care of.

The Descendant

A Conversation with Xenia Adjoubei, Nikita Khrushchev's Great-Granddaughter

In 1914 Nikita Sergeyevich Khrushchev, later the first secretary of the Communist Party and head of the USSR, married his wife, Nina, with whom he had five children: Julia, Leonid, Sergei, Elena, and Rada. Rada, the youngest of his three daughters, married Alexei Adjoubei, later the editor-in-chief of the official government daily newspaper, *Izvestia*. Rada and Alexei had three sons; the oldest, named after his father, became a biophysicist in London, where he married Svetlana, an art historian and the current director of Academica Rossica. Their daughter, Xenia, currently teaches and practices as an architect in London and Moscow.

RdG: There's no way to write about twentieth-century architecture without writing about Khrushchev.

XA: I'm no professional historian.

RdG: Neither am I, so we're a perfect match. I would like to get your take on your great-grandfather because he features in my writing. I have a curious mix of horror and admiration for his approach. I'd like to know your view on him. Not only as a person your age but as somebody with a bloodline to him. Did he factor at all in your decision to become an architect?

XA: Perhaps subconsciously. I thought that I wanted to do something creative, but it had to be functional, because I couldn't live with the idea of being so egocentric as to become an artist. I definitely subscribed to the view that architecture was a functional art form: I suppose this may have come from some of the thinking that Khrushchev propagated.

RdG: Is he discussed in your family? Does he have a presence beyond 1964 [when he was deposed]?

XA: It was an absolutely normal thing to talk about in my family; we weren't particularly traumatized, and also my grandfather Alexei was very close with him. He was an unofficial aide, so they went on many trips together, especially to the United States. My grandfather was a journalist, so it was easy for him to get press access to international trips. Once or twice they went to the White House to see the Kennedys, just my grandma and Alexei on their own as unofficial representatives. Those were the kinds of things we talked about; the liberalization, the thaw and these international trips, because he was the most well-travelled leader up until that point and perhaps even in the history of the Communist Party.

RdG: How do you view that period? I have worked in Russia, and to me it seems to me that intellectuals in the West are much more obsessed with the Soviet Union and communism than any of the contemporary Russians. They have been keen to forget; we have been keen to remind them. Where would you position yourself?

XA: To a large extent, I have a perspective from the outside. I grew up in the UK, went through all my education and my adult life here, which puts me in a very good position as an observer. I end up being shocked at lots of things, including public perception and selective blindness, or ignoring very important cultural legacies and signifiers, and I would agree with you that it's still the case [that people choose to forget]. But it's also difficult because Khrushchev's rule happened over a transitional period. To me, that's more fascinating, because it's always on the cusp of whenever change is about to start happening, that history—and certainly the history of architecture and design—is at its most interesting. So the things that he put in motion—for example, the enormous scale of his industrial building program that came to fruition much later—his time in power only ever saw the start of that. He can therefore be blamed for a lot more than he was actually responsible for.

RdG: It's almost always easier to blame people after a mission has been accomplished and the good things have been reaped as rewards. One of the things I've found out by doing my research on this, both in Germany and in Russia, is that there was a huge amount of devastation and a housing crisis after the war. The rebuilding program was rather ruthless and efficient—these two often go hand in hand—as a way of dealing with crisis. In East Germany, the figures indicate that the system solved these problems—before the system collapsed, that is. After, it's easy to say: "Oh, but it's so gruesome," or "Oh, but it's all the same." But that's a perspective you can only take today, when the problems no longer persist in the same way.

XA: As you started by saying, it's astounding to see the amount of time that has passed. The situation then was indeed that of a horrific housing crisis; in Russia, the population balance between rural and urban areas had tipped over 50:50 by 1955. That was truly a breaking point for cities; of course a lot of families were living in communal apartments. The standard was one family—actually, in 40 percent of the cases even two or more families—to a room, so in that context, the response was the prototype Khrushchyovka buildings, which took about fifteen days to erect. There were two typologies initially: the temporary and the permanent ones. The temporary ones had a projected lifespan of 25 years and the permanent ones had a 50-year life span, which has now been certified up to 150 years. Today, 10 percent of all housing stock in Russia consists of Khrushchyovka.

RdG: If you take the original planned lifespan of 50 years, and the bulk was built in the early sixties, that means that right now, about 10 percent of Russian housing stock is obsolete. . . .

XA: I think this approach was actually very utopian and had a positive view of the future. In terms of resources, these buildings were very economical and they were designed to last either 25 or 50 years.

RdG: Were they also designed as intentionally temporary—implying that a more lasting solution would present itself over the course of this time?

XA: Yes.

RdG: In East Germany there was very much this lineage to the *Plattenbauten*. What were the permutations that the Khrushchyovka spawned? I assume that the 10 percent of the housing stock today only refers to the initial types, and that there is a significant percentage that descends from them.

XA: Absolutely. It expands and expands with every iteration. I'm not an expert on the types, but every generation of buildings was made better, more resilient, and of course taller, with the help of lifts. The revolutionary thing about the Khrushchyovka was that originally, they were built to the maximum height you could have without needing a lift, so they were very cheap to construct and could be built everywhere. In the seventies and eighties they just get taller and taller. Blocks get bigger too. It's a parallel world to East Germany. Khrushchev apartments were a new concept for people who never had apartments before. They came with little information booklets about what you could do in your apartment. They also affected regulations: in Russia we now have requirements, which specify the minimum amount of sunlight entering every bedroom, because UV light clears the air. So the brochures were also about how to enjoy their new space: it's about space, it's about light, it should be hygienic, it should be bright, it should be healthy. They had to warn people not to bring their own furniture from the communal flats because it simply wouldn't fit in the door. So there was this idea—as well as the reality—that it had to be all-new furniture, it was like your first TV, your first vacuum cleaner. There was the famous kitchen debate between Khrushchev and Nixon, at the American International Exhibition in 1959 in Moscow, about the progress of home appliances. And that reminds me of IKEA catalogues and how IKEA has this particular way of selling you this particular lifestyle, one which nobody can really have. Very few people actually find themselves moving into a newly built apartment.

RdG: I grew up in a four-story block, built by the same French firm that lent its expertise to Russia; it didn't need a lift and was built around the same time period that we've been discussing. What interests me is your mention of this "tipping point" in Russian history, with a population that was 50 percent urban, 50 percent rural. Now the whole world is 50 percent urban, 50 percent rural. So fifty years later, the world at large is in the same situation. And there are still large parts of the world that face a housing crisis and rapid urbanization, much more acutely than either the building industry and the financial system can deal with. When I read about these things, I have a lingering feeling—and the West is often quick to dismiss this—that this is a past that isn't really over.

XA: But it's also a past that didn't turn into the future that it promised.

RdG: There is another aspect that I found absolutely fascinating: architects designed systems rather than buildings. A curious disappearance of the architect as a master builder, and instead their reappearance as a civil servant. Their creations saw the light of day as serial numbers, like the license plates of cars. Particularly today, when architects are either insignificant or celebrated like rock stars, there is a particular burden on architecture with regard to authorship and signature. There has always been a tension between declaring architecture either an art or a science, and to some extent, this was the pressure that was applied in that period, making Ernst Neufert almost the only worthwhile architect for them. Do you recognize that?

XA: It shouldn't be underestimated in the history of the Eastern Bloc, because it was a horrific blow to the beautiful art of architecture. These architects were turned into mechanized composers of drawings that were completely prescribed by regulations and by a set of variables. This seems a regular occurrence in architecture. Architects have an urge for self-destruction and self-annihilation, especially when faced with technology. It's particularly obvious with students, who seem curiously fascinated trying to do projects deliberately in denial of the potentials of architecture. It seems to be the zenith of their efforts.

RdG: A lot of Bauhaus members went to Russia to flee Nazism, when Khrushchev was still an army officer. Ideas of industrial efficiency and replication took root and formed the basis for these formula-based ideas. If you look at what Mies was saying at the time, you could argue that he actually performed his whole disappearing act—if you compare his later work to his earlier work—only after he moved to America. It was part of his aesthetic search for the objective, which surpasses any trace of an author. Mies fantasized that once industrialization had run its full course, it would become an automated system, wholly independent of authors. Even if you read some of Patrik Schumacher's contemporary writings on parametric systems; there is a curious pursuit embedded in the discipline, whereby the ultimate consequence of the search for the objective is a deposition of the author. You could argue that the process that Khrushchev started, carried through to its full conclusion, demonstrates the consequences of a deliberately artistic avant-garde position.

XA: If you look at it that way it's a very pure and practical expression of a philosophical concept. And it's fascinating how, in constructivism, they were obsessed with formulaic production of ideal living quarters, which they also organized in types: it wasn't only to do with minimal surface area but also with volume, with lighting conditions, all of which led to masterpieces such as Narkomfin. These values are at the root of this idea, that every human being and every family deserves an apartment of their own; these are the minimum standards and minimum combinations you can provide for this kind of family, in terms of standardization. It began with strange experiments that had very beautiful results, whether in constructivism, or in projects like Le Corbusier's Unité. As to the question of how relevant it is today, with regard to parametricism and the robotizing of architecture . . . if you look at it that way, it can be read as quite a Communist idea! There was another attempt at dissolving the author from a very different socialist perspective, by people like William Morris, for example. It was a very different approach, but with very similar aims: he said that nothing was too good for the working man, which was equally the slogan of the Khrushchev era, and Morris similarly waged a war against superfluous decoration and overcomplication of objects and buildings, which had previously been made by hand, by craftsmen. Morris's idea was that the artisan, the craftsman, and the architect would unite in autonomous, anonymous communities. He was a socialist, so he was primarily concerned with the working classes in a rapidly industrializing British countryside. His idea was that people took pride in their labor and got a lot of happiness and satisfaction by being craftsmen. He also saw a future without architects, but through the reinstatement of the hand and through the triumph of craft over industrialization. We are left with these two camps that are opposed to each other, even in agreement; one believes that architecture and construction can be merged together much more than now, while the other puts emphasis on the physical contact with the way things are made and the materials they are made of, because it is essential to being human. . . .

RdG: And so labor becomes a fundamental right, in addition to housing.

XA: Because of course Khrushchev destroyed the notions of craftsman-ship and trade. . . .

RdG: And the consequences are still apparent when one tries to build in Russia.

XA: And that's why it's so important to reinstate skills in places like Russia, and maybe China to a certain extent as well. These days, the blocks that were built in the 1960s and 1970s are being demolished across Europe, leaving even more tasteless architecture and little houses built in their place. It's the same thing, just spread out. . . . They're all the same little houses that don't involve architects in their conception, they're made by developers.

RdG: The housing sector, particularly in the Netherlands—a notoriously stingy country when it comes to spending money on buildings—has a concrete prefabrication component which is extremely adept at developing standardized parts. Once you strip away the facade and analyze the construction system, they are always made of a limited number of parts. I'm sure that practice is very similar to that of the East Bloc. The differences between the East and the West are far smaller than one would one imagine. I remember reading all 17,000 words of Khrushchev's speech from the 1954 National Conference for Builders. It's a sort of stand-up comedy, where he ridiculed and mentioned some of Stalin's protégés and made them look like fools. Stalinist architecture is dismissed as completely wasteful. But if you look at popular opinion in Moscow now, the real estate that is appreciated is the Stalinist stuff, and the period after seems to be completely dismissed. That seems to coincide with recent laws which effectively prevent the possibility to really criticize Stalin anymore. Do you think there is a relation between prevailing political strands and the type of architecture that is in favor? Do you think there might be a political motive behind or invested in the demands of the real estate market?

XA: Do you mean is there an aim to re-create Stalinist architecture?

RdG: Not so much, but I find it a bizarre coincidence that overall, the re-appreciation of Stalinist architecture follows a decree by Putin, which prevents any negative discussion around Stalin as a figure. I initially thought it was an understandable form of postmodernism: that Russia didn't need to build postmodernism if you already had it at hand from the 1950s, in which light the country was curiously a step ahead. One of the Seven Sisters makes better real estate sense than an anonymous block, but these shifts in preferences seem to coincide with, rather than mirror, the shift in politics.

XA: You're absolutely right on both accounts. Stalin is going through a mild rehabilitation; well, not even mild. Apart from that, there have been large developments constructed in neo-Stalinist style lately, in the University District in particular, which is absolutely terrifying to somebody who reads history in a visual way. Stalinist names are being reinstated in metro stations, as of two or three years ago. The barriers to Stalinism are being removed; it's becoming OK to be a Stalinist— especially for young people, who have no baggage or family history to avoid. And it is becoming a political move, a very conscious one.

RdG: I wonder, are there any Khrushchyovka that have become particularly popular for buyers?

XA: More young people are becoming interested in Khrushchyovka as a phenomenon, especially the "real" or early ones. If you see the blocks today, they are drowning in greenery; the trees have grown taller than the buildings. They are often in a quite central location in Moscow, because of the subsequent expansion of the city. This puts them in a very good position and in a very unique, desirable environment. The same problems endure, in terms of the poor building techniques and sound insulation—the heat insulation is not good either—but there is a rekindling in the interest and appreciation for these first instances of the Khrushchyovka. But these moments are unique to where modernist blocks have not been demolished and where the greenery has been left to mature to the proportions found in Le Corbusier's sketches. Maybe we're just going through a period where we're being spoilt by the investment that was done in the twentieth century, in the name of our social protection and equality in our city. I don't know if you know this, but Khrushchev was one of the people in charge of the first phase of the Moscow Metro, built under Stalin. And he always praised Stalin for this project, because he felt it was an impactful and unparalleled insertion into the infrastructure of Moscow. When he came to power, his ruling to rid Moscow of superfluous decoration in architecture also extended to the metro; he had documents set up on how to build and how not to build stations, along with all the possible typologies. He extended the radial lines to the new residential districts he was building and developed typologies of metro stations that worked like transport hubs, connecting to overground transport, which was innovative at the time. And this is another example of enormously generous public and social infrastructure that no one has really attempted over the last fifty years.

RdG: I never realized that; I always thought that was all Stalin. Hearing you say this, I begin to wonder how much of the Stalinist metro is actually Khrushchev's metro. . . . The extension of the radial lines to the new quarters, with different types of stations that embody a revision and a comment on the architecture of previous stations.

XA: You probably already know a lot of Khrushchev stations; they're elegant and very pared down, but they're still marble and have wonderful proportions. They're some of the simplest stations but have a lot of beauty to them.

But I would like to ask you, Reinier, in the context of this conversation: what do you think is the biggest loss in the achievements of the twentieth century?

RdG: I worry that in the course of the twenty-first century, a lot of the things that we simply assumed were done, were accomplished, and now take for granted—our acquired rights and emancipatory standards— will once again become exclusive. I always believed that the twentieth century, despite all the wars, bloodshed, and terror, was the outcome of a long evolution. But increasingly, the twentieth century looks like a historical anomaly. That can mean two things: either you have to aspire towards its ideals more aggressively, or you simply resign to the fact that this period was an exception, simply too good to be true. My major worry is that from a sociological perspective, 2100 might look dangerously like 1900.

28

Undesirable Work Styles

October 15, 2014: Chinese president Xi Jinping addresses an artists' and writers' symposium in Beijing. The transcript of the entire speech at the China Art Festival is not made available to the general public. Snippets of the transcribed speech pieced together online suggest that Xi is broadly referring to art and literature, and not to architecture specifically.

> *Socialist culture and art is, in essence, the culture and art of the people. The creation of art can fly with the wings of imagination . . . but make sure art workers tread on solid earth.*

This is not the first time that a Chinese leader defers to the country's proletariat as the object, inspiration, and leading arbiter for art and culture; Mao Zedong did the same as early as 1942, saying: "There is in fact no such thing as art for art's sake, art that stands above classes, art that is detached from or independent of politics." Mao echoed Stalin's announcement of socialist realism as the official style of all Soviet artistic (and architectural) output. Xi expounds further:

> *Fine art works should be like sunshine from blue sky and breeze in spring that will inspire minds, warm hearts, cultivate taste and clean up undesirable work styles. [Communist Party of China committees need to] fully implement the Party's art policy [and] select eligible cadres who have both ability and political integrity, and are able to work well with art workers.*[1]

Xi effectively calls for a revival of art under the auspices and watchful eye of the Communist Party of China (CPC). He values art not only for its "bones, morality, and warmth," but for its power to bring about a revision, denial, and perhaps even outright annihilation, for surely that is what "clean up" means, of "undesirable work styles."

The president's uncharacteristically long speech is picked up by the *People's Daily* (the mouthpiece of the CPC) as well as several other outlets, including newspapers. The Hong Kong–based Chinese language news agency Wen Wei Po additionally reports:[2]

> *In the future, grotesque buildings such as the "big pants" [a popular nickname for OMA's CCTV headquarters] will be less likely to rise up in Beijing, as General Secretary Xi Jinping has asked [architects] not to engage in odd and strange buildings during a literary forum.*[3]

The above is the result of an original Chinese text put through a Google translation. From it, it is not clear whether Xi himself singled out the CCTV headquarters, or whether it was summoned up as an example by a creative journalist in Hong Kong. Anyway, the question is not relevant. Within days, news outlets pick up the line, with headlines broadly following the same formula: "No More Weird Architecture, Says China's President." The international press also compiles "best of" lists featuring the "weirdest" Chinese architecture. By and large, these roundups contain OMA's CCTV building, Zaha Hadid Architects' Galaxy Soho in Beijing, the Guangzhou Circle by Joseph Di Pasquale, Tianzi Hotel in Langfang, and the Teapot building in Wuxi, which rotates.

Architects and developers rush to defend themselves. The head of the developer Soho China, Pan Shiyi, believes that Xi "might have been referring to ugly buildings," which would be fine because his company plans on continuing to make "beautiful" ones. "It could be a message to governments and officials to think about where to put the hard-earned money for greater good, not a showcase of your tenure," says Calvin Tsao, cofounder of the Shanghai-based developer Octave. "The city doesn't need another museum that is empty or another concert hall that doesn't have a program."[4] Rem Koolhaas is forced to defend OMA's CCTV project when he visits Seoul Design Week in November of that year, clarifying that the building was not dismissed as weird by Xi himself and further stating:

> *[CCTV is] a building that introduces new ways of conceptualizing, liberating, and realizing structure that did not exist in China before, and of which I'm sure Chinese culture and Chinese architecture will benefit. It articulates the position and the situation of China.*[5]

Roughly half a year later, in 2015, Patrik Schumacher, then one of the principals and intellectual rudders at Zaha Hadid Architects, is interviewed by the online magazine *Dezeen* and shares his thoughts regarding the impact of Xi's pronouncements on the situation of foreign architects in China.

I feel that there is this attempt by the Chinese leadership to try to make itself more independent and rely on its own talent. . . . I know that there has been criticism in the media and critical voices in the cultural debate that China has been relying too much on foreign architects putting their foreign stamp on the skylines of China. . . .

There was this kind of worry about foreigners doing projects. The temptation was maybe to exclude them and let the Chinese come forward. . . .

The debate from the central government in terms of criticizing weird architecture caused certain ripples. It had some ripple effect on one of our current Beijing projects . . . for instance, we were asked to tone down a little bit the exterior expression or rework it. It was precisely the time when these notions came out into the open and we did make changes and then we got planning for something more neutral. This was an example where you felt that this wasn't against foreign architecture, it was against unusual architecture. Of course at the same time you can still see some of the construction boom has muted, with a lot of the damping down of residential projects. I think there is temporary cooling-off of the building boom in China.[6]

Schumacher makes another interesting point: the economic and construction slowdown in China means that there is overall less work for architects, and with that in mind the People's Republic might be trying to keep its domestic workforce employed, rather than favor foreign (or weird) workers. The fact remains that China's construction boom has slowed significantly, from an average of 9.3 percent year-on-year growth between 2010 and 2014 to a projected average of 4.7 percent between 2014 and 2019.[7]

It is not until February 21, 2016, however, that the CPC's Central Committee and its State Council release revised guidelines regulating urban growth, noting that the country has at this point reached a 50-50 split between urban and rural populations. The last such document to have been released appeared nearly four decades ago, in 1978, when only 18 percent of the Chinese population lived in urban areas. The government's website reports on the publication:

> The document calls for greater oversight from city legislative bodies and harsher punishments for anyone contravening urban planning regulations. Any modification or revision of local urban planning policy should also be approved by legislators first.
>
> Bizarre architecture that is not economical, functional, aesthetically pleasing, or environmentally friendly will be forbidden, while construction techniques that generate less waste and use fewer resources, such as the use of prefabricated buildings, will be encouraged, according to the document.
>
> It is projected that in ten years, thirty percent of new buildings will be prefabricated.
>
> To further monitor urban sprawl, governments should use a variety of methods including remote satellite sensing to locate buildings that violate existing urban planning policies.
>
> Within five years, a map of all such illegal buildings across China's cities will have been drawn up and action taken against violators.[8]

The document also proposes more thoughtful approaches to preservation, mandates that a larger percentage of trips in cities (perhaps 30 to 40 percent) be made on public transport, imposes norms on green space within urban plans, and calls for abolition of gated communities and their territorial claims on the urban tissue. It emphasizes again that violators will be prosecuted.

Like the increased vigilance by the central government over the creative and artistic sector, the seeming U-turn in China's official policy on architecture is reminiscent of Soviet history. In particular, it recalls Khrushchev's overturning of Stalin's favored architecture practices. Just like Khrushchev's new policies in the 1950s, China's change of heart is ultimately founded on rational arguments. A similar desire for a less wasteful, more environmentally conscious architecture exists in the West, but in the Communist world these shifts tend to occur more suddenly, and when they occur, they are translated into official policy even more abruptly.

Still, China's "undesirable work styles" are no more desirable to leaders anywhere else in the world. The announced policies hardly differ from those so frequently preached in the West. The main difference can be found in the resolve of the Chinese authorities to enforce them. This is a capacity to which we might aspire while at the same time finding it deeply disturbing. China's policies leave us with the usual dilemma: we strive to be politically correct but refuse to stand politically corrected.

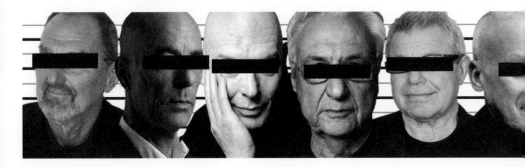

Starchitects
© Office for Metropolitan Architecture (OMA)

29

A Benevolent Dictator with Taste

Architecture is a negotiated art and it's highly political. If you want to make buildings, there is diplomacy required. I've always been interested in an architecture of resistance—architecture that has some power over the way we live. Working under adversarial conditions could be seen as a plus because you're offering alternatives. Still there are situations that make you ask the questions: "Do I want to be a part of this?"[1] In France I would refuse to work for the extreme-right party, but all around the world you have good reasons to say yes, because you don't build only for a client; you build for a city.[2]

Certainly I question working anywhere, but my position as an architect is to work in the spirit of international civilization and cooperation. You have to make a contribution.[3] As an architect, if you can in any way alleviate an oppressive situation, or elevate a culture, then I think that you should. It's different if someone asks you to build a prison—I wouldn't do it, but if I'm doing a museum or a library, I think that's different.[4] If the Beijing government said, "Can you build us a center for democracy?" I'd be the first to line up.[5]

I'm a guy who has on my wall a picture of the guy in front of the tank, but I've never turned down a project in Russia and China.[6] I think we are in a state of denial, while the Chinese are making decisions in the spirit of the Victorians. They have the courage to try it.[7] What attracts me about China is that there is still a state. There is something that can take initiative on a scale and of a nature that almost no-body that we know of today could ever afford or contemplate.[8] You have to throw out those English morals and weedy thoughts about world problems: here is architecture as ultimate statement of theatre.[9]

Only an idiot—and not a person who thinks in moral terms would turn down these opportunities—would say no. I know that there are architects who now claim that they would never consider building in China. This is both a naïve and arrogant position, one that reflects a lack of knowledge of and respect for the incredible cultural achievements this country has continuously provided over the last 5,000 years and still provides today.[10] I find it rather fatuous that the west is always only critical. The west is critical, nothing but critical. This form of uninterrupted criticism only leads up a blind alley. . . . We simply have to recognize that the right of the individual, which we hold so holy, has no tradition in countries like China.[11]

Clearly no one can approve of the miserable conditions under which people work there. It isn't just the migrant workers, but the entire factory system in China, which produces jeans, shirts and toys for the world, that works under such conditions. It is not within our power to change the conditions for migrant workers, nor is it our responsibility.[12] I have nothing to do with the workers. I think that's an issue the government— if there's a problem—should pick up. Hopefully, these things will be resolved. . . . I'm not taking it lightly but I think it's for the government to look to take care of. It's not my duty as an architect to look at it. I cannot do anything about it because I have no power to do anything about it.[13] As an architect, if you are involved in every layer then honestly you don't do anything. I'm not saying I shouldn't be thinking about it, but I think it's a job for the politicians, for the media, for the locals, to deal with it.[14]

We need to reform the public process. It's so out of control. It's an absolute orgy of public process basically, we can't get anything done.[15] The more centralized the power, the less compromises need to be made in architecture. The directions are clearer.[16] Democracy, obviously, is something we don't want to give up, but it does create chaos. It means the guy next door can do what he wants, and it creates a collision of thinking. In cities, that means people build whatever they want.[17] Somebody's got to reeducate those people that there's a pot of gold at the end of the rainbow if they follow it.[18] Some of the most amazing places were built because of dictators. Architecture is always related to power and related to large interests, whether financial or political.[19] I think the best thing is to have a benevolent dictator—who has taste![20]

QUOTES

1 Tom Mayne, *New York Times,* June 22, 2008, http://www.nytimes.com/2008 /06/22/arts/design/22pogr.html?pagewanted=all&_r=0.

2 Jean Nouvel, *New York Times,* June 22, 2008, http://www.nytimes.com/2008 /06/22/arts/design/22pogr.html?pagewanted=all&_r=0.

3 Steven Holl, *New York Times,* June 22, 2008, http://www.nytimes.com/2008 /06/22/arts/design/22pogr.html?pagewanted=all&_r=0.

4 Zaha Hadid, CNN, August 21, 2014, http://edition.cnn.com/2013/11/01 /sport/zaha-hadid-architect-profile-superyacht/.

5 Daniel Libeskind, *New York Times,* June 22, 2008, http://www.nytimes.com /2008/06/22/arts/design/22pogr.html?pagewanted=all&_r=0.

6 Eric Owen Moss, *New York Times,* June 22, 2008, http://www.nytimes.com /2008/06/22/arts/design/22pogr.html?pagewanted=all&_r=0.

7 Norman Foster, *Intelligent Life,* November 2012, http://moreintelligentlife .com/content/arts/norman-fosters-new-world?page=full.

8 Rem Koolhaas, *Democracy Journal,* Summer 2008, http://www.democracy journal.org/9/conscienceofaconstructor/.

9 Peter Cook (on Zaha Hadid's Heydar Aliyev Arts Centre), *Architectural Review,* December 20, 2013, http://www.architectural-review.com/buildings /heydar-aliyev-centre-baku-zaha-hadid-architects/8656751.article.

10 Jacques Herzog, July 30, 2008, *Der Spiegel,* http://www.spiegel.de/international /world/herzog-on-building-beijing-s-olympic-stadium-only-an-idiot -would-have-said-no-a-569011.html.

11 Rem Koolhaas, *Die Zeit,* June 5, 2008, English quote, http://www.zeit.de /2008/24/koolhaas-interview/scite-8.

12 Jacques Herzog, *Der Spiegel,* July 30, 2008, http://www.spiegel.de/international /world/herzog-on-building-beijing-s-olympic-stadium-only-an-idiot -would-have-said-no-a-569011-2.html.

13 Zaha Hadid, *Guardian,* February 25, 2013, http://www.theguardian.com/world /2014/feb/25/zaha-hadid-qatar-world-cup-migrant-worker-deaths.

14 Zaha Hadid, CNN, August 21, 2014, http://edition.cnn.com/2013/11/01/sport /zaha-hadid-architect-profile-superyacht/.

15 Andres Duany, *Planetizen,* April 26, 2010, http://www.planetizen.com/node /43935.

16 Peter Eisenmann, *New York Times,* June 22, 2008, http://www.nytimes.com /2008/06/22/arts/design/22pogr.html?pagewanted=all&_r=0.

17 Frank Gehry, *Foreign Policy,* June 24, 2013, http://www.foreignpolicy.com /articles/2013/06/24/epiphanies_from_frank_gehry.

18 Frank Gehry, *Atlantic/Citylab,* January 9, 2012, http://www.citylab.com/design /2012/01/frank-gehry-city-building/900/.

19 Bernard Tschumi, *New York Times,* June 22, 2008, http://www.nytimes.com/2008/06/22/arts/design/22pogr.html?pagewanted=all&_r=0

20 Frank Gehry, *Foreign Policy,* June 24, 2013, http://www.foreignpolicy.com/articles/2013/06/24/epiphanies_from_frank_gehry.

30

Royal Approval

May 30, 1984: Charles Philip Arthur George Mountbatten-Windsor is about to give a speech for the 150th anniversary of the Royal Institute of British Architects (RIBA), held at Hampton Court Palace; the speech will also honor that year's winner of the Royal Gold Medal, Indian architect Charles Correa. The matter is considered a formality; after all, Mountbatten-Windsor, the heir apparent to the throne of the United Kingdom of Great Britain and Northern Ireland, is not an architect. A perfunctory thank you and goodbye is all that is needed, and indeed all that is expected.

Instead, that night, the unelected hopeful head of state launches a comprehensive attack on the practice of architecture in general and modernist architecture in particular. Warming up, Charles thanks the participants for having had the opportunity to serve as honorary president of the RIBA in its 150th year and jokes about the "architectural hypochondria" suffered by Prince Albert, the prince consort of Queen Victoria and his great-great-great-grandfather, when he was redecorating the royal palaces of Osborne and Balmoral. He goes on to commend some of the best practices in urban regeneration, which by that point have already produced enough resident consultations and participation exercises to imply a modicum of concern for the communities of "ordinary" people who invariably inhabit most cities (save for the Vatican, Monte Carlo, and a few other exceptions). Then he abruptly shifts gears.

It is hard to imagine that London before the last war must have had one of the most beautiful skylines of any great city, if those who recall it are to be believed. Those who do, say that the affinity between buildings and the earth, in spite of the City's immense size, was so close and organic that the houses looked almost as though they had grown out of the earth and had not been imposed upon it—grown, moreover, in such a way that as few trees as possible were thrust out of the way. . . . What, then, are we doing to our capital city now? What have we done to it since the bombing during the war? What are we shortly to do to one of its most famous areas—Trafalgar Square? Instead of designing an extension to the elegant facade of the National Gallery which complements it and continues the concept of columns and domes, it looks as if we may be presented with a kind of municipal fire station, complete with the sort of tower that contains the siren. I would understand better this type of high-tech approach if you demolished the whole of Trafalgar Square and started again with a single architect responsible for the entire layout, but what is proposed is like a monstrous carbuncle on the face of a much-loved and elegant friend. . . . Why can't we have those curves and arches that express feeling in design? What is wrong with them? Why has every-thing got to be vertical, straight, unbending, only at right angles—and functional?[1]

The described extension to the National Gallery has been designed by the architects Ahrends, Burton and Koralek; its overall massing, rhythm, and even a little turret—added after the practice beat off seventy-seven others in the 1982 competition—responds to the architecture of the ad-joining classical building. (Prime minister Margaret Thatcher has insisted that the building pay for itself, and therefore needs to include a commer-cial component—the aforementioned turret.)[2]

Shortly after his speech Charles meets the architects of the building; within the year a new, closed competition is held. This time, thanks to a £50 million donation from Lord Sainsbury, the commercial component is dropped from the brief. The competition is won by the American prac-tice Venturi Scott Brown, which revels, not without irony, in the kind of classical embellishments, both inside and out, that so delights Charles.

If Ahrends, Burton and Koralek misses its chance of a lifetime because of Charles, it is Mies van der Rohe who is most cruelly robbed (posthu-mously) of his only chance to build in London by the monarch-to-be. On that same night in 1984 the prince indelibly lambasts Mies's Mansion House Square proposal, an austere, sixteen-story rectangular tower block, by then well known,

On that note, I can't help thinking how much more worthwhile it would be if a community approach could have been used in the Mansion House

Square project. It would be a tragedy if the character and skyline of our capital city were to be further ruined and St Paul's dwarfed by yet another giant glass stump, better suited to downtown Chicago than the City of London.

Shortly after Charles's speech, in 1985, Mies's scheme, which had enjoyed a notably warm reception when it was first unveiled in the 1960s, is refused planning permission by the Secretary of State for the Environment, Peter Jenkin. Palumbo (incidentally a former polo partner of Charles) goes on to commission Britain's leading postmodernist, James Stirling, whose cartoon-classical project for 1 Poultry is completed in 1997 (ironically, another posthumous achievement).[3] The prince later observes that the finished building, rather than being a glass stump, "looks rather like an old 1930s wireless."[4] It remains unclear whether he thinks that this is an improvement on the previously proposed scheme.

By the time Venturi Scott Brown finish with the National Gallery's new wing in 1991, Charles has firmly established a pattern. In 1987 he says of the proposed development on Paternoster Square by Richard Rogers:

You have to give this much to the Luftwaffe, when it knocked down our buildings, it didn't replace them with anything more offensive than rubble. Surely here, if anywhere, is the time and place to sacrifice some profit, if need be, for generosity of vision, for elegance, for dignity; for buildings which would raise our spirits and our faith in commercial enterprise. . . . On such a site, market forces, I would suggest, are not enough. . . . I would like to see architects working with artists and craftsmen, showing that pleasure and delight are indeed returning to architecture after their long exile.[5]

After a series of delays, the Paternoster Square that is built in 2003 is a midrise private office development with a quasi-public accessible area (no loitering, of course).

Prince Charles goes on to self-publish *A Vision of Britain: A Personal View of Architecture*, in 1989, in which he advocates a return to the traditionally constructed, small-scale morphology of preindustrial British towns. Five years later Charles launches a magazine, *Perspectives on Architecture*, based on the same messages as the book. Although the magazine lasts for only four years, it is one of the fiercest opponents of Zaha Hadid's 1994 scheme for the Cardiff Opera House in Wales. The project is initially won through an open competition entered by some 267 other practices, but takes two further rounds of judging—the first design is deemed too radical—before Hadid's (adapted) scheme finally emerges triumphant.[6] *Perspectives'* editor, Giles Worsley, writes of Hadid's project:

> A monument must express the hopes and aspirations of the people. It must bring people together, not create division. Hadid's Modernism, for all the vociferous campaigning of her supporters, is likely to seem alien to large numbers of the population.[7]

Hadid's project is rejected for the last time just before Christmas in 1995, and the Wales Millennium Centre is built in its stead in 2004. Whatever its architectural merits, the Millennium Centre can scarcely be considered the kind of traditional building that will please the Prince of Wales.

All the while, Charles has been involved in commissioning Poundbury, a village in the Duchy of Cornwall, the prince's personal fiefdom, which supplies much of the United Kingdom's middle class with organic jams and preserves. The Luxembourg architect Léon Krier, an avowed traditionalist and court favorite of the prince, is put in charge of the town's planning. The project begins in the late 1980s, and by the time it is complete around 2025, it is intended to house 5,000 inhabitants—a mere drop in the ocean compared with the 240,000 new homes needed in Britain annually.[8] Despite the supposed virtues of craftsmanship and traditional Albion urbanism, Poundbury's new inhabitants have already complained of problems: the gravel of the footpaths disappeared with the first winter's snow; the nails used in construction are not galvanized; the wood is not properly conditioned; and the fake chimneys don't drain well, leaking disappointingly into people's homes.[9]

Prince Charles continues to wield his scepter of influence to lobby for personal (apparently "popular") taste behind closed doors. In March 2009 he once again crosses Richard Rogers (by now, Lord Rogers of Riverside) when the latter's project for the Chelsea Barracks, a development of 450 luxury flats in western London by Qatari Diar, is suddenly dropped by the developer. The letter that Charles wrote to his Qatari royal counterparts goes as follows:

My heart sank when I saw the plans that have been produced for the old Chelsea Barracks site. . . . I am so sorry to have to write to you on this subject, and thus be so interfering, but it is a site of great importance in London and therefore deserves something that is appropriate to its context and worthy of its position next to the Royal Hospital.[10]

Three months later the developer withdraws the planning application, just days before it is supposed to be discussed by the Westminster council. The prince then encourages the classicist architect Quinlan Terry to submit an alternative scheme.[11] In December 2014 Prime Minister David Cameron appoints Terry to sit on a government panel on new housing standards.[12]

Over the course of his entire campaign, Charles has attacked the architects and planners of each scheme as the villains of the piece. However, by the time he makes his "monstrous carbuncle" speech in 1984, the tides in Britain have already turned against the architect's role in public life. Margaret Thatcher begins the wholesale sell-off of the nation's social housing stock in 1980 with the infamous Right to Buy policy; the idea of architecture as a purely capital investment has thus been well planted at the very roots of British society. Today, architects and planners are unable to resist the onslaught of developers' demands for taller and flimsier buildings. While the (overseas) elite can now partake in speculatively built modernist dreams, the back-door campaigning by Prince Charles and the actions of the British government mean that even the cheapest homes for domestic buyers come with a pitched roof and brick facades (double leaf or at least brick veneer, applied in wide panels predecorated with tile-like "brick slips"), along with far less space and lower specifications than were ever allowed under the previous generation of modernist architects.[13]

At the end of his speech on that fateful night in 1984, Charles quotes Goethe: "There is nothing more dreadful than imagination without taste." Perhaps the German poet had simply never met anyone who has taste without imagination. In the words of Richard Rogers:

The Prince does not debate and in a democracy that is unacceptable and in fact is non-constitutional. I think he pursues these topics because he is looking for a job and in that sense I sympathize with him. He is actually an unemployed individual, which says something about the state of the Royal Family. I don't think he is evil per se; he is just misled.[14]

Such public confrontations have become rare recently. It is believed that these days some developers informally seek the prince's approval before officially submitting their proposals for planning permission. There is no formal obligation to do this, but Charles's unsolicited 1984 "monstrous carbuncle" intervention must understandably have worried developers as a harbinger of potentially long and expensive delays.

Clarence House has repeatedly states that there is no evidence of developers directly seeking Charles's approval for building projects. When in 2013, after Richard Rogers makes such claim , the *Independent* asks the question directly, a spokesman for the prince replies:

> *Developers do not seek planning approval from the Prince of Wales as planning development approvals lie with local planning authorities. If developers choose to send the Prince of Wales information about upcoming developments that is up to them, but the Prince does not, and cannot, grant planning permission. The Prince does regularly receive letters from members of the public complaining about developments and planning decisions. The Prince has received this sort of feedback from the public for decades, which is why his interest in the built environment goes beyond individual developments and architectural style to encouraging a sense of community and pride of place, improving the quality of people's lives overall.*[15]

Still, the rumors that the prince's prior approval is now a mandatory benediction for developers reflect a wider concern regarding the influence that Charles wields in public life. In the same year in which the *Independent* publishes Rogers's claims, it emerges that three members of the Prince of Wales's staff are seconded to work full-time in Whitehall. In 2012 House of Commons records show that six government departments have sought the heir to the throne's consent before proceeding with bills on a wide range of issues, including the London Olympics, gambling, road safety, and even shipwrecks, since 2005.

Prince Charles's interest in architecture may have great comic potential and indeed is a source of wry laughter among architects, particularly those outside Britain. But ultimately, the interference of an unelected future head of state in matters beyond both his mandate and competence—and in the case of Charles this isn't just limited to architecture—is actually far from funny. The National Gallery extension, Mansion House and Paternoster Squares, the Cardiff Opera House, and Chelsea Barracks—in a respectable democracy, the personal power of a member of the royal elite to informally exercise his influence appears to go unchecked. That is a serious matter indeed.

31

His Architect

We all know him. He is a colleague, but then again, he isn't. He has no office, nor is he employed by one. He is employed directly by the client. This particular client deserves respect—not for employing an architect but for having worked his way up in the real estate world with virtually no prior education. His exact fortune is the subject of perpetual guesswork. Some people claim that published numbers are a gross exaggeration; according to others, they hardly do justice to the real extent of his wealth. The client has one problem: although he knows exactly what he wants, he has trouble articulating it. What starts with words and phrases, bound by grammar, generally ends in a primal grunt. Sound rather than language is his preferred instrument of communication. These grunts are perfectly intelligible to his colleagues (who express themselves similarly), but communicating to architects is an altogether different matter. It is for this reason that he employs his own architect: to convey his wishes to other architects in a way that they will understand without being offended. An unnecessary detour, some would say. Why not commission his architect directly? That would be cheaper and faster. Still, it is some time since his architect made a building, and even then he never completed the final stages. None of his designs have ever had to withstand the harsh check of reality. His skills are an unknown quantity; commissioning him to do a building would constitute a major risk.

Moreover, it is not the intention of his architect to be an architect. He made up his mind long ago to forgo a career as a designer. Instead, he has pursued a career where he gets to comment on the designs of others. In school he was never very good; poor grades left him with a sense of inferiority he has been trying to fight off ever since. He needs to get even. That is his primary motivation in life, more than money, more than recognition. He needs to get back at all those who mocked his poor skills, shunned him as a friend, kept him out of debating clubs, and frowned on his limited intellect. His current position offers him that golden opportunity.

When he was younger, people regarded him as somewhat of an oddity. Still, he has one talent: he understands money. He is not "from" money—his family is of modest means—but in the absence of other passions, money becomes a kind of quaint pastime. As a young boy, he charges his classmates for little things he smuggles from home. Whenever they can't pay, he doesn't withhold the goods but offers them the possibility of paying a slightly higher amount later. It's a generous ultimatum, but the supplement is nonnegotiable. His disposition toward money gives him a kind of independence, a freedom from the need to be liked. When he is alone, he can always count up his worth.

In university he finds himself different from his fellow students. They aren't interested in money. To them, it is uncool to admit that money even exists. This vulgar capitalist reality—most of his fellow students claim to be Marxists—needs to be kept at bay as long as possible. There is a theory that the first step to acquiring money is to be interested in it. He is. While his fellow students are busy planning the next revolution, he starts a small business, consulting for people on their home conversions. Generally, these conversions are too simple to require the services of a qualified architect but too complex for people to handle on their own. It is the perfect opportunity for a nongraduate to earn money. His best financial move might have been to delay graduation forever, but eventually his age would have given him away.

When he does graduate, in the early 1980s, he finds a markedly different world than the one he experienced in school: geared not toward the left but the right wing, fed up with socialist rhetoric and outmoded political theories that forever fail to deliver. This is a world that has reinvented architecture as real estate. Not composition or ideology but profit is the main driver. Understanding the mechanics of money—of only peripheral concern to his contemporaries—becomes his main competitive advantage. For the first time in his life, he feels good about himself. No longer are his skills a means to compensate for his lack of other skills; they are the only skills that matter—all that life is about. Life is wonderful.

He befriends a young property developer who at the start of his career is similarly unwelcome in the circles where he does business. People say the developer's methods are unlawful, but that is not the way he sees it. To him, his methods are just about using the law to his best possible advantage. The law is not a moral code but an instrument with which to organize his labor; the residual space left over by the law is just as much part of the law as the articles of the law. The two men are a match. The hierarchy between them is established with the first handshake. The developer is stronger and handsomer than the architect. He grants the architect access to a glamorous world, including introductions to women who would never otherwise have cast him a second glance. It is through this new friendship that the architect meets his first wife. The developer appears ever confident, but that is largely a facade. Underneath he feels deeply insecure, always conscious that the aura he has created—largely based on bluff—could be seized from him in an instant. (Decades later it is, by the tax authorities.) He needs somebody around to reassure him, agree with him, laugh at his jokes, be his sidekick. This is the only way he and his architect can survive. That is their (unwritten) contract.

They go into business. The way in which the shares are divided gives the developer full control; nevertheless, they agree to make important decisions by mutual consent. The division of tasks is evident because real estate is governed by a simple law: maximizing return while minimizing cost. The developer takes care of the first part, his architect of the second. Whenever his architect discusses projects with other architects, he is not to mention money. He is to ensure that what makes the project—any project—profitable is discussed only in terms of beauty. He diligently does so. In the name of beauty, he persuades architects to commit to major cost cuts, revisit their position, and change their designs beyond recognition. He becomes an author in his own right; if he ever puts pen to paper, he insists, it is not to design but merely to offer benign suggestion for alternatives. Over time, he perfects his art, rehearses his act, trains his voice, and finely tunes his timbre between bass and baritone—a second career manifests itself—to the content of his message: gentle but firm, tentative but pressing, open ended but ultimately definitive.

He recently divorced. His undivided loyalty to his developer friend proved too much even for a loyal wife. But at this stage that no longer matters. He can use his divorce as a testimony to his independent mind. He has done well for himself. He wears Armani suits, smokes Cuban cigars, and drinks vintage wines. Access to the finer things in life serves as evidence, underlining the validity of his approach to his struggling colleagues.

He is finally even.

32

A Property Developer for President

The Announcement

"We need Trump now!" It is a random outburst from somebody in the audience, but it is the only conclusion possible in the context of the oration that is being delivered: an endless rant about everything that has gone desperately wrong in America in the past eight years. America doesn't have victories anymore. The incompetence and stupidity of its (elected) representatives are about to squander the country's great history. America needs fixing. The intervention seems unscripted, but given the speaker's quick response ("You're right!") and knowing his long history of playing the media, one cannot help wondering whether the "spontaneously" interrupted monologue is anything other than a carefully rehearsed theatrical exchange.

It is June 15, 2015. We are in the atrium of Trump Tower, New York, where the property tycoon to whom the building owes its name is about to announce his intention to run in the 2016 U.S. presidential election. The performance he delivers is undeniably entertaining. In the context of a race that had seemed business as usual before his announcement, his openly obnoxious manner is a breath of fresh air to many. In the present political landscape, dominated by fears of alienating potential voters by saying the wrong things, it seems that authenticity alone, however abrasive, suffices to generate political clout.

Until Trump's announcement, the question whether a property developer could make a good president had been hypothetical. Berlusconi, it is true, became prime minister of Italy, but his fling with the construction industry was limited to a single project. Spanish real estate mogul Jesús Gil y Gil went on to become the mayor of Marbella, but there his political career ended, and few would regard Jeb Bush, Trump's main contender for the Republican nomination, who also has a background in real estate, as a developer rather than a politician. Generally, the involvement of the property world in politics has remained limited to financing the political careers of others, usually in the form of donations to their campaigns.

(Trump claims to have made many, including ones to Hillary Clinton.) Political influence has been something people from the property world have bought but seldom exercised as officeholders. Before Trump, no developer had ever seriously attempted to become a head of state, let alone head of the United States. Still, if the polls at the time of the announcement are anything to go by, Trump has a fair shot.

Donald Trump isn't just any property developer; he is, in many senses, bigger than that. Trump has owned his own airline; he is a TV personality, an author, a political commentator, and, as of late, also a potential president. Trump's ambitions seem to know no limits, and, with the exception of a few bankruptcies, neither do his abilities to accomplish them. His carefully cultivated image as an all-American "universal entrepreneur" makes him a role model for thousands of other property developers who—as architects have before them—aspire to godlike powers. In Trump's slipstream we may witness the birth of a whole new generation of politicians, eager to reinvent the posts left by the stagnant officeholders they intend to replace.

Trump sets the bar high. Whereas the political aspirations of architects have not reached above the position of mayor, developers might well aim higher. Trump certainly does. With a developer for president and an architect as mayor, society becomes a perfect reproduction of the construction industry's pecking order. One may wonder whether that is a good thing. When the construction industry becomes a blueprint for governance, what will ensue? Will society develop the smooth logistics needed to deliver to its citizens on time and on budget? (Trump wastes no opportunity to suggest that it will.) Or will society fall victim to the type of underhanded deals (another reality of the construction industry) that you would expect to find only in a banana republic?

In a democracy, people from all walks of life, provided they earn their living legally, should be able to pursue political careers. There is no reason to exclude property developers. Still, if one studies more closely the arguments with which Trump presents himself, certain questions arise. He repeatedly quotes his success in business as *the* reason that he would make an ideal public official. The mind-set that creates success in business, he claims, is exactly the mind-set needed to put an entire country back on the road to success. The public sector as it stands, dominated by dedicated career politicians (whom he habitually calls "losers"), is morally and spiritually bankrupt, deeply incompetent, and above all, fundamentally unwilling to solve America's problems.

The position Trump takes is curious, not least because the Trump family business owes its success, in large part, to the same public sector that the Donald so vehemently criticizes. During the Great Depression, Trump's father, Fred, leveraged public programs to construct single-family homes in Queens and Brooklyn, using mortgage commitments from the newly created Federal Housing Administration (FHA) to obtain construction loans. During the war, he used government funds to construct no-frills houses for the navy. When the government was trying to jump-start the postwar construction industry to house veterans, he built large FHA-backed projects, financed through public bonds issued by the state. When Donald took over in 1971, the reliance on public funding in no way diminished. In New York, he was the first developer to receive a public subsidy for commercial projects under programs initially reserved for improving slum neighborhoods. Because of his family liaisons with then-mayor Abraham Beame, he won a forty-year tax abatement to rebuild the crumbling Commodore Hotel at Grand Central Station—a deal that cost taxpayers $60 million. In the 1990s Trump sought and got federal help to build sixteen luxury towers on Manhattan's Westside (estimated cost: $1.9 billion), and it was government funding that enabled Trump to develop his hugely profitable Trump Hotels and Casino Resorts.

It can be argued that the public sector made Trump, and that therefore, his current stance, which decries government involvement with businesses as a threat to the "American dream," seems more than slightly incongruous. The public sector, in his political narrative, is portrayed as incompetent and its officials as spineless—giving him and his lobbyists whatever he asks for. However, had that public sector shown the kind of spine Trump evidently admires, it would have curtailed his success and made it difficult for him to pursue public office. It would seem that Trump's political views are, at least partially, the product of a deeply flawed assessment of his success. Trump may well say it like it is, but there is a lot he doesn't say. If indeed the public sector is dysfunctional, then Trump is the monster it created.

It is hard to know whether Donald Trump would make a good president, but it is worthwhile to question the desirability of an active role of the property world in politics. As a trade, property development surged in the 1980s when the conservative revolution across both America and Europe sharply reduced the public sector and privatized a number of formerly public tasks. These tasks became "business," and in the case of formerly public building programs, it became big business indeed. More than any other professional community, the property world has stood to gain from conservative politics. It is no coincidence that whenever developers commit themselves politically, it is firmly to the right of the political spectrum. Property tycoons are among the most prominent donors to the Republican Party in the United States and the Conservative Party in the United Kingdom. They are also among the most vocal critics of large government. For the past forty years, the property world has coauthored the largest sell-out of the public sector in the history of man. For developers to now pose as potential saviors and leaders of that public sector seems disingenuous at best.

In regard to assuming political office, the property world may want to exercise discretion. So far, even with the alignment of interests, real estate and politics have been two different things; checks and balances are still in place (if only to ensure the continuation of the mutually beneficial relation). Once the two converge in a single person, a fundamentally different situation arises. The political sphere is no longer a corrective against the forces of the market economy; it becomes its champion.

The candidacy speech approaches its finale. There isn't much left to be said. Everything on the agenda has been discussed or, rather, dismissed: from the state of the United States' nuclear arsenal ("It doesn't work") to Obamacare ("A disaster") and even what the government spends on its own websites ("Astronomical"). Trump embarks on a final rhetorical question, this time posed to himself: "But Mr. Trump, how are you going to get people to vote for you? You are not a nice person." He is barely given the opportunity to finish his sentence. A female voice in the audience cries out, "We don't need nice!" For a moment, even Trump seems overwhelmed. He pauses. The right corner of his mouth betrays the immense joy he takes from the moment. Then he regains his composure and proceeds to answer: "That's true. But actually, I think I am a nice person."

I keep thinking back to the 1991 documentary *What's the Deal?* about the old Donald Trump who made (and lost) it in the 1980s. Residents of 100 Central Park South give an account of the Trump they got to know. Trump had bought the building with the intention to demolish it and build luxury apartments in its place. Tenants, many on moderate incomes, were advised to move out or face eviction if they didn't.[1] When they refused to comply, services in the building were discontinued, and a specialized "relocation" firm was hired to "work on the tenants' weak spots."[2] The case was brought to court, which ruled in the tenants' favor. In a last desperate attempt to get the tenants to move, Trump embarked on a major publicity stunt in which he offers vacant apartments in the building to New York City's homeless. The stunt is Trump all the way: never give up, always present your goals as a pursuit of the greater good, and never forgo a good PR opportunity. Listening to him announcing his candidacy, I wonder to what extent the old and the new Trump are one and the same.

Trump and Architecture

Like his political convictions, Donald Trump's taste for opulence, in both architecture and other matters, tends to divide opinions. Author Harper Lee once wrote to a friend, "The worst punishment God can devise for this sinner is to make her spirit reside eternally at the Trump Taj Mahal in Atlantic City."[3] In 1979, before Trump Tower on Fifth Avenue is built in New York City, the inimitable architecture critic Ada Louise Huxtable writes about the blueprints for a "dramatically handsome structure"[4]; once the tower is finished in 1983, fellow architecture critic Paul Goldberger describes the building's atrium as "warm, luxurious, even exhilarating" in the *New York Times*.[5] Writing for the *Chicago Tribune* in June 2014, Pulitzer Prize–winning critic Blair Kamin writes the following of Trump's latest Chicago skyscraper and its large TRUMP sign that is being installed at the time:

> It is hard, however, to miss Donald Trump's sign or to dismiss the anger it's provoked in some quarters. When finished, the sign will measure slightly more than 141 feet long—nearly half the length of a football field.
>
> Not surprisingly, the developer and reality TV star, a man of no small ego, wanted the sign to be even bigger. He originally proposed that it cover 3,600 square feet, according to Peter Strazzabosco, a spokesman for the city's Department of Planning and Development. City officials cut that by roughly 20 percent, to 2,891 square feet.

Despite the building's enormous girth and subpar spire, Trump's 96-story hotel and condominium tower is a plus for the skyline. Architect Smith and his former firm, the Chicago office of Skidmore, Owings & Merrill, endowed the tower with stainless steel fins that catch the light beautifully. From certain angles, like the one on Wabash Avenue looking north, it dazzles. No one expected refinement like this from the Prince of Glitz. People formed a kinship with the skyscraper—which helps explain why they now feel betrayed.[6]

But generally, such words of praise are few. The *Economist* describes Trump as a "poor-man's idea of a rich man" and notes that this sensibility is carried over to the property developer's taste in architecture and design.[7] For his part, Donald Trump is unafraid to strike back at his detractors in a style all too familiar. Responding to Kamin, he writes on Twitter (where else?), "A third rate architecture critic—who I thought got fired—for the failing @chicagotribune likes the building but doesn't like the Trump sign."

It is Kamin's predecessor at the *Tribune,* Paul Gapp, who first draws the Donald's ire. In August 1984 Gapp has gotten word that Trump is planning to build a 1,940-foot (591-meter) tower at the southern tip of Manhattan. Gapp points out that building to such height on the plot that Trump proposes will merely be an uneconomical vanity project, and he also questions the developer's means to muster the $1 billion ($2.3 billion in today's money) necessary to build the record-setting tower. Gapp dismisses the plan outright, saying, "The world's tallest tower will be one of the silliest things anyone can inflict on New York or any other city."[8]

Unhappy with this assessment and with a *Tribune*-sanctioned artist's impression of what the tower might look like, Trump sues the newspaper for libel, demanding $500 million in damages. Perhaps this is just a way of getting half the funding for his project; in any case, the judge dismisses the case in September 1985.[9]

After a careful review of the record, this court has no doubt that the statements contained in the Tribune article are expressions of opinion. The very presentation of the article in the Sunday Tribune Magazine section, under the heading of the "Design" column, with a byline identifying the author as the Tribune's "Architecture Critic," informs the reader that the article embodies commentary by a Tribune columnist, and is not a news story reporting factual material. From the first sentence, which describes the "only remotely appealing aspect" of the Trump project, the prose is cast in subjective terms; the very words Trump objects to, which refer to the proposal as "one of the silliest things anyone could inflict on New York" and describe the asserted aesthetic balance between the proposed tower and the World Trade Center as "eyewash," convey to the reader the highly personal and subjective nature of the judgments expressed.

Plaintiff, having sought publicity for his proposal, finds that defendants do not like his proposed structure. He, on the other hand, does not like their conception any better. The words of the Latin proverb are particularly appropriate here: De gustibus non est disputandum, there is no disputing about tastes.[10]

Just as in politics, Donald Trump never looks back on this setback. Although he doesn't get to build his record-breaking tower, his attitude to his opponents, both architectural and political, is apparent early on in his career in property. In 2016 little seems to have changed.

The Nomination

"Those in favor of the rules package will say: Aye!" A loud and prolonged "Aye" responds from the floor. "Those opposed shall say: No!" An equally loud and prolonged "No" follows. "In the opinion of the speaker, the Ayes have it!" The speaker flees the stage; chaos ensues.

It is July 18, 2016, the first day of the Republican National Convention, held in Cleveland, Ohio. Eleven states have issued a petition asking for a roll call about the rules on the allocation of delegates. It is the last hope of the Never Trump camp to disrupt his candidacy. Still, the floor has reached a verdict: the rules as printed and distributed will be followed. The next morning, Donald Trump Jr. presents the vote of the state of New York, pushing his father's delegate count over the top. Donald J. Trump is the official Republican nominee for president of the United States of America.

Traditionally, conventions—Republican or Democratic—are carefully orchestrated displays of unity. Not this one. Like Trump, the convention to crown him as the Republican presidential nominee defies conventions.

In a rare exception, the streets of the hosting city seem calmer than the convention floor. The general order of speakers does not rise to a rousing climax, with each speaker building on the previous one, but rather plays out like a mismatched variety show—a platform from which to broadcast the apparent divisions within the party's ranks. When Ted Cruz, one of Trump's former opponents, is granted the stage, he fails to endorse the victor and therefore de facto opposes Trump's candidacy. The speech of Trump's wife, first lady hopeful, shamelessly plagiarizes segments of a speech by Michelle Obama, first lady hopeful eight years earlier for the opposing side. Upon critical exposure, first the Democratic camp and then the biased media are blamed. Once indisputable, the similarity is dismissed with a reference to Twilight Sparkle in "My Little Pony," putting the ball back in Michelle Obama's court and implying that it was she who set the precedent for plagiarism. Various musicians or their estates object to the unauthorized use of their recordings: the Turtles (for the use of "Happy Together"), Queen (for "We Are the Champions"), and Luciano Pavarotti (singing "Nessun dorma" from *Turandot*—a moment of supreme irony because the aria refers to a sleepless night of fear, and to Princess Turandot's threat of death to all her subjects in the approaching morning). The campaign team offers neither remorse nor contrition. Controversy is handled in line with the Trump brand, in which apologies play no part.

If the Republican convention is anything to go by, this great nation, built on immigration and tolerance, is now gripped by nationalism of the nastiest stripe. The openly professed hostility to illegal immigrants feels suspiciously close to a rejection of the idea of immigration altogether, admitting blind prejudice instead. Indeed, the call for a ban on Muslims entering the country, unconstitutional though it might be, enjoys wide support. The convention's lineup of speakers consists largely of disgruntled war veterans who feel betrayed by the ruling political class. The audience regularly breaks out in chants calling for the imprisonment of their main political opponent. When the leader makes his appearance, he does so as an iconic orange silhouette against a gray screen, surrounded by a dramatic fog of dry ice. Trump inspires a personality cult so far unseen in the United States. The scenes are all too familiar, reaching their apex when a certain conservative radio talk-show host honors Trump's giant image with the Nazi salute.

In search of a more uplifting note, the American press turns to Trump's children. In view of the demographic abyss represented by their father's following, their somewhat more progressive views, in combination with their more polished demeanors, might appeal to a wider range of voters. Still, when the time comes, there is little to celebrate. Donald Trump Jr. takes the opportunity to describe himself as a Fifth Avenue redneck, and daughter Ivanka Trump, demonstrating her acute business sense, offers the dress she wears during her speech (from her own clothing line) on Twitter.

In any other case, such displays of tastelessness—and that is the right word—would have ruined the nominee's chances. Not so for Trump. Less than twenty-four hours after the convention ends, Clinton's double-digit lead shrinks to less than a percentage point, and Trump even overtakes her in some of the polls.

Time and again, Trump demonstrates that the conventional rules of politics do not apply to him. His campaign has been anything but wrinkle free, but the more any notion of editorial control is abandoned, the more he seems to thrive. His "university" has been exposed as a form of fraud; his dubious business past, insofar as it wasn't already, is now public knowledge, as is his history as a philanderer—usually something the Republicans like to stick to their opponents. But in no way does any of this seem to affect his popularity or his ratings. Candor is the ultimate key to being forgiven. If that doesn't work, there is always indifference, which, with an estimated fortune of eight billion dollars, is easy to afford.

Trump defies not only political conventions but also logic. If his candidacy were a prospective film script, it would be thrown out after the first read: too unlikely, in the proper sense of the word, too incredible. An obscenely wealthy businessman becomes the voice of average Americans who believe that they are victims of unlawful corporate greed; the chief of a global business empire becomes the proponent of a new American isolationism; a man with three families becomes the iconic devoted husband. "Donald is intensely loyal."[11] Nothing adds up, but everything works.

Trump's speech at the end of the convention is an almost poetic string of contradictions. He promises to restore America's infrastructure while cutting taxes; he will take care of America's vets while repealing any form of public health care; he promises to get rid of ISIS while deploying the U.S. military only at home; he will make America rich again by withdrawing from global trade agreements; he will build a wall and have those he shuts out pay for it. He will solve climate change—apparently a Chinese invention, concocted to impair the U.S. economy—by ignoring it.

Donald Trump is a property developer and therefore, almost by definition, a dreamer. Dreamers have a frictional relation with reality. Dedicated to tomorrow's reality, they believe that the realities of today are there to be altered, changed beyond recognition. As an architect, I can relate, but architects and developers have different ways of coming to terms with reality. While we deal with reality by momentarily blocking out some of its less welcome aspects—budget limitations, execution practicalities, and prevailing taste—property developers tend to simultaneously embrace all aspects of reality while ignoring all incompatibilities within it.

> *Please go for the New York grid, but make it radial. . . . Love the idea of the square, but would like it to be round. . . . The buildings should stand close together with narrow streets between them; there should be views in all directions. . . . Would like to see geometric forms that are organic. . . . Please maximize density, but make lots of water everywhere.*[12]

To an architect, Trump's lack of a sense of reality feels familiar. In another setting, one could refer to it as creativity, lateral thinking, or simply the product of an unbridled imagination. In fact, Trump exemplifies what Prince Charles dismissively described as "imagination without taste": a type of thinking that doesn't bother to check conventions and their attendant wisdoms first. Taste is what is applied retroactively—a form of editing—to help these conventions retain their legitimacy.

If we momentarily replace Hillary Clinton with Prince Charles as the imaginary opponent—the swap is not that far-fetched; both are members of a dynasty—Trump's 2016 Republican convention acquires a whole new aura. Its tastelessness becomes a form of liberation. The usual expectations of coherence, unity, and scripted addresses give way to a whole new aesthetic experience. Trump's speech becomes the twenty-first-century equivalent of Dada poetry, separating words from meaning, celebrating chaos and irrationality, and aspiring to transcend the limits of logic in pursuit of an ultimate universe of potential.

Dadaism aspired to the true democratization of the aesthetic experience against the preconceived ideals of the bourgeois. At the beginning of the twentieth century, it revolutionized first art, then literature. With Trump, Dada has finally arrived on the doorstep of politics. It is no longer a question whether a property developer can become president; Trump simply reminds us of the basic constitutional fact that anybody can become president—that in the twenty-first century democracy and Dada have everything in common.

The Presidency

How did everyone get it so wrong? The network anchorman can barely conceal his disbelief. It is November 8, 2016. In an upset victory over Hillary Rodham Clinton, Donald J. Trump is elected America's forty-fifth president. The hastily assembled panel of political commentators to whom the anchorman's question is directed fails to produce the usual swift answers. The media's race during the final weeks of the campaign to see who could condemn Trump's unabashed political incorrectness most quickly and loudly has given way to collective bewilderment. The first panelist to pull himself together poses a counterquestion: "Are you referring to the polls conducted by the various news organizations—all confident of a Trump defeat up until 24 hours ago—or to the masses of voters who have simply refused to understand Trump is not a good choice?" Who is the "everyone" the anchorman is referring to? The media's general state of denial, it seems, persists. The discussion digresses into a weird mea culpa—not about signals they might have missed, but on what more they could possibly have done to convey the obvious truth that the now president-elect is unfit to be president. For months on end they have diligently reported on everything from Trump's alleged tax dodges to his suspected business dealings with foreign despots, from his alleged ties to the Ku Klux Klan to his public misogyny. In the end, none of it mattered. For the next four years, Trump will preside over the US, the same two letters the mainstream media had been careful to omit from the word "p**sy."

Trump's acceptance speech, delivered shortly after passing the required 270 Electoral College votes, is conciliatory—a far cry from the rhetoric of his campaign. His previously announced draconian measures seem to enjoy little priority anymore. In a way, his sudden reasonableness betrays a bewilderment similar to that experienced by those who so consistently predicted his defeat. It is clear that Trump, too, never expected to win. Tonight, on stage, Trump manages to retain an aura of confidence, but already a palpable panic is pervading the Trump camp, which clearly lacked a contingency plan for the eventuality of a Trump win. How the next president plans to implement his "America First" message remains vague at best: his quick-fix solutions to illegal immigration (a wall), violent crime (lock 'em up), and rising unemployment (trade protectionism) are nearly impossible to put into practice. What's more, even if Trump's party now enjoys a majority in both houses of Congress, it is the same party he has partially estranged during his campaign. With no immediate answers at hand, Trump calls for unity. His call is not answered. Protests break out across America and a few days later take their first casualty in Portland, Oregon.

A discussion about the Electoral College flares up, as it does whenever the popular vote and the election result are at odds. Trump received fewer votes than Clinton; he received fewer votes even than John McCain and Mitt Romney, the Republican candidates who lost the election in 2008 and 2012. Trump continues a weird American tradition in which democracy does not equal the will of the majority. For the self-professed champion of democracy, different rules apply. And with voter turnout at a twenty-year low, the American system, now more than two centuries old, has just had its course set by a mere quarter of the electorate.[13] There is hope: the under-thirty vote shows an America almost entirely composed of blue states, but to the defeated majority, that more hopeful future scarcely offers consolation in the present.

After the commentators, and even Trump himself, it is now the world that looks on in bewilderment. Sixteen years into the twenty-first century, democracy's predicted universal victory has turned into a game of chance, symbolized by the presidency of a former casino owner in the world's most powerful nation. Europe, Japan, South Korea, and other U.S. allies wait in suspense to see whether and how much the United States will continue to honor its international commitments. Parallels come to mind in Philip Roth's *The Plot against America,* in which Franklin Delano Roosevelt is defeated by isolationist candidate Charles Lindbergh during the presidential election of 1940. The United States enters into a nonaggression treaty with Nazi Germany and chooses not to interfere with Japan's expansion in Asia. An alternative history unfolds, in which a deeply divided American people is brought to the brink of civil war. With the election of Trump, history could acquire a similar plot twist—this time, for real.

VI. MEGALOPOLI(TIC)S

A World of Megalopoli(tic)s
© Office for Metropolitan Architecture (OMA)

33

A Faustian Bargain

In 1950 New York and Tokyo were the only cities with more than ten million inhabitants.[1] Currently, twenty-eight cities have populations matching that,[2] and by 2025 there will be thirty-seven.[3] These cities surpass many countries in population or GDP: the population of Greater Jakarta is larger than that of Australia; the GDP of São Paulo is greater than that of Turkey.[4]

Approximately 180,000 people are urbanizing every day,[5] moving to cities to access resources, amenities, or opportunities that rural conditions do not offer, in the fervent hope of becoming "wealthier." Most find their hopes crushed on arrival. Rather than being places of shared prosperity, cities increasingly present themselves as places of disparity, where the theoretical diversity brought about by globalization takes the form of social segregation. At present, at least one-third of city dwellers live in informal precincts or developments, often without the same civic rights as the city's official residents.[6]

Despite frequent use of the term, few so-called megacities actually exist as such. When the *Financial Times, Monocle,* and the *Economist* publish their rankings of the world's largest cities, they are generally large conurbations associated with the biggest city in their midst. In reality, these conurbations are little more than a tapestry of individual towns with no overriding authority to manage them.

Perhaps because of their lack of formal status, megacities are also not a matter of public concern. Their existence is discussed mostly in the private sector. Since the economic liberalization policies of the 1980s, private parties almost anywhere in the world have come to play a key role in urban development. Only through an ad hoc mix of regulations and incentives does the public sector retain a certain illusion of control, "shaping" market-driven developments while relying on the market to allow development to happen at all.

The megacity takes that principle to another level. Nonexistent as an administrative entity, it defies political guidance. In the final instance, even the public sector's sharply reduced repertoire ceases to apply. The megacity is the physical outcome of a process of deregulation taken to its conclusion: a free-for-all enacted in the absence of a center, both literally and figuratively.

The supposed rehabilitation of urban planning within the architecture profession has done little to help. Its focus on the city serves only to mask an acute lack of mandate; it knows deep down that, in the market economy, like a Faustian bargain, urban growth has come to imply the relinquishing of urban planning—that the principle from which the megacity emerges is the same as the one that denies it guidance.

Christ the Redeemer, Rio de Janeiro
Photograph by Gabriel Fernando / BrazilPhotos / Alamy Stock Photo

34

Amanhã

Rio de Janeiro, 2014. Two weeks to go before the start of the World Cup. This is my first trip to Brazil, a country that I know only through its seductive and carefully cultivated image: samba, *futebol,* Copacabana, and Niemeyer. All of them are there, and in that sense the image is not built on lies, but it takes only a short stay to realize that the appeal of this image depends every bit as much on what is excluded as it does on its magnified clichés. Like the beauty industry, Brazil's glamour stems from a combination of selective exposure and heavy editing.

Niemeyer was a Communist. One is reminded of this only when one actually visits Brazil. The supple, seemingly effortless curves of his architecture acquire their real significance when they are viewed in the context of Brazil's daily struggles. An architecture ostensibly dedicated to the elimination of any visible sign of creative struggle serves as a promise that eventually all struggles will be a thing of the past. Niemeyer's curves, applied indiscriminately, irrespective of scale—from lush, hedonistic villas to mass housing projects—have a kind of classless appeal to connoisseurs of architecture and casual observers alike. Anyway, it is my host, a representative of the local architecture institute, who reminds me that Brazil's two most important architects were Communists.[1]

The reason for my visit to Brazil, and to Rio in particular, is the 2014 Global Infrastructure Initiative, a conference organized by the international management consultancy firm McKinsey and Co. and chaired by former U.S. secretary of state Madeleine Albright. The delegation is a curious mix of transport and technology executives, engineers, financiers, and present and former politicians. Even the U.S. military is represented. The focus of the conference is "Infrastructure and the City," and the highlight, on day two, is an appearance by Rio de Janeiro mayor Eduardo Paes, who delivers a half-nervous, half-comical account of his troubled life as a mayor whose "wisdom" sought both the World Cup and the Olympic Games in the space of less than two years. His speech is a weird combination of mea culpa and self-pity; Brazil's major cultural accomplishment, he claims, is that it doesn't hide poverty. I decide to leave. I want to see for myself.

"Brazil is a unique melting pot of nationalities and races."[2] At first, the way the country describes itself on breathless tourist websites appears to be true, at least in Rio. Whereas cities in North America often have very distinguishable racial frontiers, reinforced by politically hermetic "identities," Rio presents a full gradient of color. Yet despite the seemingly smooth spectrum of skin tone, the question of race is by no means eliminated. Racism is there alongside *futebol* and the samba, often pronounced and unconcealed by any form of political correctness. During my first night on the town, in a local bar, I hear Brazilians size one another up. The array of skin colors present corresponds flawlessly with an apparently accepted scale of beauty (the whiter the prettier). Despite earlier theorems about Brazil as a postracial country, the absence of clearly defined racial frontiers has not led to the disappearance of the issue of race.[3] Nor has it helped Brazilians emerge in solidarity as a single people. People's color is almost invariably matched by their wealth and social status (the whiter the wealthier). When it comes to race, Brazil's economic DNA is surprisingly in line with global standards.

Brazilians' frank humor about their nation typically includes a quote by a wry Charles de Gaulle in 1947 that runs, "Brazil is the country of the future . . . and always will be." In many ways Rio does feel like the announcement of a strange near-future world, in which differences are not resolved but merely juxtaposed ever more directly and brutally. They coexist, but precisely because they can and they do, they lose any sense of a shared purpose; in fact, they are defined by its absence. It is as though the juxtaposition of difference over long periods of time leads only to a kind of mutual indifference. As long as the status quo doesn't spell imminent collapse, any notion of urgency is infinitely deferred, *amanhã,* to the luxurious hope offered by a perpetual tomorrow. Perhaps this is the ultimate reality, the apex of the urban condition: a zero-sum game in regard to class struggle, racial integration, and all the other issues that the twentieth century had hoped to settle definitively.

I head to the north of the city and to the favelas, which, since the announcement of the World Cup, have become an integral part of Brazil's external image. Incorporated into the general feel-good maelstrom of modern media, the favela now sits comfortably within Rio's official DNA. Still, only the politically correct form permits viewing: the favelas directly adjacent to the city center that have made it into the director's cut, equipped with satellite TV dishes and manicured terraces. (David Beckham reportedly bought a house here for one million reals.)

In the context of a ubiquitous imperative for cities to generate "value," even favelas have turned into a form of real estate. Following the inevitable path to gentrification—legalized overnight, supplied with electricity and district heating—like so many teetering Lego blocks, they look like a kind of impromptu Moshe Safdie scheme. "Brazil doesn't hide poverty," but it keeps a safe distance between those who view and those who suffer it. Seen from the comfort of the Copacabana hotels, the favela doesn't radiate a level of poverty overwhelming enough to worry the establishment (or the accidental tourist). Close to the city center, the favelas are just another part of the varied landscape of "a city in which life is anything but subdued."[4]

Not here, though. This is Zona Norte, home to the Maracanã Stadium, the university, and most of Rio's samba schools. It is also one of the poorest and most spread-out favela districts of Rio de Janeiro. Endless shacks cover the hills like a kind of pixelated fungus. The mayor, I'm told, doesn't come here. The organization of the World Cup and the heavily militarized "pacification" process that ensued in its wake have not made him very popular. Here the city seems to be at war with itself. A large police force with bulletproof vests and M16 automatic rifles is the answer to the local weapon of choice: AK-47s—supposedly easier to come by in this area than refrigerators. Established in 2008, the Police Pacification Unit (UPP) constitutes a distributed network of specially trained and specially armed police cells that have entrenched themselves physically in a fraction of the city's "pacified" favelas. South America's history is multifariously contested, and "La Revolución" is still invoked in many parts of South America as the legitimization of its prolific violence, but in the run-up to the World Cup and the Olympics, much of that feels like belated folklore.

The official definition of a favela is constituted by the absence of "asphalt," that is, the absence of roads constructed by the municipal authorities. In the favela the roads are made by the inhabitants, improvised on an as-needed basis and not included in the city's official street plan. Giving directions to my taxi driver, I need to switch the Google map on my phone from "Standard" to "Satellite View." He concludes that my destination must be in the favela and initially refuses to take me there. Only after I pass him the phone to speak with the person I am supposed to meet does he reluctantly comply.

In the absence of street names, people in the favelas do not have a registered address. This has major implications. Favela residents cannot register for many schools or universities or access health care. Obtaining a bank account is not on the cards; without bank accounts, money transfers to pay regular bills for electricity, running water, and Internet service are inherently problematic, so these are mostly illegally tapped. People do not own their homes, and the state can at any time invoke its right to access its land, destroying anything that is built on it.

This highly precarious condition makes favela life and the economy within it part of a permanently tentative shadow zone. As long as the settlements remain illegal, so does any type of life that takes place there. Even relatively harmless economic activities, such as the trading of secondhand goods, is by definition a black market. Inside the favelas the brutal rule of drug gangs is rivaled by that of informal militias composed of off-duty (and sometimes even on-duty) policemen, firemen, prison guards, and members of the military and many local residents. Under the pretense of taking on the drug trade, these informal militias extort money from favela residents for their "protection" against the violence of the drug gangs. Subsequently the *favelados,* or inhabitants, find themselves caught between two types of crime: the crimes committed by the drug gangs and the crimes committed by those purportedly fighting the gangs.

Roughly one-fifth of Cariocas are estimated to be favela residents, many of whom live in a state of exception. The favelas constitute a kind of universe of their own: a state within the state, with an economy not included in official statistics. The first favelas were established in the late nineteenth century by veteran soldiers with no place to live. Most of the current favelas, however, expanded in the 1970s as a construction boom in the more affluent districts of Rio de Janeiro stimulated an influx of rural workers from the poorer states in Brazil. It was not until the 1980s, after the collapse of Brazil's dictatorship and its economy, that the favelas found themselves associated with drugs. Changing routes of production and consumption made cosmopolitan and glamorous Rio a prime transit point for cocaine destined for Europe. The prospects and realities of higher incomes earned through the narcotics trade propelled it to an important part of the favelas' economy.

Although the favela areas under official "pacification" have seen improvements, there has been an increase in gang activity across other parts of Rio de Janeiro that lack permanent UPP forces, which themselves have been subject to scandal and corruption. Among these areas are the neighborhoods in the Zona Norte, where I find myself today. The north zone is the frontier of the pacification process. As such, it forms a strange hybrid territory between the supposed reassertion of state control and the former free state before pacification. The policemen who patrol the streets here stick closely together. They are heavily armed, but that doesn't conceal their palpable nervousness. The whole thing sadly reminds me of photos of American soldiers in Iraq: an occupation force with the impossible task of living up to the image of being a "liberating" force.

Brazil's urban population has grown dramatically: in 1950 only 30 percent of all Brazilians lived in cities; today it is 85 percent. In the same period, Rio de Janeiro's metropolitan population has increased fourfold, from three to twelve million.[5] Rio has grown faster than its economy or its infrastructure can sustain, and the same is true of all major cities in Brazil. The spectacular growth of these cities, as we have seen over the past decades, does not necessarily mean that more of its people have become urbane; instead, more and more people who flock to the city simply continue their former rural way of life within the borders of the city. In the absence of even the most basic infrastructure and provisions, many of those who migrate to the city find a decent urban life beyond their reach. What we see in Rio is by now a global phenomenon; megacities share the feature of development outpaced by growth. What we refer to as "urbanization" (literally, the step toward the urbane) has in many ways come to constitute the exact opposite. In that sense, ever-larger numbers of city dwellers do not signal the triumph of the urban but more and more its unmasking.

Urbanization was supposed to be the world's quick ticket to prosperity. At least on paper, the average urban dweller represents five times the economy of the rural dweller.[6] When a rural nation becomes urban in the space of a decade, its economy, again at least on paper, doubles every two years. But in most cases the statistics conceal reality. The influx of new and ever-poorer inhabitants is larger than most cities can handle. Consequently, many cities resort to an elaborate repertoire of denial in the face of mounting problems. Inhabitants who "overload the system" are not recognized by the city's administrative systems and are denied access to a city's administrative body. They are forced into a situation where they officially do not exist. Rio's favela residents do not have an address; immigrant workers in Dubai and Moscow are not counted as part of the cities' populations. In China the hukou system makes being a city dweller a "birthright" and denies many of China's rural city dwellers any hope of gaining the right to live in the city legally. The contemporary city breeds a kind of schizophrenic reality. On the one hand, there is the official version, expressed in censuses and municipal data; on the other hand, there is the unofficial or real city with a large number of nonregistered (illegal) residents, creating a vast but administratively invisible urban population and an economy unrecognized in official statistics.

Within ten years all of the world's largest cities will be located outside the West. Of the thirty-seven megalopolises predicted for the 2020s, twenty-eight will be located in the world's least developed countries. The metropolis, once the zenith of Western civilization, is now the property of the third world. What are the real implications of the seemingly triumphal statement that "more than half the world's population lives in cities"? So far, arguments for the city have mainly been defined in terms of opportunities: social, cultural, economic, academic. Those who inhabit the city are defined as cosmopolitan: citizens of the world. When we use this word, we generally think of a comprehensively mobile (affluent, educated) group of people, unhindered by traditional loyalties to place or nation. As the urban condition becomes universal, we can all be "cosmopolitan." It is precisely this false promise that constitutes the most venomous aspect of our current fixation on the city. The more the world aspires to a shiny, urbane life, the more it finds this kind of life unattainable. For the illegal migrant worker in Moscow, an idealized, tech-driven urban environment is no more a reality than it is for the inhabitants of Rio's favelas. In the wake of a massive influx into cities, we are witnessing the emergence of another kind of "citizen of the world": those who have drawn the short straw of globalization and for whom living in the city simply amounts to being a new kind of "cosmoproletariat."

If globalization has exported metropolitan conditions into the third world, it has also imported third-world conditions into the metropolis. While the economies of poorer states appear to be catching up with richer ones, the inequalities between individuals within states have only grown. We have not progressed; we have just changed location. The move to the city was long assumed to be a major step in upgrading the lives of people, but just as nineteenth-century England saw the rise of the disenfranchised urban proletariat—eloquently captured by the German term *Verelendung*[7]—the global market economy gives rise to another disenfranchised class, now elevated to a global market scale. What started as Friedrich Engels's description of the living conditions of England's working poor ultimately led to a political theory that would radically inflect the geopolitical landscape of the century to come.[8] What will be the political legacy of the new urban poor, those who are currently ignored by our collective administrative systems?

It can be argued that any system of exploitation relies on an asymmetry in the degree of knowledge and control of its operational logic. Only by barring the larger number of sufferers from access to and even information about the levers of power can the beneficiaries continue their existence as "the happy few." As soon as the asymmetry is lifted, the larger volume of sufferers will inevitably lead to an overthrow of the system. This begs the question: Can a political force be constructed from people who don't even exist? If power is ultimately a question of numbers, what happens when the number of people whose existence the system formally denies (but on whose compliance the system ultimately depends) reaches a critical mass—large enough to rival the forces that have denied them access? What if the seemingly inevitable "way of the world" is exposed as merely the temporary consensus of a minority?

The second half of the twentieth century was characterized by a precarious standoff between two competing political hegemonies. In a battle between dollars and demographics, the leading economies of the West were challenged by an ideology fueled by those it had left behind in Korea and Southeast Asia and later in Latin America and Africa. For a while, it seemed that a battle for world dominance could be decided there, on continents recently liberated from colonial ties, looking for a future on their own terms.

The next ideological battle will be fought not over continents but over cities. The challenge will come from whoever—or whatever—will be able to galvanize the support of all those denied a voice in the (breakup of the) urban condition. It will no longer be about who should govern but about governance itself, the end of which comes when it can no longer deliver on its promises.

As the conference progresses, hopes are increasingly pinned on the "digital." On our last day we are taken on an excursion to the Centro de Operações of Rio de Janeiro, a kind of digital ersatz town hall from which life in the city is "managed," created to allow the municipal authorities a quicker response time to imminent trouble. Data collected from GPSs, sensors, and video cameras throughout the city are processed through advanced computer algorithms, helping predict the probability of floods, rainfall, traffic jams, garbage avalanches from hillside favelas, and even certain crimes, from armed robberies to violent protests. The place evokes a curious mix of euphoria and discomfort. The possibilities of (digital) technology are clearly impressive, but the metaphor underlying the design of the Centro's interior—channeling NASA's control room in Houston—conveys a rather disturbing flip side where the city is encountered like an inevitable fact of nature: "outer space." Confronted with a hostile environment, employees are prescribed to wear jumpsuits, observing their subject from a screen. No longer is the city "made by us, for us," our own creation over which we exercise free will; it is something that happens to us, an extraneous phenomenon whose roles shape our daily lives, and the behavior of which we can at best, armed with the latest in artificial intelligence, hope to predict.

The digital was meant to make things visible, but in regard to the governance of our cities, it has largely obscured our view. The supposed omniscience of the digital has allowed the political sphere to do a Houdini act, whereby the endless simulation of reality also permits the infinite deferral of political choices. We can now monitor the favela residents on a computer screen, study their informal patterns, and possibly predict when they are about to make trouble. But in no way does their surveillance constitute a step toward any real civic recognition and all that may come with it. In systematically escaping the question of political responsibility and in simply analyzing ground conditions, on a par with natural disasters, we inevitably set the city on a course to become one.

Centro de Operações, Prefeitura do Rio
Photograph by Reinier de Graaf

35

Smart Cities of the Future

I don't know what prompted me to speak at the conference, but I did. Perhaps it was a strange need to assert myself in a setting where I felt out of place. Anyway, there I was, on stage in front of a large crowd of digital technology experts—corporate CEOs, academic luminaries, and government officials—explaining how to "engineer the smart city of the future" in line with the organizers' wishes, with a headset and a laser pointer as my only aides.

The introductory video, recorded the week before, set me up for trouble. With a bravado as calculated as it probably was misplaced, I had confessed on camera that I had no real clue what the smart city was; in my view, the main impact of digital technology on the built environment was that there was none.

What exactly is the "smart city"? Despite attending many similar conferences, I had never received a clear answer. For a long time I thought that I was the only ignorant one in the room. But the more of these conferences I visited, the more it dawned on me that perhaps I was not alone; that there were others like me; that this is a subject of which nobody has a clear notion; that maybe that's the whole point. Perhaps the smart city is such a perfect subject precisely because it allows everybody to speak in the absence of knowledge—or rather, to display his or her specific knowledge without having to go through the trouble of checking its relevance. Maybe the smart city is the ultimate free-for-all—a jam session of otherwise incompatible minds.

The smart city's momentum has built tremendously over the past decade, to the point that by now the cost of candor has become too high. Admitting ignorance of, or even professing doubt toward, the smart city is not an option. There are simply too many people who have too much to lose—not least their face—from its exposure as a potential hoax. This is a bubble that cannot burst. We can't afford to deny the smart city's many blessings, even in the absence of any real evidence.

There was that title: "Engineering Smart Cities of the Future." I decide to conduct a little experiment. The conference title contained one adjective and two nouns: smart, city, and future. I enter each term into a Google image search.

City: A collection of more or less typical images of cityscapes and skylines emerges on screen. As an architect, I relate to these images easily. I know most of the cities from personal or professional experience; our office has built in some of them. For the most part, the images look similar. The effect of modern technology (skyscrapers clad in curtain walls) seems universal. It is difficult to identify one city as more advanced or intelligent than the next. These cities are either all smart or not at all smart.

Smart: The only pictures to appear on screen are those of cars—in fact, one type of car: the smart car. Indeed, only one brand of smart car: the Smart. Corporate infiltration of the English language is apparently such that it can claim a monopoly over entire words.

Future: Road signs emblazoned with the word "Future" fill the screen, like a new screensaver designed by somebody trying to be funny. Jean Baudrillard once described highways as places of conformism: "A route that leads nowhere, but keeps one in touch with everyone. Any speculation about the future is pointless. . . . The whole point is to keep thinking about the future, if only as an existential ritual. . . . It is important to suspend any definitive conclusions. . . . We're all going somewhere, even if it doesn't matter where."[1] Google seems to have understood.

Cars, road signs . . . I am disoriented. Is the smart city about transport? Clearly the phenomenon is closely related to the computer, to the digital, but the emphatic presence of the car is new to me. Intrepid now, I continue my Google free dive; on a whim, I type in "cars" and "computers." The site that pops up is vwdieselinfo.com: Volkswagen Diesel Information. The message: "We're working to make things right." I stop.

What conclusion can be drawn from this somewhat unfortunate Google journey? In September 2015 Volkswagen's "Dieselgate" exposed the measures used to deliberately mask the polluting capacity of certain cars equipped with TDI (turbo diesel injection) engines. Does the scandal— ultimately the outcome of a combination of cars and computers—reveal the true nature of the smart city: a way of bending the rules, of beating and cheating the system? How seriously should we take the smart city as a credible way of dealing with and intervening in an ancient and complex phenomenon such as the city?

Around the world, cities from Amsterdam to Melbourne are eager to connect their infrastructure to the Internet, hoping to improve their citizens' lives while streamlining ever-shrinking budgets. Singapore is intent on becoming the world's first "smart nation." In the imagined smart city-state, traffic jams will be a thing of the past. The monitoring of traffic flows will reroute approaching autonomous vehicles from the blockages; continuous study of weather patterns will anticipate and warn the populace of an upcoming heat wave or storm and dispatch emergency service ahead of time to danger-prone areas. In the last instance, the automation of bureaucratic processes will rid the government of all unnecessary administrative work and possibly even of the need for governance itself.

Once considered to be the domain of architects and urban planners, the city is now a crowded field of creative innovators, digital entrepreneurs, asset managers, software vendors, social engineers, real estate moguls, urban consultants, start-ups, and tech giants. In offering services like health care, energy, public safety, and education, smart-city initiatives claim responsibilities formerly attributed to the public sector. The combined advertising brochures of IBM, Siemens, and Cisco (three of the largest smart-city protagonists) go well beyond the competences of the traditional urbanists. They offer solutions for climate change, dwindling resources, aging populations, rising energy prices, economic turmoil, population growth, and, however ironically, rapid urbanization.

Predicting the apocalypse in order to offer redemption, the rhetoric of the smart city unwittingly invokes a two-thousand-year-old formula: that of the Bible. And, as often happens when the Bible is invoked, the smart city reeks of hypocrisy: a desperate search for a good cause, enacted to ease a bad conscience. It is the pursuit of business that lies at the core of the smart city: nothing more, nothing less. While eager to claim a large, lucrative portfolio of public services, advocates of the smart city are uninterested in any public accountability. It is the perfect veil for an aggressive form of privatization, one that reduces the actual city to the *cadavre exquis* of corporate interests.

Corporate representatives in the audience nod approvingly as I share my thoughts. The conference is about to end. People make their way to the buffet and exchange business cards. Participants seem generally content. A middle-aged man wearing a bright green tie introduces himself as an environmental, social, and urban engineer. He congratulates me on my performance: "We need more of those!" The robustness of the smart city, echoed in an equally robust handshake, has once again been confirmed: smart enough to absorb a diverse array of viewpoints, even ridicule.

36

The Sum of All Isms

It used to be ours, at least ours to plan: the city. That no longer holds true. We have company. As the predominant form of human settlement, the city has become the subject of universal fascination: no longer the exclusive property of architecture or urban planning but the preoccupation of virtually every professional domain: technology, politics, sociology, and business.

The list is long. McKinsey and Co. is "planning" cities in India, in which it will manage both private and "public" services; Siemens proposes large-scale urban infrastructure, generally as a precursor of Siemens trains; Shell works on Chinese cities, liberally equipping them with Shell gas stations; and IKEA is methodically creating "meatball neighborhoods" in Outer London, to be furnished with still more of Sweden's finest flat pack. The tech industry has been quick to tag along: Cisco focuses on smart cities, IBM on smarter cities; Oracle is the smartest, soon to be out-smarted by Google.

In academia. too, "the city" has become a prevalent theme, the connective tissue that provides a common ground to otherwise hermetic and disconnected university faculties, a last resort for intellectual speculation. In a world that demands that education be useful and prioritizes applications over theory (or "critical discourse," those great dirty words of the 1970s), cities have become the perfect alibi. Cities are the new *studium generale*: the program through which universities once cultivated a general sort of "knowledge of the world" in parallel to the specialized programs of their individual faculties. More than half the world now lives in cities, and the other half is not far behind; knowledge of the city, more than ever before, equals knowledge of the world.

Still, looking at the number of institutions that offer the city their intellectual services, one wonders who is being served by whom. The city seems to provide a last sense of purpose in a postideological world for commercial and educational sectors alike: private companies rely on the city for their business, while academia needs the city for meaningful application of its knowledge. The honest truth is that our relationship to the city is not one of authority but one of dependence; the city now feeds and shapes intellectual debate, not vice versa. Instead of pretending to cater to the city's supposed needs, we should acknowledge that it is the momentum of the city—somehow independent of our actions—that motivates us.

The fact that the fastest-growing cities are in developing countries has caused deep discomfort in the West, once the leader in urban growth. The emergence of the megacity and its predominant manifestations outside the West is now mainly discussed as a crisis. It is interesting to observe how the change from city to megacity has created a marked shift in the tone of the discourse. The city conjures up images of cosmopolitan confidence, of the ultimate showcases of human ability; the megacity inspires only a sense of despair. It is an uncontrollable phenomenon, an unwelcome escalation, an onslaught on scarce resources, an overstretching and seemingly ineluctable breakdown of all forms of infrastructure, and a force beyond any credible form of governance. Discussions of the megacity have become synonymous with the foreboding of an imminent apocalypse. Yet the shift must entail more than just an escalation of scale: if the megacity were simply a larger version of the city, this would not explain the wholesale panic with which it is received. What if the shift is more fundamental? What if we are not witnessing a crisis of the city but a crisis of knowledge?

In the 1950s the city was still a more or less controllable entity, broadly obeying the doctrines of urban planning; the current megacity is like an organism. The tremors registering the advent of the megacity are not dissimilar to those felt in the face of climate change or natural disasters.

We stand back and observe the megacity—ultimately our own creation—as if it were an act of God, one that, at best, can be made to adjust course through a kind of retroactive acupuncture. Traffic bypasses, pedestrianized zones, deliberate amortization of certain quarters: in the same way a surgeon operates on the human body, we now perform operations on the city, intervening in its internal workings and hoping for recovery. Congestion charges, emissions taxes, widening of circulation routes, and other remedial measures are the urban equivalent of painkillers or experimental medicine; piecemeal urban renewal is the plastic surgery that keeps the city's oldest quarters forever young.

So far, the repertoire we have unleashed on the megacity has been mainly technological. However, by insisting that the megacity is a technological phenomenon, subject to "smart" solutions, we have also reduced the megacity to a mere subject of problem solving, resorting to familiar and assertive reflexes of "help" and "support" without critically questioning our position toward it. We are again banking on the blessings of technology while failing to see that in its present form, the city arises first and foremost from an escalation of the same blessings. At present there is no comprehensive theoretical framework that allows us first to understand our relation to the megacity. Without such a framework, our remedies may well be contributing to the problems we insist on fixing.

When it comes to the megacity, there is no monopoly on knowledge, either by architecture or by any other sector. No single discipline can claim to hold all the answers. Even if certain tech companies suggest that they can go it alone, providing the complete range of services necessary to create successful cities, it is only a matter of time before their claims are exposed as hubris, the same hubris that saw the utopian visions of twentieth-century architecture definitively bite the dust.

If the city is a place of exchange that progresses only through a carefully crafted form of negotiation, then perhaps this is also the best principle for any kind of intellectual constellation that endeavors to address the city: a possibility of exchange among different (and potentially competing) forms of knowledge, a kind of intellectual bazaar where viewpoints are traded. Only through a joining of intellectual forces can there be any hope of coming to terms with a phenomenon whose workings defy any singular form of logic. Rather than thinking about shaping the future of the city, perhaps we should be open to letting the city shape the future of our thinking. (Architecture has learned the hard way in this respect.) Perhaps it is time to stop treating the city as the accidental topic of choice for various sciences or professional disciplines and to emancipate it in its own right. The city is the arena where almost all forms of knowledge are acted out, simultaneously a breeding ground, test lab, and theater of operations. Consequently, the city affects all domains of knowledge alike; the city is the sum of all isms.

The city offers a platform for both the academic and the business worlds—for experts from the fields of technology, energy, sustainability, infrastructure, telecommunications, transport, finance, architecture, design, public policy, and research. It is a domain where professionals and scholars, lecturers and audience, and sponsors and actors convene in the context of a shared fascination. For all involved in the city, taking part is not just a matter of reflecting on its current state but also a matter of self-reflection: the city not as the object in need of help but, ironically, a compelling means for self-help, providing the charming comfort of a twelve-step meeting, in which we form a circle of trust and take turns admitting that we have been keeping up a front, claiming expertise in the absence of real understanding—united through the frank admission that we do not have a clue.

37

Dear Mr. Barber

An open letter to Benjamin Barber, initiator of the Global Parliament of Mayors

Amsterdam, September 23, 2014

Dear Mr. Barber:

Thank you for the opportunity to participate in the planning session of your Global Parliament of Mayors in Amsterdam last Friday. I had been looking forward to a fruitful exchange and the opportunity to receive your feedback on a number of questions, but unfortunately the lack of time allocated to nonscripted contributions did not allow for this during Friday's sessions, so instead I will make use of the form of a public letter.

There are certain persistent thoughts that I have regarding your initiative "The Global Parliament of Mayors" (GPM), which I would like to share—first and foremost, with you; second, through this public letter, also with the other mayors, deputy mayors, mayors' representatives, and other invited guests who participated in the sessions; and finally, with anyone who comes across this document because they are paying attention to your initiative.

In your book *If Mayors Ruled the World* you dismiss the current political system of nations and its leaders as dysfunctional. Defined by borders and with an inevitable focus on national interests, they are not an effective vehicle to govern a world defined by interdependence. Mayors, presiding over cities with their more open, networked structure and cosmopolitan demographics, you claim, could do it better.

Not surprisingly, your book has been welcomed by the same political class that you praise in it: mayors. This was apparent during the first planning session of the GPM: a conference about mayors, for mayors, attended by mayors, moderated by mayors, and hosted by a mayor, all triggered by a book about mayors.

I have read your book, and I recognize many of its observations. I have also encountered some of the mayors interviewed in the book personally, in my capacity as architect and planner. It is true that there are impressive figures among them and that time appears to be on their side. Nation-states (particularly the large ones) are having an increasingly hard time, and, in the context of a process of globalization, cities—particularly small city-states—increasingly emerge victorious. Cities have firsthand experience with many of the things that follow in globalization's wake, such as immigration and cultural and religious diversity, and are generally less dogmatic and more practical in dealing with them.

So far, so good.

For me, the problem arises when you suggest cities as a blueprint for global governance. I would argue that the current generation of mayors, which you describe in your book, is successful precisely because they do *not* rule the world. They are successful because they are allowed to focus on smaller, more immediate, more local responsibilities, which means that their efforts by definition generate quicker and more visible results. To remove that focus by attributing global responsibilities to them would (probably) quickly undo that success. Yes, mayors are popular—but how long would they continue to be popular once they had assumed responsibilities currently allocated to national leaders? In any case, it remains questionable whether popularity automatically equals competence to govern. Kings and queens are generally much more popular than national politicians, but few of us would want to return to a system in which they actually ruled.

One reason for the current vitality of cities is the luxury that some of the more heavy-handed political responsibilities are outside their power. Cities can thus opportunistically use the world as an arena in which they are players, free to engage in a game of global competition without the excess baggage that nations (for very good reason) find imposed on themselves. To quote the success of cities in the context of a globalized, interdependent world as a reason for cities to govern that same world is, in my view, a huge conceptual mistake. In fact, I would argue the opposite: that the very success of cities, by definition, makes them less suited to play a role in global governance. Having success in the context of globalization is something very different from ensuring that globalization unfolds in a just and fair way. Players cannot be expected to be referees. To declare the victors to be the rulers is nothing short of preaching the law of the jungle.

You frequently refer to a crisis of democracy: people no longer feel adequately represented by the elected governments of their (nation-) states anymore, but how would that improve if mayors took over? Currently half of humanity lives in cities. That is, in itself, an impressive figure, but it also implies that the other half does not live in cities. This begs the question: should mayors indeed rule the world, who would represent the other half? All nations combined include all of humanity, and the first thing that a transferal of power to cities would achieve is to cut that number in half—hardly an improvement.

Similarly, you claim that cities are more effective than nations in dealing with global problems like climate change and migration, but I fail to see how an escalation of world problems can ever be addressed through a deescalation (from nation to city) of the scale of governance. Just as cities contain only half the world's population, they also hold only half the answers to globalization's main challenges. You quote climate change as an example of where cities hold the key, but I would argue that climate change is probably the worst possible example you could use. No matter how many electric vehicles we will have driving in our cities, their effect on CO_2 emission reduction will remain negligible as long as that electricity is generated by fossil-fueled energy plants outside the city limits.

Migration is another example. Cities are bastions of cultural and religious diversity, places where immigrants—even illegal ones—can exist with a relative degree of security and recognition. But what does this say about the phenomenon of migration as a whole? Why do people choose to move in such large numbers across the world, often at their peril? How can this be explained other than as a desperate attempt to escape the fundamental asymmetries and disparities that characterize our globalized world? Africa suffers an enormous brain drain as a result of migration, as did formerly Communist countries of the Eastern Bloc after the fall of the Berlin Wall. Entire continents are being left to their own (dwindling) devices, unable to hold on to people, watching as the very disparity that inspires migration is only exacerbated as a result. No romantic portrayal of the city (not even one delivered with an Italian accent, such as by the mayor of Palermo) as "a mosaic of mosaics" contributes any substantial solution to large-scale migration as an increasingly daunting global reality. An inflated idealization of the city's current condition may well prove to be a dangerous legitimization of a deeply fraught mechanism. In short: it is true that cities demonstrate a certain creativity in the face of globalization's discontents, but that by no means makes the actions of cities a cure-all prescription. In terms of the current global challenges, cities mostly address symptoms, not the root causes.

Back to the question of democracy: how democratic are cities? In many countries, the mayor is not an elected figure. In the Netherlands and in France, for instance, mayors are appointed by the national government, often as a sign of appreciation for a role they once fulfilled within it. In that sense, mayors resemble the patriarchal leftover of a system of co-optation more closely than they do the enlightened democratic figures portrayed in your book. In most countries, voter turnouts for local elections are still significantly lower than those for national elections. In addition, when it comes to corruption and abuse of powers, mayors have an even worse track record than national leaders. There was no sign of Rob Ford, Toronto's crack-smoking mayor, this weekend in Amsterdam: not in the GPM session nor in the city's coffee shops.

It remains difficult to imagine, given the current setup of many cities, how a world governed by those cities could pose a plausible alternative to a world governed by nations (other than replacing one dysfunctional system with another). Of the one hundred largest economies in the world, thirty-seven are corporations, which, like certain cities, have outgrown nations. Walmart is bigger than Norway, Cisco is bigger than Lebanon, Ford is bigger than Morocco, BP is bigger than Greece (even after its billion-euro support package). Where previously corporations held a certain affiliation to their nations of origin, currently their affiliation lies with a largely footloose global business community. Corporate growth has spelled the end of corporate loyalty; headlines about tax dodges provide evidence on an almost daily basis. It is doubtful at best that these corporations will be any more loyal to cities. To advocate the end of the nation-state could well be advocating the unfettered rule of global capital—handing over its last alibi to go fully unchecked.

It would appear that there can be no increased role for mayors without a fundamental rethink of the office of mayor itself. A degree of introspection seems necessary to allow cities to come to terms with their own problems before mayors assume a role, let alone a responsibility, in solving global issues. Cities across the world face similar issues. However, these almost never arise because mayors lack a global mandate. It is not so much the interdependence of cities on a global scale as it is the interdependence between cities and their immediate surroundings that plagues urban areas. To give an example: very few of what we call metropolises even exist as such. We classify Moscow as Europe's only megacity, with a population of approximately twenty million, but that is actually the population of an administratively fragmented region that carries the same name, while the mandate of Moscow's mayor is limited to less than ten million inhabitants. We think of Paris as a metropolis of ten million inhabitants, but in reality, the Parisian mayor presides over just two million inhabitants, leaving the rest of the metropolitan area as a tapestry of individual towns. The scale of the metropolis is generally such that it transcends the powers of a single mayor; attempts to create larger administrative units generally hit a wall because of vested political interests, where. ironically. mayors find themselves arguing with other mayors. Paradoxically, superurban planning concepts like Grand Paris and Big Moscow have served only to erode mayoral powers and reinforce the rule of the state: Grand Paris under the Élysée and Big Moscow under the Kremlin. Only when cities are able to seize the initiative in dealing with their immediate surroundings can they hope to act as true global powers. An enhanced role of mayors on a global stage might mean that we need to have fewer mayors first—probably not a conclusion that a happily symbiotic institution, such as the Global Parliament of Mayors, is likely to draw.

The idea of a global parliament of mayors leaves one with an overwhelming sense of confusion, even long after the idea has gone public. What is the exact nature of your proposition? A parliament, or not a parliament? This is a basic summary of the discussion as it took place this weekend: "A parliament, or perhaps rather a movement" (Europe's most notorious dictators have made interesting moves in this direction). The idea of a parliament was invented as a dialectical instrument to control power once the necessity to separate powers had been recognized: to pass, modify, or reject laws proposed by kings or governments. The central question here is: Which power does this parliament control? Whose laws does or doesn't it pass? To whom does it direct its difficult questions? To itself?

Without an answer to that question, it remains difficult to identify a real use for the parliament other than for mayors to dwell on one another's greatness. If last Friday's session in Amsterdam is anything to go by, the new parliament of mayors feels suspiciously similar to the former parliaments of Eastern Europe: an endorsement machine, with free debate as its first casualty.

One notion was met with overwhelming consensus: a parliament of mayors should not be bureaucratic. But is the current, almost universal aversion to bureaucracy really such a smart idea? In a world where institutions are weak and global agreements are increasingly precarious, it would seem that the most urgent global threat, more urgent even than climate change and international migration, is that of an imminent collapse of the system itself. In that context, it is increasingly those whose rights are not secured on paper who merit our concern. To them, bureaucracy might actually constitute an exhilarating prospect.

In such a context, I would not advocate a parliament of mayors to replace "an outdated institution such as the national parliament" (as suggested by one of the delegates). I would prefer to give a new relevance to the notion of subsidiarity, in which the increased importance of cities is recognized and actively crafted, but where they are integrated into a global political system that clearly recognizes which decisions should be taken at which level. Cities are free to engage and exchange at whatever level they want, but that freedom is enjoyed under the current political system, the same system that has granted them the very freedoms that have allowed them to thrive.

After reading your book, I have often wondered what a world ruled by mayors would look like. I do not have the answer, but my best guess is that it would probably be a combination of uncertainty, difficult choices, and a fair amount of chaos: pretty much like the world we have now.

Well, Mr. Barber, these are my thoughts. I appreciate that this was not a discussion you wanted to have after a long day on Friday. However, I hope that, based on the above, you would be kind enough to reconsider.

Looking forward to your reply,

Yours sincerely,

Reinier de Graaf

38

At Your Service

Ten Steps to Becoming a Successful Urban Consultant

I

Frequently attend conferences. Don't mingle with members of your profession, but find the odd mayor looking for answers. Inevitably he or she will be disappointed. Make animated conversation, tell him or her you share his or her frustrations. Appear to be listening. Emphasize the limited value of established professional approaches in today's world; dismiss them as crude generalizations, unequipped to deal with contemporary issues. Present your own approach, rooted in particular experiences—your experiences. Upon parting, hand over your business card and politely suggest that the two of you join forces and find a reason to "collaborate."

II

Let no fewer than ten and no more than twenty-one days pass before you, or rather your company, sends a letter, reminding the mayor of your meeting. Give him or her credit for the suggestion to "work together," thereby elevating your suggestion to the status of an official invite. You can then offer to visit the city in order to conduct an X-ray of its problems. Offer to pay for your travel. (This will be the last nonreimbursable expense.)

III

When you visit the city, start by paying compliments. Of course, the essence of your presence is to be critical, but it may be wise, at least for a while, to prolong the suspense. Let people guess exactly what it is that you have to offer. On your first visit as an adviser (never admit that this is your first visit ever), mention how you are "touched by the city's history, culture, and spirit." In spite of "recent setbacks," the city's vitality seems irrepressible. (Make sure that most of your compliments pertain to the city's people and not to the city itself.) Don't go so far as to suggest that the city might not need your advice, but use your complimentary observations as the first subtle disclaimer of the validity of any eventual recommendations.

IV

Then, casually observe the remarkable similarity between the place that you are visiting and other places. This is the moment you start becoming an authority. Find a good city to reference, preferably one far away and not very well known. Draw from personal experiences; pick a city you once worked in. Trumpet the unsung qualities of that city. The experience you bring to the table doesn't have to be limited to work; a short period of residence or even a history of repeated visits will do. In offering credible advice, there is nothing like using one's hometown as the ultimate reference. As soon as the subject at hand can be related to childhood memories, all professional advice turns personal. You become the source you quote.

V

Your value as a consultant depends on the extent to which others credit you for being able to predict the future. Signal a shared transformative process between the city you have selected as a reference and the city you are serving. Claim that this process has evolved slightly further in the city of reference. The present condition of the city of reference then becomes a sneak preview of the future condition of the city you are serving. All that needs to be done is to follow—or ingeniously diverge from—the course already carved out.

VI

So as not to reinvent the wheel for every new job, make sure that the objectives and aspirations you advocate are universally applicable. Make sure that nothing you cite as a potential result of your work can be measured or quantified. In consultancy terms, the more the indexes of success and failure are interchangeable, the better. Avoid talking about form;

talk about principles. Avoid all references to the physical. Instead, talk about regeneration, vibrant communities, the public realm, cooperative planning, neighborhoods, family life, and health. All these phenomena will, in some form or fashion, already be in place. The good thing is that later you will be able to claim them as a result of your work.

VII

Avoid writing. Insist on giving verbal advice. Present this approach as a means to limit the client's financial expenditure on you. When writing becomes an inescapable part of your deliverables, avoid a narrative and stick to bullet points (Microsoft PowerPoint offers a wide array of choices). Unless you stumble across a major breakthrough that you want to claim as your own (the chances of this are slim), do not insist on taking credit for your work. In fact, it is often preferable to shield yourself behind a brand other than your own. You don't want to limit business, and future clients may not share the same interests.

VIII

As a final disclaimer, insist that recommendations notwithstanding, each place is unique and should devise its own specific solutions to its own specific problems. Again, pay extensive compliments to the city you are serving. Speak of its unlimited potential, but this time widen the perspective: reference other cities in the country, not as models but as sources of inspiration. Don't hesitate to invoke national pride. It can be a rich source of future work.

IX

Manage your itinerary. Plan appointments elsewhere by the time your recommendations materialize. In case they do not materialize, also plan appointments elsewhere.

X

Invoice early and invoice often.

The world's most livable cities (2015)

1. Melbourne
2. Vienna
3. Vancouver
4. Toronto
5=. Calgary
5=. Adelaide
7. Sydney
8. Helsinki
9. Perth
10. Auckland

Source: The Economist Intelligence Unit (EIU).

39

Rankings

The Human Development Index (HDI), published annually by the United Nations, ranks nations according to their citizens' "quality of life." The criteria for calculating these rankings include life expectancy, adult literacy, school enrollment, education, and adjusted real income. In 2007 the country at the top of this list was Iceland.

Despite its lofty claims of a thorough evaluation, what is most remarkable about this study is the eventual absurdity of the outcome. Two years later, Iceland's reputation was redefined by a de facto state of bankruptcy. If the country would top any list, it might conceivably be a ranking of nations with the highest degree of uncertainty about their future.

The indexing of human development is an extremely precarious undertaking, but the UN HDI is not the only attempt of its kind. The desire to quantify complex and ultimately subjective human conditions, such as health, happiness, well-being, or quality of life, is increasingly common and has precipitated an extremely lucrative and self-perpetuating market in unprovable projections. Among hundreds of others, both verified and independent, documents produced by *Monocle,* the *Economist,* and Mercer have emerged as the most prominent lists of the world's most livable cities. They rank cities by assessing key determinants ranging from political and social environments to recreation, housing, health, and sanitation. In 2015 the Economist Intelligence Unit's livability assessment named Melbourne as the most livable city in the world, with Vienna and Vancouver taking second and third place, respectively. The same three cities also headed the list in 2014, which was identical with the exception of Auckland and Perth outranking Helsinki.

The problem with such lists is obviously their essential premise: any system of ranking is inevitably based on a drastic reduction of the true number of variables that define a place. In their effort to quantify the unquantifiable, the lists' conclusions seem to speak more to the prescriptive absurdity latent within the whole idea of ranking than to the actual qualities of the cities they list. The fact that Helsinki overtook Auckland on the 2015 list—who knows why?—is indicative: a seemingly random shift generated by supposedly objective qualities. The pecking order of cities may well prove as fleeting as Iceland's status as the world's most developed nation after 2007.

By prioritizing a limited set of criteria by which cities will be measured—and therefore to which they must conform in order to earn their place on the list—such rankings also prompt an irreversible corrosion of diversity both within and among individual cities. Melbourne and Vancouver may be renowned for comparable levels of general convenience and affluence but—and without prejudice—hardly for a particularly unique character or authenticity. It is as though the more cities rely on rankings to emphasize their superior singularity, the more alike they become.

Perhaps the whole idea of ranking cities is a symptom of a problem. Over the past decades cities have become dependent on private initiatives for their development. In their attempt to join the ranks, cities compete to target the same mobile, business-oriented audience, and developers often apply the same standard formula to their planning: land uses that are deemed more profitable are placed in city centers to increase the value of the land with the sole ambition of producing higher returns on investment.

Small businesses, affordable housing, and even small-scale manufacturing—once the lifeblood of the city, whatever the hemisphere—must give way to the more lucrative high-end retail businesses, expensive office space, and luxury residential properties. As a consequence, new urban hot spots share the same generic composition of quasi-commercial uses everywhere, with the same generic type of architecture to accommodate them. Large government housing programs have become virtually obsolete, and today the municipal role is generally limited to granting or refusing permission to private development plans.

In the hands of these forces, urban planning becomes a strategic exercise, driven by economic rather than spatial parameters. By reducing the city to a set of checked boxes on a chart, livability indexes and rankings such as those produced by *Monocle*, Mercer, or the *Economist* unwittingly serve as evidence of the collapse of a comprehensive system, indeed, a proper comprehension, of planning.

The world's least livable cities

1. Damascus, Syria
2. Tripoli, Libya
3. Lagos, Nigeria
4. Dhaka, Bangladesh
5=. Port Moresby, Papua New Guinea
5=. Algiers, Algeria
7. Karachi, Pakistan
8. Harare, Zimbabwe
9. Douala, Cameroon
10. Kiev, Ukraine

Source: The Economist Intelligence Unit (EIU).

In the end, cities can endure only as a construct of public interests. By agreeing to compete for a number one spot on prestigious lists, they ensure only their eventual demise.

In 2016 Melbourne topped the Economist list as the world's most livable city once again. It did so for the seventh year in a row. In those same seven years the list's top ten has never featured a single non-western city. As the least livable cities it invariably cites non-western cities, in countries rife with civil unrest, war and continued threats from major terrorist groups. One wonders what signal such rankings send to the rest of the world. For the time being, they seem a striking echo of the prejudices with which the west confronts the world at large, firmly holding globalization for a western, and not a universal concept.

Top ten billionaires cities

1. Moscow, Russia
2. New York, United States
3=. Hong Kong
3=. London, United Kingdom
5. Istanbul, Turkey
6 São Paulo, Brazil
7 Mumbai, India
8. Seoul, South Korea
9. Beijing, China
10=. Dallas, United States
10=. Paris, France

Source: Forbes (2013).[1]

In August 1991, after the dissolution of the Soviet Union, Russia joined a global process of economic liberalization. From a former Communist stronghold, Russia transmogrified into one of the world's most indulgently laissez-faire playgrounds almost overnight. Although this shift has affected Russia as a whole, the effect is most palpable in its capital city. Moscow not only represents the outcome of two different ideological propositions but also (and perhaps more important) the difficulties that occur in attempting a transition between them. Once a showcase of central planning, Moscow had to adapt to the whims of the free market. Suddenly, a previously controllable territory turned into a chimerical organism, subject to its own seemingly autonomous processes and defiant of the ideas of those supposedly in control. At some point during the 1990s, "governance" devolved into a matter of "watching events as they unfolded" and trying to derive maximum economic gain in the meantime.

Moscow's official population stands at around 11.5 million inhabitants, which, discounting transcontinental Istanbul, makes it Europe's only megacity (exceeding 10 million inhabitants). Unlike that of many Asian megacities, Moscow's population growth does not reflect a national trend. During the past twenty years Moscow's population has grown by 24 percent, while the Russian population as a whole has shrunk by 3.6 percent. Moscow occupies 0.05 percent of Russia's territory, contains 8 percent of its population, accounts for 10 percent of Russia's employment and 22 percent of its GDP, and attracts 65 percent of all foreign investment.[2]

These statistics reveal a strange paradox: the more important Moscow becomes for Russia, the less it becomes like Russia. Moscow constitutes a kind of universe unto itself, a state within the state. The asymmetry transcends the city's borders: while Moscow's official residents enjoy a whole range of special conditions and privileges—special Moscow benefits, devised to help them withstand the first shocks of a capitalist system—the city increasingly relies on informal labor provided by those who are denied any rights whatsoever. This has led to a strangely divided city. On the one hand, there is the official Moscow, featuring in censuses and municipal data; on the other, the unofficial or rather the real Moscow, wherein a large number of nonregistered (illegal) residents take part in an economy disregarded by official statistics. There is Moscow and there is Moscow.

And an ever-larger bureaucracy has to go to ever-greater lengths to administer an ever more schizophrenic reality.

A small example: After the fall of communism, many of Moscow's residents moved outside the city limits in search of larger, cheaper living space, even shifting their permanent residence from their Moscow apartment to the traditional dacha, or summerhouse. As a result, some of the less savory properties within the city limits became vacant and were illegally rented out to construction workers from former Soviet republics who live in Moscow but do not have formal status as Muscovites. While Moscow's official residents are still largely employed in the city center, the construction workers find work in the construction boom at the city's perimeter. Heavy commuter flows have ensued in both directions: from the periphery to the center (the official residents) and vice versa (the unofficial residents). As a result, transportation infrastructure is stretched to the limit, and Moscow suffers congestion and traffic problems of unimaginable proportions.

In 2012 the government tried to correct this by proposing an expansion of the city area to two and a half times its previous size under a development concept called "Big Moscow." Unfortunately, the task of defining the new borders was delegated to the Ministry of Economic Affairs, which, in order to minimize the cost of special benefits for new residents, proposed a border that excluded the most densely populated areas around the city. Although much land was added to Moscow, the new borders included only 2 percent of the population of the larger Moscow region. Few additional people benefited, and the asymmetries in the city—the prime source of its planning problems—persisted.

Moscow is a textbook example of the curious paradox that is affecting many conurbations internationally. Cities are assumed to grow for economic reasons, but the faster they grow, the larger their inevitably attendant shadow economies, never officially registered, become. If the black market existed today as a nation, it would be the world's largest economic superpower, larger than the United States or China. Much of its economic activity takes place in cities. It is estimated that if the current rate of urbanization continues, 65 percent of the world's population will be working in the shadow economy by 2020.[3]

As ominous as this may sound, the shadows are not as dark as one might think. Although the activities are illegal in the sense that they are not reported as taxable services to the authorities, they are not necessarily nor even substantially criminal. Even if the drug trade has acquired vast proportions, it is only a fraction of the story. A large majority of economic activities in cities are illegal simply because those who carry them out have no legal status. This holds for a whole range of activities, varying from markets selling secondhand (upcycled) goods and running jitney buses to informal construction and necessary microfinance operations. Prostitution is an interesting example, the legality of which may be directly related to the resident status, or absence thereof, of those involved. *Gedogen* (to condone) is the magic word that describes the Dutch authorities' attitude to the more harmless illegal activities: not legalizing but also not prosecuting them. *Gedogen* is inevitably an urban concept, possible only because of the attendant level of social control.

This so-called shadow economy is of enormous but insufficiently recognized importance. In part, it is what allows cities to exist (and expand) in their present form. There appears to be a direct correlation between urban growth and the estimated size of the accompanying shadow economy. Insofar as urbanization constitutes a neck-and-neck race between the legal and the illegal economies, the latter seems to be pulling ahead. On the heels of the now-established, first-wave megacities— Moscow, Shanghai, Mumbai, São Paulo, and Mexico City—a new generation of cities is emerging, not quite as large yet, but with staggering growth rates, higher than those of any of the established megacities, and with equally staggering illegal economies.

Most of these second-generation cities hardly qualify as role models for urban growth. Abuja in Nigeria tops the list in population/headcount, closely followed by Sana'a in Yemen; Kabul, Afghanistan; Mogadishu, Somalia; and Baghdad, Iraq. These are names that bring to mind another interesting relationship: that between urban growth and war. In regard to city growth and political instability, global surveys correlate the same regions as frontrunners. This is hardly surprising if one considers the availability and distribution of basic resources. Located in areas ravaged by war and suffering major breakdowns in state authorities, large cities provide safe or at least defendable havens, strongholds against the chaos and terror contesting the territory around them.

No longer do economic opportunities exclusively drive people to the city; once again there is a political motive. In areas such as Afghanistan,

Yemen, Mali, and Somalia, the city compensates for the failings of the nation-state, providing, if not safety, at least some kind of stability, even if that stops short of granting the newcomers legal status. Such cities hardly serve as testaments of the blessings of Western democracy. In fact, the growth of these cities is largely a product of democracy's failures, or at least of the impossibility to impose it. For the war on terror in the Middle East, the war on drugs in Central America, or crimes against humanity in central Africa, it is the West that, in hoping to shape the rest of the world in its image in the name of exporting democracy and nation building, is partly to blame.

In mistaking order for peace, security for stability, and law enforcement for the rule of law, we have strangely contributed to the demise of each. In spite of everything, the city has proved unexpectedly resilient. A strange kind of déjà vu presents itself: that of ancient cities regularly under siege. Their walls represent safety, and their residents are "voluntary prisoners." The city's limited territory becomes the trade-off for larger freedoms. At the gates of Sana'a, Makai, or Abuja, the city becomes a political construct once again—the only one left standing.

The ten fastest-growing cities (in percentage) from 1990 to 2025

1. Abuja, Nigeria
2. Sana'a, Yemen
3. Bamako, Mali
4. Kabul, Afghanistan
5. Kinshasa, the Congo
6. Gaza, Palestine
7. Mogadishu, Somalia
8. Guatemala City, Guatemala
9. Bogotá, Colombia
10. Baghdad, Iraq

Source: UN-Habitat, *State of the World's Cities, 2012–2013.*

Abuja, Nigeria. After Lagos experienced Nigeria's economic boom firsthand in the 1960s and 1970s, the then capital rapidly grew into such an expansive metropolis that it was simply ungovernable. Instead of imposing regulations on its urbanization, it was decided to relocate the capital in its entirety to Abuja. Since 1991 Abuja has officially been the federal capital of Nigeria, and with an annual growth rate of at least 35 percent, it has largely been confronted with the same problems. Still much smaller in population than Lagos, it has nevertheless had to deal with a similar scale of immigration problems that have been turning the city proper into an urban agglomeration with a growing number of satellite towns. Abuja already finds itself in the center of the country, emphasizing its premised neutrality, but the needs placed on it have overtaken the original intention of allowing a fresh and new start. In 2003 Minister Nasir Ahmad el-Rufai started a brutal demolition campaign that left thousands homeless; this has left fertile ground for local clans, dealing mainly in the trafficking of drugs, humans, and political violence. More recently, ethnic tensions erupted in Abuja in October 2015, when Boko Haram carried out a series of explosions killing at least 18 people. Some 17,000 people are said to have been killed since Boko Haram began its insurgency in 2009.

Sana'a, Yemen. On May 22, 1990, North Yemen and South Yemen were officially unified into the Republic of Yemen. Mainly spurred by an interest in maximizing oil exploration, this unification put a halt to sporadic violent conflicts between the two sides and resulted in the appointment of Sana'a as the new capital city. Sana'a initially attracted many migrant workers from the surrounding rural areas, and employment was boosted further by the new jobs that were created by the recently installed government administration. However, the capital also struggled to maintain basic infrastructure, such as a clean water supply. This internal instability compounded the fact that Yemen fell prey to new conflicts between the South and the North. A new climax was reached when Houthis overthrew the government in the September 21 Revolution in 2014. Since March 2015 Sana'a is replaced by Aden as Yemen's (temporary) capital, where its internationally recognized government currently resides.

Bamako, Mali. Situated on the Niger River, at the crossroads of West Africa, Bamako has always relied on its location for trade, industry, and energy. For the same reason, it has been an interest of many other nations as well, from Berber invasions in the sixteenth century to French colonialism in the nineteenth century and strong Soviet influence in the 1960s. Since then, Bamako's population has grown almost twenty times larger (to around two million), and it has attracted many migrant workers and illegal squatters. Even though Mali installed a city government in Bamako, problems with infrastructure, sanitation, and pollution led to protests in Bamako at the end of the 1980s, demanding the final step of emancipation in the form of a free-market economy and multiparty democracy. This persistent demand was eventually met with violent oppression: on March 22, 1991, an estimated three hundred students, trade unionists and other protesters were killed. Since then, a military government has taken over; even though economic and urban expansion is going strong—largely funded by foreign investment from Saudi Arabia and China—political and ethnic tensions remain high. In November 2015, two gunmen held 170 people hostage in the Bamako Hotel attack; of the 21 people eventually murdered, 3 were Chinese businessmen.

Kabul, Afghanistan. Despite a long history of tumultuous revolutions, the city of Kabul remained relatively undamaged until the Afghani Civil War of the early 1990s. As the capital city, Kabul had grown into an economically active center for the country, although politically it had remained unstable. For a short time in the 1960s Kabul enjoyed a moderately liberal environment, but Soviet investments eventually led to a Soviet invasion at the end of the 1970s. During this invasion Kabul was unharmed for the most part, and the city's population grew from 500,000 in 1978 to 2 million in 1988. This period culminated in the civil war, which took a heavy toll on the city and ended with a Taliban regime imposing sharia law on Kabul's residents. In October 2001 the Taliban were driven out by heavy U.S. air strikes, and a new government took over, propelling Kabul's population to 3 million in 2007. Attacks on the city have since become commonplace, including a series of suicide bombings carried out in front of the Russian Embassy.

Kinshasa, the Congo. When the Congo was still a Belgian colony, major infrastructure works were realized in order to consolidate the capital (named Léopoldville at the time) as the country's first and foremost city, well connected to the ports in the west and to the raw minerals in the interior. This effort toward urbanization drew people from across the country, quickly establishing the capital as the crucible of an ethnically diverse population. Under the dictatorial regime of Mobutu Sese Seko from 1965 to 1997, Kinshasa (renamed in 1966) and its urban area continued to expand at a rapid pace. However, internal and external conflicts resulted in a fragile political situation; the civil war pursuing the end of Mobutu's reign was the deadliest in modern African history, and its effects can still be felt today. Crime, disease, and famine still threaten further development; the streets of Kinshasa have seen major protests against corruption within the Kabila government, which had tried to bypass its own constitution in order to keep its incumbent president in power.

Gaza, Palestine. In the aftermath of World War I, Great Britain took control of Gaza and subsequently made new plans for major urban expansion. This amelioration of the city's facilities was further extended when Egypt took charge of Gaza after the 1948 Arab-Israeli war. Since then, facilities and resources have grown scarce, while the population has risen exponentially. Between 1948 and 1967 Gaza's population grew six times larger because of the number of refugees flooding in from neighboring towns captured by Israel. Since the Six-Day War in 1967, basic resources have grown scarcer still through a series of territorial conflicts and strategic blockades. When Gaza was transferred to the Palestinian National Authority in 1993, violent conflicts continued; in 2006 an additional internal struggle emerged between the Palestinian political factions Fatah and Hamas. Nevertheless, Gaza's refugee population has been steadily increasing, and the population density is the same as that of New York City.[4] In 2014 Israel launched a seven-week military operation against Hamas, killing over two thousand Gazans.

Mogadishu, Somalia. In postcolonial and reunited Somalia, Mogadishu was crowned as capital of the new republic. After successive power changes and a military coup in 1969, political tensions culminated in the 1991 civil war. This accelerated migration from rural hinterlands to the capital, which heavily altered the demographic composition of Mogadishu over a period of years. During this time various Islamic factions started to emerge and eventually took control of the capital. In 2011 Somalia's armed forces finally recaptured Mogadishu from the fundamentalist group al-Shabaab. The newfound peace within the nation heralded the reconstruction of the capital, which attracted a new influx of repatriates from Somalia's diaspora seeking to invest in the surging economy of Mogadishu. Through these investments, construction in both the public sector, primarily infrastructure projects, and the private sector, for example, the real estate market, has boomed. That the threat of al-Shabaab's Islamic fundamentalist militants has not yet disappeared is proved by frequent terrorist attacks, such as the suicide bombing in early 2016 in which seventeen civilians were killed at Mogadishu's Central Hotel.

Guatemala City, Guatemala. A civil war that had been ongoing in Guatemala City since the 1960s officially ended in 1996, but it so deeply affected all layers of society that it created an atmosphere of persistent violence and corruption. As the capital and economic center of the country, the capital attracted refugees from Guatemala's hinterland during the civil war. However, its sudden growth was unanticipated, and the city's infrastructure was woefully unprepared. Despite the thousands of civilian lives lost during the war, the city's population kept rising, and it became the most populous urban agglomeration in Central America. A military coup in 2009 did nothing to improve circumstances: according to the *New Yorker* magazine, in 2009 fewer civilians were reported killed in the Iraqi war zone than were recorded as shot, stabbed, or beaten to death in Guatemala, and 97 percent of the city's homicides "remain unsolved."[5] Besides the violence, corruption has persisted and even thrived. Major protests against widespread corruption practices (mainly related to vast drug-trafficking operations) led to the resignation of President Otto Pérez Molina, who was replaced by a banana seller turned television comic.

Bogotá, Colombia. One of the longest civil wars in history, the ongoing conflict among Colombia's conservative, liberal, and Communist factions has ravaged the country, causing a death toll estimated in the hundreds of thousands. Since the nineteenth century Bogotá has experienced a very mixed and fast-growing population, witnessing successive waves of violent conflict over the years. La Violencia, for instance, was the name of a ten-year uprising between 1948 and 1958 that cost over 200,000 lives in a battle over agricultural land. According to the United Nations High Commission, over the past fifteen years more than two million people have moved to urban areas to escape the violence. This violence has nevertheless infiltrated deep within cities and certainly within the capital, in which narcoterrorists hold sway over its urban development. Finally, on November 24, 2016, FARC and the Colombian government signed a peace agreement, which the Colombian Congress approved on November 30.

Baghdad, Iraq. At the nexus of the Arab world, connecting Iran, Jordan, Kuwait, Saudi Arabia, Syria, and Turkey, Baghdad has always been a cosmopolitan city. In the Middle Ages, Baghdad was considered the largest city in the world, with a population of 1.2 million. In addition to its location, its status as the capital of one of the largest oil states makes Baghdad a place of globalized interests. In the aftermath of Saddam Hussein's dictatorship, the Iraqi invasion in 2003, recent sectarian conflicts, and IS bombings, the New York consulting firm Mercer ranked Baghdad as the worst of 221 major cities in "quality of life." Nevertheless, Baghdad is still the second-largest city in the Arab world, with a population of over seven million people.

VII. PROGRESS

Wendel O. Pruitt, St. Louis, 1944
Staff Photo / *St. Louis Post-Dispatch*

William Igoe, 1914
Photograph by Harris & Ewing/Harris & Ewing Collection/Library of Congress
Prints and Photographs Division, Washington, D.C. (LC-DIG-hec-03473)

40

Coup de Grâce

Pruitt-Igoe Revisited

Surrounded by trees, we are struck by the strange scent of autumn: sun-dried leaves mixed with the stink of rot. Underneath our feet lies a brownish carpet of foliage and litter. We plough through shrubs, hoping to look out into the open again, but the longer that takes, the more we lose any sense of space and time. Is the wilderness in which we find ourselves post- or preurban? Are the occasional fragments of rubble evidence of an earlier occupation? Just as we begin to question where we are, we reach the edge: a vast plain opens up in front of us. There was a city here once, this much we know. But there is little evidence of it left. A lonely church, with no apparent community to serve, is the only human artefact.

July 15, 1972 (3:32 p.m.): The first building of the Pruitt-Igoe housing estate in St. Louis, Missouri, is demolished through a planned implosion. Less than eighteen years after it opens in 1954, the estate is considered beyond repair and is torn down. Despite or rather because of its demolition, Pruitt-Igoe makes history. If we are to believe the critics, it wasn't just a block of flats that received its coup de grâce on that July afternoon in 1972, but the whole of twentieth-century avant-garde thinking. The demolition is featured live on national television and definitively acquires cult status when it is featured in the 1981 film *Koyaanisqatsi,* with a soundtrack by Philip Glass. In *The Language of Post-modern Architecture* Charles Jencks writes that "Modern Architecture died in St. Louis, Missouri on July 15, 1972 at 3.32 pm (or thereabouts) when the infamous Pruitt-Igoe scheme, or rather several of its slab blocks, were given the final coup de grâce by dynamite,"[1] a view further adopted by artist Peter Blake (*Form Follows Fiasco,* 1977) and writer Tom Wolfe (*From Bauhaus to Our House,* 1981).

Not only is modern architecture considered finished in stylistic terms, but also the project's failure quickly becomes a symbol of modernity's failure to address the city. In 1976 Colin Rowe and Fred Koetter, with explicit reference to Pruitt-Igoe, write that "the city of modern architecture has been rendered tragically ridiculous. . . . The city of Hilberseimer and Le Corbusier, celebrated by CIAM and advertised by the Athens Charter: the former city of deliverance is everyday found increasingly inadequate."[2] It is not difficult to complete Rowe's list; after Pruitt-Igoe, it isn't just Le Corbusier or Hilberseimer but also Team 10 the Japanese Metabolists, Constant's New Babylon, Yona Friedman, Archizoom, and any other visionary movement that have been rendered "tragically ridiculous."

The prevailing reading of events around Pruitt-Igoe is enough to make any architect uncomfortable. The repeated use of the demolition footage sends a clear message: Dear architects, when it comes to solving societal issues, do not get above yourselves—it will (literally) blow up in your face. Still, there is a strange disjunction between the powerlessness that emanates from the imagery of Pruitt-Igoe's demolition and the blame that is attributed to the architecture. Surely if architecture's power to fix societal issues is limited, then so must be its power to create them. One cannot help but wonder whether the critics, with their singular focus on architecture as the culprit of Pruitt-Igoe's demise, made themselves part of a cover-up. What lies beyond the truism that modern architecture died in 1972? What story is buried under the rubble left after Pruitt-Igoe's demolition?

January 14, 1947: While most U.S. cities recover from the Great Depression, St. Louis is one of only four facing a declining population. Its housing stock has been deteriorating since the 1920s. Middle-class residents are leaving and their former residences are occupied by the poor. Slums threaten to engulf the city center.

At the request of Republican mayor Aloys P. Kauffman, the City Planning Commission devises a development plan for the next twenty-five years to bring (the right) people back to St. Louis through private-sector gentrification in the city's poorest neighborhoods. The DeSoto-Carr neighborhood is one of these designated for renewal; the initial plan calls for three-story blocks with a public park.

George Hellmuth, Minoru Yamasaki, and Joseph Leinweber viewing Pruitt-Igoe model
Courtesy of the Archives of Michigan

Things take a twist in 1949 when the U.S. Housing Act is passed, which makes federal funds available for slum clearance, urban redevelopment, and public housing, creating a construction wave across the United States. St. Louis's new mayor, Joseph Darst (a Democrat), seizes the opportunity and revises the existing development plan, quipping, "We'll take Manhattan," in reference to the high-rise structures imagined for the future.

In 1950 St. Louis receives a federal commitment for 5,800 public housing units; DeSoto-Carr is slated for public housing at densities higher than those of the original slum dwellings. Half of the units are allocated to a relatively modest tract of land, the design of which is awarded to the architecture firm Leinweber, Yamasaki and Hellmuth. Minoru Yamasaki, who later designs New York's World Trade Center, is the project's main designer. He conceives a neighborhood of thirty-three eleven-story slabs, containing 2,700 units to house fifteen thousand people.[3] The widely acclaimed design is marketed with great confidence; in 1951 *Architectural*

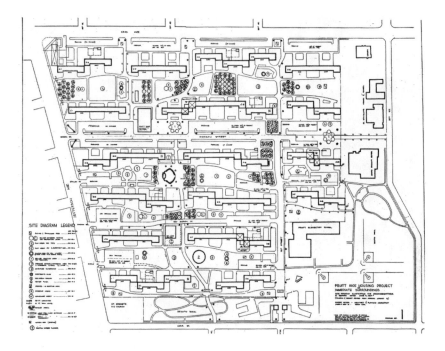

Pruitt-Igoe Housing Project and Immediate Surroundings
St. Louis Housing Authority, as reproduced for the documentary film *The Pruitt-Igoe Myth: An Urban History* (2011), directed by Chad Freidrichs

Forum runs an article, "Slum Surgery in St. Louis," in its praise.[4] *Architectural Record* applauds the unique design features, such as skip-stop elevators and glazed internal galleries, intended to create "individual neighborhoods" within each building.[5]

The area is planned as a racially segregated development, named for Wendell O. Pruitt, a black military pilot, and William Igoe, a white congressman; both men were from St. Louis but would never meet. (According to the segregation laws, blacks would live in Pruitt, while whites would live in Igoe.) However, the Supreme Court holds racial segregation illegal in *Brown v. Board of Education of Topeka* in 1954, and so by the time the project is completed in 1956, Pruitt-Igoe is destined to become one of the first and historic models of a racially mixed inner-city neighborhood.

In 1957 occupancy rates peak at 91 percent, and it would only be fair to say that before its eventual demise, there are a number of good Pruitt-Igoe years. Footage from a 1950s documentary, made shortly after the

Pruitt-Igoe, St. Louis, 1956
Photograph by Henry T. Mizuki / Mac Mizuki Photography Studio Collection, Missouri
History Museum

project's completion, paints an almost euphoric picture of the increase in
living standards: Pruitt-Igoe is labeled "a cure for the disease, rising above
the polluted slums, lifting its residents out of poverty. . . . Here in bright
new buildings on spacious ground, they can live, with indoor plumbing,
electric light, fresh plastered walls and other conveniences that are expected in the 20th century."[6]

Meanwhile, another trend takes hold in the American city: industrial
bases move out, and residents follow. The 1949 Housing Act is notably
vague; although ample funds are available for affordable housing, it remains
ambiguous where these homes should be built. Inner-city regeneration is
facilitated through high-density developments, but this regeneration is un-
dermined by subsidizing the private sector to build low-cost single-
family units in the suburbs. By the mid-1950s the suburban lifestyle has
become the dominant trend in the United States, celebrated in TV shows
like *Father Knows Best* and *Leave It to Beaver*.[7] By the mid-1960s St. Louis

Pruitt-Igoe, St. Louis, 2011
Photograph by Sam Jacob, *Blueprint 340*. Courtesy of *Blueprint* magazine.

has lost more than a quarter of its midcentury population. The white middle and upper classes leave the city; those who cannot afford to do so stay behind. It is ironic that in the decades immediately after the *Brown* decision, racial segregation is perpetuated through the free market: white neighborhoods in the suburbs, black neighborhoods in the inner city.

This trend drastically affects the Pruitt Igoe project. Occupancy rates start to fall, and in 1965 only 2,500 of its original 12,000 inhabitants are left. Average tenant income declines as unemployment grows, and a disproportionate number of families in the estate live on welfare. Pruitt-Igoe is increasingly inhabited by the poorest strata of black society; segregated and publicly vandalized, it begins to resemble the slums it had replaced. In 1965 *Architectural Foreum* publishes a second article on Pruitt-Igoe, "A Case History of Failure," now labeling as hazards many of the features praised in its 1951 article: "The undersized elevators are brutally battered, and they reek of urine from children who misjudged the time it takes to reach their apartments. By stopping only on every third floor, the elevators offer convenient settings for crime. The galleries are anything but cheerful social enclaves. The tenants call them gauntlets, through which they must pass to reach their doors."[8]

Pruitt-Igoe's deteriorated living conditions make the national press in February 1969, when its residents begin a rent strike—the first of its kind—in protest. The 1949 Housing Act had ruled that maintenance for public housing should come from tenants' rents, but the falling number of tenants has resulted in insufficient funds, causing the buildings' dilapidation. The rent strike continues for nine months; Pruitt-Igoe's residents have a short-lived moment of political engagement. Much of this takes place in the context of a backlash against government spending: "The government no longer has an open check book!" is a phrase attributed to Housing and Urban Development Secretary George Romney (Mitt Romney's father, chairman of American Motors, and presidential candidate in 1968). Public housing is increasingly seen as un-American, a Communist erosion of the free market. In the end, the forces against Pruitt-Igoe prove too strong. On July 15, 1972, the first of the thirty-three blocks is brought down by explosives.

November 11, 2014: We head east on Highway 70 from Lambert Airport in the direction of downtown St. Louis. We exit the freeway at Grand and take a few turns to get to the junction of Jefferson and Cass, the northeast corner of the site where once the Pruitt-Igoe housing estate stood. "We need to fix St. Louis," the *Washington Post* declared recently, portraying a town where urban decline and the demise of civic values are inextricably linked.[9] There is an eerie sense of abandonment to these streets, not quite the same as the postapocalyptic, posturban condition of Detroit, but somehow calmer, more accepting of its fate. In Detroit the scarce remains of the city—the ruins—provide the shock effect, but in St. Louis the shock is in the absence of remains. One would never know that this rural town has organically sprouted where at one time there was a city.

St. Louis constitutes a revolution in reverse: the city is not the apex of human civilization but simply a passing phase in the way humans choose to settle the planet. After a few traffic lights (why do traffic lights tend to keep one waiting longer, the less traffic there is to regulate?), we arrive at our destination. Despite our heightened anticipation, reaching the site is bizarrely underwhelming. Insofar as there is an experience, it is one of an absolute lack of spectacle, especially given this place's legendary significance. This supposed burial ground of modern architecture is free of ceremonial aura. Where there were once thirty-three buildings, there is currently a weird urban forest: a green relief in a context that needs no such thing, a void within emptiness.

Not too long ago a documentary was made about the deeper reasons for Pruitt-Igoe's failure.[10] In the opening scene a former resident recounts a recent visit to the site, where he was attacked by a dog. For a brief moment, even forty years later, he is overcome by the fear he had felt while living here. All the former residents interviewed in the documentary relay a similar story: good memories of the early years, when a Pruitt-Igoe address meant a considerable step up, followed by the dystopian latter years. To those who have lived through the demise, even the relative peace of the forest proves fragile.

Still, the most surreal part of our visit is not the complete absence of any evidence of Pruitt-Igoe, good or bad; rather, it is the eerie disappearance of the city around it, transformed into a boarded-up urban wasteland. The street grid serves hardly any buildings; the streets have names, but the numbers resemble complex mathematical sequences—2, 14, 38, 152. Amid these empty streets, the weird forest symbolizes not the failure of America's public housing program but rather the losing battle for the American city.

What was accomplished by blowing up the thirty-three slabs of Pruitt-Igoe? It did not solve St. Louis's housing crisis; this much is clear. A 2010 documentary, *The Hidden Homeless*, suggests that for every recorded homeless person in St. Louis, there are three to four more unaccounted for, pushing numbers well beyond anything in the city's history. In 2013 the rise in homelessness in Missouri was more than 14 percent, well above the national average.

And there is the crime. One of the main reasons cited for the demolition of the Pruitt-Igoe estate was the excessive rate of violent crime. Recent successes notwithstanding, St. Louis has seen a steady, uninterrupted rise in violent crime in the past decades. The recent IBM Smarter Cities grant of $400,000 to the city is as much an award for the St. Louis police as it is an indication of the intensity of crime in this city.

Indeed, for some time St. Louis and IBM have been partners in (fighting) crime, using predictive analytics and computer technology to help forecast likely acts: "Stopping crime before it happens." (At this point it would not be unfair to say that IBM largely awarded itself.) Nevertheless, in 2014 St. Louis ranked as the fourth most dangerous city in the United States, with more than 1,800 violent crimes per 100,000 inhabitants, ranging from assault to shooting and from arson to robbery.

In recent years petty crime—or rather penalizing petty crime—has become a major source of municipal revenue. This is also known as the "Money Ball approach." At present, St. Louis derives up to 40 percent of its annual revenue from fines and fees collected by its law-enforcement agencies, fining anything from loud music to unkempt property; even a fine for wearing saggy pants has been proposed. (Proceeds are in turn used to pay for the services of IBM.) IBM's partnership with the city of St. Louis is part of a larger trend, whereby former public tasks are increasingly claimed by private corporations. In the face of the public sector's supposed failings, an increasing number of tech companies rise to the occasion to take its place. The "smart city" becomes the new "city of deliverance," addressing everything from the well-being and safety of citizens to overcrowding, pollution, inadequate infrastructure, and the need for continuing economic growth.[11]

The rhetoric of the smart city echoes that of several traditional nineteenth-century philanthropists. But for all the elevated language of its manifestos—and there are many—the smart city is driven by the pursuit of business interests, something that stands in stark contrast to the grand urban visions of the twentieth century, which celebrated the city as a public phenomenon. Almost fifty years after the demolition of Pruitt-Igoe, we are confronted with a wholesale sell-off of public services, which inevitably leaves the city at the mercy of private interests. After the urban flight of the 1950s and the 1960s, it is now the public sector that is fleeing the city. During the last years of Pruitt-Igoe the refusal of the authorities to fulfill their responsibilities provoked a rent strike by the residents; this time there is nobody left to protest and nothing left to protest against.

Nearly half a century after the demolition, the same issues are ever present, and there is still no adequate repertoire to deal with them. Thinking of Pruitt-Igoe, one wonders: was it really the buildings that bothered us, or was it something else? Does its failure serve as an uncomfortable reminder that the American dream—even at the moment of the great civil rights movement—was not available to all? In historic terms the demolition of Pruitt-Igoe seems to sound the death knell of political ambition rather than of buildings, where Charles Jencks's coup de grâce becomes exactly that: a mercy killing, not of a movement in architecture but of a commitment to progress in solidarity—a sigh of relief. After Pruitt-Igoe, we should simply stop trying.

On our way back to the airport we drive through Olive Street. We pass the new offices of the St. Louis Police Department. We have read that the building was bought in 2011 from Wells Fargo, and that the purchase was financed through so-called criminal asset forfeiture funds. It seems that the "Money Ball approach" is paying off. The building is a curious brick box. A tiny entrance door is buried under a giant arched window, an awkward attempt to reconcile the utilitarian with the representative—not the kind of architecture likely to catch the eye of the architecture critics. It seems that St. Louis got shortchanged even when it comes to postmodernism.

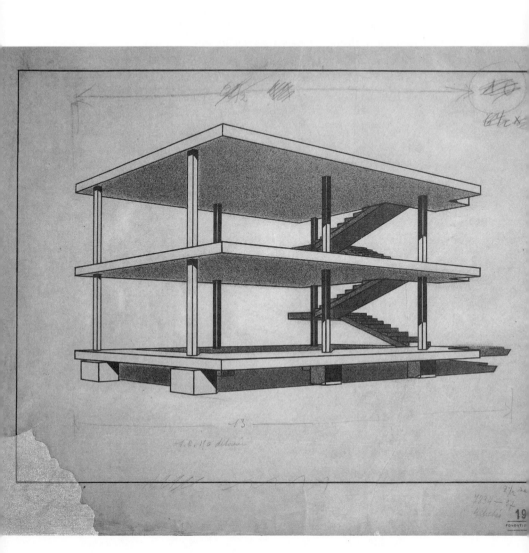

Maison Dom-Ino, Le Corbusier, 1914

41

The Century That Never Happened

In 2013 Thomas Piketty published his book *Capital in the Twenty-First Century*.[1] If Piketty is right, we can once and for all bury the illusion that the present economic system ultimately works in the interest of all and that its benefits will eventually trickle down to the poorest in society. Contrary to what every economist since Keynes has been telling us, the inequality produced by capitalism may not be a temporary phase that the system, left to its own devices, will overcome; rather, it is a structural and inescapable long-term effect of the system. Piketty's analysis is exceedingly simple. He identifies two basic economic categories: income and wealth. He then defines social (in)equality as a function of the relation between the two over time and concludes that as soon as the return on wealth exceeds the return on labor, social inequality inevitably increases. Those who acquire wealth through work fall ever further behind those who accumulate wealth simply by owning it. Only in the three or four decades after 1945—following two world wars and under pressure from social unrest, revolutions, labor unions, and the daunting presence of a global alternative to the capitalist system in the form of communism—only during this unique capsule of time did ordinary laborers improve their economic standing faster than the owners of capital.

Whether the twentieth century was merely a brief escape from the otherwise unavoidable mechanism of a deeply fraught economic system remains to be seen. Much will depend on what happens next; the twenty-first century will determine the legacy of the twentieth. So far, the signs are not encouraging. Since the late 1970s, after the great conservative revolution that Reagan and Thatcher set in motion, the promise of accumulating wealth through work has steadily lost ground for all but CEOs and other economic celebrities. The fall of the Berlin Wall (generally claimed as a victory of that same conservative revolution) and, in its wake, the wholesale collapse of the Communist bloc have exacerbated this trend. If current indicators are right, we could soon be faced with a situation where, for the first time since the end of the nineteenth century, returns on wealth through ownership will again exceed those of labor.

Indeed, if Piketty's argument holds true, the twentieth century will have been no more than an anomaly, a brief interruption in the systemic logic of capitalism, in which the inherent accretion of capital through capital remains an unbreakable cycle. This simple economic conclusion may have social and cultural implications beyond our wildest imagination. When a lifetime of labor can no longer match the returns on an acquired fortune, inherited wealth once again becomes the defining factor of class distinction, reducing any notion of social mobility to a remote possibility at best.

If the twentieth century really was an anomaly, then perhaps so were its ideals; an entire period characterized by an enlightened belief in progress, social emancipation, and civil rights can be retroactively discarded as a fleeting moment of self-delusion—no more than a footnote in the long course of history. For the generation currently in a position of power, raised and educated in the twentieth century, this is difficult to acknowledge. For them, the moral imperatives of the twentieth century are beyond question, irrespective of political choices. (Even the most ardent supporter of the current free-market economy probably believes that the system ultimately acts in the interest of all rather than explicitly supporting the notion of extreme inequality.) The current generation, whether Left or Right, has not (yet) had its faith in the great emancipatory mechanisms shaken in any way. It is all they know and all they have ever known.

I was born in the Netherlands in 1964, started primary school in 1970, and graduated from university in 1988, one year before the fall of the Berlin Wall. I received eighteen years of public education, during which the notion that one progressed through study and hard work was firmly instilled. One earned one's rights and did not inherit privileges. Education was received on the proportional basis of one's talents, not the size of one's wealth. We lived in the conviction that despite cultural and religious differences, Protestant and Catholic alike—there was no sizable Muslim population yet—would eventually merge into a single middle class. The absence of a poor underclass was generally interpreted as the logical consequence of the (apparent) absence of an upper class. Insofar as we were aware of an upper class, in no way did we have to reckon with or even acknowledge it. Sure, we had a monarchy, but even its implication in an occasional corruption scandal in no way shocked our faith in its absolute irrelevance. Monarchs were a symbolic necessity, there to represent the unity of a nation that in every other respect was getting by without them. Power was in the hands of an elected government, independent of our royal head of state. (It was not until much later, when Dutch Greenpeace activists were mysteriously released in Russia after a visit of the Dutch king and queen, that I realized that things were perhaps not that straightforward.)[2] Wealth existed, but it did not guarantee a right to power, nor should it. Our leaders were chosen by us, for us, and from us.

If Piketty is right, those self-evident truths may well have been based on quicksand. The many blessings of a life in the later twentieth century, particularly in Western Europe, were not the natural outcome of a progressive evolutionary process but the result of a short-lived and unsustainable suspension of the real fate dictated by its contemporary economic system. Only under severe (political) pressure did capital refrain from showing its true face. In that context, Western Europe got a good deal: it was protected by American intolerance of communism but threatened—or savvy— enough to maintain a generous welfare system, dissuading its citizens from entertaining any real Communist sympathies. With the dissolution of the Communist bloc, much of that threat is now gone, and the economic trends of most European countries since 1989 speak loudly: cuts to welfare, the erosion of pensions, the reduction of public services, and so on.

Although my training as an architect might make me utterly unqualified to comment on Piketty's economic theories, I cannot help but notice the resonance between Piketty's narrative of "economic history" and the context of my profession. If one studies the history of architecture, and particularly that of the twentieth century, a striking confluence emerges between what Piketty identifies as the period of great social mobility and the emergence of the modern movement in architecture, with its utopian visions for the city. From Le Corbusier to Ludwig Hilberseimer, from the Smithsons to Jaap Bakema: after reading Piketty, it becomes difficult to view the ideologies of modern architecture as anything other than the dream of social mobility captured in concrete.

Let's take a closer look. Until 1914 the returns on capital enjoy a comfortable lead over economic growth; from 1914 to 1950, the period of the great wars, that relationship reverses.[3] This period not only signifies a turning point economically but also marks a major cultural shift as the time during which the great modernist visions emerge. Shortly before the outbreak of World War I, the Futurist manifesto is published in *Le Figaro*.[4] The spirit in which it is written is one of a deliberately reckless and unconditional embrace of the new. The manifesto glorifies speed, machinery, and violence as the dawning of a new era. In announcing great crowds excited by work, pleasure, and turmoil, it describes the Russian Revolution before it happened.[5] The Futurists insist that "man will not be overtaken by progress, but instead Man will absorb progress in its evolution . . . reacting against the potentially overwhelming strength of progress, and shouting out his centrality."[6] This "triumph of the will," more than the aggressive nationalism with which it is generally associated, is a definitive reckoning with the laissez-faire of nineteenth-century Italy and the lethargy of its ruling class, to be abolished in favor of cultural rejuvenation and an aggressive modernization.

A belief in the promises of modernization continues to dominate much of the rest of the century and results in a curious alternation between brutal industrial wars and utopian blueprints, the latter of which hope to deploy the ensuing maelstrom of industrial development for the greater good. In this respect there is a clear resonance with Piketty's book, which observes a close relationship between the progress made during the twentieth century and the upheavals that went with it, noting that somehow no manifestation of the new ever unfolds without unsettling old vested interests and established relations of power. The great visionary actors in architecture—from the Futurists to the Constructivists, from CIAM to Team 10, from the Metabolists to Archizoom—invariably seemed to have coupled their embrace of the new with a need to settle scores with (that is, destroy) the old. Despite its mostly social(ist) mission, there is an element of unabashed cruelty in the depiction of the "city of tomorrow," with its repetitive, industrially produced housing blocks and oversized infrastructure systems. Good intentions are dressed up in harsh vestments, as if to convey the brutal truth that progress comes at a price.

Piketty has been viewed as a Marxist. This is wrong. Where Marx saw social relationships and class struggles, Piketty sees only economic categories: wealth and income. Marx envisaged proletariat rule through revolution; Piketty's description of the system is rather apolitical. Indeed, if Piketty's analysis is at all political, it is only because he recognizes the power of political choices in curbing capital's natural tendency toward inequality, which is best hindered by ongoing political opposition. In this view, the emancipating achievements of the twentieth century owed their existence largely to a contest between opposing political camps and would last only as long as victory for any one party is suspended.

Thus the concept of struggle moves to the center, not as a conflict between social classes but as a form of necessary agonistic pressure on the system, perhaps even an indispensable part of it, one that can never relent if the system is to remain fair. "Except in struggle, there is no more beauty," wrote the Futurist Filippo Tommaso Marinetti, followed by "No masterpiece without an aggressive character."[7] Again, an interesting echo of the modern movement emerges. Modern architecture is invariably considered to be political, but by and large its political life has proved promiscuous. Italian Fascists sponsored modern architecture, as did Communists until Stalin. Le Corbusier served both the USSR and the Vichy regime. It is mostly in a desire to overthrow the old that commonalities between these systems can be found: a shared belief that whatever the consequences of action are, the consequences of inaction would be greater. In hindsight, then, the social mobility of the twentieth century becomes not a victory of the Left over the Right but of new over old: a cleansing of the existing social order in the name of leveling the playing field. Maybe that is the main idea encapsulated, albeit strangely, in the choice posed by Le Corbusier's "Architecture or Revolution," which presents architecture as a way to prevent violent revolution, embodying an ideological revolution in itself.[8] Despite all the hallmarks of leftist rhetoric, somehow this slogan proposing that architecture replaces politics remains apolitical. Political oppositions dissolve in a battle between new and old—in a choice between progress and regress.

The resonance of Piketty's historical analysis of capital with the progression of architectural history is eerie at times. The first intersection (economic output exceeding the returns on capital) just before World War I clearly coincided with the emergence of the avant-garde, but the resonance also applies through more subtle distinctions within the twentieth century. From the early to the mid-1970s, for the first time in the twentieth century, the lead of economic output over the returns on capital begins to diminish, and toward the end of the 1970s a different political wind begins to blow. The conservative revolution first sweeps the United States and later Europe, forcing an agenda of economic liberalization and the slashing of government spending. The size of the public sector is steadily reduced, and large public housing projects become a thing of the past. This period essentially and concurrently marks the end of an unfettered belief in the merits of modern architecture. In 1972 the Pruitt-Igoe public housing estate in St. Louis is demolished, an event that critics generally herald as the "end" of modern architecture and, on a larger scale, the end of modern utopian visions for the city. After the demolition of Pruitt-Igoe, confidence in the architectural profession is severely shaken. The mood becomes pensive; the seminal works of architecture are no longer plans but books, no longer visions but reflections. It is telling that the most noteworthy architectural manifesto of 1989, the year of the fall of the Berlin Wall and the onset of an uncontested global rule of capitalism, is *A Vision of Britain* by Prince Charles. The modern age prefigured in the Futurist manifesto, at the tail end of the Ottocento with its hereditary hegemonies, ironically concludes with an antimodern manifesto written by a member of the British royal family.

If the egalitarian climate of the 1960s and 1970s had made top-down modern architecture generally unpopular, the neoliberal policies of the 1980s and 1990s make it obsolete. The initiative to construct the city comes to reside increasingly in the private sector. "Thought production" by the architectural profession, in the form of theoretical manifestos or wholesale urban visions, gradually comes to a standstill. The form in which the city is constructed changes. Large interventions in the city, using public housing projects as the texture from which to compose a new and alternative urban fabric, become virtually impossible.

As part of a wholesale privatization program, public housing associations are privatized, and home ownership rises dramatically. By transforming large numbers of people from tenants into home owners, the prevailing powers also hope to garner political sway. As soon as people own their homes, a mortgage will give them a vested interest in keeping interest rates and inflation down. Locked into an inescapable financial reality, they will have little alternative but to sympathize with the economic agenda of the Right. Home owners—so the reasoning goes—will form an instantaneous conservative constituency.

Over the decades to come, however, the new allegiance between the middle class and the Right turns out to be a marriage of inconvenience. The conservative revolution had relied on two pillars: the endless rise of property values (to maintain the desire for home ownership) and wage moderation (to maintain the economy's competitive power). It was matter of time before they would clash, exposing the whole system that allowed people to buy in as a Faustian pact. With property appreciating in value more than incomes rose, homes became ever more unaffordable; each generation of buyers suffered from the price increases that guaranteed the first owners profit.

Piketty's observations about the power of returns of wealth over income are clearly manifested in real estate narratives of the past decades. Real estate is a prime example of how capital, after a first wave of seeming to work to people's advantage, inevitably acquires a worrying dynamic of its own. Over time, the basic possibility of owning one's home becomes progressively beyond the reach of more and more people.

After the conservative revolution, the built environment and particularly housing acquires a fundamentally new role. From a means to provide shelter, it becomes a means to generate financial returns. A building is no longer something to use but something to own (with the hope of increased asset value rather than use value over time). Through the general deployment of the term "real estate," the definition of the architect is replaced by that of the economist. This is also the moment at which architecture becomes definitively inexplicable (at least by the criteria according to which architects usually explain architecture). The logic of a building no longer primarily reflects its intended use but instead serves mostly to promote a generic desirability in economic terms. Judgment of architecture is deferred to the market. The architectural style of buildings no longer conveys an ideological choice but a commercial one: architecture is worth whatever others are willing to pay for it.

Architecture and marketing become indistinguishable, leading to a curious reversal of the process: computer renderings precede technical drawings, the sale of apartments precedes their design, the image precedes the substance, and the salesman precedes the architect. Perhaps Aldo van Eyck's famous tirades against postmodernism in the 1980s were nothing more than an expression of desperation or indignation that somehow our work had been hijacked.

Indeed, if we take the Piketty analogy to its full conclusion, we may wonder whether there was ever such a thing as postmodern architecture at all. Perhaps what we witnessed was not a succession of architectural styles engaged in mutual polemics but a shift toward a fundamentally different role of buildings. If before the 1970s (roughly speaking) buildings were primarily regarded as (public) expenditures, after the 1970s buildings became mostly a means of revenue, a shift that caused further downward pressure on construction budgets. Once buildings are discovered as a form of capital, they can operate only according to the logic of capital. In that sense there may ultimately be no such thing as modern or postmodern architecture, but simply architecture before and after its annexation by capital.

Recent decades have seen the emergence of a new sobriety, a new modernism, at least in aesthetic terms. But how modern is the modern architecture of today? Modernism had a rational program: to share the blessings of science and technology universally. Recent decades have shown that modern architecture can easily be deployed to work against its original ideology. Once buildings are identified as a means of return, modern architecture's economy of means is no longer a way to reach the largest number of people but a way to maximize profits. The same repertoire of rational production, incorporation of industrial products, celebration of the ninety-degree angle, and aesthetics of sobriety that once made buildings affordable now make buildings cheap. Marketing plays a crucial role here. Once modernism can freely be reinterpreted as a style rather than an ideology, it becomes relatively easy to dissociate a high selling price from a low cost base and reap record profits as a result.

Ironically, this development affects both rich and poor. When sale values exceed production costs to the extent they now do, the quality of a building is no longer judged by its physical or aesthetic attributes but by its potential to sell for profit. The whole notion of physical luxury is superseded by a value on paper. However, the value on paper in no way represents the real material value of the product. The price of property is created by a combination of size and location. Unless major technical flaws come to light, the material or technical quality of buildings barely plays a role. As long as the hype continues, the investment is safe.

A small anecdote: in 2016, in one of the wealthier boroughs of Central London, a high-end residential project was completed, consisting of some fifty luxury apartments. The legal obligation under London planning policies to realize a percentage of the apartments as affordable homes has been met by offering an alternative site in a somewhat poorer neighborhood some distance from the development. The project is targeted at the expatriate market, broadly known to settle purchases in cash, without a bank loan. Sales go more quickly that way. The cheapest apartment in the project costs £11 million. (The price of the most expensive apartment remains privileged information between the buyer and the developer, covered by a confidentiality agreement.)

The sales brochure speaks of "a rare place to live, in and around outstanding modern architecture in a park." For quite a few of the prospective residents (rich Russians, perhaps), the idea of modern architecture in a park will evoke memories of a system whose collapse funded their personal fortunes. The architects are rumored to have considered weather-resistant cardboard as a facade material, underlining the supreme irony of asking some of the world's richest people to pay record prices for a cardboard box. The client, an old hand in the development business, has remained unfazed by the irony and has allowed the project to proceed, albeit on condition that there be a "slight change" in facade material.

Despite its aesthetics of poverty, the building is already substantially over budget. By coincidence, the surveyor releases his report (urging major cost cuts) the same day the estate agents release their list of buyers: an interesting collection of superwealthy Americans (many with Dutch surnames), Russian oligarch-billionaires, and Arab oil sheikhs. The poorest of the prospective buyers is worth a little over £2 billion, about fifty times the project's construction budget. To ensure that "finances will add up," the cost of the project is subsequently cut by 40 percent.

This anecdote, despite some of its farcical aspects, is symptomatic of overheated residential markets such as Central London, where even record prices paid by astronomically rich residents do not prevent downward pressure on construction costs. Meanwhile, the upward trajectory of residential prices created by the expatriate market has had a predictable effect at the other end of the spectrum in forcing moderate-income groups to live ever farther from the center. Nurses, teachers, policemen, firefighters, and other professionals earning moderate wages no longer qualify for mortgages for even the most modest properties inside Central London. The fire sale of council property in Central London boroughs, supposedly created to enlarge the stock of affordable homes, has done little to mitigate the process. After the first generation of tenants is offered the opportunity to purchase their rental apartments at subsidized rates, the next round of sales quickly conforms to market rates, generally making the apartments unaffordable for the income groups for whom they were originally intended. Even a well-intended piece of architecture, with all the right references to the enlightened modernism of the twentieth century, cannot avoid becoming an accessory in promoting an ever-widening gap between value and quality, a downward spiral where ultimately even the happy few get shortchanged.

Trellick Tower, a thirty-one-story building with 217 flats in North Kensington, built in 1972 and very familiar to architects, long had a reputation for antisocial behavior and crime. When "right-to-buy" council homes were introduced in the mid-1980s, many of the flats were bought by the tenants. A new residents' association was formed, and several security improvements were undertaken, including the employment of a concierge. After the buildings' Grade II* listing in 1998, property prices rose sharply, and flats in the tower came to be regarded as highly desirable residences. Despite serious technical problems within the building, properties inside the tower have sold for between £250,000 for a small one-bedroom flat and £480,000 for a fully refurbished three-bedroom flat. The maximum obtainable mortgage on an average annual gross income of £32,188 in the United Kingdom in 2014 was £152,000.

Central London is not the only place affected by this phenomenon. The Park Hill Estate in Sheffield, North Yorkshire, a council estate built in 1957, went into decay in the 1970s.[9] In 1998 the complex was Grade II* listed, and English Heritage, together with a private developer, launched a renovation scheme to turn the flats into upmarket apartments and business units. (The renovation was one of the six shortlisted projects for the 2013 RIBA Stirling Prize.) According to Sheffield's website, the city has "the lowest annual average salary of UK's core cities" at around £24,000, allowing a maximum mortgage of around £115,000. Outside the United Kingdom, the original units of Le Corbusier's Unité d'Habitation are currently being sold for €151,000 (for a thirty-one-square-meter studio), €350,000 (for a three-bedroom flat), and €418,000 (for a four-bedroom flat). The average annual wage in France is €30,300, allowing a maximum mortgage just under €120,000. The *existenzminimum*: the establishment of a universally acceptable minimum standard of living in the twentieth century seems to have become a privileged condition in the twenty-first.

The twentieth century taught us that utopian thinking can have precarious consequences, but if the course of history is dialectic, what follows? Does the twenty-first century mark the absence of utopias? And if so, what are the dangers of that? Piketty's framing of the twentieth century echoes the familiar notion of "the short twentieth century," the historic period marked by a global contest between two competing ideologies, running from the beginning of World War I to the end of communism in Eastern Europe—starting in Sarajevo, ending in Berlin.[10] If we are to believe Piketty, we may well be on the way back to a patrimonial form of capitalism. With that, modern architecture's social mission—the effort to establish a decent standard of living for all—seems a thing of the past. Once more, architecture is a tool of capital, complicit in a purpose antithetical to its one-time ideological endeavor. Nearly twenty years into the new millennium, it is as though the previous century never happened. The same architecture that once embodied social mobility now helps prevent it. Despite ever-higher rates of poverty and homelessness, large social housing estates are being demolished with ever-greater resolve. Perhaps Piketty's theory, the final undoing of the twentieth century, finds concrete proof in the methodic removal of its physical substance.

Maison Dom-Ino, Iran, 2006
Sadr Concrete Consultant / *Iran Banner*

42

In Memoriam

A Photo Essay

Pruitt-Igoe, St. Louis, 1954–1972
Photograph by Lee Balterman / The LIFE Images Collection / Getty Images

Sutter Housing Project, New York City, 1955–1987
Photograph by David Rentas / New York Post Archives / © NYP Holdings, Inc. / Getty
Images

Christopher Columbus Homes, New Jersey, 1955–1994
Photograph by Spencer A. Burnett / New York Post Archives / © NYP Holdings,
Inc. / Getty Images

Minguettes, Lyon, 1965–1994
Thomson Reuters B.V. (PHOTO) / © ANP Photo B.V.

Lexington Terrace, Baltimore, 1959–1996
Photograph by Afro American Newspapers / Gado / Getty Images

432 PROGRESS

Norfolk Park Estate, Sheffield, 1960s–1997
Photograph by Dan Chung / Thomson Reuters B.V. (PHOTO) / © ANP Photo B.V.

Robert Taylor Homes, Chicago, 1962–1998
Photograph by Scott Olson / Thomson Reuters B.V. (PHOTO) / © ANP Photo B.V.

St. Vincent's Hospital, Dublin, 1960s–2001
Photograph by Chris Bacon / PA Archive / PA Images

Breezy Point, New York City, 1979–2002
Photograph by Education Images / Universal Images Group Editorial / Getty Images

Vela H, Naples, 1974–2003
Courtesy of SIAG SRL—www.esplosivi.it

Barres Ravel et Presov, Paris, 1963–2004
Photograph by Philippe Wojazer / Thomson Reuters B.V. (PHOTO) / © ANP Photo B.V.

Churchill House Offices, Belfast, 1965–2004
Photograph by Paul Faith / PA Archive / PA Images

Marzahn, Berlin, 1977–2004
Photograph by Bernd Settnik / Picture-Alliance / © ZB–Fotoreport

McDermott Tower, Ballymun Estate, Dublin, 1966–2005
Photograph by Haydn West/PA Archive/PA Images

Le Tripode, Nantes, 1972–2005
Photograph by Alain Denantes / Gamma-Rapho / Getty Images

Barres du Pré de l'Herpe, Lyon, 1974–2005
© PHOTOPQR / LE PROGRES / MAXIME JEGAT / Maxppp

Cornouaille, Meaux, 1960s–2007
Photograph by Olivier Laban-Mattei / AFP / Getty Images

Zwarte Madonna, The Hague, 1985–2007
Photograph by René van Harrewijn / Beeldbank Haags Gemeentearchief

Pollokshaws, Glasgow, 1964–2009
Photograph by David Cheskin / PA Archive / PA Images

La Duchère, Lyon, 1962–2010
Photograph by Philippe Desmazes / AFP / Getty Images

Bijlmermeer, Amsterdam, 1968–2010
Photograph by Sergio Felter, 2010 / sergiofelter.tumblr.com

Aylesbury Estate, London, 1977–2010
Photograph by Lewis Whyld / PA Archive / PA Images

La Cité Balzac, Paris, 1967–2012
Photograph by Eric Feferberg / AFP / Getty Images

Derby Street Blocks, Dundee, 1967–2013
Photograph by David Cheskin / PA Archive / PA Images

Brewster-Douglass Public Housing Projects, Detroit, 1955–2014
Photograph by Jim West / Alamy Stock Photo

Tour 13, Paris, 1960–2014
Photograph by Christophe Herou / PA Archive / PA Images

AfE Tower, Frankfurt, 1972–2014
Photograph by Boris Roessler / AFP PHOTO / DPA / Getty Images

Red Road Flats, Glasgow, 1964–2015
Photograph: © Carol McCabe Photography

Joseph Plunkett Tower, Ballymun Estate, Dublin, 1967–2015
Photograph by Brian Lawless / PA Archive / PA Images

Neubrandenburg Plattenbau, 1974–2016
Photograph by Stefan Sauer / © DPA / Picture-Alliance / ZB

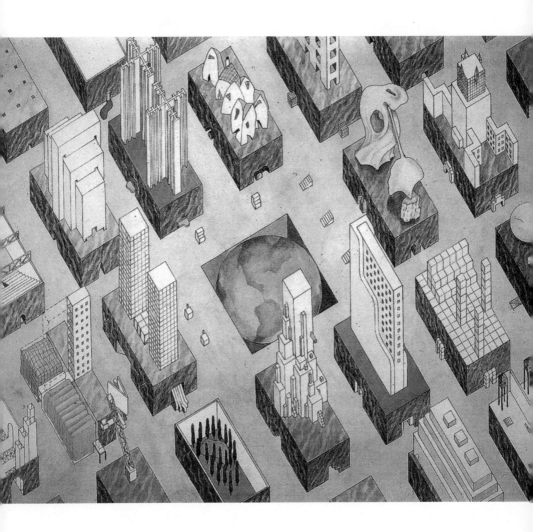

The City of the Captive Globe, 1972
Rem Koolhaas, with Zoe Zenghelis, "City of the Captive Globe," 1972.
Reproduced from Rem Koolhaas, *Delirious New York: A Retroactive Manifesto for Manhattan* (New York: Oxford University Press, 1978), 242.

The Captive Globe

This essay is about a drawing—or rather, about the insight embedded within that drawing and the life it has taken on in the forty-five years since it was made. The drawing in question is *The City of the Captive Globe*. It was created in 1972, first published in 1978 by Rem Koolhaas in *Delirious New York*, and cocredited to Zoe Zenghelis, partner in the then newly formed Office for Metropolitan Architecture. *The City of the Captive Globe* illustrates in large part the thesis of a later book, which identifies Manhattan as the mythical laboratory for the invention of a new revolutionary lifestyle: the "culture of congestion," simultaneously informed by an explosion of human density and an invasion of new technologies.[1]

The drawing shows a roughly twenty-block fragment of a theoretically infinite grid. The proportions of the individual blocks suggest that it is the Manhattan grid, but because it lacks identifiable landmarks one cannot be quite sure. To the extent that the drawing owes its origin to Manhattan, its debt is to the idea of Manhattan rather than the physical place. In the absence of a specified location, the grid becomes an autonomous ideological statement.

In *The City of the Captive Globe*, "each Science or Mania has its own plot. On each plot stands an identical base, built from heavy polished stone. To facilitate and provoke speculative activity, these bases— ideological laboratories—suspend unwelcome laws, undeniable truths, to create nonexistent physical conditions. From these solid blocks of granite, each philosophy has the right to expand infinitely toward heaven."[2] *The City of the Captive Globe* indiscriminately absorbs architectures that were previously thought incompatible. In it we glimpse El Lissitzky's Lenin's Stand, Dalí's *Architectonic Angelus of Millet*, Le Corbusier's Plan Voisin, Malevich's Architecton, Raymond Hood's RCA Building, and Wallace Harrison's Trylon and Perisphere for the 1939 New York World's Fair. "All these Institutes together form an enormous incubator of the World itself; they are breeding on the Globe. Through our feverish thinking in the Towers, the Globe gains weight. Its temperature rises slowly. In spite of the most humiliating setbacks, its ageless pregnancy survives."[3]

The language is celebratory, but the message remains ambiguous. Are we looking at an endorsement, a warning, or simply an observation? When pregnancy is ageless, birth is infinitely postponed. Potential takes the place of deliverance. Progress becomes a self-fulfilling prophecy. The question of what one is progressing toward must forever remain unanswered.

"The City of the Captive Globe is devoted to the artificial conception and accelerated birth of theories, interpretations, mental constructions, proposals and their infliction on the World. It is the capital of Ego, where science, art, poetry and forms of madness compete under ideal conditions to invent, destroy and restore the world of phenomenal Reality. Each science or mania has its own plot."[4] The "capital of Ego" no longer supports architecture in any absolute sense. In exchange for that withdrawal, however, it gives back to architecture its status of perpetual experimentation. It replaces a commitment to architectural modernism with one to modernity, for it is the experiment that is the essence of modernity, not modern architecture's overblown pretense of any definitive answer. The architectures featured in the drawing are pursuits; their value lies in their endeavor, not in their finite states. The experiment can be conducted only when its sole and nonnegotiable condition is met: the permanent suspension of all judgment.

The drawing is ostensibly about architecture, but it is also a comment on architecture's relative importance. Former visionary utopias, embodied in singular tower blocks, are lined up like products in a department store. The drawing makes a pointed statement about the futility of architecture's larger pretensions; it mocks architecture's aspirations to control. The ideology of the grid spells the end of architecture as a totalizing discipline. After *The City of the Captive Globe,* architecture exists only in the plural, suggesting an apex of multiple choice. Formerly absolute ideologies are confined to the walls of their facades; their validity is limited to the boundary of their plots. Their simple coexistence within a single territory makes them relative; each vision cancels out the validity of the next. In *The City of the Captive Globe* architecture has agreed to disagree.

Although the drawing has a distinctly postmodern flavor, it signals the end of postmodernism as the prevailing style. Like any other style, postmodernism is just one of many. At the same time, *The City of the Captive Globe* makes a convincing case that modernity itself is now postmodern—a trope to be worn lightly, like the rest. The drawing announces a distinctly agnostic phase in architecture, a form of architectural nihilism, intended to cleanse the discipline of its false projections and delusional tendencies. The grid is intentionally blind to the architectures that inhabit it. They are interchangeable ingredients within a larger order that exists with or without them. In *The City of the Captive Globe* the accumulated masterpieces within the grid do little to disguise the fact that the real masterpiece is the grid itself. The grid precedes the individual architectures and will outlive them all.

At the time of its publication in 1978, the drawing sparked controversy. The implied rejection of architecture's potential to embody absolute truths, or even to express any meaning at all, was considered to be a cynical and philistine proposition. It is unclear to what extent *The City of the Captive Globe* was ever intended to serve as a model. If it was, time has overtaken it. Nearly half a century later, the metropolis, for which New York served as the case study, is no longer an exclusively Western concept. As the challenge of incorporating the idiosyncrasies of an ever-expanding spectrum of diversity becomes central, it is no longer a culture of congestion but rather a congestion of cultures that is the leading paradigm. The metropolis of the twenty-first century is in every sense more radical than the drawing, the message of which is now an understatement. As often happens, reality defies and surpasses all expectations.

Where the original drawing gathered a collection of carefully curated examples, all different, but all architecture, the more recent incarnation of the metropolis pushes the idea of what can exist together further still. Ultimately this metropolis negates the difference between architecture and nonarchitecture, reserving judgment not only on its varied manifestations but also on the necessity of architecture altogether. It is the essence of the modern metropolis that both everything and nothing qualify as architecture. Anything may become architecture. That is its most profound conclusion. Conversely, anything considered architecture can stop being so, at which point architecture is liberated to become history; it can retire.

It can be concluded that the Office for Metropolitan Architecture emerged from the annihilation of its subject. As soon as architecture becomes "metropolitan," it is no longer architecture—at least not architecture as it lived in the minds of architects until that moment. From there on, architecture exists in the knowledge of its own relativity. Metropolitan architecture is like religion after Einstein.

That is not to say that architecture is no longer practiced. The effect of the destruction of any possible shared truth seems only to have been a general increase in architecture's productivity; the past four decades have produced an architectural big bang. Thus, the drawing can be read as modern architecture's graveyard, as well as the site of its rebirth. As the death of God produced an infinite proliferation of deities, "metropolitan architecture" has legitimized (and promoted) an infinite proliferation of architectures. It has relieved later generations of excess baggage and enabled a new breed of modern architectures to arise, produced in the knowledge that architecture no longer matters in the same way.

The implications of the drawing are not limited to architecture. Nor is the metropolis a testament only to architecture's limited relevance; like the infinite grid, its mockery extends to all attempts to create order on a larger scale. After architecture, urbanism is equally unable to establish any semblance of ideological consensus. If the twentieth-century metropolis was the bond between the skyscraper and the grid, the metropolis of the twenty-first emerges from its dissolution. The Manhattan grid is no longer an absolute, one-size-fits-all solution but merely one of many ways to organize the coexistence of individual fragments. There is a choice among square grids and radial grids, morphed grids and organic grids, impossible grids and, with increasing frequency, no grid at all. The metropolis of the twenty-first century is like a theme park. Formerly totalizing principles reappear in a buffet of orchestrated experiences; memories of particular cities make their encores as products of choice. Composition gives way to impression, cohesion to fragmentation, urban planning to Photoshop.

Does the modern metropolis express the essence of modernity, or does it signal its complete undoing? Does it announce not the triumph of a single style or system but simply the legitimacy of agreeing to disagree, of pushing any finite system to its limits? Whenever coherence proves untenable within the confines of a certain discipline, we simply move on to the next discipline, and an endless process of deferral is set in motion: architecture gives way to urbanism, urbanism gives way to planning, and planning gives way to politics. The professional authority of each domain is valid only as long as it is able to contain the disarray created by the previous one. Modernity becomes about accommodating dissent, and acquiring incremental degrees of abstraction. Modernity's final and unexpected plot twist is the revelation that the highest degree of abstraction and the lowest common denominator are one and the same. Only in abstraction is the lowest common denominator tolerable, exposing matters of "taste" for what they really are: a form of folklore.

In pursuit of greater and greater abstraction, modernity turns art, religion, culture, and architecture into successive terrains of scorched earth. They become "free" expressions, irrelevant to our historical destiny. Still, this freedom exists only because they are subcategories which are light, easy to digest, and even easier to dismiss. Casual bloggers are search-engine-result neighbors alongside major intellectual authorities (insofar as the latter can be said to exist). Obscure political parties acquire major parliamentary followings overnight, only to disappear in the next election cycle. Diversity signifies irrelevance more than it does freedom. Perhaps this explains the sense of impoverishment we experience as we watch modernization unfold: the sense of trading in previous certainties for unknown multiplicities. In religion, this is the promise of the ever after; in modernity, it is the promise of a future that may never come.

The only remaining absolute resides in the collective embrace of economic values. Even the political sphere has become a subsector of the economy. In the late twentieth century political theorist Francis Fukuyama attempted to make a case for the universal embrace of economic values as the triumph of Western liberal democracy. Authoritarian regimes that perform every bit as well as democracies, if not better, have definitively rebuked this theory. The current world consumes the political and its doctrines à la carte. China does so literally: one country, two systems. Western liberal democracy is perceived now as just one of multiple political options, with more need than ever to argue its universal claims. The political—like art, religion, culture, and architecture before it—is professed in the knowledge that it no longer matters, at least not in the same way.

It is the global economy, subject to absolutely nobody's control, that defines us as a collective. Modernity's evolution toward abstraction ultimately divorces it from the exercise of political will; our apparent consensus defies our collective judgment. Disorientation ensues. We talk about freedom passionately yet we do so without describing freedom from what; we talk about progress without stating what we are progressing toward. The appearance of freedom becomes inversely proportional to real freedom, which is ultimately the ability to control our own destiny. Modernity now finds itself at odds with democracy. The economy *tout court* becomes the sole remaining source of cohesion in the modern world, the only real form of objectivity, and the only central organizing principle.

In identifying the economy as its endgame, the evolution of modernity runs into trouble. Understanding the economy used to be about discerning the control of the means of production, a notion that implies an end that lies outside the economy. Money is surely to be converted into a value other than itself, the measure of which is the elevation of man's existence. Insofar as art, culture, and perhaps even architecture may constitute such a value, they are what constitute richness. Where the economy is the means, they are the end. But in the absence of either intrinsic or shared value, only exchange value determines worth. The cycle of exchange of which they become part ultimately leads to a conceptual reversal where the end becomes the means, and the means become the end. Art has become a high-risk asset class, generating both stratospheric returns and catastrophic losses. Architecture in the form of real estate creates booms and busts alike and played its part in bringing the world to the brink of the financial abyss in 2008. Ironically, having been shorn of their ideological values, art and architecture have become more dangerous than ever.

Approaching five decades since its publication, *The City of the Captive Globe* presents a form of dystopian foresight extending well beyond the professional realms of architecture. What the grid was to the various buildings, the economy has become to art, culture, religion, and politics. Yet the apparent ability of architecture to disrupt the economy also allows a new interpretation of the drawing with an unrecognized potential. The individual architectures depicted in it are not mere expressions of their own simple instability; collectively they embody the complex instability of the system as a whole. Metropolitan architecture becomes the sum total of architectures, whose combined weight could topple the stock market. The power of the multifarious towers lies not in the individual ideologies represented by each but in the collective capacity to derail an otherwise authorless consensus. Thus the drawing's second message becomes a rejection of its first: architecture's apparent descent into chaotic volatility becomes the source of its revenge—a way to reclaim the globe from captivity.

Shoreline of Far Rockaway, New York City, 2008
Photograph by G. Paul Burnett / Redux Pictures / Hollandse Hoogte.
Published in "Beaten Down, and Not Only by Nature," *New York Times*, January 17, 2008.

44

Remains of a Brave New World

It is hot, but even at the height of summer, the roads are not particularly busy. The light traffic brings to mind outdated complaints about jammed roads obstructing access to the once-thriving beach resorts out here. The image of summer resorts flooded with armies of Manhattanites seeking relief in the unassuming horizontality of the Rockaways' beaches seems a distant memory.

We enter the peninsula by crossing the Marine Parkway Bridge from Floyd Bennett Field in Brooklyn. First, we head to Breezy Point, also known as the Irish Riviera, the westernmost neighborhood of the Rock-aways—a gated community, albeit a hospitable one: the barriers flanking the main road can easily be opened if they are not already. We enter. A casually strewn vernacular array of beach houses is, for the most part, accessed by sandy or unpaved roads. The area has the air of a semiperma-nent campsite, with apparent indifference to formal order and absence of self-consciousness. Houses are added onto or expanded at will, giving them a kind of nonchalance that somehow enhances their beauty. Sport utility vehicles litter almost every driveway, often several at a time. The Stars and Stripes flutters from the low-pitched roofs in great numbers. There is no festive holiday today, according to my company of native New Yorkers; people here simply celebrate the fact that they are American each and every day.

We head east and pass other affluent areas, such as Neponsit, Belle Harbor, and Rockaway Park. Then, when according to the map we're about halfway across the peninsula, the road joins up with the elevated tracks of the A train line as it moves through the neighborhoods of Hammel, Arverne, and Edgemere. The view abruptly changes, along with the ethnic makeup, as is often the case in American cities. This is the other side of the Rockaways. Grim high-rise slabs stand in the middle of a wasteland, alternately animated by trash-littered lots and shabby little clusters of bungalows. Rickety frame dwellings line the elevated railroad, while burned-out and vandalized buildings dot the landscape. The area exemplifies the fate that has hit many outer urban areas in the United States. Average income is low; unemployment and crime rates are supposedly among the highest in New York City.

Then, suddenly, nothing. Across and over the garbage and the overgrown lots, we finally glimpse the boardwalk for the first time, and beyond, the Atlantic Ocean. A beachfront high-rise springs up out of nowhere, followed by more empty seaside lots. We are now in the Arverne Urban Renewal Area, which, after thirty years of vacancy, has returned to a feral, almost rural condition. Street signs running from Beach 62nd to Beach 81st mark little more than asphalt rubble piles or overgrown pathways. There is something strangely moving and heroic about these signs, the last remaining testaments of an ancient civilization.

The degree of neglect makes it difficult to picture what sort of development could happen here. Ever since the area was razed in the name of urban renewal, Arverne has challenged the meaning of the term. Whereas in most parts of the Rockaways recent projects have leeched off an existing urban fabric, Arverne has nothing to renew; there is no urban fabric left.

We continue our journey. Just before we cross Doughty Boulevard, the boundary that separates Nassau County's affluent five towns from New York City, things change again. The cityscape switches back into the comfortably suburban mode of the first part of our journey, but here the streets are remarkably busy, lined predominantly with groups of men sporting three-piece suits, black coats, and black hats, out of keeping with the hot weather and in sharp contrast with the generally pale faces. Today is the Sabbath, and members of Far Rockaway's sizable community of Orthodox Jews are on their way home from the synagogue.

This community carefully protects and cultivates the area's image as a good neighborhood. In order not to scare off potential homebuyers, real estate brokers advertise this area as "West Lawrence," the bucolic-sounding neighbor to Lawrence, Nassau County. It is perhaps sad that such a poetic name as the Far Rockaways is traded in so easily, but apparently one can't be too careful: reputations make or break the value of one's home, and in most parts of the Rockaways the aura of distress clings firmly.

Our trip was made almost twenty years ago, in the summer of 2000, in the context of potential work in Arverne, which, at the time, seemed to hold great potential. New York was different then. The attacks on the World Trade Center had not yet taken place, and the dreaded "millennium bug," contrary to unfounded and hysterical fears, had failed to materialize. There was little to suggest that the coming century would do anything but extend the good ride we had been enjoying at the end of the previous one.

In 2012 Arverne made headlines again as one of Hurricane Sandy's victims. Today, in 2016, the area is still suffering from the devastation. Since our first visit, new and profitable housing developments had started to take shape, but after the storm this "ideal beach location" had suffered yet another major setback. In the words of Mayor de Blasio: "The storm only made clearer some inequities that had existed for years and even decades."[1] In the purgatory between opportunity and misfortune, Arverne remains locked in the double identity that has characterized most of its history.

Arverne-by-the-Sea

1832: An epidemic of cholera ravages Manhattan. In search of refuge, hundreds of families make the journey to the ocean beaches of the Rockaways. The Rockaway Peninsula gradually develops into a playground for the well-to-do, and beach resorts prosper along its shoreline. In September 1895 a developer literally builds on this success by incorporating a large stretch of land halfway along the peninsula as a village, Arverne-by-the-Sea, after his signature, Remington Vernam. By the end of the nineteenth century Arverne is recognized as one of the great summer resorts of America, attracting glitterati from all over the world.

Arverne's decline sets in at the turn of the twentieth century, when the Rockaway Peninsula, as a result of relocation of the boundary with Nassau County, becomes part of New York City, and the old exclusivity and aristocratic air of the former village begin to fade. In 1922 a devastating fire destroys about 150 structures in Arverne. The dense construction that follows consists primarily of small bungalows and summer rental units. The remaining grand buildings of the earlier years are turned into boarding houses and apartments. Old street names are abandoned for a numbering system that runs the length of the peninsula.

Spectators watching a tennis match in front of the Edgemere Club Hotel, Edgemere, New York City, 1910

Byron Company (New York, N.Y.) / Museum of the City of New York, 93.1.1.15161

Indirectly, the fire of 1922 clears the way for Parks Commissioner Robert Moses to take matters in a different direction. In the 1930s, facing a surge in population growth, New York City suffers a massive housing shortage that is especially acute for the poor. At the same time, larger segments of the city are declining into slums. Now that Arverne and the entire Rockaway Peninsula are part of New York City, they should do their fair share in alleviating the city's problems. In a letter to Mayor La Guardia dated November 30, 1937, Moses writes, "The whole Rockaway Peninsula should be immediately placed within the fire limits, as plans have been and will continue to be filed for the construction and reconstruction of dangerous frame structures, such as those destroyed in the two recent fires. As there is entirely too much property zoned for business purposes, a considerable part of the area between the boardwalk and Rockaway Beach Boulevard should be rezoned for residential purposes."[2]

Slum-Clearance and Relocation Program

Not until the early 1950s is Moses's call for a massive renewal effort in the Rockaways answered. Under his chairmanship, a committee on slum clearance is appointed on December 17, 1948. (By now, Moses is designated "city construction coordinator and planning commissioner.") The committee's task is to study and expedite specific slum-clearance projects by private capital under anticipated federal law, later enacted as Title 1 of the Housing Act of 1949.[3] After a number of fierce legal battles with local opposition groups, the committee acquires legal and constitutional status from the state and federal courts in 1954 to embark on a program that encompasses the whole of New York City.

The subsequent slum-clearance and relocation program is unprecedented in scale and ambition. In 1954 areas totaling about 9,000 acres in New York City are designated as slums. During the following three years a total of 135,000 new dwellings are constructed, 75,000 of them by the public sector. The total expenditure by the federal government at the time is estimated at $1.18 billion (about $10.37 billion in 2016, adjusted for inflation). As of October 31, 1954, some 68,000 families faced displacement from government-acquired sites. Site tenants are kept informed on the purpose and progress of the project in the hope of ensuring their cooperation.[4]

By the time the committee cast its eye on the Rockaway Peninsula, eighteen other clearance projects throughout New York City are already under way. Residential development in the Rockaways is justified by the need to relocate low-income tenants from densely overpopulated areas of Manhattan and Brooklyn.

The clearance project for the Rockaways (Seaside Rockaway and the Hammels) is introduced as part of an overall plan to eliminate substandard areas in the city and to replace them with sound fabric for housing and community facilities. The site has many advantages for permanent, year-round occupancy. It faces the Atlantic Ocean, and is accessed by the old Rockaway branch of the Long Island Railroad, which has recently been opened as a branch of the rapid transit system of the City of New York.

Another reason, never officially stated, for the popularity of Rockaways' "renewal" plans is its status as a beach resort. Structures at the Rockaways are mainly occupied during the summer months and are often vacant during the rest of the year. Consequently, opposition from local groups is expected to be more sporadic and less problematic than in areas with year-round occupation.

In the twenty years that follow, the city moves forward with public housing at the Rockaways in full force. At the time, state and local legislation contains statutory restrictions against discrimination or segregation in housing, assuring families of any race or religion equal access to low- and middle-income housing. The pleasant surroundings are supposed to have a therapeutic effect on the behavior of the former ghetto residents. An active relocation policy is launched, under which thousands of poor black and Hispanic citizens, uprooted by the city's efforts to demolish the supposedly crime- and drug-ridden slums, are rehoused in the new beachfront projects. As a result of this policy, the population of the Rockaways more than doubles by 1973, and the total number of built and planned publicly aided housing in the Rockaways amounts to some twenty thousand units, roughly half of the area's total housing supply.

Several major projects are built west of old Arverne, which remains dominated by bungalows that their owners gradually abandoned or turned over to slumlords. On the eastern periphery of Arverne, between Beach 54th and Beach 56th Streets, the city opens the Arverne Houses in 1951 (Simeon Heller, 1950). The complex consists of fourteen six-story buildings housing four hundred families. Two years later the sixteen-

Jacob Riis Park, Rockaway Beach, New York City, 1937
Photograph by Percy Loomis Sperr / © Milstein Division, The New York Public Library

building, six-story, 450-unit Redfern Houses (Andrew J. Thomas, 1952) open farther west in Far Rockaway. Also in Far Rockaway is the privately financed Wavecrest Gardens (Maxon-Sells, 1952), consisting of fourteen six-story redbrick buildings. Wavecrest Gardens is a rare example of a large public project for middle-income tenants. This is plainly expressed in its architecture: six underground garages accommodating 721 cars are built between the buildings, each topped with a landscaped leisure area on its roof. A two-acre, one-story shopping center serves Wavecrest's 1,656 families. The housing project proudly occupies only 20 percent of its site. Its architectural ambitions suffice to make front-page news in a Sunday issue of the *New York Times.*

The vast majority of new public housing in the Rockaways, however, is for the poor. In 1955 the 712-unit Hammel Houses are opened immediately west of the earlier Arverne Houses and directly north of the Seaside Rockaway Project, later known as Dayton Towers. Hammel Houses are vaunted as an exemplary Title 1 project in a report to Mayor Wagner and the New York City Board of Estimate in 1955. In the early 1960s other public and publicly aided projects follow, such as the 1,395-unit Edgemere Houses and Nordeck, a middle-income cooperative in the center of the peninsula.

Even with efforts to improve housing under way all across the Rockaway Peninsula, major restructuring bypasses Arverne, and its old bungalows continue to deteriorate. In 1964 the area is declared a slum. Things are supposed to change when Mayor Lindsey launches his "Plan for New York City" in November 1969, an all-out effort to complete the campaign of slum clearance and renewal begun in the early 1950s. As part of this plan, sizable sections of the Rockaways are designated as "urban renewal zones," destined for immediate government intervention in the form of sponsored development, including Arverne, Hammel, and Edgemere. The city begins to bulldoze large swathes of them but suddenly stops halfway when it transpires that the money has run out. The urban renewal process in Arverne it put on hold before it has even properly begun, with no immediate prospect for a restart.

The 1970s arrive. The momentum of the 1950s and 1960s has not yet entirely exhausted itself in New York. A few more large-scale projects go up in the Rockaways, although not on the razed lands of Arverne. Projects include Roy Reuthers Houses (1971) and Ocean Village (1974), both in Far Rockaway and both aimed at people with low and moderate incomes; the latter consisting of 1,094 units across eleven buildings, two day-care centers, and twenty-five thousand square feet of ancillary commercial and community space. Built by the New York State Urban Development Corporation (today known as Empire State Development), it is one of the city's few realized experiments in prefabrication.[5] The uniqueness of this venture, even materially, earns it an award from the Prestressed Concrete Institute soon after its completion in 1974.[6] Ocean Village is the last project of its kind in the Rockaways.

The Gateway National Recreation Area

By the end of the 1960s few people share the appreciation of the concrete industry. In the Rockaways, as everywhere else by this point, opposition to the presence of publicly aided high-rise developments begins to take serious forms.

Trouble begins at the western end of the peninsula, about seven miles from Arverne. Here, on four hundred privately leased acres at Breezy Point, a community of privately owned bungalows and year-round homes has stood since 1910. In 1960 Breezy Point was sold to the Atlantic Improvement State Corporation (AISC); the home owners, in turn, purchase half of this land to form the Breezy Point Cooperative, a gated community of 2,650 houses. The AISC retains ownership of the 2.5-mile-long tract on either side of the cooperative. The city's Regional Plan Association proposes that the entire area be turned into a vast waterfront park, a plan supported by most civic groups but opposed by a coalition of local government officials, the new cooperative homeowners, and the AISC. When the developers for AISC announce plans to build a "city within a city"—including high-rise apartments, malls, private clubs, schools, and other community facilities—opposition from New York City quickly materializes.

Construction nevertheless begins amid a swirling debate. In 1963, just as structural work reaches the eleventh floor of the apartment buildings, the city announces that it is going ahead with its proposed waterfront park and begins condemnation proceedings on Atlantic Improvement's holdings. In 1969, after six years of debate and litigation, the federal government steps in and proposes to include Breezy Point in a massive twenty-six-thousand-acre national park that will also include Fort Tilden, Jacob Riis Park, Jamaica Bay, Floyd Bennett Field, Great Kills Park, and Sandy Hook in New Jersey. The owners of the Breezy Point Cooperative are permitted to keep their homes, but they must forfeit their mile-long ocean frontage to allow for an uninterrupted stretch of beach from Jacob Riis Park to Rockaway Point. Three years later, on October 28, 1972, legislation is signed approving the national park, which comes to be known as the Gateway National Recreation Area.

Changing Political Winds

When Mayor Lindsey announces the plan to demolish the slums of Arverne and the adjacent areas of Hammel and Edgemere in 1969, the decision is both too early and too late. It is too early to be read as part of the looming economic crisis that casts its shadow over New York City for most of the 1970s, but it is too late for confidence that anything much will happen on the razed land. By 1969 the mood in the United States has turned against the idea of an omnipotent welfare state. The relentless optimism of the 1960s and the state's ability to manufacture an "all-inclusive Great Society" is quickly becoming a thing of the past.

The year before the launch of the Plan for New York City, Republican candidate Richard Nixon has been elected president by a narrow margin in the aftermath of the bloody race riots and antiwar protests that had plagued the last years of Lyndon Johnson's administration. With Nixon as president, a new wind of conservatism is blowing across the United States, ushering in harsh financial austerity and radical cutbacks in public spending. The Vietnam War is at its peak, and government spending on anything other than the military ranks as a low priority. In 1971 the average American family pays taxes of $65 for housing programs, $135 on education, and more than $1,300 on military programs.[7] The Vietnam War exposed America's vulnerabilities not only militarily and politically but also socially and economically. According to the Census Bureau in 1971, more than twenty-seven million people live in poverty (a quarter of the nation's elderly, one-seventh of children, and a third of the African American population). Reelected in 1972 in a sweeping victory, Nixon sheds all political inhibition and pursues an even tighter agenda. In 1973 he sets out to impound funding for the Office of Economic Opportunity (perhaps the centerpiece of Johnson's "Great Society" program) and thereby withdraws all support for the Fair Housing Enforcement Program. The effects of the new policies prove disastrous for many of America's major cities. In 1974 the Kerner Commission's report on city life concludes that welfare rolls are climbing, housing is bad, the air is polluted, and crime is soaring. Like most cities in the United States at the time, New York suffers from slums, drug addiction, and widespread homelessness.

1973: The Rockaway Plan

On November 18, 1973, the *New York Times* breaks news of the Rockaway Plan, a report released by Mayor Lindsey that revisits many of the elements put forward in his earlier Plan for New York City.[8] The notion of ever more public housing projects in the form of high-rise construction in the Rockaways has caused concern among the Rockaways community, which has demanded to have a say. Partially in response to this demand, the new report is jointly authored by the Office of City Planning and the Rockaways' neighborhood government. Not surprisingly, it calls for significant cutbacks in the number of proposed public housing units for the Rockaways, as well as construction of a major east-west artery across the peninsula, rehabilitation of the eroded beachfront, and construction of facilities to "meet the needs of the community."

The report is a historic milestone in signaling a retrograde shift in attitudes to the Rockaways, a rejection of the assumptions of the previous twenty years. The opening statement describes how long-term residents of the Rockaways have been unsettled by the changes brought about by rapid growth and by the racial turnover caused by the insertion of public housing projects into the established neighborhoods of the peninsula. It is time to pay attention to this troubled community of one hundred thousand people.

The report proposes a drastic reduction of the number of proposed public housing units. Under the earlier Plan for New York City, 65 percent of the total housing stock on the Rockaways would have been public. Even though it contains only 1 percent of New York City's total population, the Rockaway Peninsula would have accounted for at least 5 percent of its public housing stock. The cuts proposed by the Rockaway Plan—from 10,164 to 5,414 public units—reduce that share significantly.

The Gateway National Recreation Area Project, giving impulse to the ongoing cleanup of Jamaica Bay—a prime dumping ground for New York's industries since the 1920s—becomes the main focus. Its main aim is to bring about a better climate for private investment in the entire peninsula, attracting also developers of unsubsidized housing for the richer pickings of middle-income families. The marketing language accompanying the Gateway project paints a rosy picture: "Eventually, the underutilized bay will be available for the full range of watersports: boating, fishing, sailing or even swimming."[9]

In the context of the Gateway project, the derelict sites of the Arverne Urban Renewal Area are identified as a major opportunity for beach-to-bay recreation. In line with new priorities, a reduction of planned public housing units is proposed (from 5,720 to 4,720), and there is pushback against types of buildings generally constructed in public housing projects. The report recommends that all public family housing be placed in low-rise buildings, and that only studios and one-bedroom apartments be accommodated in towers. Low-rise housing is thought to minimize the amount of shared space—hallways, lobbies, elevators, and staircases—and therefore to be less vulnerable to antisocial behaviors. Low-rise building is also thought to be more in keeping with the lifestyle of the existing Rockaways communities.

1976: Near Bankruptcy

In the late summer of 1976 New York City comes within a hair's breadth of becoming the first major city since the Great Depression to go bankrupt. President Gerald Ford turns down pleas from Mayor Beame for federal help, leading to the famous headline in the *Daily News* of October 30, 1976: "Ford to City: Drop Dead!"

The crisis affects the Rockaways directly by causing panic about its envisioned future. Development policies for the peninsula are scrutinized during a hearing of the New York State Legislative Committee on November 2. Arverne is also discussed. Development of any kind on its razed lands now seems highly uncertain. Local leaders denounce the city for its inaction. Assemblyman Brian Sharoff suggests that in the face of pending financial disaster, the city make part of Arverne available to private developers, who might want to build a recreational complex similar to Tivoli Gardens in Copenhagen. This desperate suggestion is indicative of how New York's near bankruptcy marks the end of an era of engaged governmental agency in planning the city. In the depths of despair, the City Planning Commission goes so far as to approve trailers as temporary relocation homes in Arverne. A long and spotty policy of active government involvement in slum clearance, public housing, and infrastructure is finally and definitively abandoned. Even the sharply reduced quantity of public housing for Arverne proposed under the Rockaway Plan remains forever unbuilt.

There are no records of any major proposals for the Arverne Urban Renewal Area in the late 1970s or through most of the 1980s. This period is the great black hole in the history of the Rockaways: a period of reflection, necessary to shake off the major hangover resulting from too many high-rise towers and an aura of unresolved urban misery. Policies on slum clearance and public housing have to be reformulated and synchronized with a prevailing mood that declares public spending innately suspect. "Government doesn't invest, government spends."[10] Particularly in the domain of subsidized housing, government involvement remains a touchy subject during much of the 1980s and early 1990s, synonymous with ill-advised policies and abuse of tax funds.

It is not until 1989 that the first new proposal of any significance pops up for the site. By then, the approach to low-income housing has shifted in an entirely new direction: away from big projects with rental units and toward public-private deals promoting subsidized home ownership.

1989, Forest City: Restart

In 1989 the Forest City Development Corporation announces the largest proposal for the Arverne Urban Renewal Area to date: ten thousand units of market-rate housing intended for middle-income residents.[11] The launch of the scheme coincides with a *New York Post* interview with Queens borough president Claire Schulman in which she lauds the area's tremendous natural resources, including the Atlantic Ocean and a beach every bit as good as the Hamptons: "Arverne's development could boost the entire Rockaway Peninsula."[12] Forest City's proposal consists of four-story townhouses, to be reached via landscaped courtyards raised over one level of parking. This design intends, according to its planners, to encourage "emphasis on public spaces, privacy, and community of great diversity and complexity."[13]

The shift in architecture is as striking as it is significant, and it is worth noting how carefully this scheme adopts the recommendations of the Rockaway Plan from 1973. "Mid-rise apartments and shopping will be scattered throughout the neighborhoods. To meet a relatively modest budget, the architects are considering industrialized modular units to be assembled on site."[14] Would there be awards this time? The proposal even includes civic plans and details about schools, firehouses, and extensive parks.

In 1990 the Forest City developments proves ominous enough to spark a shadow design competition at the Pratt Institute for alternative schemes for the site. Construction of Forest City is slated to begin in mid-1991, but as Borough President Schulman later tells the *Post*, "The market sank and their proposal fell apart."[15] In 1995, after numerous local meetings and public hearings and consideration of changes in the economy and housing market, the Rockaway Community Board concludes that the needs of the Rockaway community have changed since the approval of the original plan in 1990. It can no longer support the Arverne Urban Renewal Area project as approved by the New York City Board of Estimate in 1990, with its idea of building 7,500 units (already slashed from the original 10,000) of large-scale, market-rate, high- and midrise residential housing. In 1997 the board, along with the New York Housing and Preservation Department (HPD), hires a consultant and completes a feasibility study for the Arverne Urban Renewal Area. The study has widespread community input and participation through still more public hearings, held district-wide. The resulting plan proposes retail space, a golf course, a cinema, and a mere 800 housing units.

Technodome

In the midst of this revision (June 1997), plans are announced for a billion-dollar sports and recreation complex, "Destination Technodome," for the Arverne Urban Renewal Area site. Developed by the Canadian firm Heathmount Arts and Entertainment Corporation, the Technodome will have over two million square feet of space for indoor activities, as well as a thousand-room hotel. The abundant employment opportunities that would be spawned by the ambitious recreational facility promise a bright future for the feeble economy of Arverne. A dramatic increase in property values is also expected. However, after four years of waiting in vain, a community district needs report notes that "However, after three years of waiting in vain, Queens officials report they "have abandoned hope that a $1.2 billion sports and entertainment complex will ever be built."[16]

At the end of 2000 Borough President Schulman puts it more straightforwardly, again speaking to the *New York Post:* "That one is out of there too! They wanted to do an ambitious recreational facility; I jumped on it because it promised thousands of new permanent jobs. I thought: 'That's great!' So we played around for several years, but the developer refused to commit to necessary infrastructural developments, like highways. It just didn't seem to work; I felt I couldn't wait any longer!"[17]

Largely because of its enviable location, the area continues to inspire optimism. In the spring of 2000 HPD commissioner Jerilyn Perine speaks about a "once in a lifetime opportunity to create an entirely new, thoughtfully planned waterfront community!"[18] "Once in a lifetime" have been applied to Arverne regularly in the past, but this time the city is convinced that things will work. "Given the excellent economic climate and pressing housing shortages faced by the City of New York, it seems Arverne's time has finally come."[19]

RFP

In the fall of 2000 the HPD issues a request for proposals (RFP) for 100 of the total 375 acres of the Arverne Urban Renewal Area. The overall terms of the RFP echo those of the feasibility study of 1997. "HPD sees this RFP as an opportunity to create an attractive, middle-income residential community, known historically as Arverne-by-the-Sea, that includes market-rate housing, commercial / retail space, open spaces, and other amenities that will capitalize on the spectacular ocean-front location."[20]

The resurrection of Arverne's historic name, evoking the era when the Rockaways had not yet been part of the greater city, constitutes a convenient form of amnesia: it was the relocation of New York City's municipal boundaries a century earlier that had sparked Arverne's decline. Arverne-by-the-Sea was successful precisely because it had not been part of New York City. Still, the RFP's most striking break is with New York's more recent past. The adjective "market-rate" appears at least once in every paragraph. The days in which Arverne had been used for public housing experiments are clearly over. This conclusion is probably best encapsulated by the following clause: "Proposals should draw from successful residential communities both long standing and more recently completed in New York City and elsewhere. Preference will be given to proposals that consist principally of single family, owner-occupied housing."[21] The preference for single-family home ownership stated in the RFP is part of a wider trend: in the wake of numerous failed public housing experiments in the 1960s and 1970s, the single-family home once again dominates housing production across the United States. In less than thirty years home-ownership rates rose from around 50 percent to almost 70 percent. In 1999, 1 million of the 1.4 million new homes built were single-family homes.[22]

It is strange but also somehow exciting to think that land in the Rockaways—consistently labeled "prime oceanfront property"—was as recently as the 1970s meant to be parceled out among the poor. Today such policies would seem unthinkable. The Great Society has given way to the Great Sell-off. Ever-larger segments that shape the future of the American city—for that matter, the city anywhere—have been consigned to the domain of private initiative. This transition has marked the end of almost all public housing programs, and with it, the end of an architectural tradition that had great moments of effectiveness and raw beauty.

Arverne by the Sea 2.0

Eight proposals are received in response to the RFP. The winners are the Beechwood Organization and the Benjamin Companies, two local developers familiar with the area. Their proposal literally parrots the terms of the RFP, adopting the neighborhood's new-old name both for the development and the developers' joint venture: Arverne by the Sea LLC.

The new Arverne by the Sea will consist of four quarters: the Sands, the Breakers, the Tides, and the Dunes, consolidating the sea as the prime thematic marketing element for the development. The New York firm EE&K is responsible for the design of the neighborhood. It introduces a typical townhouse configuration, using the two-family-home concept common in other parts of New York City, to allow for higher levels of urban density, as well as a mix of owned and rented homes.

Although EE&K claims to deliberately avoid the traditional home typologies more typical of new urbanist communities, the overall look and feel of the development is remarkably similar.[23] Inside the four quarters the plan introduces a new street system, replacing parts of the typical New York grid. The quarters have fewer through streets because the new angled arterials supposedly create a better orientation to the transit station. To make the plan work, the previously existing numbered streets on the site had to be removed from the map; they no longer exist.

The approach is successful. Despite the events of 9/11 and the crash of American Airlines Flight 587 into one of the Rockaway neighborhoods later that fateful year, plans for Arverne remain on course. The mayor's office gives approval for the development in December 2003, and the land conveyance agreement is finalized in May 2004.

Supposedly, a large part of the success of the Arverne by the Sea LLC bid is due to the storm-protection and other resiliency measures integrated into the design of the new development, incorporating Beechwood's experience with oceanfront property in Florida in the face of Hurricane Andrew. This proves a sign of great foresight. When Sandy hits the Rockaways in October 2012, the developers of the new Arverne by the Sea development claim that it survived the hurricane largely intact.

> Located directly adjacent to the Atlantic Ocean, the Rockaway Peninsula was hit hard, and the developers of Arverne returned to the site after the hurricane with considerable trepidation, wondering whether their well-laid plans for the project had been enough to withstand the onslaught. But they also approached the site with some confidence, knowing that they had prepared the development for such an event. In fact, they discovered that Arverne had survived the hurricane largely unscathed, with minimal water and wind damage and no fire damage. The community and building designs and the systems they had put in place, together with strong dunes and a boardwalk along the oceanfront, had allowed the majority of the project to escape the destruction that affected other nearby areas.[24]

The triumphant lines seem almost too good to be true. Sixteen years after my initial visit, I decide to head out for Arverne again to see for myself.

July 2016: Somehow, I have managed to take the wrong train. Even though I have followed all my directions carefully—from my Soho hotel, I have taken the C at Spring Street, changing at Canal to take the A train to the Rockaways—the surroundings don't look anything like I remember. My overall sense of direction fails me. From memory, I was sure that the train should have veered course sharply to the left, but instead it gently bends to the right. As it turns out, after Broad Channel, across the bay inside the Rockaways, the A train can go in one of two directions: either east toward Arverne and Far Rockaway—final stop Mott Avenue—or toward Breezy Point and Rockaway Park, where I am now mistakenly headed. My verification expedition to Arverne is about to be literally derailed.

I get off the train as soon as I realize my mistake, at the first stop on the southerly branch: Beach 90. The next train in the other direction won't arrive for a while: today is Saturday, and weekend service on the A train, particularly this far out, is infrequent. In addition, I would have to ride back to Broad Channel Station to transfer to the right branch. Rather than crossing to the other platform immediately to turn back, I decide to exit the station and wander around.

Earlier, on the train, I had seen on and off over several miles a yellow school bus evidently headed in the same direction. There is something odd about a school bus traveling this way on a weekend, and I wonder what purpose it could be serving. Yellow buses are certainly not part of any of the other municipal services.

Two blocks from the station, I get my answer when I stumble across a venue called the Rockaway Beach Surf Club, a bright yellow but otherwise inconspicuous building along the line of the elevated A train. The bus—properly called the NYC Beach Bus—provides regular service from downtown Manhattan for a new community of hipsters who use the Rockaway beaches as a surfing location. The Rockaway Beach Surf Club is its first stop on the peninsula.

The club fosters the type of scene one would expect in Southern California rather than on the shores of the North Atlantic; evidently, the effects of global warming aren't all bad. Surfboards, apparently of a rare and expensive kind, adorn the walls and ceiling of the interior. The menu includes tofu tacos, watermelon and pineapple mint drinks, and the rather didactically titled surf 'n' eat breakfast. The cocktail menu boasts Surf Club margaritas, but at 11 a.m. it's a little early for those. Creatively bearded men walk in and out to use the outdoor shower. They have been surfing since sunrise, and it is time to evaluate the morning's waves over Mexican beer.

I head toward the ocean to Rippers, another surf shack. This one is on the beach, directly connected to the boardwalk that straddles the length of the Rockaway Peninsula. The ocean is calm today, with no signs of any storms. On a sunny day even the seemingly endless ranks of 1970s public housing slabs acquire an aura of glamour, as though they were the grand hotels of an elegant and thriving beach resort. Just behind the last slab I can see a tip of Arverne by the Sea and its pale townhouses with single- and double-pitched roofs. From afar, the facades look like natural timber, but from the project specs, I know that this is "HardiPlank fiber cement siding shaded in gray, beige or taupe." I make a rough guess at the time it would take to walk there and decide instead to settle on the terrace of Rippers for an early lunch, oddly content with the alternate ending of my trip.

Exit

I have managed to change my flight out of JFK to the early evening. Flying out over Jamaica Bay, I catch a last glimpse of the area. From the air, Arverne by the Sea looks like a classic application of Photoshop: a deliberate insertion—largely for effect—of an incompatible fragment into its context, its angled streets at odds with the surrounding city grid. Like the Rockaways' nascent surf scene, this "small town in the big city" feels off-key. Apparently, the marketing-speak about a development that withstood the forces of nature by complying with nature is all true. Apartment sales have been a resounding success; there is a car in almost every driveway. I catch myself feeling almost disappointed. But then, maybe not. There is also something exhilarating about the opportunistic exploitation of the site's natural features—sand and beach—intentionally unaware of the burden of its difficult history. Perhaps, in the end, that is where history's resolution lies: in oblivion.

Arverne-by-the-Sea under construction, New York City, 2013
Photograph by Nathan Kensinger

Notes

5. BLOODY FOOLS!

1 Hubert Bennett, "Departmental Philosophy," in *GLC Architecture 1965/70: the work of the GLC's Department of Architecture and Civic Design,* ed. Greater London Council (London: GLC, 1970), 8.

2 Ibid.

3 "The Westminster Tradition," *The Architects' Journal* 152 (1970): 992.

4 Tom Cordell, *John Bancroft: Utopia London,* http://.com/www.utopialondon /john-bancroft

5 Building Schools for the Future was the name of the previous United Kingdom government's investment program in secondary school buildings, overseen by Partnership for Schools, a nondepartmental public body formed through a joint venture between public- and private-sector parties.

   Nick Mathiason, "Venture Capitalists Go on the School Run" *The Observer,* December 9, 2007, http://www.theguardian.com/business/2007/dec/09/private equity.schools.

6 "Pimlico Academy, Westminster," ArchitecturePLB, http://www.architectureplb .com/projects/schools/pimlico-academy-westminster.

7 Elizabeth Hopkirk, "John Bancroft's Widow Backs Campaign to Save London School," *Building Design,* May 18, 2012, http://bdonline.co.uk/news/john-bancrofts -widow-backs-campaign-to-save-london-school/5036889.article.

8 "Common Ground" was the theme of the Thirteenth International Architecture Exhibition at the Venice Biennale, 2012, for which "Bloody Fools!" was originally written.

6. ARCHITEKTUR OHNE EIGENSCHAFTEN

1 Oliver Hirschbiegel, *Der Untergang* (Munich: Constantin Film Produktion, 2004).

2 After World War II, 600,000 apartments lay in ruins in the city of Berlin alone. Joachim Palutzki, *Architektur in der DDR* (Berlin: Reimer, 2000).

3 Christine Hannemann, *Die Platte: Industrialisierter Wohnungsbau in der DDR* (Berlin: Verlag Hans Schiler, 2005).

4 "Refugees Take Up Home in Berlin 'Container Town,'" *The Local,* December 29, 2014, http://www.thelocal.de/20141229/first-refugees-take-up-home-in-berlins -container-town.

5 "Berlin Marzahn (Großsiedlung Marzahn als räumlicher Schwerpunkt in der Stadtumbaumaßnahme Marzahn-Hellersdorf)," Städtebauförderung von Bund, Ländern und Gemeinden, September, 2014, http://www.staedtebaufoerderung

.info/StBauF/DE/Programm/Stadtumbau/StadtumbauOst/Praxis/Massnah
men/Marzahn/Marzahn_node.html.

6   Reinier de Graaf, "After Pruitt Igoe," *Huffington Post*, October 2, 2015, http://www
.huffingtonpost.com/reinier-de-graaf/after-pruitt-igoe_b_8220592.html.

7   Nikita Khrushchev, address to Western ambassadors at the Polish Embassy in
Moscow, November 18, 1956, "We Will Bury You," *Time*, November 26, 1956,
http://content.time.com/time/magazine/article/0,9171,867329,00.html.

8   DDR government declaration at the fifth SED party congress of 1958.
Sozialistische Einheitspartei Deutschlands, *Protokol der Verhandlungen des
V. Parteitages der SED, 10. bis 16. Juli 1958 in der Werner-Seelenbinder-Halle zu
Berlin* (Berlin: Dietz, 1959).

9   Nikita Khrushchev, Speech at the National Conference of Builders, Architects, Workers in the Construction Materials and Manufacture of Construction and Roads Machinery Industries, and Employees of Design and Research
and Development Organizations on the extensive introduction of industrial
methods, improving the quality and reducing the cost of construction, December 7,
1954. Published in *Volume*, March 1, 2009:
Nikita Khrushchev, "On the Extensive Introduction of Industrial Methods,
Improving the Quality and Reducing the Cost of Construction," *Volume* 21
(2009): 26–30.

10 Khrushchev's secret speech was a denunciation of the deceased Soviet leader Jo-
seph Stalin at a closed session of the Twentieth Congress of the Communist
Party of the Soviet Union, February 25, 1956.
Nikita Khrushchev, "The Secret Speech—On the Cult of Personality," Modern
History Sourcebook, 1998, http://www.sourcebooks.fordham.edu/halsall/mod
/1956khrushchev-secret1.html.

11 Alyssa Abkowitz, "Xi Jinping Isn't a Fan of Weird Architecture in China," *The
Wall Street Journal*, October 17, 2014, http://blogs.wsj.com/chinarealtime/2014/10
/17/xi-jinping-isnt-a-fan-of-weird-architecture-in-china/.

12 Nikita Khrushchev, *Besser, Billiger und Schneller Bauen* (Berlin: Dietz, 1955).

13 Gregg Castillo "East as True West," in ed. György Péteri, *Imagining the West in
Eastern Europe and the Soviet Union* (Pittsburgh: University of Pittsburgh Press,
2010), 94–95.

14 Hannemann, *Platte*, 63.

15 Hannemann, *Platte*.

16 Nikita Khrushchev, "On the Extensive Introduction of Industrial Methods, Improving the Quality and Reducing the Cost of Construction," *Volume* 21 (2009): 26.

17 However, some Russian sources credit USSR engineer Vitaly Lagutenko as the
pioneer who invented a prefabricated assembled housing system in 1947. They
state that Raymond Camus visited Lagutenko in Moscow and consulted him for
many hours before he patented his Camus system.
"D_Marija Drėmaitė and Vaidas Petrulis. Modernism in Soviet Lithuania:
The Rise and Fall of Utopia," Architekturos Fondas, http://www.archfondas.lt

/ leidiniu / en / alf-02 / dmarija-dremaite-and-vaidas-petrulis-modernism-soviet
-lithuania-rise-and-fall-utopia.

18 "Das Portal für Plattenliebhaber und Alle, Die Es Werden Wollen," www.jeder
-qm-du.de / ueber-die-platte / plattenbau-typen / .

19 Eli Rubin, "Concrete Utopia: Everyday Life and Socialism in Berlin-Marzahn,"
German Historical Institute, 2011, https://www.ghi-dc.org/fileadmin/user
_upload/GHI_Washington/Publications/Supplements/Supplement_7/029.pdf.

20 Thomas Topfstedt, Städtebau in der DDR, 1955–1971 (Leipzig: E. A. Seemann,
1988).

21 Sandra Keltsch, "Stadterneuerung und Städtebauliche Denkmalpflege in der
DDR zwischen 1970 und 1990. Dargestellt an der Entwicklung vond Denkmal-
städten in Sachsen-Anhalt.," Ph.D. diss., Leipzig University, 2012, http://www
.qucosa.de/fileadmin/data/qucosa/documents/12123/Sandra%20Keltsch%20
-Stadterneuerung%20und%20st%C3%A4dtebauliche%20Denkmalpflege%20
in%20der%20DDR%20(1970-1990).pdf.

22 Günter Peters, Historische Stadtplanung für den Berliner Nordosten (Berlin:
Bezirksamt Marzahn von Berlin, Abt. Jugend, Bildung und Kultur, Kulturamt / Hei-
matmuseum, 1997).

23 Günter Peters, Platten, Hütten, Wohnquartiere: Berlin Marzahn; Ein junger
Bezirk mit alten Namen (Berlin: MAZZ Verlagsgesellschaft, 1998).

24 Ibid.

25 Christine Hübner, Herbert Nicolaus, and Manfred Teresiak, 20 Jahre Marzahn:
Chronik eines Berliner Bezirkes (Berlin: Heimatsmuseum Marzahn, 1998).

26 "Kosmoswimpel Ansporn im Wettbewerb," Berlin-Marzahn Aktuell 2, no. 11
(September 28, 1978): 1.

27 DDR government declaration at the SED party congress of 1955.
    Sozialistische Einheitspartei Deutschlands, Protokol der Verhandlungen des
V. Parteitages der SED, 10. bis 16. Juli 1958 in der Werner-Seelenbinder-Halle zu
Berlin (Berlin: Dietz, 1959).

28 Rubin, "Concrete Utopia."

29 "New States of Germany," http://en.wikipedia.org/wiki/New_states_of_Germany.

30 Simon Ward, " 'Representing Normality': Architecture in Berlin," in German
Culture, Politics, and Literature into the Twenty-First Century, ed. Stuart Taberner
and Paul Cooke (Rochester, NY: Boydell & Brewer, 2006), 75–88.

31 Angelika Mettke, projektleitung, "Wiederverwendung von Plattenbauteilen in
Osteuropa," Brandenburgische Technische Universität, January 31, 2008,
http://www-docs.tu-cottbus.de/bauliches-recycling/public/publications/1
_Rueckbau.pdf.

32 "Das Fördergebiet Marzahn-Hellersdorf," Senatsverwaltung für Stadtentwick-
lung und Wohnen, April, 2017, http://www.stadtentwicklung.berlin.de/staedtebau
/foerderprogramme/stadtumbau/Marzahn-Hellersdorf.254.0.html#c16377.

33 "The New Face of East Germany," Al Jazeera, April 12, 2011, http://www.aljazeera
.com/photo_galleries/europe/20101123133736357393.html.

34 "The 'Happy' District in the Eastern Outskirt," Guthmann and Guthmann Estate, http://www.guthmann-estate.com/en/market-report/market-report-berlin /marzahn.html; http://www.guthmann-estate.com/en/facts-figures/marzahn -hellersdorf.html.

35 "Cut Down to Size," *Guardian,* November 14, 2005, http://www.theguardian.com /artanddesign/2005/nov/14/architecture.germany,

36 Vladimir Lenin, "Our Foreign and Domestic Position and Party Tasks," V.I. Lenin Internet Archive, 2002, https://www.marxists.org/archive/lenin/works /1920/nov/21.htm.

37 Mies van der Rohe, "Industrielles Bauen," *G* 3 (1924): 8–13.

38 Cor Wagenaar, Jörn Düwel, Wolfgang Kil, Györgi Konrád, Anna Tilroe, Bohdan Tscherkes, e.a., *Idealen in Beton: Verkenningen in Midden en Oost-Europa* (Rotterdam: Nai Uitgevers, 2004).

7. NEUFERT

1 Neufert's built output remained extremely modest over the course of his lifetime in comparison with his wider influence, and all his buildings were built in Germany. The earliest of these was the Abbeanum and student house in Jena, completed in 1930; in 1955 he built the Ledingenwohnheim flats in Darmstadt, and he completed the Quelle Mail Order headquarters in Nuremberg in 1958 and an Eternit factory in Leimen in 1960. In the course of his residencies, Neufert contributed designs for various anonymous buildings in industrial complexes, but these have not been recorded in history.

2 "Architect's Data," (Wikipedia, last revision November 15, 2016), https://en .wikipedia.org/wiki/Architects%27_Data.

3 "Bauleiter in Bauatelier Gropius, 1922–1925, Ernst Neufert," 100 Jahre Bauhaus, https://www.bauhaus100.de/de/damals/koepfe/freunde/ernst-neufert/index.html.

4 Frank Zöllner, "Anthropomorphism: From Vitruvius to Neufert, from Human Measurement to the Module of Fascism," in *Images of the Body in Architecture: Anthropology and Built Space,* ed. Kirsten Wagner and Jasper Cepl (Tübingen: Ernst Wasmuth, 2014), 64, http://www.gko.uni-leipzig.de/fileadmin/user_upload /kunstgeschichte/pdf/zoellner/Publikationen/unselbst_Publi/Anthropomor phism_from-Vitruvius_to_Neufert.pdf.

5 Nader Vossoughian, "From A4 Paper to the Octametric Brick: Ernst Neufert and the Geo-politics of Standardisation in Nazi Germany," *Journal of Architecture* 20, no. 4 (2015): 692.

6 Nader Vossoughian, "Standardization Reconsidered: Normierung in and after Ernst Neufert's *Bauentwurfslehre,*" *Grey Room* 54 (Winter 2014): 41.

7 Ibid.

8 Ibid., 38–39.

9 Vossoughian, "From A4 Paper to the Octametric Brick," 684; Vossoughian, "Standardization Reconsidered," 39.

10 Vossoughian, "Standardization Reconsidered," 43–44.

11 David Adler, preface to *Metric Handbook: Planning and Design Data,* 2nd ed., ed. David Adler, https://www.uop.edu.jo/download/research/members/%5bArchi tecture_Ebook%5d_Metric_Handbook_Planning_and_Design_Data.pdf (first published as *AJ Metric Handbook,* 1968).

12 Vossoughian, "Standardization Reconsidered," 36.

13 Ibid., 45.

14 Ibid., 46

15 Vossoughian, "From A4 Paper to the Octametric Brick," 688.

16 Ibid., 686.

17 Ibid., 688.

18 Ibid.

19 Ibid., 690.

20 Ibid., 692–694.

21 Ibid., 688.

22 Andrew L. Russell, "Modularity: An Interdisciplinary History of an Ordering Concept," *Information and Culture* 47, no. 3 (2012): 269, http://arussell.org/papers /47.3.russell.pdf.

23 Ibid., 270.

24 Ibid., 269.

25 Neufert Consulting GmbH, http://www.neufert.de.

8. REFERENCE WITHOUT A SOURCE

1 As part of the development process, in June 2015 the City of Atlanta and the Department of Aviation issued a request for proposal (RFP) for the "Modernization of the Landside of the Central Passenger Terminal." The RFP provides for a growth of the airport from 96 million passengers to roughly 130 million. Although there appears to be consensus on the potential of Atlanta Airport to achieve major improvements, the RFP calls mainly for cosmetic interventions: new awnings over the passenger arrival zones, refurbished retail kiosks, and improved baggage conveyor belts.

2 International Olympic Committee, "FACTSHEET: Legacies of the Games," update, December 2013.

3 Stevens and Wilkinson, Smith Hinchman and Grylls, and Minority Airport Architects and Planners.
    "Hartsfield-Jackson Atlanta International Airport," Wikipedia, https://en .wikipedia.org/wiki/Hartsfield%E2%80%93Jackson_Atlanta_International _Airport#cite_ref-23.

4 Dave Williams, "New Atlanta Airport Master Plan Eyes New Gates, Sixth Runway," *Atlanta Business Chronicle,* August 27, 2014, http://www.bizjournals.com/atlanta /blog/capitol_vision/2014/08/new-atlanta-airport-master-plan-eyes-new-gates .html.

5 Kelly Yamanouchi, "Hartsfield-Jackson Plans for Nearly $800 Million of Construction in One Year," *Atlanta Journal-Constitution,* December 4, 2015, http://

airport.blog.ajc.com/2015/12/04/hartsfield-jackson-plans-for-nearly-800-million
-of-construction-in-one-year/.

6 J. F., "The Economist Explains: What Is an Aerotropolis?," *Economist Online,* December 11, 2013, http://www.economist.com/blogs/economist-explains/2013/12
/economist-explains-6.

7 Rem Koolhaas, "Atlanta," in *S,M,L,XL* (New York: The Monacelli Press, 1995), 832–859.

8 Jean Baudrillard, *America,* trans. Chris Turner (London: Verso, 1989). https://
monoskop.org/File:Baudrillard_Jean_America_1989.pdf.

9. THE INEVITABLE BOX

1 Examples are Anfield and Stamford Bridge in England, Westfalenstadion in Germany, and more recently Bordeaux Stadium in France.

2 The original Greek word for the box in "Pandora's box" was *pithos,* a large jar, sometimes as large as a small person, used for storage of wine, oil, grain, or other provisions or, ritually, for burial of a human body. Erasmus, in translating Hesiod's tale of Pandora into Latin, confused *pithos* with the Greek *pyxis,* meaning "box." The phrase 'Pandora's box' has endured ever since.

3 Tomb of the Unknown Soldier, Arlington National Cemetery.

4 Donald Judd, "Specific Objects," in *Donald Judd: Early Work, 1955–1968,* Thomas Kellein (New York: D.A.P., 2002), http://atc.berkeley.edu/201/readings/judd-so.pdf.

5 Rem Koolhaas, "Typical Plan," in *S,M,L,XL* (New York: The Monacelli Press, 1995), 334–353.

6 Cf. Genesis 3:1.

7 Ludwig Mies van der Rohe, the Farnsworth House, Plano, Illinois, 1948.

8 Paraphrase of Jean Baudrillard, *Cool Memories* (London: Verso 1990), 3.

9 Demolition of the Pruitt-Igoe estate in St. Louis, heralded by Charles Jencks as the end of modern architecture in Charles Jencks, *The Language of Post-Modern Architecture* (New York: Rizzoli, 1977), 9.

10 Paraphrase of Baudrillard, *Cool Memories,* 3.

11 Limitless, Dubai, http://limitless.com/en-GB/home.aspx.

12 Peter Blake, *Form Follows Fiasco: Why Modern Architecture Hasn't Worked* (Boston: Little, Brown & Co, 1977).

10. SPACESHIP EARTH

1 Stanford Research Institute, Long Range Planning Service, *The World of 1975* (Menlo Park, CA: Stanford Research Institute, 1964).

Aureli Peccei, "The Challenge of 1970s for the World of Today," in *The Club of Rome—"The Dossiers" 1965–1984,* ed. Pentti Malasaka, Matti Vapaavuori, http://clubofrome.fi/wp-content/uploads/2014/10/Dossiers.pdf.

2 The Club of Rome adopted the written work of the Massachusetts Institute of Technology, headed by Jay Forrester, and titled its first report *The Limits to Growth.* It intentionally targeted the leaders of Western Europe.

Donella H. Meadows, Dennis L. Meadows. Jørgen Randers, William W. Behrens III, *The Limits to Growth* (New York: Universe Books, 1972).

3 Buckminster Fuller, *Operating Manual for Spaceship Earth* (Global Solutions Lab), http://designsciencelab.com/resources/OperatingManual_BF.pdf.

4 World Commission on Environment and Development, *Our Common Future* (Oxford: Oxford University Press, 1987).

5 J. R. R. Tolkien, *The Hobbit; or, There and Back Again* (London: George Allen and Unwin, 1937).

6 Hobbit House, Private Residence, Cynghordy, Wales, SA20 0LT, United Kingdom, http://www.beingsomewhere.net/hobbit.htm.

7 "Nine Houses, Dietikon," The International Greenroof and Greenwall Projects Database, http://www.greenroofs.com/projects/pview.php?id=354.

8 *Concise Oxford English Dictionary,* 11th ed. (2008).

9 George Orwell, *The Road to Wigan Pier,* https://libcom.org/files/wiganpier.pdf.

10 Henry George, *Progress and Poverty* (New York: Doubleday, Page & Co, 1920), Book IV, Chapter 2, http://www.econlib.org/library/YPDBooks/George/grgPP20 .html#Book%20IV,%20Chapter%202.

11 Alexander King and Bertrand Schneider, *The First Global Revolution: A Report by the Council of the Club of Rome,* 1991 ed., Scribd, March 17, 2008, https://www.scribd .com/doc/2297152/Alexander-King-Bertrand-Schneider-The-First-Global -Revolution-Club-of-Rome-1993-Edition.

12 Nicholas Dawidoff, "The Civil Heretic," *New York Times,* March 25, 2009, http://www.nytimes.com/2009/03/29/magazine/29Dyson-t.html?pagewanted =all.

11. MIES EN SCÈNE

1 Website of Lord Peter Palumbo, http://lordpeterpalumbo.com/biography.html.

2 "Flood Mitigation Project," http://farnsworthproject.org/.

3 Carol Vogel, "Landmark Mies House Goes to Preservationists," *New York Times,* December 13, 2003.

4 Adelyn Perez, "AD Classics: The Farnsworth House / Mies van der Rohe." Republished on ArchDaily, May 13, 2010, http://www.archdaily.com/59719/ad-classics -the-farnsworth-house-mies-van-der-rohe.

12. INTRUDERS

1 "Hello Barbie at the 2015 New York Toy Fair," February 18, 2015, https://www .youtube.com/watch?v=6LH9ChHoSpw.

2 "Shape of Things to Come: A Peek at Tomorrow from Today's Top Designers," CNN, August 21, 2015, http://edition.cnn.com/2015/06/30/design/tom-dixon -james-dyson-yves-behar-best-design/.

3 Jim Edwards, "Ford Exec: 'We know Everyone Who Breaks the Law' Thanks to Our GPS in Your Car," *Business Insider,* January 8, 2014, http://www.business insider.com/ford-exec-gps-2014-1?international=true&r=US&IR=T.

4 "Home, Hacked Home, The Perils of Connected Devices" *The Economist,* July 12, 2014, http://www.economist.com/news/special-report/21606420-perils -connected-devices-home-hacked-home?zid=291&ah=906e69ad01d2ee519601 00b7fa502595.

13. "PUBLIC" SPACE

1 Catenaccio is a strategy in soccer, originating in Italy, that is purely defensive and intends to take the opponent out via unexpected counterattacks.

2 Lord Justice Sedley, decision in *Redmond-Bate v. Director of Public Prosecutions* (1999). The existence of Speakers' Corner is frequently upheld as a demonstration of free speech because anyone can turn up unannounced and talk on almost any subject, although always at the risk of being heckled by regulars. The ruling famously established in English case law that freedom of speech could not be limited to the inoffensive but extended also to "the irritating, the contentious, the eccentric, the heretical, the unwelcome, and the provocative, as long as such speech did not tend to provoke violence," and that the right to free speech accorded by Article 10 of the European Convention of Human Rights also accorded the right to be offensive. Before the ruling, prohibited speech at Speakers' Corner included obscenity, blasphemy, insulting the queen, or inciting a breach of the peace.

3 UNESCO, Social and Human Sciences, http://www.unesco.org/new/en/social -and-human-sciences/themes/urban-development/migrants-inclusion-in -cities/good-practices/inclusion-through-access-to-public-space/.

4 Jane Jacobs, *The Death and Life of Great American Cities* (New York: Random House, 1993).

5 UN-Habitat, http://unhabitat.org/public-spaces-for-all-2/.

14. FROM CIAM TO CYBERSPACE

1 Sigfried Giedion, ed., *CIAM: A Decade of New Architecture* (Zurich: Editions Gersburger, 1960).

2 The Smithsons, "The Doorn Manifesto," article 1: "It is useless to consider the house except as a part of a community owing to the inter-action of these on each other."

   Team Ten, "The Doorn Manifesto," in ed. Alison Smithson, *Team Ten Primer* (Cambridge, MA: The MIT Press, 1974), 75.

3 Team 10 Online, http://www.team10online.org/.

4 Alison Smithson, *Team 10 Meetings: 1953–1984* (New York: Rizzoli, 1991).

5 Aldo van Eyck, "The 'Otterlo Circles,'" diagram presented at the last CIAM congress in Otterlo in 1959.

   Francis Strauven, *Aldo van Eyck: The Shape of Relativity* (Amsterdam: Architectura & Natura Press, 1998), 350.

6 Team Ten, "Doorn Manifesto", 75.

7 Ibid., 75.

8   Jaap Bakema, *Van stoel tot stad: Een verhaal over mensen en ruimte* (Zeist: W. De Haan, 1964).

9   George A. Hillery Jr., *A Research Odyssey: Developing and Testing a Community Theory* (New Brunswick, NJ: Transaction Books, 1982).

10 Joan Grossman, "About Drop City," http://www.dropcitydoc.com/#!about/c1ofk.

11 Ibid.

12 Ulrich Enzensberger, *Die Jahre der Kommune 1: Berlin, 1967–69* (Berlin: Kiepenheuer & Witsch, 2004).

13 Ibid.

14 Charles Knevitt, "Community Architect Mark 1: An Interview with Rod Hackney Who Works in Small Scale Community Rehabilitation Projects," *Building Design,* July 11, 1975, 8.

15 Nick Wates, "Community Architecture: CA Is Here to Stay," *Architects' Journal* 175, no. 23 (June 9, 1982): 42–44.

16 Julien Freund, "German Sociology in the time of Max Weber," in *A History of Sociological Analysis,* ed. Thomas Burton Bottomore and Robert A. Nisbet (New York: Basic Books, 1978), 152.

17 Ferdinand Tönnies, *Community and Civil Society,* ed. Jose Harris, trans. Jose Harris and Margaret Hollis (Cambridge: Cambridge University Press, 2001), 27–28.

18 Margaret Thatcher, interview with Douglas Keay, *Woman's Own,* September 23, 1987, retrieved from *Thatcher Archive: COI transcript* available at http://www.margaretthatcher.org/document/106689.

19 "Charter of the New Urbanism," http://www.cnu.org/charter.

20 Douglas Frantz and Catherine Collins, *Celebration, U.S.A.: Living in Disney's Brave New Town* (New York: Holt Paperbacks, 2000).

21 Claudio Vignali, "McDonald's: 'Think Global, Act Local'—The Marketing Mix," *British Food Journal* 103, no. 2 (2001): 97–111.

22 Economist Intelligence Unit, *Best Cities Ranking and Report* (New York: Economist, 2013).

23 Larry Beasley, "Planning the Global City: Vancouver, Abu Dhabi and the World," address given at the University of Toronto Urban Lecture Series, Toronto, November 16, 2011.

24 City of Vancouver, "About Vancouver," November 17, 2009, http://vancouver.ca/about-vancouver.aspx.

25 World Wide Web Project, Tim Berners-Lee and Robert Cailliau invented the internet while working at CERN (European Organization for Nuclear Research).

26 Milan Kundera, *The Unbearable Lightness of Being* (New York: Harper and Row, 1984), 8.

27 Neal Stephenson, *Snow Crash* (New York: Bantam Books, 1992).

28 "Mayo Clinic," www.secondlife/destinations/mayo-clinic.

29 Jakob Nabuoka, "User Innovation and Creative Consumption in Japanese Culture Industries: The Case of Akihabara," *Geografiska Annaler,* ser. B, *Human Geography,* 92, no. 3 (2010): 205–218.

15. WITH THE MASSES

1 Eventually the whole university would split into two, and its entire French-speaking community would move to other locations, most notably the start-from-scratch new town of Louvain la Neuve.

2 Dutch king Willem Alexander, "Troonrede 2013," annual address delivered in the Ridderzaal, The Hague, September, 2013, https://www.rijksoverheid.nl/docu menten/toespraken/2013/09/17/troonrede-2013.

3 The last adjective, Kroll later confessed, was added in case the word "participation" in the name of his office made it sound less serious. At the time, somebody had just donated a computer to him, *et voilà l'informatique.*

18. HOW IS DENMARK?

1 Mike Davis, "Sinister Paradise: Does the Road to the Future End at Dubai?," TomDispatch, July 14, 2005, http://www.tomdispatch.com/post/5807/.

20. FACING THE FACTS

1 Author's guesstimate.

2 Charles Roxburgh, Susan Lund, Charles Atkins, Stanislas Belot, Wayne W. Hu, Moira S, Pierce, *Global Capital Markets: Entering a New Era,* McKinsey Global Institute, September, 2009, http://www.mckinsey.com/industries/private-equity-and -principal-investors/our-insights/global-capital-markets-entering-a-new-era.

23. ON HOLD

1 "Iraqi and U.S. Officials Calling Election Successful," *CNN Transcripts,* December 16, 2005, http://transcripts.cnn.com/TRANSCRIPTS/0512/16/lol.01.html.

2 "Kurdistan, the Legend," from the *Sharafname,* a history of the Kurdish tribes, written by the Kurdish emir Sharafuddin of Bitlis. See Sharaf Khān Bidlīsī, trans. Mehrdad R. Izady, *The Sharafnâma, or, the History of the Kurdish Nation* (USA: Mazda Publishers, 2005), 1597.

3 An aromatic resin, the main ingredient in the making of Arabic perfumes.

4 "Emaar Erbil: Developing a Dynamic, Smart City of the Future," https://www .emaar.com/en/what-we-do/communities/iraq/downtown-erbil.aspx.

5 "Kurdistan: The Other Iraq," *CBS News,* February 18, 2007, http://www.cbsnews .com/news/kurdistan-the-other-iraq/.

24. AFTER THE END OF HISTORY

1 Francis Fukuyama, "The End of History?," *The National Interest,* 16, Summer, 1989, https://www.embl.de/aboutus/science_society/discussion/discussion_2006 /ref1-22june06.pdf.

2 Ibid.

3 Ibid.

4 The term "managed democracy" was originated by Vladislav Surkov, Russian presidential aide and formerly deputy chief of the Russian presidential adminis-

tration "Poroshenko Says Evidence Shows Kremlin Aide Surkov Directed Snipers in Kiev," *Moscow Times,* February 20, 2015, http://old.themoscowtimes .com/mobile/news/article/516310.html.

5 Patrick Kingsley, "Denmark to Force Refugees to Give Up Valuables under Proposed Asylum Law, *The Guardian,* January 12, 2016, https://www.theguardian .com/world/2016/jan/12/denmark-to-force-refugees-to-give-up-valuables-under -proposed-asylum-law.

26. SOCIALIST IN CONTENT, REALIST IN FORM

1 "Soviet Palace," *Time,* March 19, 1934, http://content.time.com/time/magazine /article/0,9171,747172,00.html.

2 William J. R. Curtis, *Modern Architecture since 1900,* 3rd ed. (London: Phaidon, 1996), 359.

3 Donald Leslie Johnson, "Frank Lloyd Wright in Moscow: June 1937," *Journal of the Society of Architectural Historians* 46, no. 1 (March 1987): 67–79.

4 Hugh D. Hudson Jr., "Terror in Soviet Architecture: The Murder of Mikhail Okhitovich," *Slavic Review* 51, no. 3 (Autumn 1992): 448–467.

5 Arkhitektura 1, 1933 Quoted in Alexei Tarkhanov and Sergei Kavtaradze, *Stalinist Architecture* (London: Laurence King, 1992), 49.

6 Andrei Zhdanov, "Soviet Literature: The Richest in Ideas, the Most Advanced Literature," Marxists Internet Archive, 2004, https://www.marxists.org/subject /art/lit_crit/sovietwritercongress/zdhanov.htm.

7 Anne Visser, "Lenin in Art: The History of an Illusion: The Romanticism of Art of Art after Stalin's Era," Azerbaijan International. 2006, https://www.azer.com /aiweb/categories/magazine/ai142_folder/142_articles/142_lenin_art.html.

8 Nikita Khrushchev, "On the Extensive Introduction of Industrial Methods, Improving the Quality and Reducing the Cost of Construction," *Volume* 21 (2009): 28.

28. UNDESIRABLE WORK STYLES

1 Last three paragraphs, "China's Xi Points Way for Arts," *Xinhuanet,* October 16, 2014, http://news.xinhuanet.com/english/china/2014-10/16/c_133719778.htm.

2 "China's 'Weird' Buildings: President Xi Jinping Wants No More of Them," *Building Design + Construction,* October 23, 2014, http://www.bdcnetwork.com /chinas-weird-buildings-president-xi-jinping-wants-no-more-them.

3 "Xi Jinping: Do Not Engage in Strange Buildings," *Wenweipo,* October 16, 2014, http://news.wenweipo.com/2014/10/16/IN1410160085.htm.

4 Esther Fung, "Architects Brush Off Chinese President Xi Jinping's Disapproval of 'Weird' Buildings," *Wall Street Journal,* November 25, 2014, http://blogs.wsj .com/speakeasy/2014/11/25/architects-brush-off-chinese-president-xi-jinpings -disapproval-of-weird-buildings/.

5 Dan Howarth, ""Chinese Architecture Will Benefit" from CCTV Building, Says Rem Koolhaas," *Dezeen,* November 26, 2014, http://www.dezeen.com/2014/11/26 /rem-koolhaas-defends-cctv-building-beijing-china-architecture/.

6 Marcus Fairs, "Zaha Hadid Architects Embraces America as China Turns against "Weird Architecture," *Dezeen,* July 15, 2015, http://www.dezeen.com/2015/07/15 /zaha-hadid-architects-patrik-schumacher-embraces-america-china-turns -against-weird-architecture/.

7 "Our View Playing Out: China's Construction Slowdown," *BMI Research,* June 18, 2015, http://www.bmiresearch.com/news-and-views/our-view-playing-out-chinas -construction-slowdown.

8 Zheng Jinran, "China Looks to Regulate City Growth," The State Council of the People's Republic of China, February 22, 2016, http://english.gov.cn/news/top _news/2016/02/22/content_281475294306681.htm.

30. ROYAL APPROVAL

1 HRH Prince of Wales, "A Speech by HRH The Prince of Wales at the 150th An- niversary of the Royal Institute of British Architects (RIBA), Royal Gala Evening at Hampton Court Palace," May 30, 1984, http://www.princeofwales.gov.uk /media/speeches/speech-hrh-the-prince-of-wales-the-150th-anniversary-of -the-royal-institute-of.

2 Rhodri Marsden, "Rhodri Marsden's Interesting Objects: The Monstrous Car- buncle," *Independent,* May 30, 2014, http://www.independent.co.uk/arts-enter tainment/architecture/rhodri-marsdens-interesting-objects-the-monstrous -carbuncle-9447869.html.

3 Alastair Jamieson, "The Prince of Wales on Architecture: His 10 'Monstrous Car- buncles,'" *The Telegraph,* May 13, 2009, http://www.telegraph.co.uk/news/uknews /theroyalfamily/5317802/The-Prince-of-Wales-on-architecture-his-10-monstrous -carbuncles.html.

4 HRH Prince of Wales, *A Vision of Britain: A Personal View of Architecture* (New York City: Doubleday, 1989), 10.

5 HRH Prince of Wales, "A speech by HRH The Prince of Wales at the Corpora- tion of London Planning and Communication Committee's Annual Dinner, Mansion House, London," December 1, 1987, https://www.princeofwales.gov.uk /media/speeches/speech-hrh-the-prince-of-wales-the-corporation-of-london -planning-and-communication.

6 Alastair Jamieson, "The Prince of Wales on Architecture."

7 John Darnton, "Britain Rejects Welsh Opera's Plea for Financing," *New York Times,* December 25, 1995, http://www.nytimes.com/1995/12/25/arts/britain -rejects-welsh-opera-s-plea-for-financing.html.

8 Rowan Moore, "Britain's Housing Crisis Is a Human Disaster. Here Are 10 Ways to Solve It," *The Observer,* March 14, 2015, https://www.theguardian.com/society /2015/mar/14/britain-housing-crisis-10-ways-solve-rowan-moore-general -election.

9 Steven Morris, Robert Booth, "Cracks Appearing in Prince Charles's Dream Vil- lage in Poundbury," *The Guardian,* August 17, 2009, https://www.theguardian .com/uk/2009/aug/17/prince-charles-dream-village-poundbury.

10 Stephen Adams, "Prince of Wales's Emotional Chelsea Barracks Letter Revealed," *The Telegraph,* June 24, 2010, http://www.telegraph.co.uk/culture/culture news/7850091/Prince-of-Waless-emotional-Chelsea-Barracks-letter-revealed .html.

11 Deborah Duke, "Quinlan Terry Design Tops Chelsea Barracks Poll," Building, April 14, 2009, http://www.building.co.uk/quinlan-terry-design-tops-chelsea -barracks-poll/3138296.article.

12 Robert Booth, "Architects' Vision of London Takes Inspiration from 19th-Century Paris," *The Guardian,* January 2, 2015, https://www.theguardian.com /artanddesign/2015/jan/02/architects-vision-future-london-inspired-by-paris -skyscraper.

13 Roger Graef, "The British Don't Want to Live in New-Build Homes. No Wonder," *The Guardian,* October 26, 2012, http://www.theguardian.com/commentisfree /2012/oct/26/new-build-homes-british.

14 Robert Booth, "Richard Rogers: 'Prince Charles Wrecked My Chelsea Project,' " *The Guardian,* June 16, 2009, https://www.theguardian.com/uk/2009/jun/16 /richard-rogers-prince-charles-architecture.

15 Adam Sherwin, "Prince Charles Has 'Veto' over Major New Developments, Claims Leading Architect," *Independent,* August 22, 2013, http://www.independent .co.uk/arts-entertainment/architecture/prince-charles-has-veto-over-major-new -developments-claims-leading-architect-8780507.html.

32. A PROPERTY DEVELOPER FOR PRESIDENT

1 Tracie Rozhon, "A Win by Trump! No, by Tenants!; Battle of the 80's Ends, with Glad-Handing All Around," *New York Times,* March 26, 1998, http://www .nytimes.com/1998/03/26/nyregion/win-trump-no-tenants-battle-80-s-ends -with-glad-handing-all-around.html?pagewanted=all.

2 Ben Mathis-Lilley, ""Suppressed" 1991 Trump Film Released Online by Documentary Producer," *Slate,* July 31, 2015, http://www.slate.com/blogs/the_slatest /2015/07/31/_1991_trump_documentary_released_online_by_filmmaker_libby _handros.html.

3 Alison Flood, "Donald Trump's Taj Mahal Casino Is 'Worst Punishment God Can Devise', Says Harper Lee Letter," *The Guardian,* March 29, 2016, https://www .theguardian.com/books/2016/mar/29/harper-lee-donald-trump-taj-mahal -letters-auctioned.

4 Ada Louise Huxtable, "Donald Trump's Tower," *New York Times,* May 6, 1984, http://www.nytimes.com/1984/05/06/magazine/l-donald-trump-s-tower -170724.html.

5 Paul Goldberger, "Atrium of Trump Tower Is a Pleasant Surprise," *New York Times,* April 4, 1983, http://www.nytimes.com/1983/04/04/arts/architecture -atrium-of-trump-tower-is-a-pleasant-surprise.html.

6 Blair Kamin, "Donald Trump: Giant Sign on His Chicago Tower Is Like Hollywood Sign," *Chicago Tribune,* June 5, 2014, http://articles.chicagotribune.com

/2014-06-05/news/ct-trump-sign-kamin-met-0606-20140606_1_hollywood
-sign-chicago-tower-donald-trump.

7   "Yuge Erections: The Mysterious Power of Trump's Garish Buildings," *The Economist,* April 29, 2016, http://www.economist.com/blogs/democracyinamerica
/2016/04/yuge-erections.

8   Paul Gapp, "Will New York Get New 'Tallest Building'? Don't Bet on It," *Chicago
Tribune,* August 12, 1984, http://archives.chicagotribune.com/1984/08/12/page
/266/article/design.

9   Whet Moser, "That Time Donald Trump Tried to Sue a Tribune Architecture
Critic into Oblivion," *Chicago magazine,* August 20, 2015, http://www.chicagomag
.com/city-life/August-2015/That-Time-Donald-Trump-Tried-to-Sue-a-Tribune
-Architecture-Critic-Into-Oblivion/.

10 Edward Weinfeld, "Trump v. Chicago Tribune Co.," *Leagle,* September 3, 1985,
http://www.leagle.com/decision/19852050616FSupp1434_11833/TRUMP v. CHI-
CAGO TRIBUNE CO.

11 Melania Trump at the 2016 Republican National Convention.

12 Reinier de Graaf, "How Is Denmark?," quote appears in Chapter 17 of this
volume, slightly modified.

13 Gregory Wallace, "Voter Turnout at 20-Year Low in 2016," *CNN,* November 30,
2016, http://edition.cnn.com/2016/11/11/politics/popular-vote-turnout-2016/.

33. A FAUSTIAN BARGAIN

1   United Nations Department of Economic and Social Affairs, Population Division, *World Urbanization Prospects: The 2005 Revision* (New York: United
Nations, 2006), 19.

2   United Nations Department of Economic and Social Affairs, Population Division, *World Urbanization Prospects: The 2014 Revision Highlights* (New York:
United Nations, 2014), 1.

3   Len Rosen, "In 2025 630 Million of Us Will Live in 37 Megacities," *21st Century
Tech* (blog), March 6, 2013, http://www.21stcentech.com/2025-630-million-live
-37-megacities/.

4   Sao Paulo—Turkey: "Comparing Brazilian States with Countries: Brazil's Closest
Matches," *The Economist,* June 12, 2014, http://www.economist.com/blogs/graphic
detail/2014/06/comparing-brazilian-states-countries.

Jakarta - Australie: Bernard Salt, "Population of 24 Million Smaller than
Texas but We're Doing Well," *The Australian,* February 13, 2016, http://www
.theaustralian.com.au/business/opinion/bernard-salt-demographer/population
-of-24-million-smaller-than-texas-but-were-doing-well/news-story/b71ab315b
b393495ad89d591d90f98b4.

5   Keith Hansen, "Cities: The New Frontier of Social Protection," *The World Bank,*
November 9, 2015, http://blogs.worldbank.org/voices/cities-the-new-frontier-of
-social-protection.

6   "Ricky Burdett, 'Cities in an Urban Age: Does Design Matter?'" YouTube video, 1:24:37, from a lecture at the Harvard University Graduate School of Design on August 13, 2013, posted by "The Harvard GSD," August 13, 2013, http://youtu.be /doWkdKdJx-Y.

34. AMANHÃ

1   Oscar Niemeyer and Vilanova Artigas.

2   Amelia Meyer, "Brazil Culture," *Brazil*, 2010, http://www.brazil.org.za/brazil -culture.html.

3   For the earlier theorems, see Gilberto Freyre, *Casa-Grande & Senzala* (Rio de Janeiro: Maia & Schmidt Ltda, 1933); English translation, *The Masters and the Slaves* trans. Samuel Putnam (New York: Alfred A. Knopf, 1946).

4   Regis St. Louis, "Rio de Janeiro: Make My Day," (Carlton, Victoria: Lonely Planet Publications, 2016), http://trove.nla.gov.au/work/209296303?selectedver sion=NBD57619276.

5   "Brazil Population," Worldometers, http://www.worldometers.info/world -population/brazil-population/; "South America, Brazil," Central Intelligence Agency, The World Fact Book, https://www.cia.gov/library/publications/the -world-factbook/geos/br.html; "Population Estimates for Rio de Janeiro, Brazil, 1950–2015," Mongabay, http://books.mongabay.com/population_estimates/full /Rio_de_Janeiro-Brazil.html.

6   The suggestion that urbanization is a requirement for economic development is Borne out by the empirical evidence: few countries have realized income levels of $10,000 per capita before reaching about 60 percent urbanization; and simple bivariate regressions, while no indication of causality, suggest that urbanization is a very strong indicator of productivity growth over the long run (Figure 1.1) (Annez and Buckley 2008). http://siteresources.worldbank .org/INTPOVERTY/Resources/060310_Simler_Dudwick_Rural-Urban _Welfare_Inequalities.pdf; Li and Luo (2007) re-estimate the rural-urban in-come ratio taking urban welfare into consideration and find that the income of urban residents is 5 times higher than that of rural residents. http:// eprints.lib.hokudai.ac.jp/dspace/bitstream/2115/55374/1/WANG_Xuelong .pdf.

7   Karl Marx, *Das Kapital*, first edition 1867 (Washington DC: Regnery Publishing Inc, 1996).

8   Karl Marx, Friedrich Engels, *The Communist Manifesto*, first edition 1847 (London: Penguin, 2002).

35. SMART CITIES OF THE FUTURE

1   Jean Baudrillard, *America*, trans. Chris Turner (London: Verso, 1989). https:// monoskop.org/File:Baudrillard_Jean_America_1989.pdf.

39. RANKINGS

1 Ricardo Geromel, "Forbes Top 10 Billionaire Cities - Moscow Beats New York Again," *Forbes,* March 14, 2013, http://www.forbes.com/sites/ricardogeromel /2013/03/14/forbes-top-10-billionaire-cities-moscow-beats-new-york-again /#1c6214bc464b.

2 OMA research for Big Moscow Competition, 2012.

3 "Rising Informal Employment Will Increase Poverty ," OECD, August 4, 2009, http://www.oecd.org/development/risinginformalemploymentwillincreasepov erty.htm.

4 "Gaza City," (Wikipedia, last revision of page on March 25, 2017), https://en .wikipedia.org/wiki/Gaza_City#Population.

5 David Grann, "A Murder Foretold: Unravelling the Ultimate Political Conspiracy," *New Yorker,* April 4, 2011, http://www.newyorker.com/magazine/2011 /04/04/a-murder-foretold.

40. COUP DE GRÂCE

1 Charles Jencks, *The Language of Post-Modern Architecture* (New York: Rizzoli, 1977), 9.

2 Colin Rowe and Fred Koetter, *Collage City* (Cambridge, MA: MIT Press, 1983) 4, 6.

3 Katharine G. Bristol, "The Pruitt-Igoe Myth," *Journal of Architectural Education* 44 (May 1991): 163–171.

4 Ibid., 165

5 Ibid. "Four Vast Housing Projects for St. Louis: Hellmuth, Obata and Kassabaum, Inc.,"*Architectural Record* 120 (August 1956): 182–189.

6 Chad Friedrichs, *The Pruitt-Igoe Myth: An Urban History* (Columbia, MO: Unicorn Stencil Documentary Films, 2011), DVD.

7 *Father Knows Best,* CBS, 1954–1960; *Leave It to Beaver,* ABC, 1958–1963.

8 James Bailey, "The Case History of a Failure," *Architectural Forum* 123 (December 1965): 22–23.

9 Radley Balko, "Why We Need to Fix St. Louis County," *Washington Post,* October 16, 2014, https://www.washingtonpost.com/news/the-watch/wp/2014/10 /16/why-we-need-to-fix-st-louis/?utm_term=.429a9dc8c634.

10 Friedrichs, *The Pruitt-Igoe Myth.*

11 "Smart+Connected Communities," Cisco, http://www.cisco.com/c/en/us/solu tions/industries/smart-connected-communities.html.

41. THE CENTURY THAT NEVER HAPPENED

1 Thomas Piketty, *Capital in the Twenty-First Century,* trans. Arthur Goldhammer (Cambridge, MA: The Belknap Press of Harvard University Press, 2014; initially published in French as *Le capital au XXIe siècle* in 2013).

2   The crew of the *Arctic Sunrise,* a Greenpeace ship under the Dutch flag, was released shortly after a state visit of the Dutch king and queen to Russia in November 2013.

   "Greenpeace Arctic Sunrise Ship Case," (Wikipedia, last revision of on page April 3, 2017), https://en.wikipedia.org/wiki/Greenpeace_Arctic_Sunrise_ship_case.

3   Piketty, *Capital in the Twenty-First Century,* 356, fig. 10.10.

4   Filippo Tommaso Marinetti, "The Futurist Manifesto," first published as "I Manifesti del Futurism" in the Italian newspaper *Gazzetta dell'Emilia* on February 5, 1909, then in French as "Manifeste du futurisme" in *Le Figaro* on February 20, 1909.

5   "Futurist Manifesto," Article 11.

6   "Manifesto of Futurism," (Wikipedia, last revision of page on February 9, 2017), http://en.wikipedia.org/wiki/Futurist_Manifesto.

7   "Futurist Manifesto," Article 7.

8   Le Corbusier, *Towards a New Architecture,* trans. Frederick Etchells (London: Butterworth Architecture, 1989), 269. "Architecture ou révolution" was the original title of "Vers une architecture."

9   The estate was designed by Jack Lynn and Ivory Smith.

10   The term "short twentieth century," originally proposed by Iván Berend (Hungarian Academy of Sciences) but defined by Eric Hobsbawm, a British Marxist historian and author, refers to the period between the outbreak of World War I and the fall of communism in Eastern Europe.

   Eric Hobsbawm, *Age of Extremes: the short twentieth century, 1914–1991* (London: Abacus, 1995), 3.

43. THE CAPTIVE GLOBE

1   Rem Koolhaas, *Delirious New York* (New York: The Monacelli Press,1994).

2   Ibid, p. 294.

3   Ibid, p. 294.

4   Ibid, p.294.

44. REMAINS OF A BRAVE NEW WORLD

1   David Giambusso, "De Blasio kicks off Sandy jobs programs in the Rockaways," *Politico,* October 15, 2014, http://www.politico.com/states/new-york/city-hall/story/2014/10/de-blasio-kicks-off-sandy-jobs-programs-in-the-rockaways-016666.

2   Robert Moses, "Improvement of Coney Island, Rockaway and South Beaches," November 30, 1937, https://archive.org/stream/improvementofconoonewy/improvementofconoonewy_djvu.txt.

3   Housing Act of 1949, Title 1, Section 105: "There shall be a feasible method for the temporary relocation of families displaced from the urban renewal area, and there are or are being provided, in the urban renewal area or in other places generally not less desirable in regard to public utilities and public and commercial

facilities and at rents or prices within the financial means of the families displaced from the urban renewal area, decent safe and sanitary dwellings equal in number to the number and available to such displaced families and reasonably accessible to their places of employment."

4   "Slum Clearance Progress: Title I, NYC," July 15, 1957, https://archive.org/stream /slumclearanceprooonewy/slumclearanceprooonewy_djvu.txt.

5   In 1971 the UDC engaged Carl Koch and Associates to determine the feasibility of an innovative system of industrialized housing (Techrete) on a thirteen-acre site at Arverne. Koch and a group of consultants in allied fields completed their study early in 1970. An affirmative recommendation was made, both the city and the UDC approved, and construction commenced in 1971.

6   The Prestressed Concrete Institute gave awards to Laura Spelman Rockefeller Hall at Princeton University, designed by I. M. Pei and Partners, and to Arverne Houses, designed by Carl Koch and Associates and built by the NYS Urban Development Corporation.

7   U.S. Bureau of Economic Analysis (BEA), https://www.bea.gov/.

8   Hart, Krivatsky, Stubee, Planning Consultants, "A Report to the Borough President of Queens and the Queens Borough Improvement Board," February, 1973, http://www.laguardiawagnerarchive.lagcc.cuny.edu/FILES_DOC/WAGNER _FILES/06.021.0058.060281.32.PDF.

9   Ibid, 3.

10 "Government doesn't invest, government spends" was one of the one-liners successfully applied by George Bush Sr. during his 1988 election campaign against Michael Dukakis.

11 1989 Forest City, put forward by Forest City Development Corporation under Mayor Ed Koch.
    Alan S. Oser, "The Arverne Solution; Courtyard Housing with Parking Below," *New York Times*, June 25, 1989, http://www.nytimes.com/1989/06/25 /realestate/perspectives-the-arverne-solution-courtyard-housing-with-park ing-below.html?pagewanted=all.

12 Claire Schulman, Queens borough president, interview, *New York Post,* August 28, 1989.

13 Paul Goldberger, "On a Desolate Beach in Queens, a Point of Departure," *New York Times,* July 23, 1989, http://www.nytimes.com/1989/07/23/arts/architecture -view-on-a-desolate-beach-in-queens-a-point-of-departure.html.

14 Alan S. Oser, "The Arverne Solution"

15 Steve Cuozzo, "Will the Beach Have Its Day?—City Tries Once More to Develop Rockaway Stretch," *New York Post,* January 2, 2001, http://nypost.com/2001/01 /02/will-the-beach-have-its-day-city-tries-once-more-to-develop-rockaway -stretch/.

16 Donald Bertrand, "Technodome Plans Dying—City Eying Housing Instead on Rockaway Site," *Daily News,* December 5, 2000, http://www.nydailynews.com

/archives/boroughs/technodome-plans-dying-city-eying-housing-rockaway
-site-article-1.879777.

17   Steve Cuozzo, "Will the Beach Have Its Day?"

18   Jerilyn Perine, Statement to the Press, 2000, quoted in "City Seeks to Develop Arverne Request for Proposal Issued," *The Wave: Rockaway's Newspaper,* December 23, 2000, http://www.rockawave.com/news/2000-12-23/Front_Page /City_Seeks_To_Develop1223.html.

19   James Lima, New York City conference on Arverne, February 2001.

20   Arverne by the Sea RFP, HPD website, nyc.gov/HPD.

21   Ibid.

22   "Quarterly Residential Vacancies and Homeownership, Fourth Quarter 2016," U.S. Census Bureau, January 31, 2017, http://www.census.gov/housing/hvs/files /currenthvspress.pdf.

23   "Arverne by the Sea," Urban Land Institute, September, 2014, https://casestudies .uli.org/wp-content/uploads/sites/98/2014/09/Arverne_by_the_Sea.pdf.

24   Ibid.

TELL THE WORLD THIS BOOK WAS

GOOD	BAD	SO-SO

Acknowledgments

The events and people that have informed this book are too many to list. As an architect, one is never alone. Buildings are the result of infinite collaborations, to the point that one may question whether the concept of "an author" even exists in architecture. Much of this book has tried to argue that it doesn't.

Writing is different, done in solitude by definition and forever plagued by doubts that what one is working toward will ever exist. If buildings emerge from responding to pressure, books emerge only from keeping pressure at bay. To achieve that, the support of others is crucial. Ultimately the tasks needed to complete a book—whether editing, proofreading, or simply commenting—serve a bigger purpose in that they invariably help an author overcome doubts.

I would like to thank the people of Harvard University Press and Ian Malcolm in particular for reaching out and offering this opportunity, Jeremy Higginbotham for urging me to take it, Shumi Bose for making my English read like English, Peter Smisek and Maarten Lambrechts for the research that underlies some of the more serious essays, and Laura Baird for creating sneak previews of what a finished book might look like. Above all, *Four Walls and a Roof* owes a special debt of gratitude to Jacqueline Tellinga, whose critical comments in ways known and unknown to her helped ensure that there was no way back.

Chapters Previously Published

The following chapters were previously published. Many appeared under different titles, and most were substantially revised for publication in this book.

1. I WILL LEARN YOU ARCHITECTURE!

"I Will Learn You Architecture," in "Learning," special issue, *Volume* (Stichting Archis, the Netherlands), no. 45 (September 2015).

Online:

"Charisma Allows the Architect to Speak with Authority, Even When He Has No Clue," *Dezeen*, September 29, 2015, http://www.dezeen.com/2015/09/29/reinier -de-graaf-amo-oma-opinion-architects-charisma-eisenman-rossi-van-eyck/.

3. LET ME FINISH!

Online:

"Academics Need to Break out of Their Loop and Get Back into the Real World," *Dezeen*, November 4, 2015, https://www.dezeen.com/2015/11/04/opinion-reinier -de-graaf-american-architecture-academia-insular-get-back-to-real-world -chicago-architecture-biennial/.

"Let Me Finish!," *Huffington Post*, November 9, 2015, http://www.huffingtonpost .com/reinier-de-graaf/let-me-finish_b_8504054.html.

4. FOUR WALLS AND A ROOF

Online: "The Vast Majority of the Built Environment Is of an Unspeakable Ugliness," *Dezeen*, December 10, 2014, http://www.dezeen.com/2014/12/10/reinier-de-graaf -opinion-oma-the-built-environment-unspeakable-ugliness/.

5. BLOODY FOOLS! THE STORY OF PIMLICO SCHOOL, 1970–2010

"Bloody Fools! The Story of Pimlico School, 1970–2010," in *Common Ground: A Critical Reader*, from the 13th International Architecture Exhibition at La Biennale di Venezia, 2012 (Venice: Marsilio Editori Marittima, 2012).

6. ARCHITEKTUR OHNE EIGENSCHAFTEN

In German: "Architektur ohne Eigenschaften," in *Baukultur in Deutschland: Von der Architekturqualität im Alltag zu den Ikonen der Baukunst*, edited by Wüstenrot Foundation (Stuttgart: Kraemer Verlag, 2017).

In English: "Architecture without Qualities," *Real Review* (REAL Foundation, London) 2 (Autumn 2016).

8. REFERENCE WITHOUT A SOURCE: THE APPEAL OF ATLANTA AIRPORT

"The Possibility of an Airport," in "Terminus: Transportation Special Issue," *Art Papers Magazine*, January / February 2016.

Online:

"The Possibility of an Airport," *Huffington Post*, January 18, 2016, http://www .huffingtonpost.com/reinier-de-graaf/the-possibility-of-an-air_b_9007496 .html.

12. INTRUDERS: HOW SMART TECHNOLOGY INFILTRATES ARCHITECTURE

"Smart Technology Infiltrates Architecture," *Britannica Book of the Year 2016* (Encyclopaedia Britannica, 2016).

Online:

"Intruders: How Smart Technology Infiltrates Architecture," *Icon Magazine*, November 23, 2015, http://www.iconeye.com/architecture/features/item/12333 -intruders-how-smart-technology-infiltrates-architecture.

"Smart Devices Introduce a Fundamental Ambiguity about Who Is in Charge," *Dezeen*, March 11, 2016, https://www.dezeen.com/2016/03/11/opinion-reiner-de -graaf-smart-devices-cities-data-collection-control-privacy/.

"Apple's Backdoor," *Huffington Post*, March 16, 2016, http://www.huffingtonpost.com /reinier-de-graaf/apples-backdoor_b_9475904.html.

14. FROM CIAM TO CYBERSPACE: ARCHITECTURE AND THE COMMUNITY

"From CIAM to Cyberspace: Architecture and the Community," *PROJECT: A Journal for Architecture* (New York: Consolidated Urbanism), no. 3 (Spring 2014).

15. WITH THE MASSES: THE ARCHITECTURE OF PARTICIPATION

"With the Masses," *Architectural Review* (Emap Publishing), no. 1433 (July / August 2016).

Online:

"Few Architects Have Embraced the Idea of User Participation; a New Movement Is Needed," *Architectural Review,* July 26, 2016, https://www.architectural-review .com/rethink/viewpoints/few-architects-have-embraced-the-idea-of-user -participation-a-new-movement-is-needed/10008549.article.

18. HOW IS DENMARK?

"A Year in the Gulf," in "Al Manakh," special issue, *Volume* (Stichting Archis, the Netherlands), no. 12 (2007).

21. NAUKOGRAD

Online: "Naukograd," *Stylepark*, August 1, 2014, http://www.stylepark.com/en/news/naukograd/346870.

25. THE OTHER TRUTH

"The Other Truth," *Metropolis*, February 2015.

Online:

"The Other Truth," *European*, December 2, 2014, http://www.theeuropean -magazine.com/reinier-de-graaf/9307-competing-histories-create-a -controversial-present.

"OMA's Reinier de Graaf on the Berlin Wall and Histories We Tell Ourselves," *Metropolis*, February 19, 2015, http://www.metropolismag.com/February-2015 /The-Other-Truth/.

32. A PROPERTY DEVELOPER FOR PRESIDENT

Online: "A Property Developer for President," *Huffington Post*, September 8, 2015, http://www.huffingtonpost.com/reinier-de-graaf/a-property-developer-for-_b _8098036.html.

33. A FAUSTIAN BARGAIN

"Megalopolitics," *Log* (Anyone Corporation) 32 (Fall 2014).

34. AMANHÃ

"Where the Streets Have no Name," *Blueprint* (Progressive Media International) 337 (November / December 2014).

35. SMART CITIES OF THE FUTURE

Online:

"The Smart City," *Huffington Post*, August 12, 2015, http://www.huffingtonpost.com /reinier-de-graaf/the-smart-city_b_8729496.html.

"The Smart City Is the Ultimate Free-for-All," *Dezeen*, December 4, 2015,
https://www.dezeen.com/2015/12/04/reinier-de-graaf-opinion-smart-city/.

36. THE SUM OF ALL ISMS

Online: "The Sum of All-isms: An Unsolicited Manifesto for the New Cities
Foundation," *New Cities Foundation*, June 2, 2014, http://www
.newcitiesfoundation.org/sum-isms/.

37. DEAR MR. BARBER

Online:

"If Mayors Ruled the World," *This Big City*, September 30, 2014, http://thisbigcity
.net/if-mayors-ruled-the-world/.

"Mayors Ruling the World? Let's Hope Not," *European*, October 2, 2014,
http://www.theeuropean-magazine.com/reinier-de-graaf/9068-why
-benjamin-barber-and-the-global-parliament-of-mayors-are-wrong.

38. AT YOUR SERVICE: TEN STEPS TO BECOMING A SUCCESSFUL URBAN CONSULTANT

"At Your Service: Ten Steps to Becoming a Successful Urban Consultant," in "Al
Manakh Cont'd," special issue, *Volume* (Stichting Archis, the Netherlands),
no. 23 (2010).

Online:

"At Your Service: 10 Tips for Becoming a Successful Urban Consultant," *Dezeen*,
February 5, 2015, https://www.dezeen.com/2015/02/05/oma-reinier-de-graaf
-opinion-10-tips-becoming-successful-urban-consultant/.

39. RANKINGS

This chapter is a merger of two essays:

"Look past the Ranks," *Financial Times*, April 7, 2010.

"Moscow after Moscow," in *New Geographies 6: Grounding Metabolism,* edited by
Daniel Ibañez and Nikoz Katsikis (Cambridge, MA: Harvard University Press,
2014).

40. COUP DE GRÂCE: PRUITT-IGOE REVISITED

"Coup de Grâce: The Rise and Fall of Pruitt-Igoe, 1956–1972 and Beyond," *Blueprint*
(Progressive Media International) 340 (May/June 2015).

Online:

"After Pruitt-Igoe," *Huffington Post*, October 2, 2015, http://www.huffingtonpost
.com/reinier-de-graaf/after-pruitt-igoe_b_8220592.html.

41. THE CENTURY THAT NEVER HAPPENED

"Building Capital," *Architectural Review* (Emap Publishing), no. 1419 (May 2015).

Online:

"Architecture Is Now a Tool of Capital, Complicit in a Purpose Antithetical to Its Social Mission," *Architectural Review*, April 24, 2015, http://www.architectural -review.com/rethink/viewpoints/architecture-is-now-a-tool-of-capital -complicit-in-a-purpose-antithetical-to-its-social-mission/8681564.fullarticle.

The names and some identifying details of certain individuals described in this book have been changed to protect their personal privacy.